# Daygame Mastery
## By Nick Krauser

# DAYGAME MASTERY

DAYGAME MASTERY

MASTERY

www.krauserpua.com

# CONTENTS

SECTION ONE
## INTRODUCTION
6

SECTION TWO
## VIBE
15

SECTION THREE
## STREET
82

SECTION FOUR
## MESSAGING
150

SECTION FIVE
## LONG GAME
186

SECTION SIX
## DATE
266

SECTION SEVEN
## CLOSE
336

SECTION EIGHT
## SPECIAL SITUATIONS
360

SECTION NINE
## CARE AND MAINTENANCE
394

SECTION TEN
## BANTER CLINIC
412

# INTRODUCTION
## section one

# INTRODUCTION

**W**elcome to *Daygame Mastery*, a complete deconstruction of what dedicated skirt-chasers call the London Daygame Model. The model provides specific, detailed, actionable advice that takes you from approaching a girl to sleeping with her. There are no more mysteries. No more "black boxes".

Feel the weight of this book in your hands. Savour it! This is what a golden brick feels like. Contained in these pages is everything on what to say and what to do in order to excel at picking up girls during the daytime. Not only that, but every single element of the model is broken down into painstaking detail. If you encounter a problem out on the street, you'll find the answer somewhere in these pages.

You are going to learn pick-up inside and out. Everything!

Treat this book as your reference manual. Consult it as you progress on your journey towards sexual abundance. You'll be dipping into this for years to come.

## The player's journey

Seduction is fun, but it is no trifling matter. We are engaged in a strenuous uphill task against the combined forces of nature. We are trying to seduce more women– better women–with less bullshit than nature would prefer to allow us. This is why the London Daygame Model is so complicated. If you wish to chase skirt at the peak of your potential, you must hone your technique to a keen edge. In that sense it is no different to any other art, sport, or science. You can coast on 'easy mode', sweeping up the scraps nature throws you, or you can buckle up and chase the girls you really want. I've written this book to help the second type of man.

I suggest you conceive of seduction as a journey. You begin at a level vastly below your ultimate potential. You dedicate yourself to improvement. You take steps relentlessly toward that promise. At some point you realise you have become a **player**. You understand women, you understand seduction, and you are achieving sexual success you'd not dared think possible before.

Within the daygame community, we carve this journey into three stages: beginner, intermediate, and advanced. It's a somewhat artificial distinction but it's helpful in marking your progress and in choosing your waypoints as you move forwards.

# What is the goal of this book?

This book is designed to take the beginner daygamer to the intermediate level. It provides the foundation – both inner and outer game – from which we can build a successful player. I hope to impart a solid understanding of what daygame is, at its core, and of what women respond to during seduction. Based on this solid theoretical understanding, we can naturally develop specific tactics and gambits. We become empowered to root out bad habits and replace them with good practice.

The primary focus of this manual is to drill you with correct technique. The majority of material here consists of analysing and interpreting potential scenarios with women in order to identify, extract, and perfect the most successful techniques for handling them. The purpose is to polish our *technical* game. We want to draw as close as possible to the utopian state of **perfect daygame technique**.

We'll never quite get there, but you'll be surprised how close you can come.

With this in mind, I've created a highly detailed system. Each stage contains numerous named techniques to practice, and a number of theoretical structures to follow. These are abstract. You'll find your daily interactions with girls can be highly varied but, as you settle into your favourite chair afterwards to debrief your day's work, you begin to notice deep underlying patterns. It's these **abstract patterns** that I've sought to bring into sunlight.

# Notes on the second edition

The original *Daygame Mastery* was released in early 2014 and revolutionised street pick-up. I'm pleased to report the content has held up remarkably well and it's as helpful now as it was at launch. Therefore this second edition does not re-write any of the original content. The human courtship ritual is hard-wired and a few years haven't changed it.

The model has evolved and developed at the highest/higher levels, but the intervening years haven't changed the fundamentals.

The most striking visual difference of the second edition is the move toward full colour and the adoption of *Daygame Infinite*-style graphics. These are purely cosmetic changes.

More significant is the extra content. Additional paragraphs have been added here and there to expand on topics, and further commentary has been added to the many texting exchanges used as examples. The **Vibe** section has been considerably expanded. I've added an entirely new section at the end consisting of real-life examples of texting banter with girls. In total, the new content comes in at approximately twenty-five thousand words.

## The path ahead

Daygame is an art form with hidden depths. As you grow to love it, it'll likely consume you. Chasing skirt is so addictive and the rewards are so high that once you acclimatise yourself to the art you'll throw yourself into it with wild abandon. It is empowering to realise there is a system to seduction and that it can be learned. It's exhilarating to realise there are hundreds of men on the streets doing exactly that, and you'll soon meet many of them. Once you're committed to the player's journey you'll probably want to see just how much you can achieve. You'll likely not rest until you've reached your potential.

The next step is *Daygame Infinite*, the companion volume to *Daygame Mastery*. That book was crafted to move enthusiastic players from the intermediate to the advanced level. It's meant for those who have already implemented the techniques contained in *Mastery* and are looking to keep pressing ahead. The journey is long but you'll get there in the end.

There is a whole world of opportunity out there waiting for you. This volume you hold in your hands right now is going to help you seize it.

I wish you fun and success in your journey.

*Nick Krauser*
*London, February 2018*

# OVERVIEW

Spend a few minutes examining the **Krauser Daygame Model** flowchart. This is the master graphic of how daygame proceeds from the moment you hit the streets (Vibe), to engaging the girl to get a number (Street), the transition phase to get her out on a date (either Short Game via texting or Long Game for logistically difficult girls), then meeting and escalating her in person (Date) so you can extract her to a sex location (Close).

Your first thought was probably "Fuck me, that's complicated!"

Yes, it's a complicated graphic so let's spend a few pages explaining why it's there and how this book works through it.

## The book structure

Daygame Mastery follows the backbone of the Krauser Daygame Model. Each of the four phases (Vibe, Street, Date, Close) have a section, and within each section is a chapter for every sub-stage in the chronological order they generally occur during sets. These sub-stages form the vertebrae of the **Backbone**. Any time you get lost in the details, just check the flowchart to recover your bearings.

Every other element on the chart is discussed within the body of the text at some point in the above-mentioned structure.

## How to use the chart

Players must always strive for the perfect balance between being in the Now and planning the rest of the set. They must respond moment-by-moment to the ebbs and flows of the interaction, while exercising discipline to keep it moving towards sex. Nature has equipped us with hard-wiring to follow the mating dance. There is a clear logical progression from meeting to sex, which is mapped out in this flowchart. You must drill it into yourself until it becomes a part of your consciousness, which can only happen from taking action on the streets and later on dates.

I suggest an iterative process. Study this book, internalise the model and then try to flow free in set. Debrief afterwards and re-examine how you performed compared with the ideal progression. After months of practice you'll feel your "muscle memory" respond while proceeding through the structure, which will become second nature.

The model is designed to deconstruct every element of daygame so that you can iron out all your flaws and fully develop every element of your game. While you may feel clunky at first, this becomes precision engineering over the long haul.

But when you're in any given set, looking into a girl's eyes, don't sweat the details. It's too much to keep the whole thing in mind at any one time. This is why we practice.

## How to read the flowchart

Starting at the top we have the **Control** bar. Game is about imposing your reality upon a girl and drawing her onto your wavelength, what we'd call Frame Control. It's not simply matching wavelengths — you can't be pulled onto hers or you'll lose the frame. You gradually take control of her on two meta levels(her mind and her body) until you have sexual control. Control strengthens as the set moves forward, but it is not a sequential linear progression. Always be aware of how strong your Hand is.

Below the Control bar, her **Heartbeat** represents her level of emotional involvement and excitement at each moment in the backbone. She is hit with masculine dominance on The Stop, which causes an initial flutter. You then build up excitement and electricity while Vibing. After reaching Hook Point, you can dial the energy down to trigger Investment, and then spike it at the Commit step to take the number on a high. Her heartbeat is then steady and low during the digital communication, with occasional spikes to keep her interest until slight momentum buildstoward the Date invitation. Dating begins calm, but spikes in Venue One and builds up to a crescendo in Venue Two. She is on a high for The Kiss. More calm and comfort follows, so she will follow your lead to Venue Four when you heat her up again to beat LMR.

The **red energy bar** throughout the model represents your forward momentum towards sex. In the beginning you use sexual state (horniness plus intent) to motivate your approaching, with your masculine Vibe being modulated by your emotional control. When you get in front of the girl on the Street and on the Date, you use matched-pairs push-pull to entice her along for the ride. After the kiss, you replace it with strong leadership.

Every successful seduction has a small number of key milestones that you must reach — **Leaps Of Faith**. Regardless of the level of your game, you instinctively know that everything that between these milestones is merely setting up the next one. These are the moments when you feel nervous about rejection. In order, these are:

- The Run-up: Making up your mind to open a girl and then getting your feet moving is the first big Leap Of Faith. Usually once you are moving towards the girl the nerves subside.

- Conveying Intent: At some point you have to hit on the girl, letting her know you want to have sex with her.

- Date Invitation: You can spin out your top-notch text and Facebook game indefinitely, but unless you tell her you want to meet at a specific time and place you will never be able to escalate to sex.

- The Kiss: This is the first time you overtly agree that you are sexually attracted to each other and there's no LJBF weirdness.

- Pulling The Trigger: This is the biggest Leap Of Faith. When you push her into a taxi you are saying "let's have sex tonight," and if she gets in she's saying "ok." The most nerve-wracking moment of all.

Each Leap Of Faith results in a response. Along the bottom of the flowchart are the girl's major moments of **Compliance** representing the outcomes you are seeking. When you have one, you progress to the next stage. When she refuses, the circular arrows give a short-form version of how to recover from the knock-back and build towards a second compliance test.

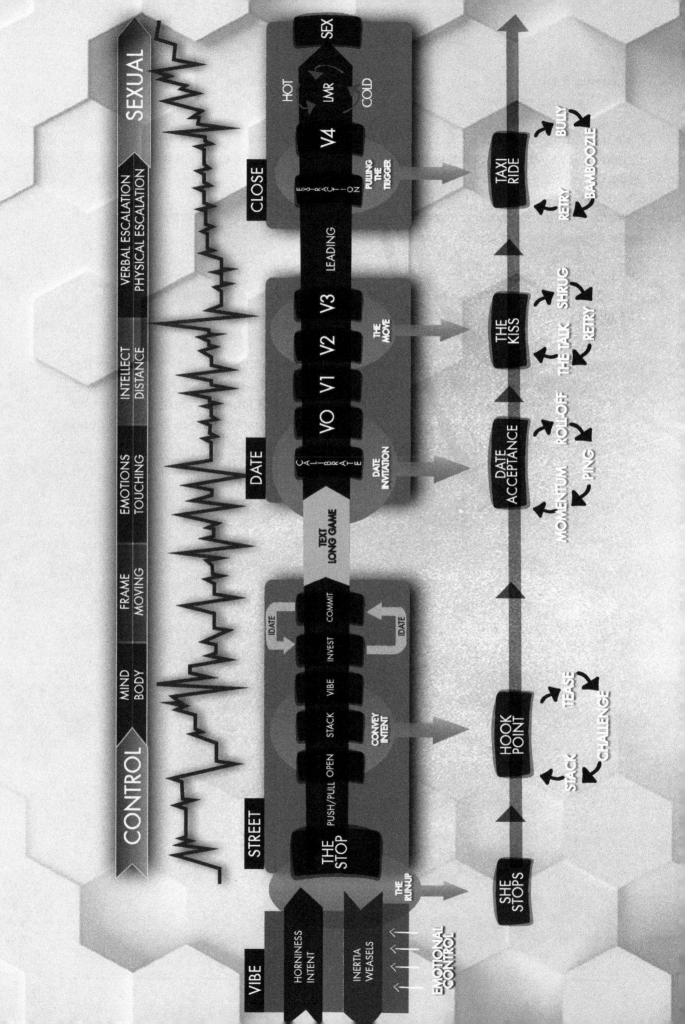

# DAYGAME MASTERY – NAVIGATION SUMMARY

## Vibe

Mental Game **16**
Mindsets **33**
Sexual Selection **38**
The Symphony **42**
The Bubble **50**
Targeting **52**
Find The Girls **63**
Three-Tiers **67**
Approach Anxiety **74**

## Street

The Stop **82**
Open **95**
Stack **110**
Vibing **117**
Investment **134**
Commit **145**
iDate/SDL **385**

## Text Long Game

Text Phase **150**
Feeler Text **155**
Rebase **168**
Sample Chats **177**
Long Game Process **193**

## Date

Calibration **266**
Venue Zero **283**
Venue One **287**
Venue Two **299**
Venue Three **310**

## Close

Extraction **336**
Venue Four **342**
LMR **350**

# VIBE
## section two

This chapter covers everything that happens before you stop the girl. We begin with a discussion of precisely what we are trying to achieve with daygame and what meta-level mindsets underpin it. Fundamental misconceptions about daytime pick-up are dealt with such as being too nice and showing too much of the Provider Chump weaknesses. I outline the deep rhythm of seduction, Composing The Symphony, and the importance of continuous push-pull to drive the interaction towards sex.

Next I outline how to find the right girls for you and how to use cold-reading to build a mythology around each one in order to unlock your creative energies. I provide a typology of common girl archetypes to give you a headstart. Once the girl is chosen you must deal with Approach Anxiety so I excavate to the core psychological process that inhibits you from freely opening any girl you like.

Emotional control is the basis of strong Game. This phase equips you with the correct attitudes and beliefs to manage your state while chasing girls.

# VIBE

## THE MENTAL GAME

**Y**ou are embarking upon a path that is very challenging, but which delivers high rewards. If you half-ass it, your results will be worse than half-assed. Daygame has a formidable difficulty curve for the first year / first thousand sets. The curve softens considerably after that, but it's *always* challenging. It's not simply "out there" on the streets which is tough, persuading pretty young women to sleep with you. It's also difficult "in here" as you challenge your ego and reconstruct your own identity.

Commit to taking it seriously.

This book is not something you can read once and expect to learn much from. It is very densely packed with new information and many pages contain enough suggestions that it can take hundreds of sets just to internalise those on that page alone.

Commit to reading this guide at least three times. Commit to testing your newfound knowledge on the streets until it sticks.

The chances are that if you made it as far as buying this book (and let's face it, it's not cheap), then you're a highly motivated man who very much wants to be a *cooler* and *more attractive* man. You are willing to invest a lot of time and emotion into improving yourself and improving your success with women. That's good. You will need that motivation when things get tough. It's what will separate you from the coulda-shoulda-woulda crowd of losers.

But what if you're worried that while climbing the mountain you'll lose your grip and tumble back to the bottom? What can you do to ensure you don't tumble back into the crowd of coulda-shoulda-woulda losers?

You will commit to seeing this through to the end.

That's how. You make the mental decision, here and now, that you will see it through. When the punches come at you, you will tuck your chin, bite down onto your mouthpiece, and fight your way through the storm. There are two key targets.

1. Your first hundred sets.

2. Your first thousand sets.

After that things get *considerably* easier. Well, it's not so much that the challenge gets easier, it's just that by then **you are stronger**. You are better able to surmount that challenge. Later in your journey, as *Daygame Infinite* explains, you'll move away from willpower-based daygame and towards vibe-based. Don't worry about that for now because that's a solution to a different problem that you won't encounter for a long time yet. For now, **willpower** is your greatest asset. You have the same blood coursing through your veins as the warriors of yesteryear who charged into battle with mount and blade. It's already in you.

For those first hundred sets you'll just get it done. It'll exhaust you, just like your first day in the gym would. But one hundred sets really isn't so much, perhaps ten days of work. Each day you psych yourself up, get the work done, and then recover. Then the next day, and the next, and then suddenly....... you've done one hundred sets.

More importantly, you are now *the-guy-who-did-one-hundred-sets*. You own that achievement. It's all yours. You earned it. You just proved to yourself that you can do something challenging and your confidence will shoot up. Next time you're wavering over something difficult you can draw on that reference experience.

"How hard can it be? I did one hundred sets."

You're ready for the second challenge, your first thousand sets. That's considerably more work, and a much rockier journey, than the first hundred. It might take you all year. But that's okay because you're a stronger man than you were one hundred sets ago. The challenge is formidable but you are better able to surmount formidable challenges. You won't always need to rely upon willpower, but for the earliest toughest part of the daygame learning curve, that's your greatest ally.

# Confidence

There are two schools of thought regarding confidence, namely:

1. Confidence is a state of mind that you can talk yourself into.

2. Confidence is the outcome of achieving things in the real world.

Those men advocating the former will generally advise you to work on the structure of your cognition, attempting to tweak and restructure the way you think. For example, "a problem is an opportunity in disguise". This aphorism attempts to reframe you from a pessimistic to an optimistic approach to the same reality. Self-help literature abounds with such aphorisms: eyes on the prize, pain is just weakness leaving the body, problems mean God is frightened of your progress etc.

The latter school advises you to take on challenges in the real world, overcome them through struggle, and then the natural outcome of winning is that your confidence improves. You are training yourself into success, and what is confidence if not the anticipation of eventual success?

**Bechdel Test**

*Does a work of fiction feature at least two women talking to each other about something other than a man? This is a feminist test intended to identify if a book or movie is misogynist.*

So, one school attacks the 'problem of confidence' through inner game, and the other through outer game. As you've likely guessed from my presentation here, I think both have merit and it's possible to work on both approaches concurrently. Straighten out your mind, straighten out your life. Each reinforces the other.

When it comes to women, confidence is king.

Women want to feel protected from the dangers of the world. Nature has evolved them into a particular biological role which is highly specialised: mobile womb carrier. A woman's job is to select a high value man to inseminate her, and to fend off the advances of everyone else. There are all kinds of other things women can do but that is her primary role in life. She is highly specialised for precisely that role. Consider women's interests and skills:

- Obsessed with gossiping about, judging, and ranking men. That's most of their conversation with other women. Women in real life fail the **Bechdel Test**.

- Obsessed with diet, weight loss, and weight gain.

- Obsessed with skin care, hair care, tooth care, and grooming.

- Extremely sophisticated self-presentation skills using make-up and fashion.

- Sharply attuned bullshit detector to sort out cool men from fakers.

Women spend their entire post-puberty lives honing their ability to look attractive to men and to choose from the best they can attract. There's nothing superficial or silly about this. They are focusing on exactly the thing they are supposed to be doing.

It's no surprise they are shit at everything else. Women can't fight, can't lift, can't build, can't reason, can't keep their mouths shut.

This makes women vulnerable in dealing with the real world which, in pre-modern times, was extremely dangerous. Don't let the relative ease of early-21st century life in civilised countries fool you as to the reality of human history. For most of recorded time, people were besieged by pestilence, war, famine and death. It was the man's job to protect her from all that and we still carry the same biological programming now that adapted us to deal with the world then.

So what has this to do with confidence?

Each man is just a speck of dust on the arse of the world. Nature doesn't care about us. There have been comets that wiped out the dinosaurs, volcanos that wiped out entire towns, and wars that wiped out nations. The world has an unshakeably strong frame. It overpowers us. As a man, you stand against that. You go out into the world and wrest from it what you need for your tribe. The world pushes back and you must stand up against it. This is where confidence matters: your anticipation of eventual success. It is confidence that emboldens you to strike out with your fellows and take on the world. It is confidence that whispers into your ear that this is *your* world and you're going to take what you need from it.

A confident man is *good at being a man*.

Confidence is all-conquering.

There are many other things that helps a man make his way in the world. Height and strength will aid his struggles against the world and rival tribes. Intelligence will aid his solving the problems encountered in nature and also his out-thinking and out-plotting of rivals. A strong disgust reflex and a preference for cleanliness will keep him free of disease. A handsome symmetrical face suggests DNA free of problematic mutations. All of these attributes will help him make his way through the world.

What they won't do is strengthen his resolve against adversity. Without confidence, all of those gains can be wiped away by a sequence of adverse consequences. Confidence is the engine that powers everything else.

# Confidence in Pick-Up

Confidence is a highly-prized character trait and women are evolved to spot it, test it, and be attracted to it. Throughout a seduction, the women is pinging your confidence.

When first encountering the seduction community it's easy to form the impression that the **techniques** are what gets you the girl: the funny openers, the cocky rejoinders, the DHV-compliance-test-IOD loops and so on. This is the kind of thing that is easy to write into textbooks and when you watch experienced players in-field you'll see them use these techniques. It seems simple:

*He explained this technique + he's demonstrating the technique + he's having success = it's about the techniques*

You try the same thing and..... it doesn't work as well. Why is that?

It's because the techniques are simply a vehicle for expressing your character and of moving through the process of the seduction. They aren't what powers the seduction. Confidence is the power. Think of it by way of analogy.

You watch Mike Tyson working out in the gym (there's a lot of footage on YouTube). He's bobbing, weaving, hitting the bag. You can see him drilling specific techniques, practising his footwork and the same combos over and over. That's his technique. Then you see him "in field" in a professional fight doing exactly that. Boom! He's knocked the guy out. Heavyweight champion of the world.

Now imagine putting Bruno Mars in the gym, drilling him a few months in boxing techniques, then throwing him into a heavyweight fight. What's the odds he becomes heavyweight champion of the world?

Even if he executed the techniques perfectly his opponent would simply walk right through him and smash him into the canvas. Little Bruno could land a perfect punch right on the point of his opponent's chin and it wouldn't matter at all. Because he's Bruno Mars not Mike Tyson. He doesn't have the power. Confidence in pick-up is like power in boxing. Your game is just the delivery system that gets your punch onto the target. You still need the power behind it to score the knockout.

## Levels of Confidence

I use a boxing analogy because there are two things that every man thinks he's good at: pulling women, and fighting. Of course deep down we don't really think that, but we don't go through our lives spending much time thinking about what's deep down. Most days, we are just waddling through life comfortable in our own delusions. I'll give you an example.

Pre-game, I used to think I was pretty good with women. I wasn't, but I *thought* I was. I actually once said to a friend:

*"I'm pretty good with women if I can just get through the first five minutes"*

That's a staggering level of delusion. Let me translate it into real English:

*"I'm pretty good with women if I can just get through the bit that's actually difficult, where nearly all the filtering happens, and where if a girl is still there afterwards then she's likely interested in me."*

I'm good at football if I just get tap-ins from the edge of the six yard box. I'm good at boxing if I can just get through to the bit where my opponent is lying on the mat and the referee's count is already at "six".

A chode isn't confident with women. That's why he's a chode. But even once you're out there approaching it's easy to delude yourself that you've now *become confident* just because you've summoned up the willpower to run after a girl, get in front of her, and tell you excuse-me-a-minute-I-just-want-to-say-quickly-you-look-nice.

I'll grant it's progress. Cold approaching is no little thing. The fact you are doing it at all means you are growing in confidence. However, there are levels to this. Stopping a girl and telling her she looks nice is not some death-defying stunt, no matter how much it *feels* like it during those first hundred sets. You are still resting on the crutch of canned lines. It isn't confidence in yourself that enables you to approach the girl, it's confidence in **the material**.

That's a limited form of confidence and the girl knows it.

If you were truly confident you'd stop the girl spontaneously no matter where she was and you'd initiate a conversation without having prepared a single line. This is exactly how I daygame: I just stop the girl, knowing full well I'll think of something to say and handle her however the interaction goes.

If your mind is jumbled up with a knot of routines, lines and canned stories then you're not really confident. Fortunately, you can still have success at this level. Some girls are going to like you and the simple fact that you can do *something* competently will be enough to separate you from the crowd and intrigue the girl. This keeps you going and begins the process of accumulating reference experiences, attacking the "problem of confidence" from the outer game side.

It's common at this stage to be overly concerned about what other people think of you in your daygame. You may feel the 'spotlight effect' of thinking everyone else on the street is watching you, judging you, perhaps laughing at you. You may be worried the girl will react badly to your approach, letting her opinions overrule your opinion of yourself. These are both signs that your confidence hasn't peaked.

That's good: however well you're doing now, there is still some headroom above you to **get better**.

A man with rock solid confidence doesn't really worry what other people think of him, especially strangers. He's relaxed and comfortable wherever he goes and with whatever is going on around him. He says what he thinks because he's confident girls will like him for who he is. He anticipates success.

## How To Build Your Confidence

We will talk about confidence from the inner game side later. For now, I'll focus upon attacking the "problem of confidence" through outer game. There are two main ways to build it.

1. Increased experience of daygaming.

2. Overcoming challenges in life.

> For the purposes of this discussion, we can analytically separate two types of confidence. There is the type that comes from being good in a specific narrow skill or situation. Violinists are confident playing violins, but not so much clarinets or bass guitar. Boxers are confident in the ring but perhaps not delivering a best man's speech at a wedding. This is **situational confidence** and you'll already have several areas in your life where you already have it, such as in your job specialism. The challenge is to bring street pick-up into that list of areas for you.
>
> You do this by doing daygame.
>
> Remember my earlier pep talk about biting down on the gum shield and wading into the fight? That's how you establish your early beginner-level situational confidence. By the time you've gotten one hundred sets under your belt you've begun to get a feel for the basic elements of daygame: walking the streets, spotting girls, psyching yourself up, getting in front of them, delivering an opener, asking for numbers etc. You aren't yet comfortable with it, but it's no longer unknown territory.
>
> By the time you hit one thousand sets you'll be pretty sure of yourself. Not necessarily sure where your next lay is coming from, but sure you know *how this thing works* and what level of success, on average, you can expect for the next hundred or so sets. That's situational confidence. The more you go out, the stronger it becomes.
>
> The other type of confidence is holistic, it's about being confident in life generally. This **general confidence** is rooted in your **identity** rather than the **situation**. You don't look at a situation and think "I've been in this situation many times before, I know how it works" but rather you think "This is just another challenge. I have it in me to overcome challenges."

> ### *You are the type of person who overcomes challenges*

> To become this person you must seek out challenges and overcome them, in life generally not just with women. Take on something difficult and commit to seeing it through until you win. You can take small wins (e.g. tidying your room, buying a new wardrobe, reading that book you've been intimidated by) as well as big wins (e.g. learning a new language, getting into shape, passing an exam). Every time you win, you condition your mental muscles towards winning. You become a winner. Being "a winner" is an identity. It's considerably better than being "a loser".
>
> Confidence is not an either-or state. It is a gradual climb to awesomeness and each time you "level up" you'll notice your interactions with women improving. Women recognise winners like we recognise hotties. As your confidence grows, your techniques have power behind them.
>
> Confidence conquers all. Women know how rare a genuinely confident man is. Think how you feel when you encounter a perfect pair of tits. You can't help but

marvel at them, drawn in by them, intoxicated by them. That's the effect confidence has on women. Just as you'll overlook imperfections elsewhere if the girl has a great rack, she'll overlook many of your shortcomings if you dazzle her with confidence.

# Take A Chance

Every time you head out onto the streets you are rolling the dice. You are putting yourself into the mix and giving yourself a chance to get lucky. This makes daygame thrilling. Will you spend the next three hours getting brutally blown out by miserable girls, or will the first girl take an immediate liking to you and she becomes your fuck buddy for the next two years?

Daygamers are risk takers. There's a reason we call ourselves "players".

Chasing skirt reconnects you to the core dynamic between a man and his world. We are built for adventure. I once read that a DNA study found 80% of women who'd ever existed had successfully reproduced but only 40% of men had. The trajectory of human evolution is simple:

*Men take risks. Some win, some lose. Women choose the winners.*

We are very lucky that in our epoch we can roll the dice on the relatively safe activity of daygame. In earlier times you'd have to board a ship for a voyage into the unknown, or rise through the ranks of an army in battle, or gamble your life savings on an investment opportunity. Most men have become alienated from their core relationship to the world: **risk taking**. We have the cocoon of modern life where houses are warm, food is plentiful, and disease can be treated. Most of us have "permanent jobs" in which entrepreneurs bear all the risks of business and we just collect a monthly paycheck from them for sitting in an air conditioned office chatting on Facebook.

Unsurprisingly, our unmet drive towards adventure needs to express itself somewhere. Video games seem to bear the brunt of it, as each evening we can be super soldiers, race car drivers, or international assassins. Daygame provides a way to channel that thirst for adventure in a way that leads to getting laid.

Seduction will consistently present you with situations of high-risk and high-reward.

- Do I go for the kiss now, and perhaps try to pull her home tonight, or do I play it safe and go for it on the next date?
- She just said something a bit bitchy. Should I tell her off, or should I go along to get along?
- She's fifteen minutes late. Should I keep standing here or should I walk off and wait for her to message "I'm here"?

Most of the time, humans are risk-averse. That's very sensible from an evolutionary perspective. There are enough dangers in the world that you don't need to go seeking out more. The problem is that while you are playing it safe, more adventurous men are rolling the dice. Sure, many of them will crap out, burn out, or wear out. However, some will roll double-sixes and win big. Girls will flock to those winners and not to you.

Confidence, remember, is the anticipation of success. It's the anticipation that if you roll the dice, you'll probably win.

*Confidence is the ability to handle uncertainty with ease.*

We regret the things we didn't do more than the things we did do. When you take a chance, you find answers *even if you come up short on this dice roll*. You reinforce the identity of being *the guy who rolls the dice*. This builds confidence and it creates opportunities to get lucky which didn't exist beforehand. *Rejection is better than regret*

I'm not advocating taking stupid risks. Don't go free-climbing signal towers or picking fights with gorillas. The only men who should act like a jackass are the cast members filming a new series of *Jackass*. Assess the risk, estimate the worst-case outcome and if you can handle that, go for it. The more you roll the dice, the better (and faster) you can make these decisions. Before long you are acting through your intentions.

## Acting Through Your Intentions

Society conditions us to fit in. There is a complex web of social relationships and rules that govern them, both explicitly through the law and implicitly through local custom. Much of our childhood is spent learning those rules and being rewarded or punished accordingly. We come to internalise such behaviours. For society, this is a good thing. It keeps things running smoothly. However, you are not society. You have your own priorities and society's rules might well get in the way.

Players tend to be ruthless individualists and that's not a coincidence. Let's consider why.

We've already discussed how women are designed to pick winners. Only a small proportion of men will win, and the rest either break even or lose. Women aren't so concerned with *those* men because they are searching out the DNA that will make their children winners in the next round of life's game.

There are two strategies for winning.

1. Dominate the mainstream.

2. Dominate a niche.

The famous winners of history will usually be in the former category, the alpha males. They may dominate on a grand scale like Genghis Khan or Alexander The Great, or on a smaller scale like Frank Sinatra or Zinedine Zidane. If you were one of those guys, you wouldn't be reading my book. I'd be reading yours.

It is considerably easier to dominate a niche. Not easy, just *easier*. The specific niche players have chosen is the art of seduction itself. Rather than win big and let women come to us, we are sidestepping the world's big battle and winning the smaller one with women. This sets us against the world. We don't need to impose our frame upon the world, but we do need to resist the world trying to impose its frame upon us. To do so, we become ruthless individualists. The challenge is to do that without also becoming a horrible person.

# The Spotlight Effect

Many beginner-level daygamers report feeling like people are watching them on the streets and judging them harshly. We call this the 'spotlight effect' because you feel like an actor on stage, under a spotlight, with a whole audience focused upon you and your performance. There are both superficial immediate reasons, and also murky reasons buried deep inside your mindset.

Superficially, you're worried people will react negatively to you. Maybe they'll point and laugh if the girls blows you out. "Haha, dumb ass!" you can almost hear over your shoulder from that group of men having a pint twenty metres away. How about the old woman with her shopping who seems to be giving you a disapproving stare? She's probably thinking of calling the police. Is that guy on his phone glancing over at you her boyfriend? Perhaps he's going to come over and punch you for hitting on his girl. Just as well there's not a football match on this afternoon or the hooligans might beat you up for being a foreigner in their town.

If you let your thoughts run unguarded, you will conjure up all manner of unlikely conflict scenarios that end up (in your imagination) with you humiliated, in hospital, or in prison. It's all nonsense. After a hundred or so sets you'll realise these worst-case scenarios *never* happen. Probably the worst response you'll have in any given month is that a girl eye-rolls and hand-waves you away. That's about as bad as it ever gets. Everything else is just your approach anxiety feeding your over-active imagination.

Save that imagination for thinking up cool stuff to say in set.

There is a much deeper level of worry, and it springs from how you see your place in the world. For our entire lives we are taught the norms and values that constitute 'respectable behaviour'. PUAs tend to call this 'social conditioning' and social scientists call it 'socialisation'. Your gran will call it 'the done thing' and if you break those norms your parents may inform you 'that's not cricket, is it?'

One such social norm is that you don't walk up to random girls in the street and attempt to seduce them. Or at least, you don't make a major life project out of it. Romantic comedies at least legitimise doing it once in a while, but she's got to be The One. Not just "set number six of the session".

As children we internalised these rules following a system of rewards and punishment. We'd be praised for approved behaviours and reproached for disapproved behaviours. All that happens now, as an adult, is that the school teacher who told you off in third grade is now residing inside your head telling you off now for hitting on women. She's not real.

## Dissolving The Spotlight Effect

The first thing to fix into your mind is you're not doing anything wrong. You are, quite literally, chatting to women. That's it. Each girl is entirely free to walk away any time she pleases. There is no harm and no foul. So, on a purely rational level there's not the slightest thing to feel guilty about.

Of course it's not that easy, because our internalisation of social norms runs deep. So we'll need to work on it a bit until our emotions catch up to our logical deductions. Here's a useful mantra to repeat any time you feel the spotlight effect.

*These people are strangers. Their opinion means nothing to me.*

There will be people whose opinions do matter: your loved ones, your best friends, your wings, your co-workers and so on. These people matter because of their special connection to you, either how you feel about them or the power they hold over you. Count them all, and come to a rough estimate how many of these people exist in your life.

Now subtract that number from the world's population of **seven billion**. That rather large remaining number is how many people live in this world whose opinion doesn't mean a damn thing to you. It doesn't make you a bad guy for not giving a shit what they think about you doing daygame.

Your real friends want you to be happy. Your good wings want you to get laid. They don't mind at all that you're on the streets trying to improve your sex life. The other people you care about don't need to be told and they are highly unlikely to ever see you open a set. Close to 100% of the people who do see you open a set belong to that group of people whose opinion doesn't matter. Even if they do snigger or gossip..... who cares?

*"You have enemies? Good. That means you've stood up for something, sometime in your life."*

— Winston Churchill.

Any time you break your chains and go after what you really want, *someone* doesn't like it. Perhaps they were benefiting from you wearing those chains, occupying the role they wanted you in. Perhaps your actions remind them that they aren't doing anything to improve their own lives, and they don't like being reminded. It doesn't matter. Their opinion doesn't matter.

Over time you'll become increasingly inculcated with the seduction community's norms and values, and these will undermine and eventually replace mainstream society's norms and values. You'll start to do what daygamers do and, ironically, you'll start to feel a spotlight effect for *not* approaching ("my wing must think I'm a voyeur full of approach anxiety"). Intermediate daygamers commonly report that they begin to feel like outlaws, revelling in their transgression of mainstream norms. This feeling tightens your bonds with fellow daygamers and makes you feel part of their community. That helps you fit into your emerging identity as a 'player'.

# Be Competitive

The intermediate stage is all about perfecting your technique, drilling yourself in good habits, and raising your attractiveness. It is a stage of actively and consciously striving to improve. Embrace this. You'll still have high motivation and a high tolerance for the discomfort and grind of daygame's negative side. It is while you still feel this relentless drive forwards that you should hoover up as many opportunities for improvement as you can.

### *Don't accept anyone as your superior*

We'll need to qualify that statement.

I mean don't accept anyone as being a superior *person* to you, as having a right to lord it over you, or as doing things that you can't learn because you don't have in you whatever they have. There will always be people who are more skilled at you at some given activity. Great, you can learn from them. But it doesn't mean they are a superior human to you.

Right now you are mid-way through Project Daygamer. There is a manufacturing plant which brings in raw material (chodes) and turns out the finished good (players) at the other end. Within that plant is an R&D department, assembly, finishing, tuning and whatever else. Turning you into a player is like turning steel, rubber and fibreglass into a super-car. To stretch the metaphor a little further, as a beginner you've just been carried into the factory and some labourers have begun hammering you into shape, ready for the next stage of processing. As an intermediate you've got the skilled engineers installing all the key parts and tuning them to work together.

You are not yet a finished product, but you will be.

Those other guys you see on the streets having more success, doing better game, getting better reactions? They aren't superior humans to you. You'll both end up as seasoned players if you go through the same assembly line. Be patient and keep tuning yourself up. You'll get there.

The competitive athlete isn't trying to win the big race every day. Most of his days are spent training, in preparation for the big race. He may not be running the track right this very moment but he's still an intensely competitive man working towards his goals.

# The Competition Is Everywhere

As a daygamer you are lucky to be surrounded by a community. There are support structures everywhere: books, videos, seminars, wings, mentors, and of course what you see on the streets with your own eyes. You are surrounded by people you can learn from so take advantage of it.

Deconstruct the successful guys. Don't just listen to what he *says* is the secret of their success, but really intensely observe him. Watch how he behaves with other men. Note his speech patterns such as vocal tone, pacing, sentence construction, and word choice. Watch how his body language is, both at ease and at work. How does he dress and how does it compliment his body type, facial structure, and the male archetype he is presenting to the world?

There is a wealth of material out there. You can observe people in person or on YouTube. Don't just limit yourself to PUAs. Any time a man strikes you as cool, try to figure out why. How does he create that impression of coolness in you?

Over time you'll become increasingly confident in your own judgement. Most chodes have an image in their minds of what the 'cool guy' is, or 'the guy good with women'. As you get further along your player's journey you'll end up revising that image. You begin seeing to the core of the issue and ignoring all the chuckleheads trying to tell you what's cool.

Throughout this process, don't waver from the belief that you too can learn those things. Cool guys are not cut from a different cloth, they just seem to be because they've internalised all the right behaviours and mindsets. What one man can do, another man can do. Watch, learn, and practice.

# Be In It To Win It

Some places are considerably better than others for daygame. A hunter goes where the prey are. Many times I've had emails from readers that begin, "I live in [suburb] of [small town] where there are not many hot young women. What is the best way to daygame it?"

The obvious answer is move somewhere better.

Committing yourself to daygame means committing yourself to a formidable difficulty curve that can only be surmounted by extreme effort. If you live in a low-opportunity area then you only have four options:

1. Move somewhere better.

2. Daygame in short bursts by travelling somewhere better.

3. Resign yourself to poor results.

4. Find a different way to meet women than daygame.

It might be that you are inextricably tied to your low-opportunity area and there really isn't any viable option to move. Whatever the reason, be it caring for a sick relative, needing to be available to your children, having a full time job you can't transfer..... you'll know your lifestyle options better than I do. In the medium term you can initiate a plan to increase your flexibility but in the short term it's probably better for you to consider other ways to meet women: social circle, meet-ups, hobbies, online dating, the bar scene and so on. By all means keep your hand in with daygame theory to prepare yourself for when circumstances change.

I've met many daygamers who live in small towns who use their weekends to chase skirt in the nearest big city (or university town). They'll buy train tickets in the morning, daygame all afternoon, set up dates in the evening, and rent an apartment for the Saturday night. They'll daygame more on Sunday and get the train home that evening. Such men get the same number of sets in as a more favourably-located daygamer and have the additional external discipline of having fully committed themselves to that weekend of action. They are far less likely to bail on a session just because it's a bit chilly outside.

An additional psychological benefit of travelling is a reduced spotlight effect. You're on an adventure and won't meet anyone you already know. It has a more exciting "outlaw" feel.

By hook or crook, you have to get yourself *into the mix*. You must walk the streets, malls, and campuses where large numbers of single young women congregate. If you're unwilling to do so, you're not as motivated as you'd like to believe.

# Improving Your Value

As I stated in the introduction, *Daygame Mastery* is a textbook on how to do daygame. There are many other aspects to work on that will improve your sex life in addition to learning the techniques and mindsets for picking up girls from the streets. I'll give these a cursory overview here and recommend you find subject matter experts to advise you in greater detail.

**Health**: This is the single biggest weakness I see in beginner-level daygamers. They enter the seduction community having been sold a line that there's 'one secret method that no girl can resist'. This marketing line is effective because it reassures the customer he can get what he wants without needing to change anything about himself. Just as with diet pills and get-rich-quick schemes, there is no "one thing". If you want the results, you must make big changes.

Modern society is a sickly society. Look around you next time you're walking down the high street, or switch on the television set. The average person is, by objective standards, ill. Overweight, dehydrated, full of chemicals, weak. They wear upon their bodies the results of a lifetime spent avoiding both healthy food and strenuous exercise. This is extremely unattractive.

Statistically, most people are overweight. This probably means *you* are overweight. If you're actually one of the rare few in great shape, give yourself a pat on the back. Measure your chest with a tape measure around the nipples and your stomach around the belly button. If your chest is six or more inches larger than your waist, you're doing okay. Less than that and you're overweight. If you require more confirmation, consult a height/weight chart on the internet.

It is exponentially harder to attract women in daygame if you're a lard ass. Don't worry about your openers, body language, or teases until you've first sorted out your diet. You know it's a problem so take your head out of your ass and start addressing it. Everything in your life will improve.

**Strength**: As if it's not bad enough that most modern men are overweight and sickly, most of them are spaghetti-armed faggots too. Women admire our strength like we admire their fertility. It's very difficult to project gravitas in your body language if you look like your neck can barely support the weight of your head. Ask yourself the following questions:

- Can I bench press my own bodyweight for a few reps?

- Can I throw a hard accurate punch?

- Can I throw a girl over my shoulder, slap her ass, then carry her away at my leisure?

Just asking yourself those questions, you know if you're a faggot. If you feel a prickling irritating sense of shame on your skin or in your gut, you're a faggot. If you're frantically listing reasons why those questions are not an accurate test of faggotry and that, under your *own* criteria you are in fact *way more masculine* that I am..... yep, you're a faggot. If you have prepared a rejoinder for how strength isn't important in our modern progressive society and women are more enlightened now and more attracted to.... wait.... yep, you're a faggot.

Fortunately, there is a simple cure to faggotry. Go to the local gym and start lifting weights. Actual iron weights, the ones that make your muscles tire in the gym and then ache the next afternoon from delayed onset muscle soreness. Once you've built up some anti-faggotry momentum, poke your head into a boxing gym and learn to fight.

These things matter for daygame. Your success ratios improve considerably when you become a man able to physically handle himself.

**Masculinity**: The degeneration of modern men's health and strength is in some measure due to a decline in overall masculinity. We have been attacked on all fronts. At school boys are held back and told to be more like girls. At work we are slandered as misogynists and patriarchal oppressors. In culture we are presented with weak role models and harangued for 'toxic masculinity'. Even our diet is under attack, with soy and estrogen flooding our foods.

The feminine is attracted to the masculine. Women are attracted to *real* men.

Take actions which will reconnect you to your masculinity and boost your testosterone. Never ever apologise for that masculinity. Nurture it. Immerse yourself in masculine literature, hobbies, social groups, and modes of thought. Become better at being a man.

**Fashion**: You impress girls by standing out from other men in a positive manner. This includes how you present yourself. Women are extremely sensitive towards fashion and take it very seriously in presenting themselves. If you roll up in front of her in ill-fitting, badly co-ordinated, cheap clothes then she will quite rightly dismiss you before you've had a chance to spit your game. Why wouldn't she? You clearly don't 'get it'.

There are two ways to approach this, either:

1. Decide on a male archetype women like, then model that

2. Observe the men who date the women you like, then model them

The first strategy has the advantage of congruence, in that you construct a look that expresses who you are. The risk is you become stubborn and unresponsive to feedback when that look isn't working. This is particularly acute if you are used to dressing according to a hobbyist subculture that is tear gas to women. The second strategy has the advantage of copying a style that has already proven a measure of success, but lacks congruence. Take your pick.

It's better to have one set of high-quality daygaming clothes than many sets of cheap clothes. Once your eye is attuned to quality, you really notice cheap clothes and girls always notice. I do not suggest you flaunt brand names, as this identifies you as a herd animal. Focus on quality. You'll likely want a separate set of clothes for first dates because the social situation is different, but it's not so important.

Don't neglect your shoes, watch or any other accessories. Men often err towards functionality in dress and thus neglect what they consider extravagances. Girls will notice and more than once I've laid a girl who subsequently said my shoes were one of the things that attracted her during my initial approach.

Lastly, buy clothes that fit. Almost every man buys his clothes one size too large. It took me a long time to learn this particular lesson and in some of the photos in this book – taken several years ago when I was already an experienced daygamer – you'll notice my jeans are a size bigger than is optimal.

# MINDSETS

## Goal: Think the right thoughts for perfect daygame

I won't go too far into mindsets. If you're at the stage where this book can help you, then you're already capable of the basic aspects of the mental game: pushing through approach anxiety, committing yourself to self-improvement, and viewing sex as something you proactively seek out. So let's just touch on a few principles that directly relate to this daygame model, particularly how it fits into women's sexual selection and how to conduct what I refer to as the "symphony of pick-up." This is the one chapter of the book which **does not** compartmentalize everything into specifically actionable do-this-do-that advice. We'll get to that stuff later.

Women have two sexual strategies:

- **r-selection:** Casual sex to acquire the DNA of sexually successful men

- **K-selection:** Dating to acquire additional long-term protection and provision

**Beta Male**

*A regular guy who fits in, follows orders, and does the same things as everyone else. He is characterised by a desire to avoid conflict and is eager to please. Approximately 80% of men are beta and struggle to exceed ten lifetime sexual partners.*

For a couple of centuries, modern industrial civilisation was designed by the men who specialise in fulfilling K-selection strategies (**beta males**) to play to their strengths. Women didn't vote, weren't fully educated and didn't obtain an independent income by participating in the labour force. This essentially forced women into embracing K-selection as a means of securing a tolerable quality of life. Civilisation was created by beta males *for the benefit of beta males*. It specifically sought to hobble R-selected males (alphas) and deny or punish women for following R-selection strategies. The demonization of extramarital sex, social ostracizing of loose women, and strong pressure for both men and women to marry all existed with this one purpose in mind. You'll see beta males still try to do this informally, though the cultural tide has shifted against them monumentally.

## Scientific Aside — Evolutionary Theory

Game is based on the lessons of evolutionary psychology, which has a number of implications to a Player's epistemology and thus his conduct on the streets. Going in-field is our way of conducting controlled experiments by formulating new hypotheses (e.g. a new opener, a change in body language) and then testing them on subjects (attractive girls) to see what happens. There are no nebulous grants or grad students to do the work for us — we are personally invested in the research methods and findings by forcing women to react. In economics terms, we are inducing women to reveal their preferences.

This element of practicality is why Game is more scientific and more effective than social psychology research papers. Social scientists have long known that you can't trust what people say; to get realistic results, you must instead force them to act. Imagine a grad student inviting a few dozen peers into a lab room so he can ask them questions about attraction and seduction. This is a highly contrived situation that introduces confounding factors we would never see on the street. It is a weak form of research. When a Player approaches a thousand girls and forces each one into compliance tests, only then is he mining pure data on human behavior. The Player's experimental evidence has greater validity and reliability.

Once you've done 1,000 sets you can ignore the scientists. Your direct in-field experience is more valuable than any advanced degree or lab-based data set, both in terms of general human behavior and specifically on getting beautiful women to have sex with you. Feel free to use their ideas to inspire you to new deductive principles (which you then must test in the field) but don't change something that you know works due to anything in an academic journal.

A good example is r/K selection. The theory was initially posed in the 1970s-1980s and has been largely replaced now by a broader "life-history," where the timing of key events in an organism's life are shaped by natural selection to produce the most surviving offspring. To be more precise and faithful to the biology literature (hat tip: Tom Torero):

- The majority of organisms don't fully polarise to K or r but are on a continuous spectrum. Organisms are thought of more as an "r strategist" or a "K strategist," but often the same organism will be using both strategies at different periods and to different ends. A compromise is reached between the two extremes.

- The concept was more of a heuristic device than hard science. It doesn't affect the seduction usage of the concept for the provider/lover distinction, but it's interesting to think of men using both r and K strategies in different situations. Even on the micro level of one date, a good fractionating seducer will be at different points on the spectrum. We do not think in limiting binary terms.

r = maximum growth rate of the population (N)

K = carrying capacity of its local environment

Your direct in-field evidence will not perfectly overlay cutting-edge evolutionary science. However, the important lesson for seduction is that using r/K selection to trigger women's responses is an incredibly powerful way to up your Game. As you strengthen your inner game and calibration you'll increasingly prioritise what you see with your own eyes over what consensus opinion tells you you should see. A belief in your own firsthand experience is a characteristic of a high-value man with strong boundaries.

Feminism was women's attempt to break out of the beta control and to gain access to far more exciting R-selection strategies. It also included lots of other things, but the main sexual motivation of feminism was to free women of dependence on beta males (and the stale boring marriages that resulted) so they could pursue **alphas** for exciting encounters.

Because nearly every man is a beta, they see this as a **bad thing**. They bitch, whine, and concoct grand schemes to put women back into their old roles. It's an irony of the **manosphere** that the very men who complain of feminism as an anti-male attack are the men who want to restructure society to have sexual relations with women who otherwise wouldn't want anything to do with them. It's value-taking.

I'm not condoning the many evils of feminism, but you must understand that much of the motivation you may have (as a recovering beta male) is selfish and value-taking — you want to get access to high-quality women without doing the hard work to become the kind of man they'd freely choose based on spontaneous natural desire. To use an economics metaphor, you are like a pampered unionised public sector worker suddenly trying to survive in the private sector. It's harder. In the private sector, companies will only hire you if you bring value to the table.

The biggest single mindset to adopt for daygame is **value-exchange**. You expect nothing for free. The world doesn't owe you a living. You will neither give nor take in an unequal forced (or dishonest) exchange. Every single girl who comes to you will do so because she likes you. She knows who and what you are and has decided that engaging in sexual congress with you is a good move.

Essentially, you become the R-selected man.

These are some of the sub-mindsets that emerge once you embrace the idea of game as value-exchange:

## Respect The Hustle

There are very few men in the world who are granted lots of easy sex with hot women. Even those who appear to have it easy are like ducks gracefully moving across the water with serene calm... while under the surface their legs are kicking frantically. Game is not the only way to get laid. When you see a guy getting laid and taking what he wants from the world, you must *respect the hustle*. Many of these men will naturally trigger envy and disgust in you, but this is your ego trying to dismiss them so you can remain comfortable with your sexless mediocrity. Whether the guy has started a rock band to bang groupies, set himself up as a nightclub promoter to bang club girls, or hits the gym to develop an elite physique, you should be sure to grasp the central point: getting laid well is a hustle that requires hard work, dedication and a plan. Respect the guys who are implementing their plan, even though it's different from yours.

Once you respect them you'll begin to develop a winner's mentality. The envy and rage will fall away, causing your entire vibe to improve. You'll begin to notice things they do that work, which you can then incorporate into your own game. You'll begin to engage with the world more proactively, shaking yourself out of a passive and reactive stupor. Proactivity is a prerequisite of Game.

# You Are An Entrepreneur Of The Sexual Market

Most guys are wage-slaves. They work for The Man. Every day is a boring trudge into the office to sit tapping away in their cubicle and collecting a salary. The true wealth producers are entrepreneurs. They develop a business idea and then implement. The best entrepreneurs are those who correctly predict what consumers want and then skillfully provide precisely that product, delivered at precisely the right marketplace. To take the metaphor further, entrepreneurs are streamlining business processes, improving efficiency, mobilising labour and pursuing excellence. Consumers give them money because they want the product. Entrepreneurs are market-focused; they don't stubbornly insist consumers are wrong for not appreciating their shitty product. They instead retool, rebrand and produce a better product.

This is how you should approach your Game and your Identity in general. Hot women are the consumers of your product, so you will apply an entrepreneurial mindset to figuring out exactly how to outperform your rivals. In honing your Game, you are identifying the most lucrative market for your product and then delivering the best version of it possible. Like a constantly-innovating entrepreneur, you must be willing to change up your Game. Consider your identity fluid and malleable while you tirelessly look for tweaks and improvements.

## Pursue Excellence

Worship excellence for its own sake and let yourself be inspired by witnessing it in action. I don't care for tennis but I like to see Roger Federer play precisely because he is technically perfect. That man has spent decades on the court honing his game to a razor-sharp edge. I don't drive, but yesterday when I was standing at the bus stop a guy drove past in a Lamborghini Aventador and it was simply amazing. The sleek low profile, the aerodynamic curves, the throaty roar of the engine, the way it snaked around corners glued to the road. It was a beautiful sight, like a panther stalking prey. I like to hear music that is expertly arranged with carefully selected notes, play video games that are beautifully paced, and read books by authors at the height of their powers.

Absorb excellence. Admire it, respect it, let it fill you with the inspiration to achieve excellence in your own life. This will drive your game forward technically and shift you out of long plateaus where you lull yourself into coasting. It will straighten out your vibe so you project a sense of purpose. Once you recognize the rarity of excellence, you will be motivated to devote your life to its pursuit.

# SEXUAL SELECTION IN DAYGAME

When you see men in the streets practicing daygame, be aware that both R- and K-selection is going on even if neither party realises it. Most daygame instruction is of the nice friendly variety in which the man is auditioning for the role as boyfriend. He may *intend* to get fast casual sex, but his style of daygame is putting him into the Boyfriend Box. This manifests itself as:

- Friendly compliments with no strong push (via teasing and challenging).

- Muted sexuality like a muzzled dog. You're essentially hiding your dick and not laying a strong man-vibe onto her.

- Little risk-taking. You're not touching her or moving things fast.

- Conversation topics follow a long-term dating strategy, such as qualifying yourself on how interesting your life is and what a high quality man you are.

- Quite high investment, both in time and effort. You have long street chats, try to idate frequently, and get involved in lengthy text exchanges.

This type of daygame is fine if you're looking for a girlfriend and don't mind waiting five dates or more to get laid. You'll find girls hook quite easily and give up numbers quite easily and even come out on dates quite easily. Though you would hope this is due to attraction, it happens more because you're not being very demanding of them and they sense you're willing to invest alot of time and energy. Girls following a K-selection strategy like this will audition you for the boyfriend role if they're single or checked-out of their current relationship. Everything is sweet and flowery, smiles all around. Meanwhile, you are putting very little pressure on them to acquiesce to your compliance tests. You are not imposing a strong frame.

The downside to the friendly approach is that you don't get laid much this way. Girls who want casual consequence-free sex will screen you out. Tourists in town won't have their adventure sex with you. Dissatisfied married women won't either, nor will

**Polarity**

*Men and women are meant to be different. Polarity is the difference in energy between masculinity and femininity that acts as a catalyst for attraction. Opposites attract like poles on a magnet.*

Arabs who risk tarnishing their public reputation. When you present yourself as someone who is great to get involved with, the girl thinks: *Do I want to get involved?* You'll also find lots of dates go nowhere because her shopping list for a boyfriend is long and she has an equally long list of eager rival suitors for that job.

In contrast, being the R-selected guy is easier. Well, easier **and** harder.

It's harder because you have to be a more sexworthy guy, which most beta males have trouble with. You must exude sexuality and charisma. Whereas the K-selected guy can offset deficiencies in his attractiveness by offering to pay a higher price in attention and commitment, the R-selected guy has initial attractiveness as his main weapon. The K-selected guy is competing against other beta males, so it doesn't take much to outperform themwhile the girl grows incrementally more comfortable with the idea of his dick inside her. The R-selected guy is going for it **right now** so he has to make her hot from the initial approach. That's a bigger challenge.

And yet it's easier. Fast consequence-free sex with a girl actually requires *less* compliance than a relationship. You are having a less traumatic influence on her life and have fewer bases to cover. The boyfriend has to be of acceptable social status, no strike-outs in ethnicity or style, suitably attentive, and willing to let her keep the frame. The sex guy only needs to be attractive. She has sexual needs and if you can satisfy them she might take a little time out of her day to jump your bones before going back to her normal life (and boyfriend search).

This book is principally about R-selected daygame, but we will always be aware of how to flip into K-selection when necessary. R-selection is fun, exciting and allows you to pick off more girls for sex (while retaining the ability to girlfriend them up if you so desire). I make an analytical distinction for readability here, but bear in mind that it's not fully binary. Generally I'd recommending presenting yourself mostly as R-selected with some K-selection to soften it and let her romantic triggers fire. There are also cases where you'll do it the opposite way. Are you a wolf in sheep's clothing or a panda in a leather jacket?

Moving to r-selection has the following likely outcomes:

- Far more blowouts. Girls very quickly realise the deal you are offering, so if they aren't up for it they'll blow you out rather than tolerate a long chat. You get harder rejections, but you will also waste less time.

- Sets crackle with sexual energy and your main challenge is to dial it down into rapport and investment so it doesn't just fizzle out early.

- You can hook, date, and sleep with women considerably outside your normal parameters because you are selling yourself on one narrow proposition: sexworthiness. A girl with a millionaire boyfriend wouldn't dump him for you (K-selection) but she might desire the occasional secret rendezvous (R-selection).

- Everything happens faster. SDLs and Day 2 lays become far more common, and everything ends faster as well. You are more likely to have a great experience that suddenly disappears in a cloud of vapour when the girl stops responding to texts.

> As you become to increasingly embody the r-selected mating strategy girls will instinctively recognise you as the casual sex guy. You will also increasingly identify yourself as such. Although this will greatly increase the quality of your sex life, it will eventually lead to some negative personality traits that you'll need to deal with. This tends to become a problem for Advanced players rather than Intermediates, so it is discussed in *Daygame Infinite*."

### Falling Between The Stools

When I started daygame I had lots of initial success at hooking girls and getting numbers. These would lead to lots of dates where nothing happened, and when I did get laid I'd end up with a new girlfriend. I was happy enough, but frustrated that the promise of abundant sex wasn't being fulfilled. So I rebranded myself as more of a bad boy. I sexualised sets, pushed harder and faster. Many sets blew up in my face or went achingly close to sex before the girl suddenly vanished, but I also started getting laid more. Girls gave me "player" tests and just assumed I didn't want to see them again after scoring the notch. It wasn't until long afterwards that I realised I'd moved from K-heavy game to R-heavy game. The point is that while I was in the awkward transition period between strategies my success ratio plummeted. Be aware that when you stop presenting yourself as the perfect boyfriend you need to replace it — with the perfect fuckbuddy

**Introvert**

_A person who becomes gradually tired when interacting with groups and recharges their energy when alone. An extrovert is the opposite. A common misconception is that introverts universally have bad social skills — this is untrue. Introverts can be excellent in social situations, but they do not feed off social energy like extroverts do._

The real high-level skill of daygame is knowing when to prioritise R-selection traits and when to turn to K-selection. If you meet a beautiful leggy model which angle do you take? Until you know more about her (from calibration and probing) **you simply don't know** because until you know her character and life options she's still an enigma. Maybe she has a highly satisfying globetrotting party life surrounded by rich orbiter chodes. In this case you prioritise R-selection to extract some unobtrusive adventure sex. But perhaps she's a natural **introvert** who treats her modelling as nothing more than a job and would rather spend time with her family or read a book. In this case you prioritise K-selection. Just be aware of which route you're taking because a slapdash jumble of both K and R will confuse both of you, leading to zero sex.

This leads us to two main routes of effective daygame:

1. **Start off strong R**. Get her horny and attracted to you as the exciting sex guy. Move as fast as you can. Whenever you sense barriers or non-compliance, consider bringing in the K. If you want to keep her around throw in more K.

2. **Start off strong K**. Draw her into conversation and rapport, with just enough teasing and challenging to keep polarity. Once you're sure your hooks are into her (usually on Day 2), start amping up the R to get faster and more exciting sex, and to position her into your rotation.

Both methods work. You'll adjust on the fly according to what you want and what you sense she needs. The method outlined in this book prioritises the R with strong aggressive **frame-pushing**, but it's entirely feasible to dial it down a little without going off-model.

There is alot of sex out on the streets. Daygame is _your_ hustle. It's how you get yours.

**Frame-push**

_When you pro-actively impose your frame onto a girl in order to absorb her into yours. Your frame can be both active and passive. A passive frame is like an unmoveable object, whereas an active frame is an irresistible force._

Really drill this mindset into yourself. You are a man of action. An initiator. The world is a harsh and unforgiving place that doesn't care if you're happy. You have to go out and make it happen. The world will push you back, cold and unyielding, but so long as you keep fighting it you'll find your way through. With enough practice, you will discover your business plan and find your ideal customers.

# CONDUCTING THE SYMPHONY

**Expert System**

*A decision support designed to solve complex problems by reasoning through bodies of knowledge, represented mainly as if–then rules.*

I like to delve deep into the meta-theory of Game. That's my inner nerd coming out. All through my life I've been attracted to **expert systems** — those self-contained spheres of excellence bound by rules and stratified by levels of learnable skill, such as chess, accounting, Brazilian Jiu Jitsu, and of course Game. I like to pull apart the watch and examine the pieces from every angle. While most of this intellectualisation is tangential to improving my ability to lay women, it does carry one very practical benefit into the field: **the power of the metaphor**.

Metaphors steers us past the clutter of details. They give us an end goal, telling us what success is supposed to look like. A good metaphor is like Michelangelo's mental image of the finished David, something that spurred him on and directed his chisel while he was still staring at a blank slab of stone.

I've spent a lot of time with daygamers this year on foreign jaunts, so we've knocked our heads together trying to refine our game. We've been looking for the distillable essence of daygame. What are the central themes that run through everything, and what are the metaphors to encapsulate them? We are both dissatisfied with the hyper-detailed linear programming model that treats pick-up like a step-by-step process. While there is unquestionably a process composed of individually analytically separable units that can be learned in isolation, it is akin to learning your chords and scales on the electric guitar. You scales and music theory are the building blocks of music, but knowing them won't turn you into Eric Clapton. At best you'll be one of those fast-fret thrash guitarists belting out a technically-skilled but cluttered and graceless metal solo.

**Fractal**

*A geometrical figure in which similar patterns recur at progressively smaller scales*

So how do we arrive at mastery? Once you can race up and down the fretboard, how do you learn to pick the correct notes and, just as importantly, drop the unnecessary ones? You'll see I've already introduced my main metaphor, but we'll get back to that soon.

## Scalability of Fractals

A common visual trick in modern Hollywood movies is to fly the camera from way up in the stratosphere down into an actor close-up without breaking the camera shot. Perhaps the shot will begin high above a city, and then swoop down towards an office block until it's zooming through a window, showing the protagonist reloading an Uzi while pressed up against a wall. We see a similar effect in GTAV on the Xbox when switching characters. You'll be on the streets in an over-the-shoulder view of Michael the heist-man, then suddenly zoom out into a Google-map view, reposition, then zoom back in to ground level to see Trevor snorting coke in a trailer park.

The metaphor here is scalability.

A fashionable movement in physics and maths in the late 1990s was Complexity theory, an outgrowth of Chaos theory. They saw the world as composed of many systems operating at different levels of explanation. For example, hydrogen and oxygen molecules operate according to the laws of physics, which give predictive precision to their behaviour. However, once you mix two hydrogen molecules with one oxygen molecule, you get this thing called water. It has entirely different properties from the isolated molecules. It's wet, it runs, it finds its own level, it quenches your thirst. These are emergent properties that neither exist nor can be predicted at a lower level of explanation.

This is a fascinating topic in its own right for those who wish to construct a grand theory of everything. It applies to Game as a meta-theoretical aid to help diagnose your progress over time, within a specific set, and it's also a good way of conducting the symphony. Let's unpack it.

Your Game has many levels. It infuses every area of your life. Consider this example of a street stop, beginning with the tiny and zooming back out to the massive:

**Micro:** While looking into a girl's eyes on the street you detect a mild flicker of attraction pass through. It lasts a moment then is gone, a tiny micro-communication. "Yes, she fancies me," you note. This is a Maybe or **Yes girl**. You decide to ease off a little to release tension and slip into rapport because you have confirmation that your attraction has hit.

**Small:** You're a few minutes into the chat and probing her about life growing up in her hometown of Sigisoara, Romania. You sense you're getting too logical and Wikipedia-like in discussing the features of the town. So you pull the conversation towards emotions, hopes and dreams to inject flavour and colour to the conversation.

**Yes Girl**

*A girl who is immediately attracted to you and is sexually available. This is in contrast to unavailable or unattracted girls (No Girls), or girls who are somewhere in between (Maybe Girls).*

*A short trip to a foreign city with the express purpose of seducing local girls. The ideal trip length is ten days, to get enough time to close the Yes Girls but not so long as to flatten your vibe from over-gaming.*

**Medium:** Your internal clock has ticked off ten minutes and she doesn't seem to have much happening in her life right now. "I think I'll idate this girl," you decide. You've plotted where you are in the model and decided it's time to shuffle her into the next phase.

**Large:** You're talking to this girl on the second day of your **Euro-jaunt**. You're still number-farming. You can't afford to devote six hours to one girl because it'll suck your momentum and incur an opportunity cost in other girls not approached. As you walk her to a café you've already set a time-limit. One coffee, thirty minutes, then you'll take her number and hit the streets again. Add her to the number-filter funnel and go for a Day 2 later in the week.

**Massive:** You need to allocate an hour or two this evening to Facebook/Whatsapp maintenance for your best existing leads. Yulia from Latvia is still wavering over visiting London. You kissed her on the Day 2 a couple of months ago and have been slowly working the long game. She'll need a bit more comfort, so you should give her a Skype call tonight. She likes drawing so you should probably give her some homework to draw you a picture.

---

### Scalability as a technique

**Krauser Tip**
precision engineering

I'll discuss later in this chapter how Game's main rhythm is the use of pacing to play on the human emotional bias towards relativity rather than absolutes. Expertly pacing a set between extremes of fast-slow, hard-soft, busy-quiet, close-far is the advanced goal. One such dichotomy is micro-massive. As you talk to the girl, you should take her mind on a journey from the micro to the massive and back again. Move her attention seamlessly from the immediate sensations of the cold glass in her hand with droplets of iced water tracing snakelike paths down the outside, to the soft warmth of the roaring fireplace next to your table….. and then to the vistas of your hiking trip along the old fortified walls of Northern England, brown-green hills stretching out as far as the eye can see, meeting the grey blanket of the winter sky. The same walls that two thousand years ago were garrisoned by Roman troops at the outer extremity of their empire. In and out. Read good fiction to really master this technique. Watch how a writer describing, say, a WWII conference of men in an old gentleman's club discussing an espionage mission against the Nazis can effortlessly slip from vivid precise details of micro-movements to broad strokes of the Allied war effort, and back again. Mentally she will feel like Lois Lane being swept off the street and flown around the clouds by Superman.

---

At any point in the interaction, or the day, or the holiday, it's good to have the capability to choose your zoom level. When you're face-to-face with the girl, you must be able to zoom in close to read micro-calibrations and to monitor the tension on the fishing line from moment to moment. You must simultaneously be able to zoom back out to where the interaction is headed and the tweaks necessary for vibe or comfort or sexuality. Zoom even further back, and see how much time and effort you want to put into this girl and whether right now is the correct time to be doing it. Game is all about going in and out, in and out, in more ways than one.

# The Four-Piece Rock Band

**State**

*Your mood as it is projected onto those around you. When you feel socially free and uninhibited you can micro-calibrate to the energy of the streets. You develop an aura and your approach anxiety drops to near-zero. This is the peak flow state that impresses girls and supercharges the strength of a girl's hook.*

Consider how an expertly arranged piece of popular music is put together. On my way to the café this morning I was listening to Adele's hit Rolling In The Deep. Find it on Youtube and listen, then come back to me....

... ok? Note the emotional progression as the song picks up pace. She begins with a strumming guitar that sets a marching pace to time her vocals, soon bringing in a pounding drum beat. There is still a void, the song sounds hollow as if the drums and vocals define the boundaries of an otherwise empty room.... And then she brings in the bass and heavy guitar as the vocals are ramped up for the chorus. I'm not attracted to fat girls but I'll admit Adele masterfully arranges her intro. From the very opening moments she hooks your attention and then rides an emotional wave up and down, in and out. Just as the intensity peaks she pulls right back out into the verse and calms things down. Once we reach the middle third she breaks pacing again then ties in recurring motifs and temporarily takes us back to the empty sounds of the opener.

Good musicians are like good storytellers. They hook you, strap you into the rollercoaster, and then shamelessly play you with expertly constructed peaks and troughs. They are hijacking your emotional **state** to direct it precisely where they want it to go. Sound familiar? We'll go into the pacing later but for now let's consider the instruments.

What do I mean about creating a full sound? Listen to a modern song produced in a good studio (or a remastered classic) and listen to it with great quality headphones. Close your eyes and absorb the sounds. Focus on the melody for a while, catching the precise notes. Then pick out the bass line humming along. Be aware of the incidental instruments thrown in to highlight key notes that then fade back out. Where do the backing vocals come in and how many people are providing them. When you really listen actively to a good song it's incredible how well-layered the sound is.

Then go listen to a scratchy old 50s song with just one hillbilly and his acoustic guitar. That hillbilly may have written a catchy song but the sound quality is piss poor. Each sound has weak fidelity and there's very little going on. It's a tinny flat, crackly sound. It's like coming out a five-star restaurant and buying a hot dog from a street vendor.

The classic Western combination is the four piece band. A drummer, a bassist, a lead guitarist, and a vocalist/rhythm guitarist. This is the minimum requirement to produce a full sound. Let's apply it to Game.

**Drummer:** This is your marching beat. Drums determine the pace and timing of the band, with everyone else aligning themselves to its beat. When talking to a girl this is fueled by your sexual intent. As you talk to her you'll pull her into your frame by imposing your beat onto hers, putting her on your rhythm. The precise level of your intent, its intensity and your state will determine the BPM. It may slow down, but it never ceases.

**Bassist:** This is your masculine gravitas. The Bass fills out the sound and grounds it, giving it a weighty feel. The same goes for interacting with the girl. Your core masculine presence is weighty, rooted and immoveable. While everyone's attention is drawn to the melody, the bass is strumming away in the background below conscious awareness, filling the space, noticed only when it's absent and suddenly the sound feels tinny and lightweight.

**Rhythm Guitar:** This is your basic technical model. Most popular songs have a simple chord progression that marks the verse, the bridge and the chorus, and rely upon the chord changes of the guitar to identify each. Just as sexual energy is not enough to attract women, a basic drumbeat is insufficient to move the song along; it must utilize each chord to move the mind. When you apply the step-by-step model you are changing chords. Each time you stack assumptions, ask an open-ended question, segue into a new topic, slap her hand… these are the chord changes. They move the interaction back and forth between attraction and comfort.

**Lead Guitar:** This is the spice and flourish, the spiking. Songs need a vibrancy, they need fiddly twinky-twonky bits to break the unrelenting wall of sound. A guitarist inserting a quick lick at the vocalist's pause between sentences is a quick tease. A statement of intent. When he runs off into a fret-hammering solo, that's like when you spiral into a story, pulling the conversation to a temporary giddy height.

**Vocals:** This is the colour. As the element closest to our conscious thought, vocals are what we sing in the shower after hearing the full song. The content of the words doesn't matter much — just think how it's possible to enjoy songs in a foreign language or with otherwise unintelligible singers. It's the cadence and flow of the voice that stirs our emotions and the occasional totemic or anthemic turns of phrase. Lyrics are not a philosophical treatise. In your Game this is the content and symbolism in your conversation. It's how you paint pictures with evocative imagery, it's how you probe and draw information from her, it's the banter and the rapport.

Remember we are just talking metaphors here, not scientific fact. The purpose is to improve our Game. The main lesson is this:

*Your game should be a fully-formed sound*

Where are you lacking? Are you a bit lightweight in your impact (no bassline / gravitas), somewhat lacking in conviction and intent (weak drum beat), floundering aimlessly in set (wrong chord changes), or flat and boring (no lead guitar)?

You can self-diagnose your game by monitoring your sound. Taking the metaphor further, you can improve your game by increasing the fidelity of each instrument and fidding with the balance between them. Take some time tuning that rhythm guitar and practice new chord progressions, which will make your bassline shine even more effectively.

The whole point is to improve the girl's estimation of your value and enjoyment of the interaction. Just as when your ear perks up upon hearing a good hook on the radio, the girl will experience your presence as a fully-formed sound. Each instrument hits its notes with clarity and timing. The band is tight. Now let's look at how to arrange the song.

# Composition

The human mind is designed to react to small changes in relative states of being rather than absolute states. You'll find examples of this all around you:

- Lottery winners get a flush of emotion upon collecting their prize and soon sink back into their default level of happiness.

- Playing Call of Duty online for two hours fries your brain with nonstop adrenalin so you need to pause, make a cup of tea, then return after a break.

- When you first check into a tropical beach resort you can't wait to jump into the surf. After a few days you look at the sea, say "meh," and check your Twitter feed.

Deep within the human soul is a tendency to take our current blessings for granted. We are prone to focusing all our mental energy not on what we have, but rather on the next step up the ladder. This is the engine of progress. Natural selection favours the DNA that strives to achieve, even if it makes the vessel organism unhappy and jittery while carrying out the DNA's plan. Nature doesn't care if you're happy, it just cares if you pass on your genes. Hence we find ourselves grinding away on the treadmill, eyes on the prize. And as soon as we win, our eyes turn to the next prize and the next treadmill. To continue the music metaphor:

*You quickly fall into a new rhythm in life*

Just as the human eye detects movement, human emotions also detect movement. They seek contrast. **Contrast is King**. This is the central unifying theme in Game and we'll use the music metaphor to illustrate it.

Go back and listen to that Adele song. Or perhaps an even more bombastic entry into the musical canon — say, Bonnie Tyler's "Total Eclipse Of The Heart." Something melodramatic and overwrought brings out the learning points. As a little exercise, try to visually represent the song on paper as a graph, like a heartrate monitor in the Emergency Room. Draw the peaks and troughs in emotion with one colour pen. Listen to it again and overlay another colour for the volume. Another colour for the thickness of the sound. Another colour again to mark the incidental spikes of keyboards and guitar licks. Pretty soon you'll see a complex interplay of coloured waves ebbing and flowing, sometimes soft and slow like waves lapping along a beachfront other times the crashing and banging of the violent sea crashing against a cliff face.

*This is how your game should be.*

Let's consider a range of contrasts that can be woven together into a complex interplay of themes:

1. **Push-Pull**: You are at times teasing and challenging her, accusing her of being a pervert, or clumsy, or uncultured, or having hamster cheeks. At other times you are at the other end of the spectrum, holding her hand as you exchange names, telling her she's got great fashion sense and sexy legs.

2. **Fast-Slow:** Sometimes you are slamming into her with a strong street stop and hustling her along to the idate and telling her to drink up before the next pub. She feels harried and pressured. Other times you ease off like you have all the time in the world.

3. **Present-Absent:** Looking deep into her eyes, engaging with her immediate concerns, riding the waves of the micro-communications and being fully in the moment is intense. You are fully present and she has your attention. So when you withdraw, let your gaze wander, seem preoccupied and distant she feels it all the more keenly.

4. **Bad-Good:** You are a free-spirited, self-absorbed entitled bad boy who lives life on his own terms. No-one can control you, dominate you or wrest away what you've fought for. Yet you call your grandmother every Sunday lunchtime to ask about her week and you have to cut this date short because your friend needs you.

5. **Smart-Stupid:** You just regaled her with a story that seamlessly weaved in the cultural history of Japan with some advances in molecular biology and your thoughts on the bushido spirit. Then you pat your belly and tell her you want a cheeseburger, revelling in the baser appetites of life.

6. **Near-Far:** Sometimes you talk about the joy of sitting in a comfortable leather sofa chair, a mug of steaming coffee and the soft sounds of 1940s jazz on the radio, enjoying the sensations that make life so rich in colour. And other times you are outlining your grand theory of life, history, of male-female interactions.

7. **Warm-Cold:** Girls like it when you encourage them, reward them with approval, and make them feel like the world is a warm safe place full of fluffy bunny rabbits. They also like your hard pitiless side that won't be pushed, won't take any bullshit, and will ruthlessly crush your enemies.

8. **Advance-Retreat:** At times you are moving in on her, closing distance, touching her, eye-fucking her, taking control of her body and mind. Other times you lean back and give her space to fall into you, take your foot off the pedal, make her chase.

There are many more pairs for you to uncover. The point is that you are not travelling at one speed or overusing one chord. That's boring. Her mind will quickly adjust to the new normal no matter how cool you are and gradually your distinct outline as a man will fade into the background because her eye responds to *movement*. Keep moving yourself from one side to the other, learn to weave the strands together so you are at times hot on one pair while cold on another. Try to feel your own personal heat map and adjust on the fly. This is the rich texture of seduction.

Now we can weave together the two main principles of this chapter on mindsets, the two main metaphors. We are engaging the girl on her R-selection strategy for fast sex and we are sucking her into a symphony we conduct in fully vibrant ever-changing sound. We'll call this the Love Bubble.

Put another way, if we are to zoom out a level above the usual daygame model and abstract one step further we are doing this:

- Pull the girl in with an attractive hook

- Lead her along a complex emotional journey

- Let the crescendo rise until it peaks in sex

It should be obvious that this is an emotional journey and not a logical negotiation (the latter gets you **LJBF**d or, at best, boyfriended). This is why it is so important to be fully present in the moment and authentic in your thoughts and actions. Deep down you are mobilising well-drilled muscle memory to shuttle the interaction along a logical path (the daygame model) with a desired outcome (sex), but this rarely surfaces into your awareness while talking to the girl. You have to trust your intuition to trigger and steer at the key moments while releasing all your mental resources to enter that flow state of Now.

**LJBF**

*Let's Just Be Friends. Girls are hardwired to extract attention and support from men without giving sex in return. When she has successfully done so, you are in the Friend Zone giving her "free" attention. LJBF is the female version of the male pump'n'dump, in which the man extracts sex without providing continued attention and support*

As you hit an unencumbered flow state you'll naturally sense which girls to open. The flow state will allow you to create specific unique teases and assumptions from your opener. You'll effortlessly slide into engaging conversation and react to the ebbs and flows of her mood, micro-calibrating to the moment. The girl will feel you as a force of nature sucking her into your world.

It's hard to convey just how special an experience you are giving her. This may be literally the **one time** in her life when a high value man seduces her with beautiful artistic precision, expertly navigating her through a carefully crafted journey that hits all the highs on her emotional spectrum. She cannot create that for herself. There's no shop she can buy it from. It must come from a man and most men are woefully unable to deliver it.

## Purity of "moments"

The Love Bubble is timeless, like stopping the Matrix in bullet-time. You are fully present in the Now and pull her into it, this bubble of suspended time while the rest of the world plods by in dreary misery. Inside the love bubble every colour is rich and vibrant, every scent full of texture, every emotion strong. A girl will lose herself in it just as she may lose herself in the music on a nightclub dancefloor.

There's no logic in the moment. There's no career worries, family troubles, health worries, money worries….. and no obligations to boyfriends.

Once you've got the intermediate skillset down pat you can free yourself from it. It's no different from learning how to box. Endless repetition on the heavy bag drills your muscle memory until you couldn't throw a technically imperfect punch if you tried. You stop thinking of the mechanics and free your mind to calibrate to your opponent — figuring out his timing and distance, drawing him out of position — until you find the spot to let the punch go. Intuition takes over.

This book is a stepping stone. It's the technique work in the boxing gym. There are infinite if-this-then-that permutations that you can drill, but the ideal end state is to put this book on a shelf and never look at it again. Get the skills down and then free your mind for the higher-order concerns of creating a succession of pure moments, surfing her emotions as you guide her to your bedroom.

# TARGETING

## *Goal: Find the girl you like*

In my time teaching and reading field reports I've noticed men seem to view women as an amorphous fungible army of clones, with their only distinguishing characteristic as where they rank on the 1-10 scale. Most men embrace a one-size-fits-all approach to The Game. Imagine if a jungle was a mono-species environment with only one predator, one type of prey, and one strategy for the former to catch the later.

If only life were that simple.

Be glad it's not, because if this were true you'd be royally fucked. The reality of Game is there is a complex ecosystem in which multiple predators are using myriad strategies to snare almost infinite types of prey. The mongoose traps the snake, the leopard traps the boar, the panthers eat baboons and the parrots eat insects. Specialisation is the name of the game in the animal kingdom, and so it will be with your game. You have a particular set of strengths and weaknesses. This will predispose certain types of girls to liking you, and will better fit you naturally to certain strategies. Most of your lays will come from understanding your niche. You can still expand your horizons and go after girls you "shouldn't" in ways you "shouldn't," but only while expecting significant drop-off in your success rates.

Daygame is one group of strategies. Some girls are far more amenable to it than others, and others simply will not accept it.

So, getting back to the real world let's consider which girls are daygameable. I have spent countless hours observing targets and have found one unifying trait that predicts a girl's <u>receptiveness to day approaches</u>: femininity.

**Feminine Girls** — These are susceptible to daygame magic. They enjoy taking the submissive curious female role and respond positively to a masculine frame push and value. This book is about how to get them.

**Masculine Girls** — These girls have absorbed a caricature of the male value system. They are disconnected from their feminine essence and strive to take on masculine mindsets. They are attracted to good looks, height, buff bodies and youth (like men are). They resist forming deep connections and prefer superficial sport fucking, which is more easily achieved through night game. To get these girls you'll have to go considerably off-model.

## Value gap

The bread and butter of daygame is going after the hottest women you can reasonably expect to catch, and most of this book is written with that in mind. However, just as Einstein found that strange things happen at the extremes of speed, the rules of Game physics bend at the extremes of value. All bets are off when your SMV is a couple of points above the girl's. You can break many rules and apply only the weakest game, and you may still get her. That's why you'll see infield videos of extremely attractive men doing fast simple pulls on pretty-but-unremarkable women despite displaying weak game. The value gap is so large the girl simply doesn't care. Her hindbrain is flashing "this is your winning DNA lottery ticket, grab it now".

Most of the time we'll ignore this scenario because a man who feeds on scraps is underselling himself. We want women hotter and younger than we are. There is one exception: Once you have built your masculine value to a certain stratospheric level, you will be of higher value than pretty much every woman you could ever conceivably meet. She may be a ten but you are a fifteen. This will lead to daygame sets that have the dynamic of a groupie meeting her favourite rock star — no game needed. Most of us are a long way from that reality, but bear it in mind when watching Youtube so you are not distracted from the path of tight game.

### Green lights

*Girls will react to each attempt to move them towards sex. An easy heuristic is the Traffic Lights system. A strongly enthusiastic girl will give Green Lights by actively encouraging your escalation. A strongly unenthusiastic girl will try to block or evade your escalation, giving Red Lights. Most girls will be in the middle, passively accepting the escalation by giving Amber Lights. Beginners are usually reticent to escalate even on clear Greens, while expert players escalate on Amber.*

My expertise is in catching feminine girls, so my book focuses on that. It's what I like and it's what I'm good at. I do get the occasional mannish girl, however, so just bear in mind how you'll need to tweak your game:

- They expect to take more active control of the mating ritual and will try to lead the interaction.

- Your physical appearance and lifestyle niche are more important than your charisma. If you aren't immediately their type, you're out. Screen for No Girls faster.

- They are sluttier. Once they like you, the decision to fuck comes faster and they'll give **green lights** rather than amber.

- They will reject the MaleDom-FemSub polarity. When you find her constantly rebelling you need to stop pushing your frame and instead let her lead you to the sex.

Assume the rest of this book is talking about feminine girls unless I specifically state otherwise. So now we need to talk about animals...

*Every girl embodies the character of a specific mammal.*

That sounds like a weird statement but it's an extremely useful typology to identify girls. Putting an animal type on a girl not only shows you the best practices for gaming them, but also triggers specific teases and humour to hook the set and impose your frame. Here are the most common types:

## 1. Squirrel

*Girl waiting for her Uber*
*– Minnesota girl.*

This is the most common. Squirrels are average height with pretty soft faces, rounded cheeks and features, thick hair and a timid, unassuming character. Her fashion will have several "softeners" to indicate girlishness, such as a woolly hat and colourful mittens in winter or a little teddy bear keyring hanging from her handbag. When she smiles she'll actually look like a chipmunk.

Squirrels usually open easily and very quickly accept the submissive frame. They consider themselves ten-a-penny and are often surprised you even noticed them. They love soft teases about being cute. These girls are not used to being chased by rich orbiter chodes so they'll be more responsive to lifestyle DHVs. Even if they are not interested in you, they will appreciate your efforts and rarely blow you out despite your aggressive r-selection game.

## 2. Giraffe

*Tall receptive blonde*

This is the long-limbed upright girl with the narrow hips and angular features much loved by the catwalk industry. She has a proud bearing and a simple elegant fashion sense. Usually she'll look extremely serious and scarily off-putting while striding down the street. She's probably employed in a job that leverages her beauty.

Giraffes are initially intimidating but they are as sweet as any other girl. The initial coldness is because they are used to guys being scared of them and nervously kissing their ass. Usually they'll test you hard in the beginning to see if your metaphorical height (character) is enough to match their literal height. You have to open strong and hit them with a borderline-insulting tease delivered with an undercurrent of authentic warmth.

Bear in mind she's almost certainly got several rich provider chode orbiters and a fashion photographer promising her model agency introductions. Don't try to compete with that. Stubbornly refuse to qualify yourself on provider lines. Go 100% charisma. This girl has men of a certain type around her — polite respectful provider chodes with constant angles to manipulate their way into her knickers. She has a Prada handbag, endless VIP table invitations and a separate closet just for shoes. What she doesn't have is a bad boy who doesn't give a flying fuck about all these trappings of high society, a guy who'll just maul her and drag her to the bathrooms for a rousting. That's what she needs.

## 3. Greyhound

Commonly mistaken for a giraffe, the greyhound is almost as tall but possesses real curves and a smooth sensuality to her movements (as opposed to the cold, stilted grace of a giraffe). Unlike the giraffe's high fashion and numerous brand labels, the greyhound has an understated and idiosyncratic fashion. She doesn't look like she's trying to impress anyone. She thinks giraffes are silly fools.

Greyhounds are almost always intelligent and very engaging to talk to. They'll smile, laugh, and contribute easily. She'll have real hobbies and probably studied to be a vet, engineer or doctor. Though they usually have high self-esteem, unlike giraffes they don't need a hard opening tease. Just be open and authentic because they are immediately scanning for your intelligence and cultural sophistication.

Your main weapon is your well-rounded sophistication. You need anti-provider game because these girls already have a self-sufficient career lined up, which likely exposes them to a horde of weak beta males. They crave masculine gravitas.

## 4. Cat

These girls are prowling sexual predators disguised as lambs. They'll usualy be of medium height and possess strong curves that they accentuate with their clothing and a very subtle manner — tight jeans, little shoes, big hair. Imagine the archetypal French girl with wavy brown hair, glasses, a colourful scarf and a cigarette dangling suggestively from her fingertips.

You'll know she's a cat by how calm and comfortable she is with the sexual tension. Whereas the squirrel will blush and giggle, the cat will meet you dead-on with a simmering sexual confidence. Her outward appearances is that of a a good girl, but there's a spark to her eyes.

She'll have a languid manner and often doesn't say a lot. You'll sense she's looking you up and down, sizing you up for the potential cat-and-mouse game. Whereas your Game puts squirrels off balance and makes them run up the oak tree, cats just purr and stretch.

## 5. Skunk

This is the rebel. She'll usually be of average height and probably voluptuous (or chubby). Her hair is dyed, her ears pierced and her fashion and walk issue a challenge to the world. Like every other girl, she might be very sweet and want the same things in life, but there's an outer shell of rebellion. This is the girl most likely to inhabit a definable sub-culture, identifiable by her slogan or band t-shirts.

The skunk responds well to acceptance of her style. She's trying hard to signal how different she is from other girls, and will reward you for pointing out that fact. She's more willing to step outside normal social convention, more willing to be a bit crazy. Don't tease her identity choices in a disrespectful manner. So long as she thinks you don't look down on her pariah status, she'll take the street stop well. If you project "I think you're easy because you look like a slut" she'll get hyper-defensive. These girls actually are the easiest for toilet pulls. Just don't tell her you know it. Work the rebellion and adventure angle.

Next time you're walking around town, practice by categorising girls that you see. Start with the types I've outlined and eventually add your own. Learn to recognise the identifying signals in dress, body language, and physical makeup. This will give you a shortcut to your cold-read and easy ammunition for your first tease.

## Cold Reading Drill

The easiest way to hone your cold reading skills is to people-watch. Sit on a park bench or by a cafe window and then observe the women who walk past. Try to observe rather than simply see. Engage your mind in making speculative deductions based on the information they give you based on their fashion, manner, facial features, and mood. Don't limit yourself to only pretty girls.

Try to label the girls with a simple description, e.g. 'lost Italian tourist' or 'busy lawyer'. Then concoct a potential backstory for them, similar to those I present over the next few pages. The purpose is not to be correct but rather to train your creative energies to quickly create material that you can feed back to girls early in the interaction. This will alleviate the common worry of running out of things to say.

This drill is stress-free because you don't need to actually open the girls nor risk rejection. You can do it while hung-over or sleepy.

I will present some archetypes you can look for. Remember: they are not presented as the literal truth. Less than half of the girls you meet will fit a type. They are food for thought, ammunition to feed into your creative guns. When you identify a girl as a type, you can open up a whole world of playful assumptions. Then as she reacts and feeds back information you can refine your viewpoint until you're certain of how to play it. Combine that with a comparison to a furry mammal and you're well into the vibing stage.

# Cold Reading

As you spend more time in the field you get better at reading a girl's life situation. You'll begin to spot the nuances in dress and looks which mark the girl's particular country of origin. In the beginning it helps to study Google Images for photos of girls from different regions. It will become even easier as you travel more, because you'll see hundreds of girls in their home countries and develop a feel for their lifestyles. There's a world of difference between the realities of a Moscow barbie doll and of a Bosnian village girl. Picking up on the subtleties helps you moderate your game to connect more effectively.

At first reading my typology may sound ridiculous. "How can you distill the full complexity of female differences down to such rigid archetypes," you may protest. The purpose is not to be scientifically correct. You need triggers to build the mythology:

1. You need raw material to build a good assumption stack off the opener

2. You need fantastical elements to paint pictures with your words in the ensuing vibing

3. You need potential sources of rapport to spring to mind while getting her invested

4. You need playful stereotypes to tease her and frame her

5. You want a default mode of dealing with her until you've gathered enough information about the specifics of her character and situation.

Game is **fun**. You are tooling the girl. Pushing her, pulling her, sweeping her off her feet. Mythologise her life to draw her into a world of evocative imagery and higher meaning. So no we **aren't** going to Wikipedia to collect actuarial stats on each country in order to make dry guesses. We **are** instead leveraging cultural stereotypes to make it all fun. If she's Turkish she's a Bond Girl. If she's Russian she's a KGB assassin. With this in mind consider the following character types:

Do this for Majors at the university

# Slavic Princess

She's got long slim legs, a tight firm ass, high cheekbones and flowing soft hair. She walks in heels with studied grace and on the rare occasion she's not in a skirt she'll be sure her tight jeans accentuate her femininity. Her aunt and grandmother drilled into her the importance of always looking her best to land a good husband. Though she looks like a pouty catwalk model she can cook traditional recipes, has read all the Russian classics and has deep bonds with childhood friends. An English girl looking like her would be a horrible illmannered oaf, but she's loving and sweet to any man dominant and manly enough to win her over. She will refuse to kiss or kino on the first two dates but once she's sure she wants you, she'll go from 0 to 100mph in seconds and overwhelm you with passion.

# Silly Wop

She's from a small town in The Med where men are lazy pushovers and women nagging shrews. Her pretty-boy orbiters are all mummy's boys she leads on a merry dance. She has hairy arms and is ever so slightly overweight, but her youth and natural curves carry it well. She's commonly seen wandering aimlessly through swerving traffic, a London guidebook in her hand and Converse All Stars on her feet. She's almost certainly a squirrel at heart. Her ideas of life are and may involve a gap year, some waitressing, and an English study trip to Bournemouth. She's probably never fucked a guy from a nightclub, but almost certainly given a blowjob behind the bike shed on school camp. She assumes you want a girlfriend.

# French Smoker

She's dressed with unmistakeable panache yet looks identical to every other girl in Paris. She'll have frumpy shoes, tight faded blue jeans or dark leggings, at least one colourful scarf, and a brown bag hanging from her shoulder. She'll rarely show skin but always shows her figure. She expects your relationship to be open, a series of late-night assignations with a post-coital cigarette on the balcony. She won't lead but confidently follows. She loves The Beatles and reads existential philosophy.

# Muslim Bond Girl

This dark sultry beauty has long thick shampoo commercial hair and fiery dark eyes to complement her olive skin. She smoulders with hot forbidden sexuality and a bitchy look of disdain. She covers her skin, but the absence of headscarf and vulgar gold jewelry betray her Europhilia. Well-educated and well travelled she'll surprise you with her knowedge. Tired of constant social pressure in her homeland to protect her virtue and marry well, she's aching for a holiday fling with a discreet lover.

# Persian Princess

Easily identified by her silky thick black hair and excessive make-up. Her eyes and lips seem massive. There'll be some gold on her fingers and wrists, and likely a high-end branded handbag. Dressed mostly in blacks and greys, she wouldn't dream of being seen in trainers. We are as exotic to her as she is to us, holding excessively romantic notions of European men. Play up the gentleman side. Become Hugh Grant. As with all Middle Easterners, discretion is everything. There will be no hand-in-hand walking down Oxford Street; only a secretive succession of closed-door meetings.

# Latvanian Waitress

Her wide eyes and long legs will trick you into thinking she's living the dream life of parties, yachts, and orbiter chodes. Don't make this mistake. Until two months ago she shared a grotty one-bedroom apartment with her parents in a 1960s Soviet tenement block. She's broke and thinks the welfare state is a deeply evil attempt for Bolsheviks to rule the world again. She jumped on a Ryanair flight with her EU passport to get some adventure. Her £6 per hour waitressing job makes her feel rich, and she has a genuine work ethic and sense of self reliance. What she craves most is excitement and broader horizons.

# African Minx

This girl is all curves and wiggle. She's got a soft vibe and good fashion. You'll spend half your emotional energy concentrating on her wide round ass, totally amazed that it's not offset by a fat belly. She pipelines thoughts of steamy sex directly into your brain from her curves and mannerisms. Yet she's far tamer than she looks, raised in a traditional environment were casual sex is frowned upon. Her confidence comes from an awareness of her sexuality and her strong identification with femininity, rather than a loose sexual history. She banters well and gives you lots of serious forebrain talk about what a good church-going girl she is. However, once that hindbrain revs up she'll jump your bones in a heartbeat.

# New York Slut

This girl thinks she's empowered. She'll be walking decisively to an important meeting carrying a Starbucks in one hand while tapping a text message into her smartphone. She's slim and her fashion is discreetly high-end. Though she talks of feminism, deep in her hearts she's as sweet as the next girl. Drop in quaint old words and European turns of phrase. Tell her it's awfully nice to meet her. She wants a holiday adventure fuck for her mental scrapbook before returning home. Dance adeptly around the edges of her nonsensical American education, so as not to trigger a feminist rant. Steer the conversation towards happy thoughts. She thinks Europeans are sophisticated, so hold that frame and use it to your advantage. For her, the decision to makeout is only one step before the decision to fuck.

# Latina Preener

This temperamental headcase can barely control her wild swings in mood. One minute she's passionate, the next she hates you. On the street you'll first notice her buxom curves and shapely legs before your eyes move onto her long hair and slightly excessive makeup. Perhaps she's wearing big hooped earrings or coloured contact lenses. She's pretty and bangable but has a slightly grotty look to her, like a sex worker who hasn't yet reached burnout. This girl really fancies herself. She carrier her chin high and loves the attention of your street stop. A good push will have her laughing. From there it's a minefield. She wants to fuck and she'll be good at it, but the whole mating dance is her opportunity to derail you until you become just another orbiter chode to feed her princess fantasies. Keep resisting it. It's a fight.

# Balkan Crazy

This girl was extracted from an evolutionary goldmine of perfect genetics: Slavic bone structure and Ottoman curves. She has the long legs, long hair and high cheekbones of the Russians, but also the dark features, voluptuous curves and smoldering fire of the Turks. It's a land of giraffes and greyhounds. In summer she dons trainers, denim cut-offs, and a tight vests as she struts down the promenade. She's warm from the beginning and makes connections easily. Her local men are tall, strong, physically-masculine guys so you need some hair on your chest to hold your own against that competition. The real value-add is in showing a multi-faceted sophistication in your lifestyle and world-view. She'll insist every *other* Balkan girl is a raging slut.

# WHERE TO FIND THE GIRLS

You will quickly settle upon a standard daygame route that you inherited from whoever first took you out onto the streets. In London that's the Golden Triangle of Oxford Street-Leicester Square-Covent Garden. There'll be a reason for most guys hitting the same places: that's where the girls are. At some point, however, you'll want to get more creative. What happens when you roll into a new city or get tired of the same old places? The best way to generate ideas for new locations is to think about the girls you want, then think about where they'd go. Let's first start with the simple typologies, with a focus on London:

1. **Tourists** — London is a highly centralised city with numerous key tourist sites within walking distance of each other. The highest concentration of tourists will be found at the sites or on the main walking routes between them. These girls will be taking photographs outside Buckingham Palace, wandering along the South Bank, trying the weekend market at Camden, or hanging around Trafalgar Square and British Museum.

2. **English Students** — Girls who are staying for a few months have likely already done the sites, so now they have a small social circle of other foreigners from school. They'll be sitting in cafes doing homework or on Skype with family. You will often find them wandering through parks or sitting down to read a book. They'll be somewhere on the Primark-to-Primark section of Oxford Street doing their shopping.

3. **Arabs and Asians** — The girls who come to London to spend their orbiter's / daddy's credit card will be found in upscale department stores like Selfridges, Liberty and Harrods. Their hotels are likely near Edgeware Road, Notting Hill, or Mayfair, and they'll walk the streets nearby.

4. **Sloaneys** — Certain nationalities group together in particular areas. French girls often live and hang out in South Kensington and Earls Court. Russians and English toff girls will be found around Sloane Square.

5. **Career Girls** — She's going to be at work during office hours so you'll have to catch her on her lunch break or journey home. Hang out near a major Underground station to catch them on the way in, or alternatively to hang inside a major interchange (such as Baker Street) and catch them on the platform.

Always consider the weather. Girls are phototropic so you'll see far more of them on sunny days and they'll be in a much better mood. When the weather is good, pay extra attention to parks and wide pedestrian boulevards. When it's cold and rainy you should turn your attention to shopping malls, indoor tourist sites, and the insides of shops.

You must also consider the time and day of the week. Weekends are obviously the peak time for all types of girl, but what about mid-week? The girls you see in mid-afternoon on Monday are precisely the girls who don't have 9-to-5 careers. That's when you'll see students, tourists, kept-women, waitresses, bartenders etc. In contrast, if you like office girls you should be near major Underground stations between 5pm and 7pm.

Your timing will affect girls' moods. When you stop an office girl at 1pm she's highly likely to be fast-walking between Pret and her office on her lunch break. Stop the same girl at 6pm outside Barbican tube station and she's worn out from a day in front of the laptop. Her energy is different. Her time pressure is different. The same goes for tourists. Catching a wandering tourist at noon at Trafalgar Square is great for a twenty minute chat when she's full of energy and plans for the day. Catch the same girl at 8pm outside Primark and now she's tired and really needs to sit down. In this situation, think of idates.

How about if you've just rolled into a new city on a Euro-tour?

Your first impulse will be to check the online pickup forums for recommendations, but I would advise against this. Almost everyone on the internet is a moron and even the decent guys likely don't do proper daygame or go for the types of girl you do. Rely on the evidence of your own lying eyes.

Step one of this process is to find the main pedestrian centres. In central and eastern Europe this will almost always be the centre of the Old Town or the pedestrianised shopping strip near it. Get a tear-off map from Tourist Information in the airport and ask the staff to circle the main tourist areas. The Old Town is where you get the nice pedestrian streets, the shops, the cafes and the bars. It's a natural magnet for young women and they'll be far from their neighbourhood (and thus under less social pressure).

Next find the big meeting point for young people, usually the main square in the Old Town, probably under a big clock or in front of an imposing statue of a man on a horse. In Croatia it's Jelacic Square, in Serbia it's Republic Square, in Oslo it's by the train station, in Vilnius it's the old cathedral, in Tallinn it's the old church. That'll be where the 21-30 year old girls pass through. If you're looking for 17-20 year olds then there's probably a McDonalds nearby that gets lots of teenagers hanging outside.

You've now found your main hunting ground, but don't stop there. Every reasonably-sized city has additional venues to mix it up:

1. **Train station** — Find the central station or at least the closest thing to it near the Old Town. This will be a major hub that draws fast-moving traffic. Consider rolling past there towards the end of office hours or lunchtime on a weekend.

2. **Shopping malls** — I find these overrated because the traffic is relatively low and girls often go in groups or with a boyfriend. The high street is a better bet for solo girls. Nonetheless, sometimes it rains and you need to get indoors. Start by finding out which shopping mall is popular with the girls you like. Generally avoid the high-end malls because they attract older women and taken women. Mid-to-low-end malls are better because that's where students and young women shop.

3. **University** — This all depends on the time of year of your visit. Obviously it's only viable if term is in. If you are allowed onto the campus, that's great. If not, just wander until you find the little pockets of cafes and restaurants on the fringes and try to find the main train or bus station that students pass through. Obviously universities are great for greyhounds, especially if you familiarize yourself with their individual disciplines. If you're in a country with poor English-speaking, try to find the linguistic university or British Council because that will select for girls who speak English and have a more internationalised mindset. In the FSU you should consider Law and Engineering universities because they attract greyhounds.

4. **Resorts** — London is an all-year evergreen city and the same places are always predictably bustling. This is not so when you travel because many European cities are seasonal. Central Europe in summer is unbearably hot, so for much of the day the streets are deserted. For the two hottest summer months, girls from Zagreb all go to the Adriatic coast, girls from Belgrade go to Greece (or if they can't afford it, to Ada on the river), girls from Vilnius go to the Palanga beach, girls from Kiev go to Odessa. There are many European capitals that just empty out in summer, so research this a little before booking your flights. Consider the weather in the winter as well. The Baltics are at -20C for much of winter so the streets are deserted then too.

5. **Western Franchises** — When I was in Japan I noticed girls always did their English homework at Starbucks and gaijin groupies went to Irish bars on Friday night. If you want low-hanging fruit by chasing girls who are already strongly pre-disposed to meeting a Western man, you should go to the big western franchises like cafes, McDonalds, Apple Store, Levis etc. Cast your eye for girls just hanging out who look slightly outside the mainstream of their culture and maybe have a little identifier in their fashion, such as an I Love London badge or an English-language paperback.

And what's the best way to research local venues? When you hook your first couple of sets you ask the girls which places are popular. Find a girl you like and ask her where she and her friends usually go. Ask the hostel receptionist "which places do people tend to go just to hang out in good weather?"

### The tyranny of high standards

I've often been out with students who refuse to approach because none of the girls are hot enough. If you're in a provincial British town or downtown San Francisco I can see your point. But in central London, Paris, Moscow, New York....? No, sir, you are simply weaseling your way out of a potentially uncomfortable situation.

If you're not already fucking sevens regularly you've got no business holding out for eights. You aren't so precious. Many men, especially on the internet, will construct an elaborate reality-weave in which they are super high value, where they are only banging tens while making it rain at the club. The reality is that they aren't even getting sevens. So, how do they stop reality from crushing the fantasy? By rationalising away taking any action that could provide evidence contradicting their little fantasy world. In the context of approaching, it means dismissing all the women as not hot enough. It's full-on weaseling and it's transparent to anybody unfortunate enough to be listening to them. Don't be afraid of the truth.

# THREE-TIERED TARGETING

In all but the busiest cities, you will find that there simply aren't enough hot girls around for you to be selective and busy. Often you'll be walking down a bustling shopping street and you'll be overwhelmed by the sheer volume of dross. Fat unattractive women. Old unattractive women. Women who have destroyed their natural-given value with horrendous lifestyle choices. Being 'on' takes energy, so you'll gradually deplete your batteries if you are too selective.

So now you are actually on the street walking your route. It's time to decide exactly what you are looking for and what you are tuning your RAS to pick out. To maximise my effective catch without compromising my time or decisiveness I usually set myself to a three-tiered default:

1. Girls of exactly my type, the DNA-tug girls.

2. Girls of such rare quality that I ought to open them out of general principle, the Unicorn girls.

3. Girls who project an extremely approachable and fuckable vibe, the Spider-Sense girls.

This strategy is designed to pick up every type of girl I'm interested in. At the same time, it allows me to immediately categorise any given girl so I understand why I'm opening her, what I intend to do about it, and the odds of success.

# DNA-Tug

Somewhere buried in the depths of your soul you have an archetype for your perfect DNA-match. This goes back to hunter-gatherer times, when humans bred only within their small tribes. Genetic diversity was low in these societies, and immune systems were weak and vulnerable as a result. At some point we developed a preference to mate outside the tribe so that we could secure access to complimentary DNA and widen the scope of our immune system. As a general rule, this is why we are attracted to girls who have a different look from us. We value the exotic. Fortunately, it works both ways and exotic girls find you exotic as well.

I'm a blonde fair-skinned blue-eyed man from Northern England. I have angular features. I'm most attracted to black-haired, olive-skinned, dark-eyed girls from the Mediterranean with rounded features. When I see classically Nordic girls with angular catwalk features and long blonde hair, it simply doesn't move me. My forebrain acknowledges their obvious objective beauty but my dick doesn't stir. In contrast, when I see a dappy little wop ambling out of Primark with hair like Sideshow Bob I feel my blood stir. It's not about the 1-10 scale. It's about feeling your blood bubble. These are the girls you have instant chemistry with and are most likely to be Yes Girls. If you're pulling girls to impress other men, it means that your inner game is externally referenced and therefore weak. Chase the girls *you* like. Don't seek another man's approval.

When you first experience this blood bubble it may catch you off guard. It's like a jolt of electricity. It doesn't even matter if you're in shit state and dragging your feet from lethargy, because once you see this girl your reserves of energy are magically restored. Embrace it. When you get the DNA-tug you **must** approach. These are your strongest possible leads. Even if you're feeling so off-vibe that you approach no other girls in the session, make yourself a promise you'll at least open the DNA-tug girls.

# Unicorns

An intermediate trap is to artificially narrow the type of girls you approach based on who you've done well with in the past. Perhaps you lived in Asia and banged a lot of Japanese girls, so now you think you have a special "in" with J-Girls. Perhaps at university you were in a punk band and banged a few punk girls so now you think you have a special "in" with bohemians. Whatever it is, deep down in your identity you think there's a particular group of girls who like you and other groups who just won't ever be into you.

For me, I never believed I could get socially-savvy trophy girls such as long-legged catwalk models or girls working the perfume counter in Selfridges. Then I fucked a couple and I realised that sometimes those girls do like me. I believed Arab headscarf girls were off-limits but then I fucked a couple of them. The reality is **no type of girl is truly off-limits**. Some are long-shots compared to your normal diet, but if you open enough of them and do good work then you will sometimes surprise yourself. Shake the tree and see what falls out.

This leads into an important second-tier strategy: opening girls who are outside your usual target group, but are of such unusual beauty that it's worth rolling the dice. That's how I bagged some of my best lays. It's how I expanded my comfort zone of which girls I'll regularly approach. And it's a key component of taking your game from intermediate to advanced.

Don't worry if your success rate is way lower with these girls. That's not the point. Growth occurs outside your comfort zone.

# Spider-Sense

While I strongly advise against exclusively targeting low-hanging fruit (it conditions your hindbrain that it's all you deserve), I do suggest being attuned to when easy opportunities present themselves. Sometimes you're walking down the street and the crowds part to reveal a little squirrel wearing a rucksack, a dreamy expression and a map of London in her hand. She sees you and instinctively flashes an IOI.

You think "she's only a high six"

"Not really my type"

"I'm in this to catch the greyhounds"

Yes, this is all true. But opening this girl doesn't close the door on the leggy eights. It doesn't divert you from The Plan. Just go and sweep her up. At worst, you can treat it as your personal testing ground. Perhaps use her as an opportunity to test out an idea or two you've been thinking of. Perhaps go more overtly sexual than you'd usually be. Perhaps you just want to get an easy number / idate to pump your state. When your spider-sense triggers that's your intuition telling you the girl is sexually available so do it. **Flip the stone.**

Remember that these girls are the Fast Food of daygame. It's fine to grab a 99p cheeseburger once in a while but don't make it your steady diet. Get your close friends to monitor your "eating habits." If they pull you to one side and suggest you're fucking too many rotters, you'll want to cycle off the cheeseburgers and resume looking for filet mignon.

### Flipping the stone

*The act of opening a girl to find out how receptive she is, so you can categorise her as Yes, Maybe, or No. No matter how skilled your cold-reading, you never really know how a girl will respond to the opener until you go ahead and do it.*

---

## IOI game

**Krauser Tip** *precision engineering*

Be alive to where a girl's eyes are looking, so that you can catch any who are checking you out. Beginners sometimes find it psychologically difficult to look directly into the faces of girls who walk past, because it can feel 'rude' or 'ungentlemanly'. Not only does this attitude prevent you noticing Indicators Of Interest, but it also projects asexuality and weakness to the women. Keep your head up and your eyes level. Don't avoid their eye contact. Women like to be noticed."

# Number Farming

Once you've reached a basic competence at daygame you'll settle into a routine. At any given point in your life you'll probably turn your mind towards going out for one of two reasons:

1. Restocking your leads

2. Upgrading your rotation

These are two different motivations and require two different strategies. There'll be times when all your leads have dropped away due to inactivity and now your phone never rings. The pantry is bare. Or perhaps you've got lots going on in your hometown but now you are standing in Berlin airport with a one-way bus ticket downtown — you're building from zero in a new city. This is when you number farm. In contrast, when you've got a few locals on rotation and it's getting a bit ho-hum you'll get an itch for fresh meat. You've already got a baseline of regular sex, which will sap you of the motivation to hit the streets hard and naturally make you more picky. In this case you'll be operating a more selective sniper game that requires statelessness.

**SDL**

*Same Day Lay. Meeting a girl during the daytime and then having sex with her before the night is over.*

Number farming is essentially about brute-force opening to create mid-term momentum and state, filling your phone with new contacts, and then seeing how it all filters out. It's important to be clear about what you're doing and why. Daygame requires conviction and has no place for contradictory goals or emotions. You are not trying for long idates or **SDL**s. You are not holding to high standards of quality or suitability. You are not judging girls on the street. This is what you do:

*Open as many girls as you can who are above your basic quality threshold. Run good street game, take a number and then move onto the next one.*

It's all about time efficiency and momentum. If you start bogging yourself down in idates, suddenly the hours fly by and you've got only one lead to show for it. You emerge from the idate lacking momentum and struggle to rustle up any more numbers. Worse still is going for an SDL (which as we'll see in a later chapter always runs a high risk of being a timesink with no payoff) and losing the whole day to a girl who says no at the point of pushing her into a taxi.

When you're number farming, throw yourself into set without a care in the world for how it turns out. Keep flipping stones. When the girl hooks give her ten minutes or so of your best work, then take the number and go. Stay on the streets as long as you can without burning out. Manage your energy by taking coffee breaks every couple of hours and perhaps a beer at half-time so that your dusk/evening sets have more spice. At the end of three days' number farming you should have a fat pile of leads. Then filter them through the text game until you have dates.

## Stateless Game

Number farming leverages the short-term effects of hitting many girls in quick succession. This method forces your vibe to become dialled into the energy of the streets, allowing you to hit a good social state. It only works when you have a high approach rate with lots of girls consecutively. That requires lowering your standards to the minimum acceptable level and opening in places and situations you might not usually try.

Sniping to upgrade your rotation is different, because you will lack the motivation to grind as hard and your standards are at the "at least as good as the girl I'm dropping" level.

So get used to stateless game.

You are abandoning the idea of building momentum and raising your state, since it's simply too much emotional energy to expend when you might only do one approach in an hour. Instead of wasting energy, you will simply accept the state you are in and work with that.

**Hindbrain**

*The animal emotions and instinct in the human brain. This is the source of base desires for food, shelter, and sex. A girl will act on her hindbrain's desires if you can neutralise the controlling influence of her logical forebrain.*

Emotional control is the foundation upon which all game rests. By mastering your emotions you can direct your outward vibe, which will in turn align the numerous micro-behaviours that a girl's **hindbrain** unconsciously reads. Good micro-behaviours (i.e. subcommunication) leads to imprinting the girl with a positive intuitive assessment of you, which will lead to smoother interactions both during the approach and on subsequent dates. This is why some men can have almost comically bad conversations and still get the girl — they were excelling at the 90% of communication that is non-verbal.

*Being so emotionally invested in succeeding in a particular goal that you become anxious and self-defeating. Girls can sense when you want them too much. The best players want the girl but don't need her.*

It's generally believed that achieving good state is the core of good game. The argument goes as follows: Wake up feeling good about yourself and head out onto the streets. After a few awkward warm-up sets you'll start to slip into a social vibe, gradually building momentum. Eventually a run of good interactions will cause you to "hit state" and then you can open everything, hook everything, and pull the elusive magical sets. You are in "the zone."

*This is not wrong.*

*It's just a massive pain in the arse*

The reality of daygame is that there simply aren't enough pretty girls around to keep the momentum flowing. You cannot afford to waste the first ten sets trying to hit state. As I stated earlier, you know your game is getting tighter if you get more girls, better girls, and expend less effort. Hamstringing yourself to the goal of peak state prevents progress because:

- Trying to force yourself into state takes alot of emotional energy and is inauthentic. You are trying to make yourself feel something you don't actually feel.

*Always 6R*

- Once you start to improve your state you become **outcome-dependent**, since you are focusing on keeping that little glimmer alive. More emotional energy is expended.

- In the long periods between sets, holding your state up is like holding a medicine ball in the air. Eventually you tire and it drops, making it that much more difficult to lift again.

- Over the long term, you can frame yourself into a negative thought pattern of "I'm only successful when I'm in state" or in the short term of "I won't approach this girl because I haven't hit state yet."

- Girls can sense the inauthenticity if you're trying to state leech from them, as with your wings. You can end up in destructive state wars with your wings until one or both of you crash. Noobs should especially watch for this "value tap" behaviour from more experienced players.

When you are dependent on state to make quality approaches, daygame becomes much harder than it ought to be. You are giving yourself an internal opponent to fight, a fight that doesn't need to happen. Peak state is good. When you hit it, embrace it. **But don't try to manufacture it.** Far better is to drill yourself in stateless game. It's advanced stuff and not for everyone, but give it a try. Essentially you are following this principle:

*I feel however I feel and that's okay.*
*So I will rely on that authenticity to carry me through.*

Authenticity trumps state (and is equal to vibe). Forcing a high state is essentially qualifying to the girl by telling her "Who I am at this moment is not good enough to get you, so I will expend great effort in forcing myself to be a happier version of myself just to impress you." Instead, just accept your current state. For example:

- If you're feeling flat and low energy, work with that. Maybe do small side-on opens at a traffic light rather than run-around front stops. Let your vocal tone stay light, flat, and disinterested.

- If you're feeling cocky, go that route. Ostentatiously stop a hard-walking girl, let your eyes shine, smirk insolently and use an outrageously teasing opener.

- If you're feeling horny, go sexual. Pick out a girl who has the ovulating vibe, eye fuck the hell out of her, encroach on her space. Hold that hand a long time.

- If you're completely lacking creative inspiration, just tell the girl she looks nice and drop a generic cold read and tease on her. Leave silences, let her talk.

For beginners its actually quite helpful to tell her your emotional state. Acknowledge the elephant in the room by saying "I'm a bit nervous but I wanted to talk to you."

Stateless game is not a list of instructions to follow, it's a mindset. Fundamentally, you are shrugging the weight of "hitting state" from your shoulders. Don't be so hard on yourself. Do you think those approach monkeys running up and down Oxford Street every evening are happy? Allow yourself to instead reach a zen-like calm of "whatever-will-happen-will-happen." Just flip over those stones, let your authentic state come out, and rely upon your well-drilled Game to navigate the set for you. There's nothing to be scared of on the streets. Conserve your mental energy by exerting emotional control. You are not pushing water uphill, you are letting it find its natural level and then swimming in that.

Should peak state ever creep up upon you, milk it for everything while it's there and don't mourn its absence when it leaves.

# APPROACH ANXIETY

## *Goal: Reduce the emotional cost of opening to zero*

**M**ystery was wrong. Approach anxiety **does not** come from a hard-wired evolutionary fear of having your head bashed in for hitting on the tribal leader's girl, nor does it come from the fear of sexual exclusion if word gets around your 50-person hunter-gatherer tribe that you struck out with one of the few girls of child-bearing age. Those are just evo-psych rationalisations. Perhaps these motivations are deep in the hindbrain but that's not really why your gut churns when you think of approaching. **At the root of all AA is a lack of self-acceptance.** The process builds out from your identity as follows:

> Pain of low self-esteem ⟶ Fear you are not good enough ⟶ Fear of confronting real feedback on your value ⟶ Fear of rejection by girls ⟶ Fear of making your sexual intent known ⟶ Fear of approaching

**Buffer**

*Any construction, thought or behaviour pattern which is designed to soften the impact of negative feedback to our psyche.*

That's the emotional cycle.

Our ego requires us to create a delusional reality in which we are high value, so as to assuage the feelings of low self-worth. We construct this reality in our minds with convenient rationalisations, which require careful filtering of how much feedback is allowed into our reality. Each man will find his own answers and they are called **buffers**.

Everyone's buffers are different. They depend upon highly personal circumstances, but one commonality is that they involve finding ways to avoid approaching women with the declared intent of fucking them. Examples:

**Phase-shifting**

*Changing gears in the middle of an interaction from being non-sexual and friendly to becoming sexual and charismatic. The Krauser Daygame Model begins with sexual intent, so it doesn't require phase shifting.*

- Opening indirect and then not **phase-shifting** into hitting on the girl.

- Orbiting a girl on Facebook or social circle in the hope she'll eventually initiate courting you.

- Telling everyone the girls are no good. Too slutty, too short, too tall, pointy elbows, etc. This is the delusion of high standards.

- "Working" one particular girl for months to the exclusion of opening new leads.

- Being in a relationship and waxing lyrical about emotional intimacy while your eyes wander at all the new girls you actually want to fuck.

- Declaring that women are broken and society is misandrist and therefore you will swear off women until the revolution.

- Hitting the gym, reading books and doing meditation to "work on your value" without doing any approaching.

## Avoidance Weasel

There's nothing in Game that can't be explained using furry animals. That voice in your head constantly spewing reasons not to approach is your Avoidance Weasel. He's a sneaky fucker. He'll tell you the girl is busy, or probably has a boyfriend, or looks like a stuck-up bitch. He'll look out your bedroom window in the morning and tell you it's too rainy for daygame and the streets are deserted, so you shouldn't bother going out. He's a weasel, after all.

Recognise him for what he is — your enemy. You can't kill him, but you can suppress and overrule him. When a girl goes past who you know you should open but you don't, make a mental note: "I'll call that a weasel set." Keep a running score of how many girls you weaseled. After a couple, you'll start to build up anti-weasel momentum, telling yourself you're only allowed one more weasel set before you open. Again, don't beat yourself up about it. It's ok to weasel sets now and then, especially at the beginning of the session. By putting a name on your negative behaviour you are bringing it to the surface, flushing it out where it can be countered.

I guarantee you have buffers. We all do. You must root them out and cast them away. Like hypocrisy, weaseling is easy to see in others and hard to see in yourself. Perhaps you need to ask a friend, "What are the ways I bullshit myself into not approaching women?"

To make progress in daygame you must engage directly with reality. You must look it dead-on in the eye and welcome raw unfiltered feedback. The best way to do that is to approach 100 girls with direct sexual intent. They'll give you all the answers you need.

But now we come back to approach anxiety. It's not easy to just go out there and put yourself on the line over and over again. It's emotionally draining. Walking around the streets, hands deep in your pockets, watching pretty young girls skip by and then trying to work up the motivation to open them. It's hard work.

There are only three ways around it:

1. **Brute force:** Will yourself into so many approaches that you become anesthetized to the nausea of AA and the sting of rejection. This is the tough love approach

most prevalent in the community. AA never goes away, it just becomes less painful and you become more accustomed to overruling it.

2. **Become Delusional:** Make yourself so oblivious to reality that no negative feedback penetrates your outer shell. Shrug off all rejection like a tank being fired on by small arms.

3. **Neutralise it:** Dig deep into your identity and learn to accept yourself. Become so strongly internally-referenced that the feedback of reality can be seamlessly integrated without challenging your core self-worth.

**Social violator**

*A person who transgresses the normal code of conduct in a social situation. For example, heckling an on-stage performer is usually considered unacceptable, as would farting loudly in church. Men of higher social status are allowed greater degrees of transgression before overstepping the mark. Once somebody becomes identified as a social violator their value crashes. Men won't be their friends and women won't play the seduction dance.*

In practice you'll combine all three ways and all have advantages, but only neutralisation comes without serious side effects. Brute-forcing your way through sets depletes your mental energy and forces extreme catabolic reactions. You'll feel considerable emotional pain and have many dark nights of the soul. You'll probably fall into misogynistic phases after a run of hard rejections and develop player-hate and envy for the guys outperforming you, which I noted before is a barrier in itself to improving your game. The upside is you tremendously strengthen your willpower and develop strong control gambits to channel your hindbrain. Delusional confidence drastically limits the pain of each rejection, but it directs you towards weirdness and becoming a **social violator**. Your stubborn refusal to see the feedback for what it is (instead you have to make reality "talk to the hand" and relentlessly reframe the negative reactions) means your calibration suffers and your successes become more due to luck and volume than actually fine-tuning your game. You are also building yourself up for a major implosion when the weight of reality finally cracks the walls of your delusion and then smashes you to pieces. Who wants to live in a fantasy world? I've seen some spectacular meltdowns from guys living in delusion.

Neutralisation is the only healthy response, but it's also the hardest because of the feedback loop:

Positive results ➡ Positive reference experiences ➡ Greater confidence ➡ Better results

Negative results ➔ Negative reference experiences ➔
Lower confidence ➔ Worse results

In the beginning you need to ruthlessly weed out the negative experiences and not let them settle into your identity while you also shamelessly exaggerate the positive experiences. It's a bit weird and I don't recommend it forever, but each time you are on a plateau and striving for the next level, give it a try.

## Player Traps — Delusional Confidence

One source of frustration for aspiring players is the inevitable realisation that the men who get laid most are usually dickheads. Women respond viscerally to men displaying strong frames and delusional self-belief, so almost without exception other men are annoyed to be subject to this man's constant frame-push and social violation. It's tempting to follow the logical deduction of:

*That guy is delusionally confident. It gets him laid. Therefore I should become delusionally confident and I'll get laid too.*

No, it doesn't work like that. First of all, you can't learn this attitude. Nature experiments on the male side and throws up all kinds of mutations and anomalies. Most mutations fail spectacularly but one in a million creates the perfect storm of getting laid. This dickhead is that man. Often he has no idea what is working for him. He just has a rough plan of "Do X and sex often follows," and this Plan X is only the part of the iceberg he can see. Trying to model his behaviour is like modelling the tip of the iceberg.

Secondly, these men are unhappy. Every last one of them. Delusional confidence is great for attracting women for quick sex but it's a severe handicap in all other areas of life. The women can't be kept, high value men avoid you, and you eventually crash your car into a tree. Sometimes literally. So watch these men and model what you can, because fundamentally they are good are seducing women. But be careful you don't take on the life-destroying habits and mindsets too.

# Emotional Cost Of Opening

**Catabolism**

*Players will move through cycles of daygame immersion. Long periods of gaming will deplete your mood, breaking you down. This is catabolism. The flip side is that time away from gaming will build you up. This is anabolism.*

Every open carries a cost. We don't want it to, but the reality is that you have to marshall your resources and throw yourself in there. As the session progresses that cost goes down, but it only reaches zero for small periods when you are in the zone and in a flow state. Ideally we'd always be in that state.

Don't beat yourself up if you're feeling low and can't push yourself into set. We all have days like that. Sometimes we are ground down and can't find our vibe. Try to grind some out with mechanical work (you may get lucky and find a Yes Girl) and if it's still not working just ease off. Take a break. Sit somewhere without girls walking past and switch off. Diagnose the problem.

Is it a short term issue today because you had vibe earlier and have now gone a bit flat? Fine, just take an hour off and read a book or something. Recharge. Turn your switch from **Catabolic** to Anabolic.

Is it a long term issue because you've felt flat and worn out for days on end? The same principle applies — you've overdone the catabolic and now you need some time in anabolic until your vibe returns.

# Self-Acceptance

Always be aiming to reach a place of complete acceptance and internal referencing. Two axioms that help me are:

> *I am more invested in myself and my opinion of myself than in other people's opinions of me.*

> *I would like to be better at X, Y and Z but I'm still happy with who I am right now.*

Look deep into yourself to find what you truly value and what is the core essence of your identity. Burn away all the fat, all the trappings, all the clutter. Burn it all down until there's only a small hard rock left that is the real you. That's your internal reference point. Nothing else matters. That is you. Those are your values. You will live by those and no outside factors will change that. You know who you are.

Now when you walk up to a girl and hit on her, it doesn't matter how she reacts. She laughs, titters, and two days later you fuck her? Great! She gives a po-faced stare and excuses herself after thirty seconds? Big deal. Neither the highs nor the lows change that hard rock of identity that is You.

That's the end goal, but this is not an inner game book. Don't expect to just repeat those axioms in the mirror every morning and suddenly you're internally-referenced and self-accepting. It will take time. While you are out daygaming, organise your thoughts to keep moving in this direction. Little tricks such as:

- Don't get overly excited by good responses or overly depressed by bad responses. Both are reinforcing external referencing. Try to let all responses wash over you without shifting your core.

- Practice putting yourself in positions where the girl can say "no" and then take it, wish her a nice day, and politely excuse yourself. No harm, no foul.

- Any time a girl calls you out for daygaming / hitting on her, you agree. Don't deny it. Tell her you're a man, she's an attractive woman so it's the most natural thing in the world to say hello and make your interest known.

- Don't lose sight of the Big Target. You are trying to get better with women. So long as you are going out, provoking feedback, and then refining your Game then you are on the right track. It doesn't matter if you fail your smaller targets such as number of approaches that day or hit a run of bad rejections.

*[handwritten: ← this is critical]*

# The Game Myth of AA

So now we can go back to my opening statement about Mystery being wrong. Why is that, and why was his erroneous explanation accepted for so long? Most people enter this community with low self-esteem and a whole slew of buffers to prop up their self-image. Mystery was no exception.

Narcissists react to low self-esteem by denying it and overcompensating for it. They can't accept themselves so they create a False Idealised Self (the Super-Player) and then construct a delusional world to support it. What is the one thing a narcissist can *never* accept? What is the one thing that will lead to a complete unravelling of his FIS and the mental meltdown that results? His kryptonite:

Confronting his own low self-esteem.

**Mystery** knew approach anxiety was real, so he had to construct an explanation within his system and deal with it in his own in-field adventures. But he could not trace its cause to the real root — a lack of self-acceptance resulting from low self-esteem.

To have done that would have checkmated himself and triggered the very meltdown he entered the Game to avoid. Same with all the other noob players with similar issues. It's far safer for the ego to rationalise away approach anxiety with some plausiable comforting evo-psycho babble. It's the ultimate meta-weasel because it diverts you from finding the real path to reducing AA.

**Mystery**

*The creator of the first modern Game system called Mystery Method. Although tailored for bar environments (nightgame), his original book remains one of the most important contributions to the field.*

# STREET
## section three

This section covers the process from first stopping the girl to taking her number. There is a clearly-defined chronological progression, in which you must first impose upon her with masculine dominance (The Stop) and then initiate a conversation (The Open). The purpose is to kill her physical and psychological momentum so that she will stop and listen to you. You can then draw upon your mythology to create an Assumption Story about her (The Stack) that will encourage her to enjoy the conversation and wish to keep talking (Hook Point). You have now earned time to amplify her attraction to you (Vibing) and build some initial rapport (Investment), until the time is right to take her number (Commit Her).

This is a finely-tuned sequence of events that can be deconstructed into its many component parts, each of which should be analysed and practised. When most people think of Daygame, they focus on the ten-minute street stop. As we shall see, the approach on the street is merely the beginning of a long journey.

# STREET

## THE STOP

### *Goal: Make her stop walking and start talking*

For all the talk I just gave about coming up with interesting observations about the girl, the real key to a good stop is your subcommunication. That's what really stops the girl. In particular:

1. Eye contact

2. Vocal tone

3. Cheeky grin

4. Commanding body language

5. Sexual intensity

I'll begin with a focus upon the street stop because this is the bread and butter of daygame and the purest expression of the model. Later we can go into different situations such as coffee shops, malls, and public transport.

So you've seen the girl walking down the street and immediately set your brain to put her into a playful archetype and perform a quick cold read. Your expectation of who she is will inform your assumption stack. Don't worry too much about forming specific words for the opener — just start jogging after her and hold that playful energy. Mix in some sexual intensity by looking at her ass and legs, that long flowing hair, and imagine what you'll do to her once she's naked on your bed. This girl wants to be opened.

Don't rush your open. Read the flow of the street to predict when a comfortable space will open up in front of her and if you have to stalk for a minute or two, so be it. Watch her to figure out if she's really solo or if that guy keeping pace exactly three feet ahead is her boyfriend. Take your time and then jump in at the earliest opportunity.

Each daygamer has his preferred take on the run-around. I like to catch up and as I pass into her peripheral vision I extend my arm to lightly tap her upper arm then, leaving the arm extended horizontally I describe a semi-circle until I'm in front. My extended arm has measured the radius for me to get the distance right. I then stop her with a one-handed "stop" signal. Tom Torero does a wide drift and then his stop signal is two handed palms facing down (like the hard-wired "calm down" signal used the world over) while he visibly sits back a little on an invisible high chair. Yad often jogs straight past without even looking at the girl then counts off a few steps and does a dramatic spin to face her. Everyone is different, so experiment until you find the approach that fits your vibe.

### The Jog

The most important part of the stop is your vibe as it determines how effectively you can subcommunicate your value. Every part of your approach needs to point towards the direction of good vibe, including how you catch up to her. So think, "I'm having that one" and start your job. Make it light and playful because your physiology will determine your psychology. If you find yourself entering with a flat serious vibe, replay the jog in your mind and you'll probably find you were flat-footed and stiff on the run-up. Loosen up.

*"Play the jog in your head and be playful"*

# The Dirty Secret Of Daygame

We are not daygaming to make friends. We are all about seducing the girl and fucking her. Don't let any let's-be-friends niceness creep into your vibe. Most of you will have watched YouTube videos of daygame approaches and read marketing spiel painting us as Disney princes giving sweet happy girls a movie moment. The sun is shining in a clear blue sky, and we will cavort around the park hand-in-hand then sip a latte.

No. No. No.

Daygame is **dirty**. Very, very dirty. We are predators hunting prey. We are approaching horny girls and giving them a strong sexual come-on from the beginning. We are an r-selected sexual threat. Daygame is not puppies playing with a ball. It is tigers stalking deer and then taking them down. And this is ok because Game is the one hunt where the prey *want to be taken*.

Keep this mindset and you will avoid the lightweight smiley LJBF territory that most daygamers fall into. You are a hunter. When you walk the streets you are scanning for the straggler from the herd, or conversely you are the Big Game Hunter tracking the dangerous prey (i.e. the models and actresses). Let your gameface come on and put steel in your heart and eyes. You will take this girl. Real sexual tension comes when you are standing in front of the girl chatting about nonsense while electricity crackles between you. Your eyes are locked and you both know exactly how dirty it is, no matter what inane chatter passes between you. That's how you get the girl.

# SUBCOMMUNICATION

Don't think it's your words that are getting the girl. You are speaking to her in the hard-coded physical language of the ancients, the language that got homosapiens laid before spoken language evolved. The words are just the things that fill the space while you lay your man vibe on her. That's not to say that words are meaningless, but for the pincer attack to work you need both sides operating in tandem.

## 1. Eye Contact

*"Always keep eye contact until Hookpoint."*

Learn to put fire into your eyes to project sexual intensity and then to change it in a heartbeat to a sparkle of amused mastery. Practice looking deep into a girl's eyes and projecting thoughts. Tiny micromovements in your iris and eyelids will impress these upon her and you'll often see her eyes twitch in response. Ever wonder why women seem to comment on a man's eyes? Eyes are the single most important part of sexual attraction. Transfix her like a vampire crucified against a holy cross. Yes, it's aggressive.

As you run up to the girl, you must think cocky thoughts about how awesome you are. Let those thoughts build as you think "I'm having this girl" and "I'm going to lay some proper man-vibe on her." Let it amuse you. Not only have you got a funny assumption stack ready to drop onto her, but the very way you'll convey it is eye-opening for her. As you turn and face her, dial your eyes into "cocky and playful" until you've finished the opener and moved into the assumption stack. Then start letting the sexual predator flash through them, just fleeting glimpses at first. As she reaches **hook point** you can let the sexual threat eyes vie with the psychopath dead eyes.

Your calibration is key. At all points in the set you are keeping the fishing line at an optimal tension. Sometimes you need to reel in (pull) by increasing tension, other times you need to let out some slack to prevent the line breaking (push). Catching a big fish requires you to keep it in that sweet spot, reacting to its flailing, until it finally tires itself out thrashing and you can reel it all the way in. So it is with girls as well. Lay the tension onto her with sexual eyes to heat her up and then sense when it's time to ease off back into playful eyes or soft eyes. Then tighten the line again. Keep pushing and pulling her around with your eyes. It's the perfection of combined mechanised warfare, every unit synchronized on land, sea, and air until you've invaded her bunker.

Be dangerous. Girls feel the strongest tingle of sexual attraction when they are slightly frightened by the man. The defensive crouch is where pussies get wet. Whereas men get a fight-flight response upon encountering an aggressive interloping male, women get a tend-befriend (or appease-please) response. Scaring her increases your chances of fucking her because it makes her hornier and she takes you seriously. The issue is *how much to scare her and when.*

As a rule, don't scare her until after hook point. Before then you are mostly playful and cocky so she doesn't freak out, but she's intrigued by your confidence. Then after laying the assumption stack on her and drawing her into conversation, she's already put you into the "not a street crazy trying to murder me" box. Remember your distancing, posture, smile, and words are all beautifully calibrated so she knows you aren't a proper crazy. Turning on the sexual threat is so effective because it's the contrast. She can't tell if you're a bad boy with a heart of gold or a nice guy with a hard streak. As long as she doesn't feel in immediate physical danger, that display of **hard and soft dominance** is what keeps her around aching for more. As the hook point passes you now have enough of a safety buffer to turn on the hungry wolf eyes and the pitiless psychopath eyes. Don't overdo it. Just show flashes of the beast within, then slide back into soft comfort eyes or playful amused mastery.

Before hook point you need to keep your eyes fixed on her. Not wild-man no-blinking eyes, just keep looking into her eyes as you talk. Even in the opener when you say "I just saw you over there" you don't actually look over there, you just gesture while looking into her eyes. I see many beginners fail to hook by letting their eyes wander to follow their gesture or down to their feet. The eyes are your power, so pour that into her. It shows real confidence. Then after hook point you can start breaking eye contact occasionally to ease the tension. As she continues to invest, you break off the eyes more when she's talking. It's all about managing the tension of the fishing line.

"I usually look at where "I saw there"

**Hook point**

*The moment a girl decides that she is enjoying the conversation and wants to have more of it. This is a pivotal moment in daygame because you have killed her momentum and have time to work. She feels some attraction for you.*

**Hard dominance**

*Displays of your ability to impose yourself onto the world and take what you want from it. This includes your strength, competence, and willingness to stand up for yourself. Girls always screen for hard dominance in the early stages of an interaction, which is why subcommunication is so important.*

**Soft dominance**

*Displays of your ability to bring someone into your world and take care of them. This includes your listening skills, rapport, kindness, and sensitivity to what the girl is feeling and how to direct her mood to a happy place. Girls screen for soft dominance after they are attracted to you.*

## 2. Vocal Tone

Almost everyone makes the same mistakes in the beginning. I'll bet money that you talk too fast, too high-pitched, too much inflection, uptalk on sentence-endings, and don't leave enough silence. These are all expressions of nervousness and betray that you lack the sense of entitlement necessary for the optimal seduction. The psychology is quite simple: you believe that unless you pour lots of energy into the interaction and keep it going, she'll walk away. You fear silence because that's her opportunity to say "Thanks, bye!"

### Boxing centre line

At a muay thai class one of the retired ex-pros took me for some boxing sparring. While only softly cuffing me around he made an absolute fool of me by constantly feinting me off balance. Then at the end of the first round he explained my problem. "Your eyes follow my hands," he said. "Don't do that. Look down the centre line, at my chest or my face." He explained how the moment my eyes follow his hands he can start drawing my eyes one direction with a showy feint and then use the other hand to hit me from outside my peripheral vision. The shock of being hit by something you can't see knocks you further off balance and it becomes a snowball of defensive blunders. I learned that day to keep my eyes down the middle. Don't be distracted by the flux around you. So it is with daygame. Keep the centreline. Don't let your eyes flicker to people walking past you, or a bus blaring it's horn, and god forbid don't distract yourself with your own hands. When she moves her own head (for example to adjust her bag, to look at your shoes or whatever) you keep still and let your eyes track her. It's a very powerful masculine gaze.

Such poor vocal expression is telling the girl you don't feel worthy, and she is only too happy to accept that signal. In contrast, correct vocal tone signals to her that you consider yourself really hot shit but don't brag about it. That intrigues her. All you need is for her to ask herself "Why does this guy think he's such hot shit?" and then BOOM! You've killed any bad momentum.

Good vocal tone is low, slow, and patient. Watch old movies with famously attractive male leads such as Clark Gable or Burt Reynolds or Sean Connery. Even better, watch movies with leading men who are physically gruff and unattractive but nonetheless got girls tingling such as Clint Eastwood, Lee Marvin, and Charles Bronson. Listen to how they talk and model it.

You'll notice when girls are trying to seduce a man they'll have a high-pitched sweet voice to match their playful energy, and when the lights are down and the mood turns sexual they'll have a throaty rasp. There's a deeply hardwired way of sex-talking that we all naturally unlock. Men have the same. When the lights are on (or you're on the street) your voice is soft without being weak, low without being deep. Later on the date you'll drop your voice deeper and turn it more sexual. For now, on the street stop, concentrate on being low, slow and patient.

In the beginning you'll be doing most of the talking, but that doesn't mean you have to rush. String out the opener as long as you like and leave short pauses to build anticipation. Once the girl realises you are about to feedback something to her about herself (that's the power of saying "I'll tell you what I noticed about you") she will wait to hear it. So right after you say something like "I saw you and I thought you looked like...." You can begin to toy with her by drawing out the process of giving the answer.

---

### Chuggers

We Brits have a word for those annoying charity muggers who stop you in the street and try to get you to sign a direct debit for their cause. They are a great teaching aid as an example of what not to do. Every part of their subcommunication is anti-game. They are:

- Needy

- Talk with a rising inflection

- Bend over and make themselves seem small and harmless on the open

- Value-taking

- Dressed like shit

Watch them for a while. Break down the mechanics of how they open passers-by. Let them open you and monitor your instinctive reactions moment-by-moment. That's how sickened the girl feels if you open her the same way. Now you know what not to do.

---

After hook point you can leave longer pauses to encourage her to fall into the conversational gap. Just be sure that you've given her something to latch onto, such as an open-ended question or a statement that implies a question. If you simply stop talking she may take that as a signal that the conversation is over.

# 3. Cheeky Grin

It's likely that you are either too happy or too serious. It's a difficult tightrope to walk. If she sees you as a nervous eager-to-please lightweight, that's an attraction killer. If she sees you as a trembling serious bore that's even worse.

When your vibe is great you'll just naturally wear the correct facial expression. Try to recapture that. I like to use the assumption stack as my fuel. I've just spotted a girl, categorised her, and thought of a funny back-story for her. This amuses me. I'm now going to interrupt her day and tell her. This also amuses me. So I run up to the girl with the same mindset as if I've just remembered a secret joke. I have a barely-suppressed cheeky grin. Likewise, if I decide to do an accusational

*I've done this with the fashion girl*

opener I feel like I've just caught her with her hand in the cookie jar. This also amuses me.

Try not to smile in the normal sense of the word (full teeth, needy, seeking-approval) as that'll signal you're a **Nice Guy** while also throwing your vibe out of the sexual zone. Let your eyes flash with cocky playfulness and your cheeky grin will support it. This is the most self-amusing part of the mating dance. *You're about to accost a random girl and try to fuck her.* If that isn't surreal, what is? She's literally just walking down the street enjoying her day with whatever plans she has and you're going to squash them. She's kept herself in shape, done her hair, put on nice clothes, made herself a fine sexy young minx and now you are going to pluck her from the crowd and have your wicked way with her. Daygame is a dirty, sordid, and ***incredibly self-amusing*** business. If you're not having a bit of fun and sporting a cheeky grin there's something wrong with you.

As the chat progresses you'll wipe the grin from your ugly mug. The nature of daygame is to approach girls in a situation where they can't possibly know anything about you other than what you display during the conversation. It's not like a rock singer being on stage in front of his fans, or a footballer in a nightclub, or a rich guy on his yacht. Daygame is the great equaliser where you are competing on personal charismatic value alone (plus good looks). This has both an upside and a downside.

**Upside** — You are fighting the battle on homeground. You have spent years developing precisely the social skills and artistry to attract and seduce a girl using nothing more than your physical presence and wordplay. Once you are "in," no amount of Ferraris, yachts, or platinum CDs can matter. You are communicating directly to her hard-wired attraction mechanisms.

**Downside** — In the beginning she has no reason whatsoever to talk to you except the reasons you give her. You need that foot in the door, which becomes a beach head, which eventually becomes massed artillery smashing into her bunker. But none of that happens without getting the initial hook.

Let's relate this to the earliest moments of the street stop. In the first microseconds where she knows literally nothing about you, her hindbrain scans you for a stop-don't-stop response that is entirely emotional. Once her feet stop moving she's scanning again for a hear-him-out-don't-hear-him-out response, which is again an emotional one. The earliest moments are the most precarious because this is when she knows the least about us and is the least invested. **We** know that we are high value charismatic men but she doesn't, yet. So every detail of the stop needs to be <u>technically correct</u> to project the highest possible value. A girl's default strategy is to dismiss/**disqualify** the man and the daygame street stop effectively hijacks her emotional programming to delay the dismissal long enough for her to recognise the value and hook.

So the very first few moments are commanding but not threatening. We have a cheeky grin, not a serious glare. It's very difficult to hold a bright-eyed cheeky grin while also holding ill-intent towards a stranger. Our intuition is very effective at spotting threats in others, especially from non-verbal signals. By entering with good vibe and a cheeky grin, we immediately put the girl at rest while the commanding presence stops her feet.

*→ need to build assumption stacks*

Once we reach hook point the grin can be turned off. <u>You've gotten your assumption stack out so you've "told the joke."</u> The reason for that cheeky grin has gone, and so must the grin itself. Keeping a grin or smile when it's not warranted by the interaction is weird and inauthentic. Turn it off and only turn it back on again when you think of another playful tease or she says something funny. Once you've reached hook point your default is a straight face, unless you have good reason to animate it. She's hooked, you can be a sexual threat now.

### The Value Delivery Mechanism

precision engineering

**Krauser** Tip

When you're new to the Game you don't have much personal charismatic value. That's okay. The game changes you. A few years of approaching girls, processing their feedback, straightening your inner game, and so on will lead to a deep-level identity change. But for your first 1,000 sets you don't really have it so your game is a pretense. Your game is a Value Hologram. It projects an idealised version of you that doesn't really exist, like CGI on a movie screen. As you improve, you'll become increasingly comfortable with authenticity and game now becomes a Value Add. You use it to spice up your actual character and present yourself in the most favourable light, like applying the finishing touches in photoshop to a carefully posed portrait. When you finally get all your shit together, game becomes a Value Delivery Mechanism. The model is just an efficient way of channeling the authentic you in as short a time as possible. The street stop is an unusual glitch in the matrix that we developed to give ourselves an "in" with hot girls — we are hijacking her social circuitry for precious moments until we can channel enough real value that she decides to stick around for more.

# 4. Commanding Body Language

Sexing a girl means dominating her and gradually taking control of her body and mind until your dick is inside her. You do so by taking advantage of natural sexual polarity in which the man is the dominant active agent and the woman is the submissive passive object. This is how nature wrote the rules. So right from the beginning you are trying to increase polarity. This means:

*Immediately overwhelm her with masculine dominance*

Practiced daygamers are rare men who have aligned all of their arrows in the same direction of positive masculinity. There are lots of attractive men in the world (far less than the number of attractive women, but there's still plenty of them), which means there will always be men who have something more than you have. Perhaps they will be richer, or better looking, or more confident, or more outgoing, or better dressed, or have a cooler lifestyle. You'll never be the best at everything. There's always a King Of Kong who has dedicated his whole life to mastering one narrow area of expertise. However, even the best men are born and raised with contradictions. Perhaps a guy is a brave-hearted hero on the battlefield but was raised as a mother's boy to pedestalise women. Perhaps he's a hardballer nightclub bigshot but restless and insecure when he is idle on his own. The only way to be a fully-developed man with all chinks hammered out of his armour is to consciously work at it under good instruction.

This is extremely rare.

Rarer still is a man who has aligned all his arrows and also possesses the artistry to convey his value in a street stop.

When the girl encounters you on the street she has probably never experienced fully-developed masculinity before. Her DNA is hard-coded to yearn for it and respond with tingles, and now suddenly it's standing in front of her in the middle of the street. The archetype of masculinity. Her natural emotional response is to be transfixed like a deer in the headlights, and then flip strongly to the feminine. Instant polarity. You'll be well aware of the intense pleasure of feeling like a man, those moments in life when you've conquered a summit. The blood of a thousand warriors courses through your veins, filling you with manly satisfaction. It's a feeling we strive for and put ourselves through unendurable hardship to attain. Because it feels so good. It feels so natural and right.

Well, guess what. The girl feels just as good when she feels like a woman. When you flip a girl into the feminine, you have given her the greatest gift of nature. It's like handing the pipe to a meth head. The bossier and more careerist she is, the farther away from her biological urges she is, and the more she needs it. A great street stop does that from the very first moment.

How does the CEO walk when he enters his office lobby? How does the field marshall walk when inspecting his troops? How does the lion walk in the savannah?

## *Command presence*

You are already walking down the streets like you own the place and everyone else is your guest. Now when you stop the girl, you do so in the full belief that she should stop and talk to you. It would never enter your mind that this is weird. You are a man and you have found a woman who interests you. It's **obvious** that you should go up and say hello. *It's the most natural thing in the world.* How weird would it be if you just stood there holding your dick and doing nothing at all?

Your body language will reflect this with decisive movements, gestures that command attention, a straight back with chest proud, chin up. She will immediately sense that when you talk, people listen. It all happens at the emotional level, so her feet will stop before she's fully processed what's happening.

Don't give your power away. Don't soften your posture to appear less intrusive because that just reduces the polarity. Don't loom over her (a problem for taller men) or lean back in an excessively devil-may-care posture (a buffer to avoid putting the real you in front of her). Don't bend your back, shuffle, or commit any other tell that you feel you don't belong in conversation with this girl. Just stop her.

Once I am talking I like to use one-handed gestures to emphasise points. There's something more commanding about it than two-hands (which is a bit gay). Teachers use one hand. Drill sargeants use one hand. Don't be afraid to point. You are gradually taking command over her body. After hook point you can start prodding her, slapping her wrists, juking her shoulders, tapping her nose and so on. Your vibe and calibration will tell you how physical to make it, but it's never with apology. You command this interaction. You decide how it goes. She will fall into line. When you reach the point of dialing down your energy, your presence will become more like a statue. All unnecessary movement is removed so it's just you standing there, waiting. Perhaps your hands are in your pockets, or hanging by your sides. Now your only movements are nods of the head and occasional one-handed small gestures. You are now the oak tree and this matches the lower vocal tone, longer pauses, deadpan expression and sexual/psychopath eyes. Her feminine response will be to either increase her own energy in a playful manner (the squirrel running around the oak tree) or to match your lack of movement while entranced with your eyes (this is the strongly sexualised "vampire mesmer" set). Either one is good for you.

# 5. Sexual Intensity

Never forget that daygame is intensely sexual. You may be standing in the frozen foods aisle of a supermarket at 2pm, but the substance of the communication between you and the girl is on the sexual plane. At any moment she could be whisked into a public restroom and raw-dogged into submission.

Let your vibe carry your sexual intensity as a knowing grin. As the conversation develops, your sexual mindset will present teases, challenges, and double-entendres automatically. For example:

She says she's a gymnast or dancer

- No sexuality: "I imagine that's a very demanding profession"
- Sexuality: "You must be very…. Flexible"  ✓

She says she's on her way to the gym

- No sexuality: "It's nice to keep yourself in shape"
- Sexuality: "So you like to get hot and sweaty. In public too!"  ✓

You haven't propositioned her or called it out but there's absolutely no doubt in her mind what you are communicating. You're a sexual threat. You are the man who understands what she wants and how to give it to her.

An advanced player can effortlessly present the contrast of sexual predator and comforting nice guy, that mix of steel and velvet, of hard dominance and soft dominance, that perhaps only 1% of the world's men have. Switching your eyes from hard to soft, your words from sexual to playful, your face from cheeky smile to poker face…and doing so skillfully and at the right moments…This overwhelms the girl. She's literally never seen anything like it, especially from someone who just walked up to her on the street. She's never had a guy stab her in the heart with such stiletto precision and *she loves it*. She thinks "this man *gets it*." That makes you a member of the 1% club.

Most men struggle with the meanness of daygame. They want to be nice. They want to put the princess on her pedestal and then wrap her in cotton wool at night. So by all means spend a few months being overtly aggressively sexual. You'll blow lots of sets but the reactions you get before they explode will convince you of women's dirty secrets. If that fails, just get drunk and fuck some whores. Pay them extra to slap them around a little. Learn that women are not fragile dolls. They are sexual beasts waiting to be unleashed.

## Overt Sexuality

Most guys are too nice. They completely underestimate how sexual girls are, how much they want sex, how quickly they will have sex, and how many horny thoughts go through their minds in everyday interactions with men. So once a guy breaks out of the nice guy trap, he tends to overcompensate in the other direction and become a foul-mouthed douchebag. It's normal — swinging the pendulum to the opposite side. This will get occasional crazy lays when you happen to meet the right girl, but generally it will give you exciting street stops that lead to immediate blowouts or subsequent flakes. Why?

You scared the girl away. All girls want it rough. All girls have rape fantasies BUT they don't want their real life to be as extreme as the fantasies. When shit gets real they are likely to revert back to dismiss/disqualify. You've just given her an easy basis to disqualify you as "too aggressive," or the more modern "creepy." Secondly, girls want to communicate on the covert plane. When you have to state something overtly, it's because you failed to convey that same information covertly. This reduces the tingles.

Using your eyes to tell a girl you want to fuck her is far more powerful than using your mouth.

Using playful banter to tell a girl you might rawdog her in the toilets is far more powerful than just stating it directly.

Don't come out and tell a girl what you want to do to her until you're heating her up for extraction on the date (and sometimes, not even then). Give her plausible deniability. Let her feel the sexual vibe without calling attention to it on the overt verbal plan.

## Key Concept — The Secret Society

Most men are, in carnival terms, rubes. They are easy marks. They have been brought up in a deeply fem-centric world and are inculcated with all of its delusions. They go to work, earn money, pay taxes, buy products, watch TV, and have sex with a tiny number of homely women. Dysfunctional as this sounds, it's exactly what the grand meta-narrative of the feminine imperative wants because it holds society together and gives women power. It's a feature, not a bug. It's no conspiracy. Most people have bought into the ideology implicitly and women can't even articulate why they want it this way, much less design and administer such a conspiracy.

What matters is the result: Most men don't get it.

Most men don't realise that sex is everywhere. That innocent-looking girl in a woolly jumper sitting in Starbucks reading Proust? Last week she was picked up in Hyde Park by a player who fucked her three hours later in the disabled toilet at Charing Cross Hotel. That Iranian girl with the head scarf and wide blue eyes? Once a month her father pays for her shopping trip to Harrods and she sneaks away to spend the night with a player who picked her up outside Knightsbridge underground station.

There is a world of sex going on underneath our noses. 99% of men have never participated in it and many don't even believe it exists. While waiting in the queue at Whole Foods they see the customer in front making small talk with the cashier as she bags his items. Oblivious, the man saw but he didn't observe. A keener eye would recognise that "small talk" was a flirty indirect-direct ping that raised a smile, followed up by some sparkling eye contact. The player was screening the cashier, giving her a come-on to gauge her interest. Sometimes this leads to nothing. Other times, she gives her number and gets fucked in a hotel room three days later. Then she goes back to work with nobody the wiser.

All women have "indiscretions." These are her R-selected moments. It's just that she's not having them with the K-selected man so he doesn't even know they happen. There are precious few R-selected men in the world so they act as aggregators. Twenty women may each have only one indiscretion but they all happen with the same man. This is why when you become an Advanced Player your stories become literally unbelievable to the average man. He's literally never seen that world. He was never allowed into the Secret Society.

According to the UK Office Of National Statistics, 20% of all females living in the UK are between 15 and 30 years old. According to me, approximately 20% of them are a six or better in hotness. Depending who you believe, women of that generation will have between 10 and 20 lifetime sexual partners on average. So let's run some simple maths (it's a crude sketch, social statisticians beware!):

- 4% of women in the UK are bangable (20% of 20%).

- Each of these women will average 1 new notch per year during their bangable window.

Let's assume half her notches are within stable LTRs with K-selected men while the other half are R-selected "indiscretions," thus each girl has one Player Notch every two years. This means for one player to score 20 notches per year he is aggregating 40 girl-years of indiscretions. He's stealing the lunch money of 39 other men.

Note that we are only looking at the top 20% of the girls. This leads us to quite a startling conclusion about R-selected men:

*The hot girl population of the UK can only support a maximum of 0.1% of men being players before female notch-counts rise exponentially.*

There's a reason the society is kept a secret.

# THE OPEN

② *Goal: Initiate a fun conversation*

**T**he opener is so overrated, especially among noobs, that it's quite likely half of this book's readers skipped immediately past the first few chapters to here thinking "What opener is he using?"

There's no magic.

You can definitely display value with your words, as they give her a window into your mind, your life, and your cornerstone male characteristics. Words must be mastered, but don't neglect all that other stuff which is far more important.

I'll repeat it again: **You attract the girl with your vibe and your subcommunication**. Words are not meaningless, but they are not the engine driving the seduction. They are not a black magic incantation with the power to summon the player spirits that deliver the nubile virgin to your bed. All that words do are:

1. Provide a track for the train to follow

2. Offer a window into your core male characteristics

The train needs an engine to power itself down that track, which is your vibe and subcommunication. The most powerful engine in the world is nothing without a track to ride and a destination at the end of it. Consider your words as adding structure to move things along. It's pretty difficult to pick up a girl just by looking at her and saying nothing — just two people standing on the street eye fucking. I've done it a couple of times but only because we didn't speak each other's languages, so I had no other option. When you have words you can strike up conversation, you can make suggestions, you can plan ahead. Likewise, it's difficult to show a girl who you are without words. She can sense your vibe but she'll learn much more as you tease her, challenge her, paint evocative pictures and push back against her tests. These all happen with words.

So words matter but vibe matters more. But we've talked about vibe, so let's move onto the words, beginning with a couple of iron laws:

*You can open with anything*

*You can always use the same basic template*

When you hit good state in a daygame session you'll find the creative springs of your mind burst forth with gushing flows of clear, precise observations. You can open reflexively without conscious reference to the model. This is the proof that anything can be an opener. However we will not always be in peak state. Even when we are, we are drawing upon internalised principles learned the hard way through a dogged mechanical application of the model. This is why you must learn the structure first, and then fly free of it when your state is high.

You'll notice this book is several hundred pages, including long discussions of minor points. For example there's all the girl archetypes in a previous chapter. This can mislead you into thinking daygame is complicated. It's not. This book is about **mastery**. If I'd called it Daygame Adequate, it could've been fifty pages long. I am writing everything I know deconstructed down to the nth degree because, as time passes, you'll encounter unexpected responses or quirks and be curious what they mean. Somewhere in this book is the answer. As the years pass, you'll internalise this information until it's second nature and you needn't think about it. I don't think about it unless asked. I'm like a watchmaker who pulls apart the chronograph and polishes every part of the mechanism before reassembling it. You don't need that knowledge just to tell the time.

So to bring it back to the Iron Laws, while daygame can be infinitely complex with fun ways to run a set, you don't actually need it. I'll begin my discussion of openers by offering a set template. You can learn this and you'll get laid plenty without ever deviating from its narrow prescriptions.

# THE TEMPLATE

Probably half of my openers follow this basic structure. It's my simple bread-and-butter fallback when I feel uninspired, and yet contained within it is so much creativity and raw conversational meat that if the girl has any interest in me *at all* she'll hook. It also polarises with its frame-push so you can quickly screen out girls who aren't amenable to daygame.

| | |
|---|---|
| *Me:* | Hi! I hope you speak English... Ok. I have to tell you something... I was just back there when I saw you and what I noticed about you is... You look very... Spanish. It's your big black hair, your nice fashion... and your crazy eyes |
| *Her:* | No no. I'm not Spanish. I'm Italian |
| *Me:* | Oh...... my mother warned me about Italian girls... |
| *Her:* | Really? What did she say about us? |
| *Me:* | She said three things. That you're all beautiful, good at cooking.... And all crazy. |
| *Her:* | Hahaha... maybe! |
| *Me:* | I'm guessing that you.... *[begin short assumption story]* |

Let's break apart the watch and analyse the moving parts, beginning with the pre-frame of "I hope you speak English." I've tried many variations before settling on this such as "Do you speak English?" (too easy for her to say no and walk away) and "On a scale of 1 to 10 how good is your English?" (too long-winded and gamey). I used to skip this sentence altogether, but I soon realised that by asking about her English you are doing two things:

- Her first logical thought is you are asking for the time or directions, which is likely to stop her feet.

- If she's not a native speaker (usual for my girls) she'll immediately get mixed emotions of being pleased at a chance to practice her English, while also slightly intimidated by using her limited English with a native speaker. Remember the pussy tingle is born in the defensive crouch.

So this piece helps stop her and push her immediately into a timid submissive frame. These are just baby steps, but they are in the right direction. Emphasise the "hope" with an expectant look to indicate she will please you if she does speak English, it will encourage her to overcome her fears and try because of your positive expectation.

## Elephant in the Room

*This is the obvious context to the interaction, which is unspoken but not unknown. For example if she is waiting for a friend, or a bus. It is usually wise to explicitly state this context in order to neutralise the awkwardness it would cause if you both continued to ignore it.*

## Creepy

*The disgusted and threatened emotion a woman feels when a man of lower Sexual Market Value tries to seduce her. This is an innate response to ensure she only has sex with men of adequate quality*

Next comes "I have to tell you something." This is providing the logical reason for talking to her and differentiating yourself from the street urchins who merely want to sell or beg. Contained within you is that amusing assumption and the female archetype you put her into. You want to tell her about it, you want to share your value. She doesn't know that yet. She doesn't know if you're about to tell her she dropped her purse or has a snot hanging out of her nose, but the vibe is already giving her an idea that she's about to get some good news. Who doesn't like good news? I don't tell girls I want to ask something or ask permission to talk to them. Never ask permission. Remember the command presence.

Right after that comes the Root in which you recognise the **Elephant In The Room**. Usually on a street stop it'll be the "I was just over there when I saw you and..." but when opening in other situations it'll be things like "I know you're waiting for your friend, but..." or "I know you're busy reading your book," but..." The principle is the same: **tell her what the situation is** so you show the social savvy to know what's going on. That tends to disarm her **Creepy** Alarm immediately.

*[handwritten margin note: Call out the situation.]*

Now that we've prepared the ground with enough social fluff to enter a conversation we get to the main verbal hook: "...and what I noticed about you is... you look very...." This is absolute gold due to fundamental female psychology.

So you dangle the carrot of what you noticed, and then you draw it out to build her anticipation. Focus on slowing down your delivery and allowing pauses at this point. Think for a moment how good novels are written. You can essentially boil them down to one basic rule:

*A good novel will ask an intriguing question on the first page and then delay answering it until the last page.*

That's how a good street stop works. You get your bait in as early as possible to kill her momentum, and then once she's standing still to hear the answer you delay it. When it arrives it pleasantly blindsides her (the playful assumption story).

Next we have the initial assumption, what I'd call the compliment-tease. Hundreds of hours on the streets and many bootcamps taught has led the London Daygame elite to the same basic core compliment-tease:

*Guess her country or occupation then feedback*
*three things about her that you can see which support this guess,*
*of which two are mildly complimentary and one is a tease.*

Nationality is the easiest when gaming in an international hub such as London or Prague or New York. When practicing in a smaller town, you should consider talking about her occupation or mood instead. So take a guess about her country and then give her the three reasons. We are now introducing push-pull into the opener. Girls love being buffeted around without knowing what to expect. On the rare occasions men have tried to pick them up in daytime, the guys would've used 100% pull, something like "You are gorgeous, can I take your number?" This is overt communication, which women will always punish you for. When you drop a light nicely-calibrated tease onto her you've just given her a little spark of electricity. She realises you aren't like all the other guys. There's some spice on this food.

## Excessive Cold Reading

Once you get good at cold reading it becomes addictive. Just by looking at the girl you can figure out lots about her lifestyle and personality.
Each time you feed something back to her she rewards you with surprise and attention until… she gets bored and walks away. Never forget the goal. You are not trying to impress her with your cold reading skills. You are not trying to score 100% on your guesses. It's far better to have a creatively amusing and totally inaccurate guess than an accurate boring one. The cold reads are just fuel for the conversation. Don't become Derren Brown.

Typically she'll respond to your compliment-tease with a surprised laugh and then either confirm or correct you on the assumption. It doesn't matter which because this is not an exercise in cold reading accuracy. The purpose of the cold-read and assumption is simply to start a fun conversation that she quickly invests herself in because it is, after all, about her either way.

If she confirms your initial assumption you just riff off it with further detail. If she corrects you then express feigned disappointment that she hasn't met your standards and then riff off her actual country. If she doesn't immediately tell you her country, just plough on or take a short diversion to guess it.

Now comes the "my mother warned me about…." which is another tease stacking off the assumption. It also provides another chance to bait her with an intriguing question that she will stick around to hear answered. You are reeling her in. Notice again I stick to the magic balance of two compliments and one tease, while encouraging her to qualify herself in accordance with the standards I've laid out.

This particular tease is good for playfully framing yourself as shy with girls, a powerful contrast to the obvious confidence you display through the act of opening a stranger on the street (contrast is king). Usually she'll be bright-eyed and laughing now, but you still aren't in a conversation. That requires the assumption story to bridge into it. We'll go into that in a minute but for now it's all about the opener.

I've just spent several pages looking under the bonnet of the opener to explain what's going on, which this will allow you to easily construct your own versions. The last thing I need is a few hundred people running up and down Oxford Street using my material word for word. Just understand that having one simple pattern (and this example is my pattern) is enough to form the backbone of all of your daygame opening. It will be well-rehearsed, well-delivered, and always there when you need it. You don't need to overcomplicate things.

Let's look at how you can complicate things and have more fun.

---

### Hang Her On Her Solipsism

precision engineering
**Krauser**
Tip

Girls are completely self-obsessed. This isn't a knock against them, just a raw biological fact. A woman's evolutionary job is to protect that womb from all the dangers of the world until she's selected the best semen to inseminate it. This means a woman has zero interest in anything that doesn't concern her personally.

- Have you ever heard two women have an intellectual discussion?

- Have you ever heard of a woman running into a burning building to save a man she doesn't know?

- Have you ever heard of a woman spending years in a laboratory to invent a new technology for the advancement of humankind?

Of course not. Women are simply not interested, and this is an innate characteristic that has allowed our species to propogate for hundreds of thousands of years. The way to engage a woman's attention is to talk about her and things that directly affect her. Women are intensely interested in what other people think of them, because as the physically weaker sex they are hard-wired to seek the approval of potential allies. That's why daygame always begins with telling her what you noticed about her. It's her favourite subject and thus the best way to hook.

# ACCUSATIONAL OPENERS

Sometimes life throws you a tremendous opportunity to push a girl onto the defensive. When that happens, take it. Accusational openers are gambits that set a much more dominant frame than the standard street stop, and generate more electricity when they hit. Some examples:

## 1. From a forced IOI

A girl eyes you up while walking past on the street. So you catch up to her and start finger-wagging: "Woah woah woah! Stop *right* there.... You are *not* allowed to check me out like that and then not say hello. I'm not a piece of meat. I have a name. I have hopes and dreams." This is all done with a playful cocky smile. The power comes from her own recognition that she got caught checking you out and *you were both socially astute enough to see and ballsy enough to act on it*. This is an even stronger display of masculine presence than the boiler-plate generic street stop. Other variations:

- "One moment young lady. I can't believe you just checked me out like that. I feel so… Objectified. Flattered too… But mostly objectified."

- "Excuse me young lady. I simply cannot allow you to give me such a nice smile and then let you walk away."

## 2. From suspicious behaviour

Sometimes the girl hasn't noticed you but something in her behaviour or situation can be misconstrued as suspicious. Let's say she's standing outside a tourist site taking lots of photographs… "Excuse me, young lady. I just saw you taking lots of photographs of a site of national importance. So naturally, despite you being a pretty girl, I'm wondering…are you a terrorist? Are you casing the joint for a heist?" Never forget the cocky playful smirk because it's the contrast of aggressive words and playful subcommunication that makes it work. Other examples:

- "I saw you! You're holding a salad but looking at the cakes. You know what that means…… you have a deep dark secret. Don't worry, I won't tell"

- To a woman standing stony-faced: "Let me guess…. You're security. That's why you're standing stony-faced giving everyone evil looks."

- "I love your concentration. You look so…. Focused."

Implying suspicious behaviour is best on a stationary girl as it lets you just walk up and ignore the pre-frames. Just lead from your accusation.

Once she's responded to the opener, you still need to assumption stack into a real conversation or else it comes off as fake and rehearsed. Generally I'll transition with a phrase that both amplifies the accusation and funnels through some assumption meat for her to bite on. I use the same topics: her nationality, her occupation, her mood:

- **Nationality:**Is that what they do in your country? I thought Italian girls were more boring and well-behaved.

- **Occupation:**That's so typical of you lawyer girls. Always aggressive, always going for it.

- **Mood:** I imagine in a different mood you're a lot more normal. Reading a book and baking cakes or something.

From here you can just work the normal assumption story.

## 3. The observed incongruence

I prefer this opener for high-pressure ambush situations where the girl is sitting down and there's an audience, such as on an underground carriage or coffee shop. It's essentially an observational opener but you mix in a tease by suggesting something about her doesn't "fit." This can again put her pleasurably onto the defensive and thus trigger some self-justification / qualification, flipping the script for you and assuring the hook.

*Find two elements of her look / behaviour / fashion that don't naturally match and then call her out on it*

For example if a girl is sitting opposite you on a train and you notice her fingernails don't match her toenails, point it out. "Excuse me. I like your nail colour. But…you realise it doesn't match your toes? I'm like that wearing odd socks at times." You need higher social acuity to pull off these openers because your vocal tone and body language must balance teasing with genuine warmth so she understands it's just an opener. Other examples I've used:

- A smoking hot black girl carrying a leopard-print purse. "Excuse me, can I just say something? I couldn't help noticing you because, well, you're a rather pretty girl. But I must say that purse you're carrying. I don't mean to be rude, it's a compliment really, but you do realise what men think when they see leopard print?… prostitute." I pulled this off because she was obviously so hot she's full of herself and used to guys kissing her arse, she had a touch of the ghetto bravado, and she knew I was deliberately poking her as a challenge. So I held my frame, she paused for a second to let it sink in and enjoy the indignation… Then burst out laughing. She sucked my dick later than evening.

If you are in doubt, do the good girl / bad girl incongruence. Every girl will be dressed or acting in a manner that has at least one item in both camps. By picking it up you are doing a light cold read, putting her into a box she wants to climb out of, working a contrast, and pinging her to probe her self-image. Examples:

- The girl is studying at a table in a bookshop café: "I can't help but notice an incongruence. You are studying really hard, books open, and you have those nice sensible glasses. And yet I see a small tattoo on your wrist and those striped tights. It's like you're a combination good girl [indicate books] and bad girl [indicate tights]. Intriguing."

- The girl has a biker jacket and carries an iPad. "When I first noticed you I immediately noticed...well, I noticed you're pretty but that's not the point... I noticed this black biker jacket and your heavy eyeliner and I immediately thought hmmmm that's a bad girl, a rock chick. But then I see this iPad and I'm thinking do bad girls sit in Starbucks sipping lattes and checking their twitter feed..."

The possibilities are endless: She's dressed like a business woman but slouched in her chair or conversely she's dressed like a rock chick but has correct body posture and a fluffy gonk hanging from her pencil. Just find the incongruence and then feed it back to her playfully. An easy pattern to use is "Either you're [observation A] or [observation B]."

## 4. The burning question

Sometimes when you see a girl there's something so obviously different or interesting that it spontaneously overrides every other thought about her. For example, while walking through Covent Garden one afternoon I heard a sweet voice singing behind me. I turned around to see a cute black girl singing along to her music player, headphones on. So I immediately open and ask "Did I really just hear that? You're walking through here singing away in public. It's so sweet." I banged her three days later.

*When a question or puzzle occurs to you spontaneously, use it. It's far more authentic than constructing a template-based opener.*

They'll all spring from observations rather than being pre-prepared, but the key is that the question is burning inside and you simply must get the answer. That's your motivation for picking her rather than any of the other pretty girls you saw today.

**Screening**

*A filtering process that allows only girls possessing the things you are specifically looking for to remain. Men and women screen potential sexual partners. Much of the cold-reading and probing during the street stop is designed to make the woman feel like you are screening her*

We have focused on the street stop because that's the purest expression of the model and the best single method for accessing a large variety of women. Every girl has to walk somewhere and the sheer volume of footfall on busy streets guarantees that something will turn up. You also have the ability to quickly **screen** out No Girls. But there's more to daygame than stopping a moving target. The three other common types are as follows. What they all have in common is increased social pressure. This is where things get more difficult -- if you mishandle it, you'll likely pop the bubble and lose the girl. However, if you handle it with social intelligence, then the girl is even more impressed — like any other venture in life, high risk daygame offers the opportunity of high reward.

## 1. Opportunistic contact

You are going about your life and the girl hers when something happens to bring you into brief coincidental contact. Perhaps she bumps into you coming out a doorway, perhaps she drops something right in front of you, or trips, or you catch her yawning. The important point is you have just been handed a situational opener where it's completely natural for you to comment on what just happened (unlike the clearly contrived street approach). The best way in is an accusational opener:

- "I can't believe you just did that... [relay the opportune action back to her]... dropping your sandwich on the floor. I hope you're not going to eat it [big smile]... maybe there's a charity that will take it as a donation now."

- "I'm sorry but I simply can't let you eye me up like that without saying hello."

- "I'll pretend I didn't see that... You know we have rules about that sort of thing here. You're lucky there's no policemen here."

If you were the one caught out one standard go to is:

- "I'm sorry you had to see that [cheeky grin]... My mum always said I'd get into trouble, and now here I am... busted by you."

## 2. Queues

*Addressing a girl with covert signals (eyes, grin, posture, innuendo) of sexual intent while restricting yourself to non-sexual overt signals (words, touch). This is the most powerful type of seductive communication because you can convey high levels of social acuity and intent without violating social norms. Sometimes referred to as "plausibly deniable" direct game*

You'll often find yourself next to a pretty girl in a coffee shop queue, on a train platform, or sitting in the airport. These situations are where the world has temporarily put you into proximity with a stationary girl. If you don't act she'll naturally drift away from you.

The key here is to make an observational **indirect-direct** opener. That means say something about her that isn't a clear sign of sexual interest while making your subcommunication very flirty and sexual (i.e. cheeky grin, sparkling eyes). You don't need to overwhelm her and you don't need to make a production out of the pre-history / elephant. It's an off-hand comment that's pinging her for interest. You'll need to muster your fastest powers of observation for this scenario, so quickly run down the checklist for ideas: her look, her actions, her mood:

- She's behind you in the queue at Starbucks and quickly grabs a pannini: "Wow, now that's a decisive woman! See it, grab it. Your stomach must be rumbling" or she spends a while deliberating: "You know if you wait any longer the police might think you're a sit-in protestor"

- She's next to you on the train platform, you notice a big Fortnum & Mason's bag: "That's alot of tea you have there. More than they had at the teddy bear's picnic."

- She's sitting opposite you on the Underground carriage: "Excuse me. I can't help but notice... you've painted your fingernails red and your toenails green. Now, does that make you a patriotic Portguese or you just left the house in a hurry?"

*Indicator of Disinterest. A signal given by the girl to convey a lack of interest in you, such as checking her phone or turning away from you*

You don't need to directly come onto the girl and tell her she's nice — it's too much too soon in such a situation. You're just pinging her with an off-hand comment to see how she takes it. She'll read the twinkle in your eye and your cocky grin. If she likes it she'll bite, if she doesn't she'll maybe chuckle and then **IOD** (in which case, perhaps consider one last assumption before giving up on her).

You are always under time pressure in queues, so how to proceed depends entirely on your position relative to hers:

i. She's ahead of you. Chat to her until she reaches the cash register / the train comes etc. If she wants to keep talking she'll keep herself in a position where you can catch up. For example she'll linger by the condiments counter and look at you as you approach. If she boards a train she won't go far down the carriage and again she'll give you some kind of look or signal that the conversation hasn't ended. In contrast if she's trying to bail she'll put some distance between you and not look back.

ii. She's behind you. You are the one who lingers a while and looks at her. If she comes to you, engage her as she approaches. If she finds excuses to stay a distance, takes a circuitous route around you, or studiously avoids your eyes then that's the brush-off and you should eject.

iii. If you opened her on a bus or train, tell her where you are getting off after you reach hook point. If she doesn't immediately tell you her stop, then ask (but only after, doing it before hook point is creepy). If she's at all vague its a sign she's uncomfortable. Use her answer to judge your time and then take a number before one of you leaves. If the interaction goes really well, suggest you both actually get off the train and chat on the platform for a while.

## 3. Ambushes

The girl is settled somewhere and you must proactively go up and talk to her. Perhaps she's standing at a bus stop or waiting for friends outside an Underground station. Maybe she's sitting in a cafe doing homework. The point here is she isn't going anywhere and you have no incidental reason to talk to her — you have to actually make an effort to go over and try something.

The key concept here is to call out the Elephant In The Room. You must describe the situation you find yourselves in so you pace her reality and demonstrate your social acuity in recognising her anxiety that you might be a weirdo. The rest of the opener will be the same as the street stop, though you have more time to formulate it. So...

**RAS**

*Reticular Activation System. Human perception is designed to automatically draw attention to valuable signals, such as an approaching predator. Girls have a strong sense of when men are checking them out. Once a man has entered a girl's RAS, the clock begins ticking on how much time he has to open before he is dismissed as indecisive or creepy*

i. Observe her for a short time. Stay outside her **RAS** and try to figure out her backstory. What is she doing, how is she doing it, why is she there, has she been there long, what's her mood like. Imagine you see an Asian girl sitting in Starbucks with a laptop and book. Observe:

- How much has she drunk from her coffee? If it's almost full she's probably just settled in and the coffee is hot ("Hey, I see you've just settled down with a hot cup of coffee to start...") whereas if it's nearly empty it'll be cold she's been there a while ("Hey, I see you've been camped out here, probably for hours, working on...")

- How engrossed is she in her laptop or book? If her eyes are locked on the book, she's chewing her pen and barely noticing her drink then she's deeply engrossed ("Hey, you look absolutely engrossed in that book...") whereas if her eyes wander, she checks her watch, sips her drink, and looks into space then she's getting bored and probably working ("Hey, I couldn't help notice you staring into space, distracted...").

- How organised is her vibe? Has she neatly arranged her papers, set out a special place for her coffee cup, kept most of her belongings in her bag, and her pens in a pencil case ("I have to say, you are the most organised student I've seen all week...") or is everything spread slapdash across two chairs and its all messy ("I'm amazed you can study, it looks like a bomb hit this table")?

- What does her dress and accessorising say about her? Does she have soft knitted mittens, a novelty keyring, stickers on the laptop case, a decorative notebook or any other "softeners" that indicate a cute mindset ("Look at you, little green mittens with snowmen on them. That's so cute"), or is she dressed more severe and professional with a leather iPad cover, angled brand name handbag and so on ("You have the look of a very serious business woman...").

> You have time to observe, deduce, and build a little mythology around her to feed your assumption stack. If she's waiting for friends, try to get a sense of how impatient she is and notice the time: people tend to meet on the hour or at half-past, and girls tend to be late meeting each other so if it's 13:55 you likely have more time to work than if it's 14:05. Does she look impatient and looking around (her friend is late but expected) or does she look resigned and bored, engaged in another task such as texting or reading a book (her friend texted her she's late). Once you've sized her up it's time to open.

ii. If it's possible to approach obliquely then do so. That means if she's sitting the table next to the condiments and milk, go walk to that counter and open slightly off-hand. You don't need the big strong masculine presence of the street stop because her momentum is already killed. You've ambushed her — she has nowhere to go — so play it softer. Position your body slightly away so she has you on her twelve o'clock whereas she is on your 11am or 1pm. This subtly telegraphs that you are not going full-on (which could intimidate her and shows too much interest from you).

iii. The rest of your subcommunication will be direct. Look her full in the eye, talk slowly and surely, gesture as usual. There is no pretense of this being a chance encounter because you had to directly walk up to her with the intention of speaking. Open as usual and refer to the Elephant:

> "Excuse me. I know you're sitting there reading but I just wanted to say you look nice... what I noticed about you is you've got this very serious, very engrossed look like you're reading the world's most important book... and yet I could see those cute little green mittens, like my little niece wears to school..."

iv. The biggest difference between the ambush and the street stop are Indicators Of Disinterest. A girl on the street can just shrug you off and be on her way but an ambushed girl can't. It's a higher pressure situation for her, so you must be more sensitive to IODs. Is she giving you any "please leave me alone" signals? These include:

- Very short non-commital answers that leave you nothing to stack with

- Looking away from you and only looking back when you address her

- Finding an activity to replace talking to you, such as stirring her coffee, tapping her keyboard, looking at her book, checking her phone

> If she doesn't immediately hook give it one extra attempt to get into the assumption story and... if that doesn't hit, just roll off. Ambushes are really just pings to flip the stone and see if she's interested. There's no need to get embarrassed or self-conscious upon bailing because you were socially calibrated and did nothing wrong.

> Once you reach hook point you will have to lock in. If she's sitting at a table and you're standing, ask if you can sit down a minute. If she's standing, lean against the wall. Do this only after you've reached hook point (usually when she's asked you a question or two and clearly stopped whatever it is she was doing before you approached) and initially subcommunicate restrained attention. So if you're sitting, lean back and have your chair angled to put her on your 11 or 1 o'clock. If you're standing, just lean up against the wall and don't quite angle directly towards her. Gradually turn more into her as the hook strengthens. Reward her interest with more of your attention.

> Generally for ambushes I try to get in and out within five minutes. If she's waiting for friends you need to take the number before you're interupted. If she's busy doing something it seems strange to keep imposing and potentially idating (you could always suggest a delayed idate when she's finished with her work).

## Mother/daughter five sets riding unicycles

**AVOIDANCE WEASEL**
finding ways to avoid opening since 2009

Too many people treat daygame like it's just that -- a game. Perhaps the very word gives them the wrong idea. Do not come into the community as a hobbyist treating cold approaching like you would stamp collecting or Magic The Gathering. The purpose is not to fill an encyclopedia with every possible permutation of the Game. The purpose is not to impress other men on Youtube. The purpose is not to invent ridiculous thought experiments then argue on the internet how to approach them. That stuff is for the men who don't get laid.

Daygame is about getting laid. Focus on that. And the best way to get laid is to approach solo girls who are ambling slowly down the street. Everything over and above that is a complication you'd rather avoid.

Don't worry about two-sets, mixed-sets, father-daughter sets, girls riding bicycles or whatever. Consider those only as variety to break up the pacing of spending 95% of your effort on solo slow-walking girls. Some sets are simply not worth approaching — it can't be done. Don't be doing teary mother-daughter sets on the way out of a funeral (despite what "Wedding Crashers" might advise). Don't ask me how to open a juggler riding a unicycle. Stop using far-fetched situations to avoid the bread-and-butter sets.

## Goal: Get her talking

The biggest danger of delivering your opener (other than completely failing to stop the girl) is that you just leave it hanging out there, she thanks you, and then walks off. When you signal to her that all you wanted to do was deliver a compliment and tease she'll read that and when it's over, the interaction is over. So you need to signal that you are beginning a conversation rather than making an offhand remark.

The assumption story is the moment when you signal this intention, and thus it's at this moment when No Girls will make excuses and leave. Be ready for this and don't let it upset you. For a girl to be successfully seduced she must be:

- Available

- Into you

These are not binary conditions. Some girls are somewhat available in the sense that they are not fully committed to their boyfriends. Perhaps they only recently began dating and aren't strongly attached, or maybe they've been dating a couple of years and she's growing tired of him and starting to consider alternative options. Other girls are happy with the sex they are getting but are naturally promiscuous. Other girls still are dating a provider chump for the security, status, and emotional attention but are on the lookout for a sexy bad boy to give her tingles and rough sex. You simply don't know at the moment you open. You have to flip the stone and give it your best shot.

Some girls are available but not to you. Just like us, girls have types they go for and certain standards they operate with, which may often seem arbitrary. Again, you don't know what these are when you open. So when a girl listens to the opener, responds favourably, and then starts to disengage while you trot out the assumption story that is feedback telling you the following:

- She's either unavailable, not into you, or both

- You conveyed your sexual intent so she knew where it was headed

The first one is beyond your control. The second one is positive feedback. Getting an early polite blowout is evidence that you are doing this right. She knows you are trying to fuck her and she respects you as a man (shown by her politeness), it's just that **she's not the right girl at the right time**. If you were employing a more K-selected daygame method, she might have engaged you in a dead-end conversation and wasted precious time you could devote to other sets. So do not let early blowouts faze you. It means you are doing it right. The exception to this is if you're getting "eye-roll" blowouts or freaked-out blowouts. The former means you are shooting for women who consider themselves out of your league. Maybe they are deluded about their own value, or maybe you are the deluded one. Either way, process the feedback. If she's acting freaked-out then your calibration is off and perhaps you aren't correctly calling out the Elephant In The Room.

Accept that you are going to lose a fair number of girls at this stage. The girls who stay are the Yes and Maybe girls. It can be emotionally draining to lose all the No Girls so quickly, but in the long term they are doing you a favour by screening themselves out before they waste your time.

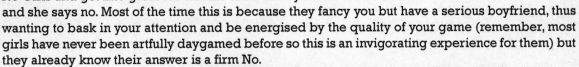

# The Story

We've finished the opener and begun the assumption story and she's still standing there. Great. The principle behind the assumption story is this:

*Tell a mini-backstory that playfully frames her*
*and gives her raw meat to accept and reject*

I've already given you a bunch of archetypes to feed this so let's put them into actual examples, picking up where the "...And all crazy" part of the opener ended.

**Brazilian:** I can already imagine it. A week ago you were lying on Copacobana beach, soaking up the sun while you sip a Caipirinha in your bikini... then you take a flight to London and now you're standing in the cold rain thinking "why did I come here?"

**Romanian:** You realise that English men are very scared of Romanian girls? We all think you live in castles in the Transylvanian mountains and drink the blood of virgins. We've seen Dracula movies.

**Russian:** I don't know Russia well but I imagine you live in a little wooden cabin somewhere in Siberia, eating potatoes and hunting wolves at night.

**French:** You fit my stereotype of how French girls are. Maybe I'm wrong but I imagine you sitting in a café by the Eiffel Tower, with a little cup of coffee, nibbling a pain au chocolat and reading Jean Paul Sartre.

**Serbia:** We don't see many Serbs in London. All we have is our stereotype that it's a land of giants. Big tall men like Djokovic and tall long-legged girls with short shorts and very serious faces like angry princesses.

There's an unlimited number of assumptions you can make once the bit is between your teeth. Freewheel. See where your mouth takes you, but try to keep it down to a couple of sentences. The best assumption stories contain the following elements:

- Borderline racist stereotyping

- Colourful imagery, sounds and taste

- Keep the story about her

- Playful ignorance

You want her to get a small dose of righteous indignation because girls **love that feeling** and will be energised to respond and correct you, opening the conversation into banter. By triggering her indignation you are giving her a soft push, which further demonstrates your boundaries and shows you aren't a kiss-ass push-over male. The indignation is the emotional bait that motivates her to respond while the playful vibe softens the edges so she understands you're not just being mean. You are also beginning the frame control and investment based on this tactic:

*Put her into a box she doesn't want to be in, then let her expend effort (investment, qualification) to climb back out of it. Then put her into another box.*

This is the essence of banter — playfully framing her according to stereotypes and mildly unflattering characterisations, then watching her try to fight back. You'll notice girls rarely start framing **you**. They are too busy defending themselves against your **reframes** and trying to maintain their own value. Solipsism 101. If your opened on the basis of her style / occupation / activity then your assumption story will reflect that. For example:

**Business girl:** I can see it now… You've spent all day in meetings, serious faced, upright body posture, nodding and writing on Powerpoint… and all the while your thumb tapping into Whatsapp, gabbing on with your girlfriends.

**Hurried girl:** I can only imagine you are saving the world today, a girl on a mission. There's an office somewhere that's descending into chaos without your steady hand on the ship. Kids misbehaving, girls chasing their tails over boyfriends, dogs yapping… until you come along to give them a stern look.

**Dreamy girl:** Your life must be one long daydream. Your feet pounding the city streets, bright lights in your eyes, your head in the clouds. Probably right now as we speak there are rainbows and unicorns frollicking through endless fields of sunflowers. Ah…. To be young and free!

**Proud girl:** You seem so determined and proud. Eyes always forwards. If you looked behind, you'll see a path of destruction.. men and women sitting dazed on the ground, head's spinning, knocked over by your aura. You need to be careful, you don't know your own power!

It never matters if you are right or wrong. So long as there's a tenuous connection between something you can see in her and the first step on your wild flight of fancy then you're good to go. She'll understand what you are getting at and laugh along.

*90% of the time, this is where you reach hook point.*

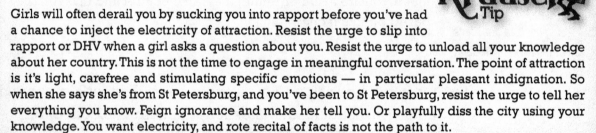

### Sucker Rapport

Girls will often derail you by sucking you into rapport before you've had a chance to inject the electricity of attraction. Resist the urge to slip into rapport or DHV when a girl asks a question about you. Resist the urge to unload all your knowledge about her country. This is not the time to engage in meaningful conversation. The point of attraction is it's light, carefree and stimulating specific emotions — in particular pleasant indignation. So when she says she's from St Petersburg, and you've been to St Petersburg, resist the urge to tell her everything you know. Feign ignorance and make her tell you. Or playfully diss the city using your knowledge. You want electricity, and rote recital of facts is not the path to it.

She'll respond to your teasing, throw a little back at you, and then give you the hook point signal. The most reliable signal is she asks you a question:

- Where are you from?
- What do you do?

Alternatively she'll rattle off a couple of sentences which continue the conversation and add a little value, such as:

- No no! We are not vampires. I'm from Bucharest. That's in the south, it's a normal city. You've watched too many movies!
- Haha, no I don't work in an office. I'm a fashion buyer for Shop X. I spend all my time in factories and shows.
- Yes, I seem to bowl people over. What can I say, I'm a determined girl!

More subtle still will be how her body language shifts as she settles into the conversation and her momentum stops. The key signs are:

- She crosses her legs and sits her weight down a little
- Her eyes open up

You don't need to check off everything on the above lists, just be aware of when you feel the girl has come to a complete mental and physical stop from what she was doing before, and has instead fully entered a conversation with you. This is hook point and the attraction phase is almost over. From here, you'll start to dial down the banter and progress into a real conversation. It takes calibration to sense how quickly this can be done following the basic rule:

*The stronger the attraction created,*
*the faster you can slip into rapport*

If you sense she's still not quite fancying you, drop in slightly more "push" through teasing and challenging. If she's responding great and you're sure she fancies you then you'll move into rapport sooner. This prevents you from overloading the set and making it too fizzy. Remember the fishing line metaphor. Attraction material tightens the tension on the line, and too much will snap it. This is the dreaded "overgaming" in action. So once you've spiked her up and gotten your hook, you need to let the line out a little so she can flap around, tire herself out, and drive the hook further into her. Upon hitting hook point your whole demeanour shifts.

- Fold your arms
- Wipe the smile off your face
- Talk less

Any further attraction material will not only prevent the interaction settling down and becoming real authentic communication, but it will also subcommunicate that you aren't confident of your own value.

## Demanding too much signal

Consider an analogy between Game and your favourite sport. Imagine a guy first developing an interest in boxing. He doesn't really know what he's watching aside from the really obvious stuff like a knockdown. He's only capable of recognising the biggest most obvious signals. As he watches more fights (and even better, trains in a gym) he'll start to pick up on all kinds of weaker but crucial signals such as:

- One fighter is throwing lots of fast flashy punches everytime his opponent comes near but he's not setting his feet. This betrays his fear and lack of confidence in his power.

- The more aggressive fighter takes a hard counter right hand. His legs don't wobble and his face never changes expression but he suddenly stops coming forward. That one hurt.

As you learn your chosen sport on a more than superficial level, you begin to see what others can't. For example, I'm told that Aussie Rules football is a deeply technical game, whereas to me it looks like one big fight with a football thrown into the middle. Guys who know the sport can see those subtle ebbs and flows that determine the game. So it is with The Game. The longer you spend in set, the more face-time you have with women, the more chances you take to provoke feedback... the more you condition and utilise your brain's innate pattern recognition system.

There are likely three reasons why you can' read the signal:

1. Lack Of Entitlement: You don't believe a girl like that would be attracted to and have sex with you, so you can't process her signals telling you that's precisely her intention. You look for over-confirmation.

2. Calibration: You are too logical and too clueless, or perhaps too drunk. You simply don't know what you are looking for and how to distinguish the signal from the noise.

3. Model: You haven't been properly taught the technical progression of an effective seduction model. Perhaps you've been sidetracked with charlatan YouTube videos or the blind-leading-the-blind of internet forums. You don't have an expectation of the appearance and timing of signals thrown out by the girl, so you aren't receptive to them

You must learn to tune out all the "noise" in a girl's behaviour and to focus in on the tiniest, faintest "signal" that betrays her real interest level in the seduction. This is a key skill in Game that can only be developed through repeated exposure in the field. This is why advanced players can seem so smooth — they literally see things that you can't. Phase: Street

# VIBING

## Goal: Have an interesting, fun, two-way conversation that gradually draws her in

Once she's hooked you'll be moving further and further away from structured communication and less concerned about loading your conversation with value. That first minute is a carefully-planned assault on the beach to establish a beachhead. You've done that, now you can focus on just channeling the value through more conventional means.

Once you are both talking about a substantive topic, keep to it for a while. Don't jump around introducing new topics and don't derail the thread of conversation. Show genuine enthusiasm in the subject and direct it in ways which satisfy your interest. Rather than cluttering your mind with specific lines or techniques at this point, it's better to just embrace the free-flowing spirit of conversation and keep yourself firmly in the Now. Free up your intuition to read her signals and nudge you in the right direction.

### Feel the strength of the hook

When the hook is dropping she'll lose some of her animation and her conversation will become less enthusiastic. So throw in some push:

- Occasional light challenges. Don't accept everything she says. If you don't agree with her then don't express agreement. Artfully indicate disagreement without triggering an argument. Ask her direct questions like "Why do you think that?" or "That sounds boring, don't you think?"

- Occasional teases. Remember the animals and the female archetypes. Work them in to frame her in a playfully unflattering light.

Conversely, when the hook feels strong you can loosen the fishing line and force her to work harder to build rapport. Draw her out with open-ended questions and by making statements that imply questions. Resist the urge to talk about yourself except in passing before turning the spotlight back onto her. To get nerdy about it, there are two basic patterns: Meat and Expand:

# CONVERSATIONAL MEAT

A good sandwich has more than just bread and lettuce. It has a big slab of meat in the middle that you can sink your teeth into. A good conversation is just as meaty. When making a statement you should load it with a couple of nouns or emotions that act as conversational meat she can bite onto. When she makes a statement look for the conversational meat she has given you. For example (meat in bold):

> *You:*　I imagine (1) **growing up** in (2) **Germany** is very different to (3) **central London**.
>
> *Her:*　Oh yes. (a) **Berlin** is a (b) **beautiful place** with very (c) **lively nightlife** but it's much (d) **more relaxed** than here.

Each sentence contains so many segues into other conversations that you should never be at a loss where to go next. Just pick a slice of meat and steer the conversation in that direction. So in this example you could continue to talk about any one of her four topics and in a manner designed to strengthen the hook or to strengthen the rapport. Bear in mind we're still in the early stages of the first few minutes so we don't want to turn the electricity off. Conversation must still be evocative, lively, and not-too-serious:

Each of the following examples takes one of her conversational slices of meat and then shows how to use it to either strengthen the hook (H) or strengthen rapport (R). So the first example (a)-H is taking her reference to Berlin and then strengthening the hook by teasing. In contrast the second example (a)-R uses the same reference to Berlin but instead I feel the hook is strong so I use the opportunity to increase rapport by waxing lyrical and painting evocative pictures with my words.

**(a)-H:** You know I heard something completely different about Berlin. Mind you, I've never been this is just what a few friends told me. Apparently everyone gets blind drunk on fruit beer in the bier haus then stumbles out at midnight to eat massive bratwursts. Shocking, really, to us timid gentlemanly English.

**(a)-R:** I'd love to visit Berlin. It's a city with unique history because of the post-war partition. I've read so many spy novels that are based there, with double-crossing agents crossing the Berlin Wall checkpoints in hidden compartments inside trucks.

**(b)-H:** I'm a little surprised when you say that. You have a grungy bad girl look. More like a girl who gets drunk in a midnight party in a beautiful park, rather than sitting under a tree with a book in the afternoon sunshine.

**(b)-R:** I've got a soft spot for European old town centres with their beautiful parks and historic old buildings. Germany also has those old cinderella castles...

**(c)-H:** I just *bet* you like the lively nightlife, you crazy party girl! Smashing tequila shots and dancing on tables. Oh my god!

**(c)-R:** That's something Europeans do differently to us Brits. Your nightlife is more...

How can I say… You just seem to enjoy it more. I'm not sure why…

**(d)-H:** Come on, you Germans have a reputation as the least relaxed people in Europe! If you're not winning the football you're starting another war. I'm pretty sure the one thing no German has ever done is sit in a conservatory with a mug of hot coffee, a newspaper crossword, and then said "Tell you what, let's just relax and do nothing today."

**(d)-R:** People don't relax enough in life, don't you find?

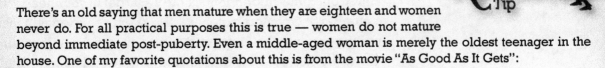

## Women are children

There's an old saying that men mature when they are eighteen and women never do. For all practical purposes this is true — women do not mature beyond immediate post-puberty. Even a middle-aged woman is merely the oldest teenager in the house. One of my favorite quotations about this is from the movie "As Good As It Gets":

- Receptionist: How do you write women so well?

- Melvin Udall: I think of a man. And I take away reason and accountability.

Men are designed to go into the world, understand the terrain, and then design and execute a plan to take what they need from it. We developed logic, discipline, tenacity, and an understanding of cause and effect over the long term. Natural selection forced men to develop a Real World Interaction Tool. Like children, women lack these additional cognitive processes. Nature selected for women who look nice, make men feel good, and provide a reliable oven in which the man can cook his bun. This means you must not treat women the way you treat men. Don't hold them to male standards. They are not men-with-tits.

Women are children. What are children like?
- Always in the moment
- Carefree
- Self-centred and self-obsessed

What do children want?
- Fun
- Happy vibes
- Shiny things
- Boundaries

Vibing is where you can inject a girl with happy vibes and free her inner child. Women have been pushed into an unnatural position in modern society, where they are constantly pressured to take on male responsibilities and function autonomously without male leadership. This makes them very uncomfortable, unhappy, and ill, and they struggle to understand why. Like children with absent parents they struggle on their own without the warm comforting blanket of responsible authority.

Lift that weight from her shoulders. Impose your masculinity and let her carefree femininity release itself so she disappears into the moment. Watch her light up with pleasure.

We wish to avoid being The Interviewer or The Hairdresser. You'll naturally jump from topic to topic if you haven't learned how to organically nudge conversations along. One way to avoid jumping is to practice teasing out further information from a girl so she expands a topic, offering more of her thoughts. The easiest way to do so is to have *genuine interest* in the topic and her opinions on it.

If you don't have genuine interest then you need to stop and diagnose why. Self-diagnosis is a crucial skill in game. Some likely culprits are:

- You're outcome-dependent. There's a target in your head ("Get a number," "Get more notches," "Do twenty sets today") that is pulling you into the future and taking away your enjoyment of the Now. When your mind is focused on the goal her contribution to the conversation is just an irritation, a necessary running down of the clock until you ask for a number. Unsurprisingly this makes your conversation inauthentic and she senses you're just going through the motions. You're not making her feel like you are both in the moment, a prerequisite due to her child-like sensibilities

- You are opening women you aren't interested in. At the beginning of your daygame career this is no big deal because you just need experience standing in front of women and trying the model. During an intensive number-farm you'll also be opening women on the borderline of what you like. So if you find yourself lacking intent and conviction with a girl, you've probably been too much in your forebrain and not established enough connection with your sexual intent. Reconnect. Visualise her naked and ask yourself how much you want her bouncing on your dick. If the answer is "meh," eject and save your energy for women who can hold your interest better.

**Mangina**

*A male who pretends to identify with women and feminine goals as a strategy to get laid. He usually does this by proactively seeking out and criticizing/ sabotaging masculine men to prove his own loyalty to Team Woman. He mistakenly believes that avoiding polarity will create attraction*

- You don't much like women. I'm reluctant to throw the misogyny card around because it's so much abused by feminists and **manginas**. However, lots of guys getting into the Game are coming from a place of pain, often because of bad experiences with nasty women. Many are recovering Nice Guys who are experimenting with swinging the pendulum too far the opposite way into Total Assholery. When you first tear women down from the pedestal, it becomes tempting to smash them into the ground and squash them like cockroaches. This stage is inevitable, but you want it to be as short as possible before you emerge with a healthy and pragmatic acceptance of female nature. If you find yourself having total disrespect for a woman's conversation and find enduring it a chore then perhaps you need to remind yourself why you like women. Visualise all those things you like about femininty.

Once you've dragged your mind back into the Now and you're engaging on a healthy, respectful level you'll find yourself having real interest in what the girl has to say. That doesn't mean you necessarily agree with her or kiss her ass, but you want to probe her more. There are a few conversational conventions that let you prod her into expanding:

1. **The Granny Move**: Have you noticed when talking to your grandmother that she just repeats the last couple of words of your sentence? For example:

> *Her:*    How was your day?
> *You:*    I went out to the shops to look for a new laptop.
> *Her:*    a new laptop....
> *You:*    Yes. My old one has a broken fan and overheats a lot so I need to find a new one.

When you find yourself in a situation where you don't really know what she's talking about, or you're a bit short on ideas and need to fill the space, just repeat the last meaty phrase back to her while softly nodding your head. It's a signal for her to expand. For example:

> *Her:*    I came over here to study at the fashion college. I'm very interesting in knitwear.
> *You:*    interested in knitwear?
> *Her:*    Oh yes. I love designing cardigans and scarves... *[blah blah]*

2. **The Vacuum:** A temptation among beginners is to talk incessantly without leaving any pauses, only indicating the girl to speak by asking a direct question. This is motivated by a limiting belief that if you stop talking the girl will lose interest and walk away. Intermediate players are normally more confident, but tend to so enjoy the act of delivering conversational value so much that it can work against them. They often forget to shut up and let the girl get involved. You must give the girl space to talk. One simple technique is the vacuum: You just stop talking and look expectantly into the girls eyes.

Remember, you've already reaching hook point. She wants to talk to you. So as she comes to the end of her sentence you just stay quiet. Nod your head, make a listening noise, and look expectantly like you are waiting for her to continue. Sometimes there'll be a little tension because you are bending the normal rules of turn-taking in a conversation. That's ok, because part of attraction is showing the girl you are more comfortable with tension than she is, and that you are not always going to play by the rules of social convention.

Usually she'll pick up the ball and start babbling. This is precisely what you want — her working, slightly off-balance, and giving you more information about herself. Encourage her with listening noises and slight smiles. Reward this good behaviour.

Sometimes she won't pick up the ball so you have a long awkward silence. Your calibration will tell you what to do about it. Your choices are:

- **Pick up the ball.** Take your turn in the conversation. I use this as the last resort because it means the vacuum was only a partial success and you may be playing into her frame.

- **Prod her to continue.** Say something like "Please, continue" or "Yes, I'm listening." It's just a stronger invitation for her to keep talking than the original vacuum.

- **Knowing smirk.** Covertly acknowledge what you are doing by deliberately leaving the silence. Use it to build sexual tension by looking into her eyes, smirking warmly so the subcommunication is now the focus. If she acts a little self-conscious, you've succeeded.

3. **The Freudian Probe:** Back in the 1970s, some enterprising psychologists took issue with Freudian psychoanalysis, believing it to be a sham. They suggested that rather than helping patients fix their problems, the analysts were really just providing a sympathetic non-judgemental ear to bored housewives starved of attention. Thus the analysts simply listened to the women's petty problems and collected a fat cheque. In efforts to prove the quackery, the psychologists wrote a computer program to act like a psychoanalyst then invited patients to communicate through typing (the patients believing it was a real analyst on the other side of the connection). This was the 1970s, remember. Very primitive IT.

The computer program had a very simple AI. It would detect certain flagged nouns (father, mother, depression, work, etc.) or emotional adjectives (happy, sad, anxious, etc.) from the patient's text and then insert it into a template. Literally the conversations would go like this:

| | |
|---|---|
| *Patient:* | I have been speaking to my mother a lot recently. |
| *Program:* | Ok. Tell me more about your [mother]? |
| *Patient:* | She's very anxious right now. She's got a health complication with her stomach and it's causing her a lot of pain. So she often calls me in the middle of the night needing someone to reassure her. |
| *Program:* | I see. What do you think about the [anxiety]? |
| *Patient:* | Probably she's still missing Dad. Because he... *[blah blah]* |

## The Russian Minute

Krauser
precision engineering
Tip

There is a particular quirk that is common among high esteem girls and Eastern European girls when initially stopping them which I call the Russian Minute. Whereas most girls immediately engage you be it positive or negative and provide feedback, the "Russians" give you nothing at all. Or so it appears to the untrained eye…

These girls stand motionless and expressionless looking intently at you. Imagine how a bored woman at an art gallery looks at the main exhibit. She'll give you this for a minute or two, which I can guarantee will feel like an hour.

Noobs are terrified of it. They are so desperate for feedback from the girl to tell them where they're at (and whether to pull the rip-cord) that this cold response unnerves them. That's precisely why she did it. To filter out men of faint heart.

Never forget the golden rule of a street stop:

*If she's still standing there, she's interested.*

When faced with a Russian Minute I smile inwardly because I know exactly how to pass this test, and I also know how few men can. So I continue to plow. I make conversation, I don't get rattled, I get to show her I'm solid. She might pipe up with a challenge:

- "Why are you talking to me?"

- "What do you want?"

For these girls that question is not bitchiness — it's a genuine inquiry to be taken at face value. FSU girls (Former Soviet Union) are high-esteem greyhounds. These girls are very direct and straight about the dating process. Let them know exactly why you stopped them. For example:

"Because I saw you and you are pretty. I'd like to find out more about you."

"I'm making conversation because I find you attractive."

First time you try this on the street you'll realise why these girls use the Russian Minute — it's a very effective filter. Very few men can stand in front of a beautiful catwalk model type girl who is giving them no positive feedback, let alone openly admit they are trying to seduce her.

---

**Mark**

*The clueless victim of a fraud. The term comes from hustling because one member of the team (spotter) would mark the victim's coat with chalk to identify him for the member who initiates the fraud (roper)*

Psychics, tarot readers and con men have long known the innate human need to be understood and listened to. It takes very little prodding to get a motivated person to talk about themselves. While they are trying to empty the **mark's** wallet, **we** are merely trying to engage in a fluid exchange. I mean, value exchange. The pattern is simple: pick out the key emotive word or topic in the girl's sentence and then ask her to tell you more about it.

> **You:** So you really are a dancer. Not just a part-timer going to the easy classes after work!
>
> **Her:** Oh yes. I love dancing. I went to ballet class since I was eight and now I'm doing hip hop and jazz.
>
> **You:** I see. Why dancing?
>
> **Her:** My mum used to watch ballet when I was a little girl... *[blah blah]*

Don't actually ask the Freudian questions outright. It would sound weird to ask her "Tell me about your father," but you can wrap it up in an implied question or generalism:

"It sounds like your father is a very traditionally strong man..."

"I find Serbian girls are often skilled at traditional arts like singing, dancing and music. Why is that?"

4. **The Other Side of the Coin:** An easy conversational topic is to draw out a contrast between two things and get her offering her own opinion. For example, if she's a tourist / student in London you can contrast London life to her home country. If she's a local you can contrast her stable current life with her hopes and dreams. Take a guess about her imagined life if she was free to do whatever she liked, and get her to engage about this fantasy. You can contrast the real her with your stereotype, and the reality of her country to the stereotypes of it (building on the mythology you created for her). It's very easy to just present two opposites and get her to fill in all the details in between. Get her talking about one and then get her to consider the other side of the coin. Examples:

## Place

> **You:** I imagine Prague feels very different to London...
>
> **Her:** Oh yes! London is so busy and exciting. There's so much to do here.
>
> **You:** Whereas Prague...
>
> **Her:** It's beautiful but it's different. People have a more close-minded attitude there and there's more pressure... *[blah blah]*

## Stereotypes

> **You:** Tell me your stereotype of English men. Don't be too diplomatic. I can handle the truth!
>
> **Her:** You are very reserved and cold. I think you don't touch or hug much and you can seem very serious.

Daygame Mastery

> **You:** So back in Romania what English people do you see. Is it David Beckham and Coldplay, or the older people like Sherlock Holmes and William Shakespeare?
>
> **Her:** We see all of that.
>
> **You:** But now you're here I guess your real opinion of English men changed...
>
> **Her:** Yes. I know some of the teachers in my English school and met a few friends of friends. They are... *[blah blah blah]* The biggest single problem men have with daygame is that they are boring. Too nice, too static, too agreeable, too... dull. Look around and ask yourself what you would find interesting and exciting about the men around you, even your friends. Almost everyone who turns to daygame is a Nice Guy. Therefore, the first order of priority is to re-attach their balls. Swing the pendulum out towards the Bad Boy side and crash the car.

Encouraging a girl to expand upon a conversational topic really isn't very difficult, so long as she has some social interest in you and can speak a common language. Early in a set, you probably haven't started escalating yet and thus you may have either a **social** or a **sexual** hook point. Both are conducive to chatting. The fundamental social skill of listening to someone with curiosity and enthusiasm is a skill we practice every day of our lives around friends, family and co-workers. If it's not happening in set, there's a barrier somewhere.

The barrier could be that she isn't much interested in talking to you. If this is the case, her sparse conversation will be matched by her body language indicating her wish to leave. This includes such actions as looking away from you, shuffling her feet away, turning her body towards the direction she'd been walking, and a look of consternation or impatience. If she is uncommunicative but her body language suggests she wants to stay, you need to slow down your vocal delivery and give her more 'conversation meat'. Give her something to feed on so she can talk.

If you find yourself hopping around topics and cutting her off, you're probably just nervous. Likely, you're worried that it you don't keep throwing new content at her she'll walk away. Calm down! Stick to a single topic and follow the golden rule of listening: *if she starts talking, you stop talking until she finishes.*

## Redlining the car

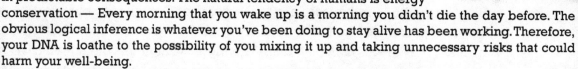

Everyone has comfort zones in which learned repeatable behaviours result in predictable consequences. The natural tendency of humans is energy conservation — Every morning that you wake up is a morning you didn't die the day before. The obvious logical inference is whatever you've been doing to stay alive has been working. Therefore, your DNA is loathe to the possibility of you mixing it up and taking unnecessary risks that could harm your well-being.

This is why people get stuck in a rut. There is a powerful evolutionary drag towards inertia and routine. Do just enough to get by. Don't rock the boat. This attitude will not get you laid.

*If you do as you've always done, you'll get what you always got.*

Clearly being a Nice Guy isn't working. If it was you wouldn't be reading this book. Even men who are getting laid regularly might be within their comfort zone. A good-looking male 9 who is dating female 8s is slumming it. He ought to be dating female 10s, but the level of effort and identity change necessary to date above his comfort level is too much — he stays in the rut, despite being better off than the vast majority of men. Most of us aren't lucky enough to be in a popular band, or a DJ, or a male model. We must shake free of the inertia and get things done.

In this area, I use the metaphor of race driving.

Imagine multi-class race day at Silverstone. Each driver brings his best car. Some guys are lucky because they inherited a Red Bull F-1 car. Some are unlucky and have a rusty old Ford Cortina. The car the guy brings is his "passive" game — it's the sum total of his life-choices, diet, genetics, gym, and so on. That's the car he drives. The driver himself is the Game element.

In investment terms, Game is your value-add (alpha) to the normal market return in the industry (beta).

Average laptimes of the F-1 cars are going to beat the supercars, which are in turn going to beat the fastbacks. But on race day the mechanics of your car are beyond your control. You must simply drive the fastest race you are able. This is where driver skill and driver intent becomes crucial.

Are you prepared to redline your car?

Are you prepared to take every corner at high speed, riding the dangerzone of turning circles, traction, and downforce? Are your prepared to slipstream a faster opponent and try to outbrake him and nip in from on the hairpin corner? Are you willing to skip a pit stop?

Some drivers are so inept and so risk-averse that they will cruise their F-1 car through fifty risk-free laps. The skilled driver who redlines his supercar will beat that guy. Redlining carries risks because the slightest error can result in a wipeout, but you need to find out how fast you can take those corners before you break. It's not until you've crashed the car that you find where the limit is. In game you redline it by pushing hard:

- Open girls hotter than you're used to
- Push for faster and wilder sex
- Try the threesome, try anal
- Tease hard, challenge hard
- Try a nuclear push in response to princess behaviour. Throw the girl out your house in the middle of the night.

You'll instinctively feel where your current limits are and every time you approach the danger zone your gut will tighten. It's similar to stretching in the gym — as your muscles reach maximum stretch they involuntarily contract to pull you back into safety. It requires mental energy and is even physically nauseous to push past that limit.

That's what you need to do. Redline the car and risk crashing it.

# ELECTRICITY AND SPARKLE

You must put electricity into the set during the vibing phase. Ideally the power of your street stop made the girl fizzy, but you won't often get that. Just getting to hook point is good enough because you now have time to work. Getting her to stand there willing to talk is the biggest hurdle for most men. Never forget vibing is about creating a sparkle. Do not go straight into rapport and investment. Tease and challenge her, draw her out. Be defiant. Let's look at some additional techniques to increase the voltage. All of them involve moving poles within the matched pairs.

## Good-Looking Guy Game

The dirty secret of the community is that most of the name coaches are the kind of big muscular good-looking guys who really ought to be getting laid plenty even without Game. These guys already have strong masculine polarity that is immediately obvious from their physical appearance. As soon as a girl sees them their "DNA jackpot" switch is flipped and the girl gives him a strong positive response. A virtuous circle ensues because the man knows his next strongly positive response is only a set or two away. He doesn't have to face long periods of cheerless grind. He can rely on IOIs and warm opens. This means he enters every set full of confidence and positive expectations, which makes the girl even more receptive.

Good luck to them. If I was good-looking I'd do the same.

The problem for the average daygamer is in ignoring the advice of these guys. The average guy's biggest hurdle is initial attraction. Give him time to work his personality and Game into the conversation and the girl will warm to him, but just getting an opportunity to be heard is tough. Yet the internet is full of men who have never needed to worry about building attraction. They just open and escalate.

There is thus a smoke and mirrors con being perpetrated. These men are opening girls who already fancy them and then giving advice on how they build attraction from a cold open. It's about as useful as a tall guy teaching a short guy to play basketball.

The time to listen to good-looking players is on the areas they genuinely have experience of, which is:

- Filtering out timewasters
- Escalating
- Closing.

Even very attractive men need to close the girl, and one thing attractive men have lots of experience of is getting girls into a position to try a seduction.

## The Statue vs. The Dervish

Every time I walk along Oxford Street I can spot the daygamers. I can even guess whose boot camp they did. What most of them have in common is they are too static. There is a community-standard alpha male street pose with legs apart, hips forwards, leaning back, and totally motionless. A coach noticed they fidget too much, betraying their nerves and lack of self-belief, so he advised them to stay still. It's good advice for the beginner but they soon outgrow it.

Standing motionless is not natural. Don't do it.

Instead learn to change your movement according to the rhythm of the interaction. On the opener, you quickly put your roots down like an old oak tree to project gravitas. That's the default position but don't hold it against natural urges to gesticulate. When she's talking you should hold steady in gaze and posture, but when you talk give your body the freedom to emphasise your words and mood in a natural manner. Kick a stone away with your foot, scratch your arse, gesture at the beautiful Christmas lights as you talk about them. Don't be afraid to move. Movement is not beta. It's normal.

## Attention And Inattention

I go into detail on attention in the Date Phase section, but you should know that it also applies in the street. Up until hook point you project masculinity on her by holding eye contact and paying attention. As she slips into vibing you can start withdrawing attention on occasion. This means:

- Make reference to something in the environment and then actually turn your eyes to look at it as you talk.

- Turn your body off slightly so she's no longer on your centre line. After ten seconds turn it back.

Don't overdo it and make sure it's actually congruent with the interaction. Occasionally put the spotlight on yourself.

## Kino vs. No Kino

I touch girls quite a lot now if the energy is fizzy. I don't have an established kino ladder (that's for dates) but sometimes it will just be natural to guide the conversation to something on her body and then touch it. Examples:

- While teasing her for being a squirrel ask if she stores nuts in her cheeks. Then softly grab her cheek between thumb and forefinger.

- While commenting on her boots give them a very light kick with the inside of your shoe for emphasis.

- While accusing her of being a pervert, lightly stiff-arm her shoulder to "protect" yourself from her coming after you.

- Say "come on, let's see what perverted sex stuff you're reading" while reaching for the book she's carrying.

- Pat her softly on the head while patronising her for being a good girl.

- Turn her around while commenting on how you'd been checking out her ass but now require a better look.

What all of these examples have in common is using kino to amplify a tease that you are delivering verbally. It's congruent because the action is matched to the subject of the conversation. Think of them as exclamation points on the sentences. It's completely non-sexual touching.

She knows instinctively what you're doing — encroaching on her personal space and taking control over her body — which signals extreme confidence and social acuity. Do it only when your vibe is strong. Trying it on low-vibe days will come off at best mechanical and at worst creepy.

## Sexual Spiking vs. Good Guy

If you sense the hook dropping and you need to fizz up the set, consider dropping in an outrageous sexualisation very briefly, like a drive-by, then immediately go back to the normal less-sexual vibe. Some examples:

- "Sorry, what was that you said? I was distracted, looking at your breasts."

- "Yes… uh huh… [listening]…You have very nice eyes. So big, like a raccoon [pattern interrupt]"

- In reply to something from her "I just bet you do, you pervert!"

Sexual spiking is very much dependent on the vibe in that particular set. Generally I do it either as a test (I sense the girl isn't much attracted so I want to try a Hail Mary before deciding to bail) or the vibe is going great so I want to push my luck and move things along while all is good. If the girl is not very flirty but you still read subtle signs of attraction, there's no need to sexually spike. It'll come off as try hard.

All the above are ways of amping up the energy of the set to make it fizzy. Girls want to have fun. You are separating yourself from the pack of Nice Guys by having the boldness to inject raw energy into what is normaly a "respectful" or "awkward" interaction. So few men have this powerfully seductive confidence that thrills the girl with the feeling of being swept up into an adventure. Get her fizzy.

After a few minutes of this, she takes you seriously as a sexual threat and you plant your name firmly on her Fuck List.

Vibing shouldn't take more than a few minutes. Get a feel for when you've achieved its purpose and then slide into Investment. You'll instinctively feel "This is fizzy enough now, she's loving it, so let's calm it down."

**Key signals**

- Her eyes are sparkling

- She's smiling a lot

- She has forgotten whatever she was doing before

- She's actively contributing to the conversation

- She makes no motions to leave

- She's reacting to your conversational lead

- She likes it when you touch her

*The Fuck List*

You are either her boyfriend or her girlfriend — If you're not fucking her then you're her girlfriend. Too many Nice Guys do daygame and fall into the trap of making friends. It's fairly common knowledge in the community that girls will quickly put you onto one of two lists (i) Men she might fuck (ii) Men she'll never fuck. Yet even modestly experience daygamers will still plod along and waste time, leading to being placed on the girlfriend list.

Often it happens in the first ten seconds (Yes and No girls respectively), and sometimes it takes a few minutes (Maybe girls). But never longer than that. This is why you need to vibe before you invest her — there's no point running rapport on a girl who doesn't fancy you, but this is precisely the strategy most men run. It's just a buffer to avoid an early rejection and a sting to the ego.

Getting onto a girl's Fuck List (or what she might call her "romantic radar") doesn't guarantee sex. It just means that she views you as a Man rather than a (sexless) Male. She may still have all kinds of logistical barriers, doubts, or whatever. Getting onto her Fuck List is a necessary, but not sufficient, condition to getting her in your bed.

# HOLD YOUR NERVE

**Shit test**

*A statement or action by a girl designed to provoke a reaction so she can then more accurately judge your SMV. Girls only test when your value or intention is not clear*

Some girls don't yet play along with the vibing because they are undecided as to whether you are worthy of their time. This is a simple **shit test** scenario, so treat it as such. There's a hierarchy of desirable responses to a test, in order of best to worst:

1. Ignore it

2. Dismiss it

3. Reframe it

4. Respond to it

That sounds obvious, but much pick-up literature is obsessed with smart rejoinders for a girl's tests and devolve into a library of witty smart-ass replies. For a regular guy who usually falls into the girl's frame by responding at face value, it's good to learn some reframes. As I said before, though, this book is not for beginners.

*The girl is testing your frame, not your wit.*

A man imposes his frame onto the girl and then leads her. He won't allow her to derail him. When you engage in a bantering exchange that responds to her test, then you are being derailed. It doesn't matter how funny you are, or even if you win the banter, the fact she derailed you means you lost. She will pick up on it. It doesn't mean you blew the set, but it was a suboptimal response you will have to make up for at a later date. Far better to just dismiss it ("Yeah, sure. Anyway… [continue talking about what you want to talk about]") or ignore it (just keep going).

The most common shit tests you'll get early in the set are:

- **Calling You Out** — This is the "Are you hitting on me?" challenge designed to filter out men who are not sufficiently comfortable with the integrity of male sexual desire. It also weeds out men who are weak because they fear rejection, forcing them to hide their sexual intent. The simplest response is "Yes, obviously" then keep your conversational thread going.

- **Boyfriend** — Calibration tells you if the girl really has a boyfriend or if she's just trying to unbalance you. Generally speaking, if she really has a boyfriend you'll sense it by observing her enjoy the chat but not really committing herself to it. You'll be told about the boyfriend late, when you go for the close. Conversely she might tell you immediately she is taken — this is a No Girl. It's usually just a test when she raises it during vibing with a challenging rather than appeasing look on her face. Simple response is "I don't care," or "I should hope so, a pretty girl like you," then continue talking as you were.

- **Busy** — If the girl was walking fast and looked busy before you opened her, then she's likely just telling you the truth. Tell her it'll only take a minute and rush to a quickie number close. If you stalked her a bit first and noticed she was walking slowly and aimlessly, then clearly she's just throwing out a test. Dismiss it with "This won't take long" and continue talking as you were.

### Orbiter

*A male who hides his sexual intent with the aim to stay in a girl's awareness long enough (usually months and months) for her to wear down and "notice" that he's better than the men she's dating. This is also dismissively called Omnipresence Game. The girls always know what he's up to, even if they won't consciously admit it*

### Chode

*A male who is mostly externally-referenced and thus fails to project attractive male qualities such as confidence, conviction, sexual desire, boundaries, and individuality*

Eagled-eyed readers will have noticed a pattern. The best way to respond to these tests is to dismiss them and get the set back on track to go in the direction you want. The girl feels this as a strongly masculine frame. In contrast to nearly every other **orbiter chode** inhabiting her life, you are a man who pursues what he wants and won't be denied. They like this.

Sometimes the girl with test you with a direct personal challenge. Now the test is about you, not about her. Things like:

- How many girls have you hit on today?

- You're a player, aren't you?

- I bet you say that to all the girls!

- Why should I talk to you?

Though these may seem more harsh on the surface, if you hear them then congratulations are in order. These tests are all signs of attraction. The very fact you are in the Player Box means she accepts you as a high value man who multiple women wish to be

*A category used by the girl for r-selected men. She recognises them as "The men who hot women have sex with," in contrast to the Boyfriend Box for K-selected men, "The men who buy us stuff and give us attention"*

with. I will usually give a cocky smile and dismiss the objection just like the other tests. Occasionally I'll use it as an opportunity to challenge (which builds attraction):

"Why would you say that?"

Then let her justify her accusation. She's investing.She's thinking about you and she's giving you ways back into the conversation.

You don't need to get too hung up on learning specific responses. When a girl shit tests you, it's only your mindset that is important. You'll sidestep them easily if you genuinely believe:

- You are good enough for this woman

- It's totally natural to hit on girls you like

- It's ok to cast your net wide and flip many stones

- You are proud of your masculine sexual desire

# INVESTMENT

## *Goal: Connect with her and make her work for you*

**A**ttraction is vapour. You can approach a girl, tease her to the point of hysterical laughter, flirt, make sexual innuendo, and then as you're walking away smugly with her number she's already forgotten you. Girls get attracted to men all the time — it doesn't mean much in itself. Normal guys who begin to get their first attraction signals during daygame are blown away by it.

"Woah! I just had a really hot young girl into me. I *saw* the IOIs. She *definitely* fancied me!!"

It's understandable. Most men's hurdle is attraction. Most men are unattractive and build up decades of reference experiences that confirm their identity of Normal Unattractive Guy. So when they actually learn the mechanics of amplifying attraction it's like giving nukes to chimps. The few attractive guys out there know full well that getting a girl to fancy you is only the initial hurdle. Actually moving it along is another game entirely.

---

### Sport Sex Archetypes

There are rare cases of men who are so incredibly attractive — to women generally, or just that particular woman at that time in her life — that sex happens quickly and without investment. It's more common in nightgame because of the self-selection involved (i.e. horny DTF girls naturally congregate at meat market clubs precisely to get fucked, whereas daygame has no such selective pressure) but some guys just immediately flip the "fuck him now" switch. That's not learnable. It's an artifact of the man's lifestyle or looks. Tall good-looking men with broad shoulders, strong angular features and brawny high-T skin will get this a lot. If you're not that guy, such fast sex cases will be very rare. Don't base your game on it. Always assume you have to invest the girl for a positive result.

---

Attraction comes and goes with the wind. In an age where women will freely give out their numbers with no intention of returning your call, if you want the number to be solid you need to put some roots down in the attraction. This means you need to calm the girl and make a real authentic connection.

Investment is really four things happening concurrently:

1. Comfort

2. Rapport

3. Making her work

4. Running down the clock

I give a fuller discussion to comfort and rapport in the dating chapters because that's where most of it is done. Street Rapport and Street Comfort are truncated forms for the sole purpose of bedding the set down. You'll reach a point where you think she's sufficiently settled-in for the number to be solid.

# 1. Street Comfort

Comfort is about her heartrate. At the beginning of the street stop, you are hitting her with a huge spike, overwhelming her with masculine presence and triggering her appease/please natural response. She gets a rush of pleasure from receiving quality male attention and all kinds of gears start spinning as she tries to keep up with the conversation, present herself well, and run quick calculations on whether she wants to see you again. There's a lot happening all at once in that little girl-sized brain of hers. This is why Vibing is "fizzy": you took a can of Coke and shook it up. Shake too hard, and the whole thing sprays onto the floor.

Energy is high. Her heart is racing. Whether she's kicking her feet and laughing or standing still like a deer in headlights, you can be sure her heart is thumping like a trip hammer. It's an intrinsically exciting experience, but anyone who has owned a dog knows how such excitement wears them out after a period of time. So, monitor the fizziness of the set and gradually lower it. The basic dampeners are:

- Keep your movements slow and patient (pacing)

- Reduce the speed with which you switch between the matched pairs (volatility)

- Allow each of your conversational turns to be longer so you can each say more each time (duration)

It will be a smooth process, much like turning a car engine off and watching it gradually slow to a stop. As she calms down her brain will be more receptive to taking in what you say, engaging with it, and offering real opinions and information about herself.

# 2. Street Rapport

Rapport is all about making a connection, breaking down barriers between you and offering your authentic selves. On the street you don't need to probe too hard and overshare. Just let some of it come out. This means you'll ask your more personal questions about her likes, dislikes, past, present, and future. Unlike Vibing you won't be deliberately framing her, making assumptions and building a mythology. When you get her story in rapport you are getting the truth, which opens up many possibilites because she is giving you a look into how her mind works.

**Fizziness**

precision engineering
**Krauser**
Tip

There is a hard-wired mating dance in us all. We instinctively realise that
the initial stages are highly ritualised and not very serious. It's a game.
So you can be a bit gamey. You can't skip the attraction phase or else you land in LJBF territory, but
you also cannot string it along past its useful period. If you find yourself getting "stuck in attraction"
you'll need to introspect to uncover your inner game weakness. Probably it's due to:

- You don't really believe you are attractive enough to get this girl. So you think you
  need more attraction.

- You are trying to impress somebody who's watching.

- You haven't read her signals correctly to know the attraction phase is over.

- You are addicted to the validation of making her IOI you.

In each case spending too much time in attraction means trying too hard. She intuitively feels your
lack of confidence and authenticity, which is an instant turn-off.

*Rapport is powerful because it shows
you are confident in showing yourself.*

**Outgrouping**

*People are tribal, instinctively
classifying others as
"my tribe" (in-group) or
"other tribes" (out-group).
Interactions with the in-group
are subject to social pressure,
reputation, harmony, and
co-operation. The out-group
is treated instrumentally. This
is why girls in your "scene" will
rarely give harsh blowouts —
they consider you in-group
and thus feel their reaction to
you will affect their reputation.
R-selection is most effective
when you are out-grouped
because it supports the
anonymous consequence-free
frame of adventure sex*

It's surprising how few people are willing to give of themselves
in the modern world. People construct elaborate defense
mechanisms or Psychic Armour to reduce their emotional
vulnerability. Many people will do anything to avoid "being
real," and thus exposing their real identity to the possibility of
rejection. Examples:

- **Sub-cultural fashion**: By dressing as a hipster, goth, punk
  rocker or whatever, you are wearing a uniform that identifies
  you as a member of that group first and an individual second.
  Therefore any rejection can be blamed on **outgrouping**.

- **Super-fly**: Suiting up with branded sunglasses, Italian shoes,
  and other fineries is an elaborate avatar in which *the avatar* is
  accepted or rejected rather than you.

- **Sarcasm / Irony**: Refusing ever to give your real opinion
  and artfully evading a real "A is A" factual statement or clear
  value judgment makes you too slippery to reject.

- **Intellectualism:** Making all subjects impersonal and
  general, or excessively pedantic and nitpicking, is another
  way of avoiding showing who you are and what you think.

- **Gamey:** Reeling off a stream of witty rejoinders is just another rebuff to attempts for someone to get to know you.

- **Ideology:** Obsessing over political causes and world views allows you to play the Clash Of Civilisations game in which your world view battles an opposed world view. At no point do individual personalities connect.

The common theme to the above is external referencing. Rather than two unique individuals connecting on a personal level, you have two avatars connecting on a symbolic level. It's not a real connection.

Spend some time introspecting on which parts of your life, routine, and personality depend upon each type of referencing. It's almost certain that, like most people, you are too externally-referenced. You care too much about what others think. You care too much about fitting in. You fear somebody finding out what you really think and then out-grouping you. Most people are excessively externally-referenced and that means they struggle with being authentic. The natural deduction is that **encountering an authentic man is refreshing**. It's powerful.

*External Referencing*

You can get your meaning in life from one of two places: inside yourself (internal referencing) or from other people (external referencing).
An internally-referenced man looks inward to decide "What do I think about this?" and "What is important to me?" He finds his answer and uses that to give himself direction and purpose. An externally-referenced man sends out pings to people around him to establish a consensus answer to the same questions, and then follows the crowd (or deliberately plays the contrarian — but that's still external referencing). Examples:

- Reading GQ and Esquire magazine to tell you which hairstyle is in fashion. (external)
- Seeing a movie and thinking, "That haircut looks cool. I'll have that." (internal)
- Buying an expensive sports car in order to look cool as you arrive at a nightclub. (external)
- Buying an expensive sports car to enjoy the act of driving it, no matter who is watching. (internal)
- Reading a book everyone is talking about so you can contribute to the conversation. (external)
- Reading a book in your room for the joy of it or to expand your knowledge. (internal)

There is nothing inherently good or bad in either pole. It's the balance that matters. A fully externally-referenced man doesn't know who he is, what he wants, or where he's going. He lets the sheepdogs herd him into the sheep pen. We call these men chodes. A fully internally-referenced man is a sociopathic drifter who can't relate to and respect other people's value systems.

Authenticity is a mindset rather than a technique, but there are some simple ways to practice it. While investing the girl you can focus on topics that allow each other to genuinely share opinions and give a window into your personalities. You are still focused mostly upon her as you try to learn about and screen her. Here are some sample questions:

### Her Past

- What is it like growing up in [her country]?
- I can't imagine you as a little girl. What were you like?
- Have you travelled much?
- What's the most impressive place you've been to?

### Her Present

- How do you find living in [city/country]?
- Tell me about your perfect Sunday. You wake up with no work, no problems. Just a free day to enjoy.

### Her Future

- Where next? Are you going to stay here forever?
- What's the Big Plan?

### Her Likes / Dislikes

- Cinema
- Books
- Music
- Hobbies
- Fashion

There's no special technique in rapport. Don't be afraid to ask direct questions but do try to keep them opened-ended rather than closed. Learn to embed implied questions into statements so you can offer some value while still triggering a response from her:

**Closed:** Do you like reading?

**Open:** What books do you like?

**Implied:** You have quite a thoughtful look about you. If I was to guess, I'd say you like reading the classics.....

When she gives an opinion you can listen, give her some respect and acceptance (now is not the time to tease and challenge), then offer your own thoughts on the matter. It's a very simple turn-taking system which in abstract terms looks like this:

| | |
|---|---|
| *You:* | Question to elicit opinion. |
| *Her:* | Offer brief opinion. |
| *You:* | Acknowledge, probe her to expand on it. |
| *Her:* | Expand on opinion. |
| *You:* | Encourage. Question on details. |
| *Her:* | Give further details. |
| *You:* | Acknowledge. Offer own opinion. |
| *Her:* | Encourage. |
| *You:* | Ask new question to elicit opinion on related topic. |

So let's use a contrived example. We are five minutes into the conversation and I've learned she's from Italy, likes the food, and is studying in London.

| | |
|---|---|
| *Me:* | I'd imagine it's not easy to adjust to eating English food. Your country is famous for its quality cuisine. *[implied question is: What do you think about English food?]* |
| *Her:* | Oh yes! Italian food is the best. English food is okay but it's very stodgy and fattening. *[her short-form initial opinion]* |
| *Me:* | Yes, we like our pies and potatoes here. There must be something about Italy's culture of food that makes it delicious… *[implied expansion question is: Why do you think this is?]* |
| *Her:* | From the time we are little girls our mothers teach us to cook. We have all the freshest ingredients and the family meal is a part of life. *[expansion]* |
| *Me:* | That sounds nice. What does the typical Italian evening meal in your city look like? *[question on details]* |
| *Her:* | I'm from Palermo so our local dish is *[blah blah… details about the meal]* |
| *Me:* | Oh god, can you hear my stomach rumbling just listening to that! One thing I heard about Italy is you have real regional variety in your cheeses and beef. Each region has a specific way of raising the cows and then curing the meats with spices. It's like a whole library full of tasty meat. That's why I love the little family Italian food shops here. I'd love to just get a motorbike, a book, a rucksack and then drive throughout the Italian countryside, each night in a different town, sampling the local cuisine. *[own opinion]* |
| *Her:* | You should. There's so much variety! *[encouragement]* |
| *Me:* | I know you're young but you must've thought about just travelling alone, going off on an adventure…. *[Implied question for related topic is: Have you ever thought of travelling somewhere interesting alone?]* |

There is an art to good conversation and it must be learned. During the set you'll be responding to the ebbs and flows of the chat, intuitively following the model to draw her opinions and strengthen the bond of rapport. You can also do some preparation as homework. Try these simple steps.

## Read A Lot

Reading allows you to borrow someone else's mind. Traveling widely gives you lots of direct experience (and I recommend it), but reading allows you to gain access to lifestyles and thought patterns beyond your individual perception. It also allows you to cram far more experience in by proxy, since reading a book is a small investment in time and effort in comparison to taking a trip. Mix up your reading between pure pleasure (e.g. genre fiction), high-brow culture (the classics), social theory, history, biographies, travel writing, and so on. It's not for me to tell you what to read, as only you know your taste. Just for illustration purposes I'll expand on my own reading habits and indicate what it adds to my abilities as a conversationalist.

- **Hardboiled detective fiction**: I love Raymond Chandler and his ilk. His heroes inhabit the shady underworld of petty criminals where everyone is on the take, everyone is hustling, and nobody can be trusted. The dialogue bristles with wisecracks and one-liners. The tale is set in old-time noir America. These books allow me to develop my own wisecracks and pull out little vignettes about the underworld when chatting to a girl (e.g. explaining to her the Long Con and the Short Con, or how a hustle gang works to do the Three Card Monte). It has the feel of forbidden knowledge. I can also wax lyrical about whiskey and cigars.

- **The classics:** I especially like Alexandre Dumas. He writes fast-paced stories dripping in the period detail of 1800s France with a window into the lives of courtiers, advisors, prosecutors, officers, smugglers, etc. He constantly references philosophers and playwrights. These books educate me on history and life in particular periods which I can then refer to. For example, I may mention to a girl how in the 1800s dueling was commonplace and expand that to talk about testosterone, respect, and the need for a man to "make something of himself."

**Value Judgement**

*A personal opinion about what is good or bad, essentially taking the form of "I like," or "I don't like." Whereas a Statement of Fact can be either true or untrue (and thus subject to empirical verification), a value judgement can only be sincere or insincere*

- **Biographies:** I like to read about great men who achieved something special. Not only does it educate me on the details of what they did (e.g. reading about a mountain climber will tell you a lot about the act of climbing) but it also provides inspiration to keep grinding at my own goals.

You get the idea. Reading widely gives you a depth and breadth of knowledge to pluck out at any moment. You have something interesting to talk about.

## Form Opinions

Get into the habit of making a value judgment on what you like and don't like. Keep your eyes and ears open then make judgments as you encounter situations. I'm not suggesting you go around forcing your opinions onto others, which comes off of as annoying and approval-seeking.It's more about learning to organise, label, and discriminate the world around you to help bring it into order. As you develop opinions you'll develop certainty and decisiveness, which enhances your internal referencing.

Don't download your opinions from the hive mind. When reading a news story, try to unpick the journalist's world view then judge it. Do you agree? What does he have right and what does he have wrong? What are the core beliefs that underlie his world view and do you agree with those?

The world is full of people trying to push their judgments, world-views, and preferences onto you. Figure out what opinions they are selling,then deconstruct them into fundamental axioms and beliefs that allow you to make your own judgement.

That's at a deep level but you can also do it superficially. Shake yourself out of the habit of being indifferent. Modern society has a rush to non-judgment and has made non-discrimination into a religion. The end result is a culture of wishy-washy grey men with no opinions on anything and no courage to express themselves. Don't be one of them.

So when you hear a song, decide if you like it. When you watch a movie, decide if you like it. When you hear someone pontificate, decide if you agree with them. Look inside for the answer. Then when you are talking to the girl you'll naturally project a sense of individuality and a command over your own mind. She senses you know who you are, what you want, and you won't be rolled over.

# 3. Make Her Work

After a minute or two in Investment you'll be engaging in an authentic two-way conversation about real things. There'll be little pressure to jump topics or to perform. You'll feel you have sunk your teeth into something meaty. Once you find yourself engaged in this wholesale communication, you can start shaping the relative energy levels and modify the work rate between you and the girl.

## You want her to do most of the work

In the beginning, the conversation is 90% you because you're the man and it's your role to initiate. You have to create something from nothing so that you can signal to the girl that you're making a play for her. As you get to Vibing it'll probably be 60-70% you talking because she's cooing and laughing at what you say, but is still reliant on you leading and pouring in value. By the time you exit Investment and take her number, you want her to be doing 70% of the work. Your role at this point is mainly prodding her in the right direction and encouraging her to open up and say more.

Don't get too pedantic about the percentages. Even if the set never gets beyond 50/50 in workrate, ten minutes of that is still a pretty good investment towards a man who was a complete stranger just minutes before. You only need enough to solidify the number. Once you are on the date, you have far more time and control to get her chasing you. Most men barely give the woman a chance to speak at all.

The primary skill in Investment is:

## Learn to shut up and let her talk.

If you've practiced your routines and explored the strengths and weaknesses of your game adequately, you'll be bursting with things to say and value to offer. Restrain yourself. Don't over-invest. She's hooked, so you can allow pauses. In the beginning you'll have to learn specific actionable rules such as:

1. Any time she talks, you stop talking.

2. Don't interrupt her.

3. Nod your head and make listening noises.


You'll also learn to instinctively frame sentences to give her subjects to talk about. When girls talk, they are always pinging you for feedback to see if you are still interested, still listening, and therefore it's okay for them to keep talking. So watch for it and when she seems to be pinging, give her a signal such as a head nod or a "Please, continue."

Girls will invest more easily if you focus on them or what is important to them. Talking about yourself on the street is usually a bad thing, so just respond to her question and then turn it back to her. You'll notice my examples of rapport above are not actually talking about *me* — I talk about Italian food, inviting her to talk about what she thinks of the topic.

# 4. Running Down The Clock

*Don't rush the conversation. Relax into it.*

It's often tempting to push the conversation along quickly to the point where you can take the number. This makes you outcome-dependent and takes you out of the moment. The early stages of the set have a natural time limit: Opening should take about a minute or less. Vibing should take five minutes or less. Once you're into Investment the time scale lengthens. **Talk for as long as it's fun and involved**. If she's showing no signs of impatience then just relax into it, lose yourself in the flow and the content of the chat. You need to be present to make the delivery of your value authentic.

It's not until you reach the ten-minute mark that you should consider whether you are overstaying your welcome. If necessary, get a countdown timer and put it on vibrate. Stick it in your back pocket so it gives you a buzz when you're ten minutes in. In time your intuition will take care of it for you.

Lose yourself in the chat, build the rapport and let her talk. You'll naturally sense once the girl is working hard for you so let her do it for a while and then turn your mind to talking the number.

## Flipping the script

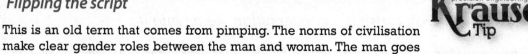

This is an old term that comes from pimping. The norms of civilisation make clear gender roles between the man and woman. The man goes out into the world to earn the daily bread, while the woman stays home to make house. The woman is provided for by the man and gives sexual access in return. Pimps inverted this relationship by sending the whores out to turn tricks, and then handing over their money in the hope of earning his favour. The script is flipped.

Try not to get too excited about pimping it up. Famous pimp biographies make it very clear that they are preying on broken women and that most women can't be turned out. When you see actual photos of the whores it really takes the lustre off the story. Slavic Princesses they are not. Just take the core concept and apply it to daygame.

### Most men pull too hard

The typical man is so imbued with the notion that he must earn the right to the girl's approval (qualify himself) that it doesn't occur to him that she should also qualify herself to him. A man with options doesn't have to eat on scraps. He can always walk away. Daygame requires you to balance your pull with some push in order to amplify attraction and make her work. But is the script ever really flipped? Is the girl ever really chasing you?

No. At any moment from open to sex she could simply say "let's have sex" and you both know you'd agree. She's not chasing the sex. At most, she's working to convey enough value to keep you around after the sex. It's smoke and mirrors on the one hand (projecting yourself as the chooser) and it's a nuanced hard-coded dance on the other.

Consider how young kids chase each other in the school playground. Both the chaser and the chased accept their role in the game and both take pleasure from it. If the chased begins to outpace the chaser he'll slow down. If the chaser begins to lose heart the chased will encourage him. Just as the chaser is looking forwards at the target, the chased is constantly looking over his shoulder to satisfy himself the chase is on. This is the "pull" of the chaser — both are keeping correct tension on the fishing line. This expresses itself throughout the pick-up:

- When you street stop a girl you want her (pull), but you know that you can approach another one 60 seconds later so you don't need her (push).
- She gives you some token resistance (push) which is really her way of seeing if you're a man who she wants (pull).
- You flip the script and get her to qualify herself (push), but you're doing this as a well-rehearsed, calculated move to get her (pull).
- You kick her out of your apartment for playing games (push) which triggers massive attraction that makes her come back and jump you (pull).

The point of this is that you shouldn't get too hung up on the idea of making her chase. The phrase "make her chase" functions more like a maxim to remind yourself that she needs to do some pull and you some push, rather than a literal description of the underlying dynamic. Also, while as men we initiate with the open, don't forget she did the first pull:

*When a girl stays in shape, dresses nice, and then walks solo down the street, she has put herself in the shop window. That's the very first pull of the whole model.*

Keep this in mind when you struggle with a run of rejections. You already rejected a hundred women before you even saw her. Every woman you saw in the shop window and passed up is one you would not give a second of your time. You may feel a concentrated sting of rejection in any given set, but women feel the soft sting of accumulated non-opens when they dress up nice and stride purposefully into the world and no man even talks to them.

# COMMIT HER

## Goal: Get contact details and an agreement to meet later

In normal sets when neither of you has a reason to rush, you'll start thinking of taking the number about 10 to 15 minutes in. Any later than this and you risk over-investing both from the girl's point of view (she feels you gave her too much time/attention) and from your own (you should free yourself to flip more stones). If circumstances force you to rush the number, so be it.

Over time you'll learn to feel when she's ready to give the number. There'll be a sense of expectation and anticipation like she's waiting for you to ask. Look for subtle signals like the conversation is beginning to stall, she's starting to nod her head and give short answers while looking at you expectantly. Perhaps she'll even drop in some hint that she has to go. This isn't a brush-off because she's already spent ten minutes chatting and giving IOIs. Each phase of the courtship has an exit point, and if you overstay your welcome the set will stall and eventually crash no matter how much attraction you initially created.

### There is no magic to "number closing"

Just ask for the number. Be simple and direct. Make it clear it's okay for her to say no. You'll have seen all kinds of creepy gambits in the PUAsphere which are trying to manipulate a girl into giving the number without realising it. Stupid things such as:

- We should hang out sometime

- We'll have to hit those places up

- Which would you prefer tea or milkshake?

- Put your number into my phone

**Frame-Creep**

*Gradually imposing your frame onto a girl over a long period of time rather than from the beginning. This is only recommended if the girl has an exceptionally strong frame or a low interest level, situations where a strong frame-push would backfire.*

There's nothing wrong with those statements in themselves. The problem is that men often employ them as a buffer to avoid rejection, making them come off as wishy-washy or creepy. Life isn't a cheesy romantic comedy. There's no grey area where she helps you take her number and co-closes you. You are the man — you ask for her number. Keep it simple.

> *Me:* Look, I should probably go now. You seem really nice. Now I have to ask, can you drink English tea like a real English lady?
>
> *Her:* Haha… I'm Italian. We all drink coffee!
>
> *Me:* Sure. But you're in England now. Can you be like Audrey Hepburn? Chin up, back straight, pinky-finger extended. Drinking tea in a proper china cup from a proper teapot?
>
> *Her:* Yes, I probably can.
>
> *Me:* Ok. I'd like to take you out for tea. Would you like that?
>
> *Her:* [yes or no]
>
> *Me:* [pull out phone on a Yes or undecided] Right then. How do I spell your name? [open new contact]

I've made a pleasurable game of it, but I've given her a very clear Yes/No opportunity at the end. The last thing I want is a flaky number that'll waste my time and energy. There's really nothing more to it. Once I've got the number I'll immediately text her my name. This is to check for mistakes and connection issues (which are actually quite common with foreign sims).

Don't feel it's weird to be checking her number. Mistakes can happen and often the girl doesn't know her number and needs to bring it up on her phone. So just tell her "I'll text you mine to check it works." If she's deliberately given you a false number (very rare) then the ensuing awkwardness is her punishment for being a stupid bitch — there's no reason for you to be embarassed.

If the set has been less playful but you are fairly sure she likes you, it can be better to close less playfully but still restating your sexual intent. This is a less showy version of the above example."

> *Me:* Look, I have to go now but… let me tell you a secret.
>
> *Her:* Okay
>
> *Me:* I think you are cute. Let's get a drink sometime. Would you like that?
>
> *Her:* [yes or no]

Once your text hits her phone, bid her farewell. You've made a successful day approach.

# MESSAGING
## section four

Now that you have the girl's contact details you must do something about it. She has disappeared into the crowd, and within minutes the electricity you created will fade and the rapport between the two of you will weaken. She is no longer directly within your aura of masculine dominance and the love bubble will pop. This section details how to use digital communication to get her out onto a date.

There are two routes: Short Game and Long Game. In increasing order of time horizon, the tools you will use are texting, Whatsapp, Facebook, and Skype. Usually you will try to get the girl out soon (Texting), but many leads will be logistically unfeasible. This will force you to put her into a holding pattern (Long Game). This section gives detailed advice on how to progress the girl quickly until she has agreed to a date. The next section considers more patient options.

# MESSAGING

## TEXT PHASE

### Goal: Get her out on a date

Notice how I say you are trying to get her on a date, not a "meet up" and not to "hang out." You want her to be showing up with the expectation of a man-woman vibe. Even if your hook was strong, you don't know what her life circumstances are or how interested she is, so the temptation to soft-pedal the invitation is strong. Don't fall into the Noob Trap of weaseling her onto a date without knowing your intentions.

> #### The Weasel Date
>
> In your early days of Game you'll be struggling to get solid numbers because your limited value conveyance and in-set work lead to extracting numbers rather than having them freely given. This means she'll give you a number to get rid of you, or maybe you turned your intent off so much that she thinks you're just a new friend. Perhaps you tried to override a genuine boyfriend objection. The result is that very few numbers lead to a text exchange. Thus, you overvalue that one lead. You'll do anything to get her onto the date for "date practice," so you low-ball it and hide your intent. Stop doing it.

Drill it into your mind that the purpose of texting is to get the date. That's it. Occasionally there'll be girls that are logistically blocked off, so we'll get into exceptions to the model later. Think of the ideal model as the motorway headed to Date City. You want to be gunning down that motorway in a straight line and the only time you turn off into a sideroad is when construction or a traffic jam make the best route impossible. The only time you stop at a service station is when you run out of petrol or need to sleep. If no extenuating circumstances present themselves, then just keep gunning it for Short Game.

> ### Text Map — Engage in a couple of light text exchanges and then after about three back-and-forths push for a date.

Remember the frame underlying a street pickup: you are initiating, you are sweeping her off her feet, you are carrying her along on the waves of your charisma. So don't dither and don't wait for her to give green lights. If a girl likes you she'll let you escalate her on amber.

## The Endless Prevarication

Most noobs are struggling with a lack of reference experiences, and thus do not have entitlement. You don't really believe you deserve the girl. Deep down you are worried that if she gets to know the real you then she won't like it and the set dies. Symptoms of this deep insecurity include becoming an Approach Machine who never puts himself on the line, a reliance on routines and always the same opener, not asking for a number, and in this case texting her for waaaaaay too long before inviting her on a date. Confront the emotional motivation for this self-sabotage. Don't avoid the moment where she can turn you down. Don't worry about what happens on the date. Just get yourself through this stage — send the invite in good time.

Most of your adherence to the model is based on information you collect while talking to her on the street. All those probing questions you should've asked and your reading of her energy levels, her keeness, her character...these all inform the tone and speed of your text game. Likewise, it depends how your own vibe came out during the approach, because you should present the same persona in texts. Be congruent. You know that she liked what you showed her on the street and will respond to that side of you. Before sending that first text you should have an idea where she fits on these scales (refer back to the Street Stop phase for how to probe):

1. Really into you or not so much

2. Staying in your city for a while or leaving soon

3. Open and uninhibited about meeting men or careful and withdrawn

4. Lots of free time or busy

5. Enjoys banter or prefers to play it straight

## The Endless Banter

Once your text game has improved to the level where girls enjoy the banter it becomes very tempting to just keep doing it. You'll find yourself mired in endless back-and-forth where she's giggling and squealing, responding to call-back humour and flirting. The problem is she never actually comes on a date, so you're just wasting your time. Why is that? Two reasons — she has a boyfriend / doesn't physically fancy you but your game is tight enough that she enjoys being in the moment with you via text, or you are enjoying your own attraction material too much and not moving forwards. Be sure to push it forward to eliminate time-wasters and to give yourself some self-discipline. After all, why would you want to entertain a girl and get nothing in exchange?

There's one more piece of information to classify her that you won't have until after the first couple of texts- Is she a texter? Fortunately, this doesn't change your method. Remember in an ideal scenario you'll push forward quickly, but the above five factors may cause you to tweak it. So here's an example of a straightforward text exchange where everything goes according to plan.

She's into you, living in the city, very open, has free time and likes banter:

|  |  |
|---|---|
| So this is the crazy French girl with crazy big hair. Nice meeting you, hon 😊 | standard feeler text to open chat |
| Hahaha, what's so crazy about me??? | she takes the bait enthusiastically |
| Everything. I'm scared. My mum warned me about French girls. | indicate I like banter |
| She's a smart lady!!!! Haha, be careful of us!! 😊 | she responds well to banter |
| I shall. I wonder if you are capable of drinking an English tea like an English lady. Hmmmmm | having seen she's keen, I can begin seeding the date |
| Hmmm I don't know about that. I can try but usually I drink coffee. | she's implicitly agreeing to date |
| I guess we can try. Tuesday 6pm is good? | so I commit to a date invitation |
| Yes, that's good. Where? | no quibbles, she wants to be led |
| Piccadilly Circus. Dress cute, so we match 😊 | playful vibe |
| I'm always cute! 😃 | agreeable to my frame |

I'll break this down in detail. First let's consider the blueprint underneath the specific words chosen

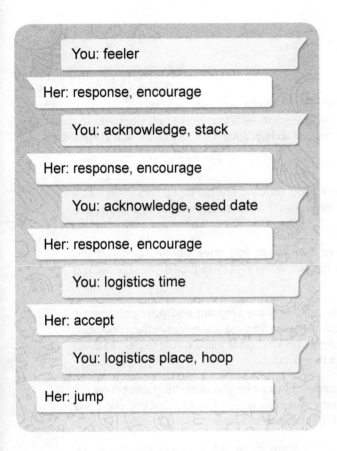

You: feeler

Her: response, encourage

You: acknowledge, stack

Her: response, encourage

You: acknowledge, seed date

Her: response, encourage

You: logistics time

Her: accept

You: logistics place, hoop

Her: jump

The man leads the interaction from beginning to end, literally from first picking out the girl in the street stop right up to leading her to the bedroom, and then telling her how the relationship will proceed. Girls are impressed with a man who takes control of the situation because he shows both the balls to chase what he wants and the competence to do it properly. Very few men have either characteristic, never mind both together. This text pattern is a smooth, repeatable system built upon literally hundreds of interactions that led to dates. The blueprint may be dry and logical, but it comes to life when you convert it into specific texts for the specific girl. With each text you are moving things forward, and her primary role is to respond to your lead and comply. It comes naturally to her if she has the proper leadership.

## Success ratios

Aspiring players are naturally keen to benchmark their results against more established guys to answer The Great Game Question — "How good is it possible to get?" The answer is the same as for the proverbial piece of string. Your success rates will depend on many factors:

- How good-looking are you relative to how good-looking she is? If you're a male 9 and she's a female 7 then it'll be very easy to get her. Switch those numbers around and it's ten times harder.

- How old are you relative to her? Every five years you have on her doubles the difficulty. If you are younger than her it becomes very easy to close girls the wrong side of 28.

- Do you have an "in" to her identity subculture? If you are a hipster and you open hipster girls then you have a home field advantage because you are already matched on social acceptability. The difficulty ramps up once you go after girls you'd never expect to meet socially, such as an English man chasing a Persian girl.

- How "on" is your vibe? You'll get far stickier numbers when you're milking an upswing in vibe than when you are grinding it out. Remember, the girl only sees what you show her in that short street interaction. If you're on, all she sees is "great vibe."

- Did she IOI you prior to the approach? Those are warm approaches and ten times more likely to get a strong hook.

To summarise, your success ratios are dependent upon how close to your upper limits you operate. If you want an easier ride you can open girls who are less attractive, older, similar identity, and only do so when you feel great and she spots you an IOI. It's not outlandish to close (i.e. have sex with) one out of every ten such girls with only moderate daygame skill.

If you redline it for hotter-tighter-younger, expect dramatically worse ratios and a far higher skill requirement. That's like asking the driver of a street-legal Porsche to beat the driver of an F-1 car at Silverstone. I tend towards redlining it. In 2013 my stable ratio abroad was 1 in 20. In London it declines to 1 in 50.

Obsessing about ratios is an internet noob trap. What really matters is your final results in absolute terms — How many girls did you fuck and how hot were they? Ratios exist only in your own head and in internet pissing contests. Girls on the street don't care. They either fuck you or they don't.

# FEELER TEXT

**Eye Sparkle**

*The wide-eyed bright stare that a woman gives a man when she is attracted to him and is excited to be chatted up*

Most numbers go nowhere, that's just a fact of life. When you get some downtime between sets on your daygame trawl take a moment to consider the timing of your first text. There's no universal right answer. You have to balance logistics with her interest levels:

- **Keen Girl / No Time**—One or both of you are on holiday so you've only got a couple of days in the same city. She was bright, smiley, full of energy. You got a strong **eye sparkle**. Send the feeler within two hours of the street stop and then keep it running throughout the day.

- **Keen Girl / Lots of Time** — It's a Yes Girl but she's living in your city for at least a couple more weeks. Try to catch her later on that night when she's home and has nothing better to do. This makes you more likely to catch her in a good exchange, where you have her full attention and she goes to bed thrilled to think about you.

- **Flat Girl / No Time** — Give it an hour. You need the texts to filter her just in case you get lucky and she perks up in the texting.

- **Flat Girl / Lots of Time** — This will probably represent half of your total numbers. Wait until lunchtime the next day to send the feeler. You don't want to look too keen nor too try-hard aloof.

Sometimes she will tell you something in-set that changes your timing. For example, you stopped her on her way to meet friends for dinner. Put yourself into her position — she's yapping on with her friends, she's got an activity that's taking her attention, her bag is probably in a cloakroom or under a table with her phone on vibrate. If you send a feeler text now she might not read it for a couple of hours, or worse she'll scan it then something in her environment takes away her attention. Or she's a weak hook and her friends sabotage you. There's no reason to fight those battles. Just wait until the evening when you guess she's home alone. Ultimately it's guesswork. We live in an uncertain world with only partial information. Take your best shot.

It's important not to over-invest so early in the interaction. Keep it short, don't try too hard with callback humour, don't over-reference how you met, don't push for a date, don't over-explain yourself, don't deny the Elephant. Here are some contrived examples of chode texts. They aren't hopeless, just sub-optimal.

- Hey Julia! It was great to meet you today. I never would have guessed you do molecular biology. Wow, you'll be a scientist :) I liked what you said about Spain and the traditional architecture there. I'll add it to my dream holiday itinerary! *[Too long, too invested, too agreeable]*

- Hi Julia! It was fun but random to meet you on the street like that. I guess life is full of opportunities. *[Denies the elephant so she'll sense inauthenticity and give you player tests]*

- Hi Julia! It's Nick from Covent Garden this afternoon. How are you? *[Bland and undersells your value because of course she remembers you. The name would've been enough. Poor thematic hook]*

An ideal feeler text will just announce your presence and covertly convey your intent that this is a man-woman vibe and you really are that charismatic, nonchalant guy she just met. If you did your street stop well enough there's no doubt at all that she's been thinking about you all day. You don't have to chase her. She's already captured. You are just moving it along. Here are some of my favoured feeler texts together with notes on how I use them:

- **Play-It-Safe Feeler:** Hey. It was nice to meet you today :) Are you always so friendly to strangers? Nick *[Used with girls who play it straight, don't especially run with the banter, didn't give off big green lights, or where I didn't get any good teases into the set that I can refer to.]*

- **High-Tease Feeler:** So this is the crazy little Romanian ewok who owes Nick a coffee?... *[Used when the girl was loving the banter, pushing back playfully and giving good eye sparkle. It's quite an aggressive frame-push so use only when you are sure of the girl, where she gave you lots of compliance and you know she responds well to spiking.]*

- **Mild-Tease Feeler:** So this is the cute Italian with the big shoes and bigger smile... You scare me. *[Used in most sets where she banters and you get a few teases it but you see no reason to hit her with a strong frame-push yet. This is safer than the High-Tease.]*

- **Boring Feeler:** It was nice meeting you :) Nick *[Used on Slavic girls who play it straight and don't joke around. Also if her English is really bad. Make sure you had lots of rapport and investment in-set, ideally an i-date, because this text assumes you are already on solid ground. It's power is in underplaying your hand to display complete confidence that she wants to keep talking to you. It's also good if you think you over-cooked the banter so you can dial it down a little and not come off as a clown.]*

- **Familiarity Feeler:** Hey, how is the museum? *[Used only after **very** long sets and idates where you hit strong rapport. Just pick up the conversation where you left off or ask about something she was planning to do. You are short-cutting the usual initial texts that would be a back-step in rapport at this stage.]*

Once you've sent out the feeler you can just turn your mind to other things. The ball is in her court. Don't be surprised if half of your feeler texts disappear into the ether and you never hear from her again. Those girls will get a ping text later (see separate section), but for now we'll assume she does reply.

# Calibrating her response

As you've no doubt grasped text game is an art and not a science. While you are trying your best to keep the car barrelling down the motorway you must constantly adjust to her behaviour, her character, and the other logistical challenges life throws at you. It's not a Need For Speed time trail where the track is cleared of cars and shows you the ideal racing line. It's more like Thrill Drive, where you are nipping between heavy traffic constantly thinking and reacting to the ever-changing flow.

The main new bit of information to glean from her response is: is she a "texter" or a "non-texter"? Most girls love the act of texting and then waiting for a reply, probably 80% of them, in which case they'll happily fall into your text model. Occasionally, you'll find one who simply doesn't like texting. Her responses will we short and unimaginative. This does not necessarilly mean she isn't into you because the basic rule of her first response is this:

*If she responds at all, she is attracted to you*

All good text game should follow the two basic tests of (1) Jumbotron and (2) Glasses Off. This means that if your text exchange was on display in Piccadilly Circus on the big jumbotron screen for everyone to see, would you be proud or embarassed? If the latter, you are doing it wrong. Secondly just scroll through the exchange without looking at the words. Just look at the relative size of the blocks of text. Is she writing more than you, generally? If so, good. You're doing it right. Always be aware of the relative investment levels.

If you ran your street stop like I tell you to then she knows the deal. She knows you're sexually interested in her, so if she isn't then she simply won't reply (or on rare occasions she'll reply with an explicit immediate LJBF). All girls have learned the hard way that any reply at all will be construed as interest. So she likes you. Your calibration job is to evaluate her level of interest and respond accordingly.

So if she's not a texter, just cut the whole model short and get her on a date asap. Here's an example of a non-texter:

|  |  |
|------|------|
| Hey. I'm still with friends. Will be free in 30 minutes. How about you? | Familiarity feeler, had a long street stop where we agreed a delayed idate |
| Hi! I'm also with friends near Harrods, will be done also in 30 mins. | Simple logistics. No frills, no obstacles |
| Ok. Let's meet at Piccadilly Circus. 7pm? | So proceed directly to invitation |
| Ok. | Agreed |
| Cool. See you at the statue. | Clear and direct |

Note how flat and logical that whole exchange is, contrary to nearly everthing I've written up to this point. The normal model won't look like this, but she's a very straightforward girl and our initial meeting had about ten minutes of good deep rapport. It would've been weird to get all flirty in this case. Much better to just get her on the date and escalate from there. For the second date I sent her two pings before I realised she's simply not into texting. I was getting full compliance so no need to overgame and come off as being weird.

| | |
|---|---|
| Hey. I've been feeding squirrels in the park. I love summer 😊 | Positive WoMW ping (see later explanation) |
| Sweet 😊 I love it too — enjoyed today at Parliament Square | Agree and encourage |
| That sounds nice. If the weather is good on Wednesday, let's try a park | Seed a date |
| Ok | Simple agreement, no frills |
| [next day] I just ate an amazing spaghetti carbonara. So happy to have a warm belly full of pasta 😊 | Another WoMW ping |
| Cool. I enjoyed sushi 😊 | Agreeable but adding little |
| Nice. What time do you finish work tomorrow? | So proceed to date invitation |
| Not sure yet but aim to finish around 6:30pm | Simple logistics, no obstacles |
| Ok. We'll figure it out tomorrow afternoon. Maybe eat somewhere. | Loose agreement of time |
| Ok | Simple |
| [next day] What do you think about 7pm at Piccadilly? I know a good Chinese place with comically rude waiters. | Clear and direct, with a little positive vibe |
| Hi! 7pm Piccadilly sounds reasonable to me 😊 | Agreed |
| Ok. Same place 😊 | |

This is all bland logistics and pushing forwards because she's going along with my plans but simply won't bite on any of the entertaining and creative stuff. Several times she declines to pick up on a thematic hook I've given her. Remember the rule of compliance — **If she's complying, you don't need to game**. So now that we've dealt with the rare case of non-texters, lets get back to the model that works for the vast majoriy of the female population...

The tell-tale signs of a strongly invested girl are the following:

- Long messages

- Lots of smiley faces and exclamation marks

- Tries to add value by including additional things that are not a direct response to your message

- Tries her own callback humour

- Gives you "hahaha" and rewards any little bit of humour

- Agrees with everything you said and possibly expands on it

- If you've been bantering, she returns the banter with some creativity

To the extent her response embodies the above signs, you know its strong. In contrast, if she replies with a terse acknowledgement without any real encouragement or potential thematic hook to latch onto, then she's fairly unmoved by your existence. Moving along a Yes Girl is different than reeling in a Maybe Girl (and much less work).

# Acknowledge and Stack

Try not to get lost in all the detailed analysis and various branching off points. Your basic job following the initial feeler is to keep driving down that motorway towards the first date, fending off any attempts of hers to grab the steering wheel. If she's replying to you, she's attracted. She wants you to set up that date but also... she wants you to do it properly. I find the best way to covertly communicate your confidence and competence is to briefly acknowledge her reply but do not directly reply to it. Never be afraid to snip and stack. Just acknowledge (not "respond" or "reply") and then push forward in the direction you've chosen. You might need a few of the Ack-Stack exchanges before you are ready to seed the date. Play it by ear but try not to get past more than three exchanges.

### Letting her snatch the frame

This early in the seduction she is still subconsciously testing you to figure out what kind of man you are. A crafty ploy she'll pull is to ask you questions or drop in little comments that you can't help responding to. Then she'll do it again. All of a sudden she's leading the conversation into no man's land and you're following her around like an obedient puppy. Don't let that happen. She should be reacting to you, not the other way around.

The best stacks will flow organically from what you talked about in set, your assumptons about her, and the flirty responses she gave. Here is a sample of real Ack-Stacks from a French girl I dated. The street stop was flirty but she gave some resistance to the "date" frame on the close, so I decided to turn off the teasing in the beginning:

Hey crazy. It was nice to meet you 😊 are you always so friendly to strangers? Nick

It was nice to meet you too! I do as long as they're funny and not too blunt 😊

she likes texting and seems fairly keen

I'm in St James Park with the ducks :)😊

ping test, low investment as a test to see what I can draw from her

Be careful ducks are wild and might be dangerous! 😊 I was wondering, if I sign a one year contract as a waitress but quit 2 months later, what do I risk? Sorry to ask but you might be more reliable than my french roomies 😊

Compare to list of tell-tale signs. Also note attempt to snatch frame

Realistically, no risk.
They'll just find a new waitress.

Acknowledge, would be rude not to but don't go into a long conversation about it

Ok, I think I can handle it!

How was your day? I'm still walking around central London

ping

I'm on my way home, I went in Camden, what a gorgeous place, I wish I had stayed there forever! How was your day?

a classic respond/encourage

I'm with friends in Soho. Great fun. Let's meet tomorrow. 7pm?

so I acknowledge and push forward with logistics

What do you want to do?

[one minute later] I'm not free tonight, let's meet another day!

counter-offer, still keen

Sure. Suits me.

[six hours later] I just saw a man walk into a lamppost. I thought that only happens in comedy shows.

ping

Did you?! Ahahaha painful but hilarious! I've found a job as a room attendant in a high quality hotel, not the job of my dream but that will do for less than 2 months! Call me nafissatou diallo!

respond/encourage, lots of text, hands me thematic hook

Who is she.... The one who had a "liason" with Dominic Straus Kahn?

I realise I can steer this towards a sexual spike to change the tone to a better one for the date

Indeed!

Good grief! You'll seduce me then call the police.

spike

[next day] Good morning. I'll be in the centre today. Afternoon tea?

push forward with logistics

Sure, I just have to go to the bank first. 3pm?

compliance

Sounds good. Meet me at Trafalgar Square by the lions.

lead

Ok!

As you can see, real text chats are messier than contrived chats to illustrate a model. As we get through this section of the book you'll start to see the other things going on under the surface and why I had to diverge from the model in places. No matter how far you diverge, though, always try to get back onto that motorway whenever the opportunity presents itself. Women will constantly try to sabotage their own love lives, acting as a force of chaos in any text interaction. In texting as in real life, only the keenest of Yes Girls will roll out the red carpet for you.

# Setting up logistics

Tight game requires you to be aware of relative investment levels at all times. We are not hiding our intent nor disguising our interest in the girl but neither are we rolling over for her like an obedient dog. You need to push for the date but you don't have to overinvest in doing so. That's why I like to set up logistics in two steps — time, then place. Consider the pitfalls of suggesting time and place together... not only do you seem keener but she has two different things to disagree with. Realistically nailing her down to agree to a time is more difficult than to an actvity or place because your real interference is from her other appointments / plans rather than her preferences on what she likes to do. The former might not be breakable for a man she just met whereas girls generally are happy to just go whereever / do whatever if she likes the man. So get the time agreed first. Don't come off over-precise as that is an attraction killer.

- **Good:** [acknowledge previous text then...] Wednesday 7pm is good?

- **Bad:** Let's meet Wednesday at 7pm. In front of Top Shop on Oxford Circus.

We are always assuming the sale. She responded well to you in the street, she gave you her number, she replies to your texts.... she likes you! Don't ask for a date or weakly suggest it. Why would she be texting you if she *didn't* want a date? The fact that you are this far along is a sign that things are going well and its 'on'. So exercise some dominance and leadership by taking control of the direction and making the move. Look for it at the end of this exchange with an African girl I dated. It was a five minute street stop with light teasing and flirting. I pick up the texting after she'd rainchecked the first agreed date two days earlier:

> Another roasting hot day to lie in my hammock and catch up on reading 😊

ping after 24 hours of radio silence

Heyy Nick!! Beautiful day indeed, I would gladly do that only am stuck in the library working on my dissertation! How are you doing?

She immediately replies with more tell-tale signs of interest

> I'm gonna have a relaxing day. What's your dissertation title?

ack-stack

My dissertation is on the implication of property led development on urban economic development. Why relaxing day? No work today?

respond/encourage

> Sounds Keynesian. I never work in summer. Weather is too good to be trapped in the office.

ack-stack

OHHH that makes sense since the English weather is usually horrible all year around. So what are you doing today??

See her feminine wiles — she deftly moves away from anything that could kill the vibe, such as discussing her dissertation, and moves towards happy energy. This is good Girl Game

> Mostly I'll be in my hammock reading Agatha Christie 😊 when do you finish? BTW I like rain. Very English.

probe logistics before I go out on a limb

That sounds really relaxing and summery. I plan to finish around 7. Why am I not surprised you like rain!! Typical English.

respond/encourage

> Ok. What time can you get to Oxford Street, 8pm?

logistics time

Wow.... you are quite upfront! You didn't even ask if I had other plans for the evening 😊

I'm like that

Ohh I see. Do you think that's always healthy?? Just asking

girls rarely call out the Elephant of assuming the sale, but note how she likes the confidence

I follow my instinct. 8pm at Top Shop?

Acknowledge, don't get derailed. Just push forward with logistics

Haha. 8:30?

Ok. 8:30pm. Dress cute 😊

hoop

Dress cute??

Yes. So we match 😊

OHHHH I will have that in mind

Now get back to your study! 😊

Sure! Enjoy your afternoon with Agatha Christie

You too, hon

# MOVING ON FROM THE INITIAL SEQUENCE

We've just gone through what can be considered the basic boiler-plate "What to do after you get the number" sequence. You'll be sticking to this as closely as possible. Consider it the skeleton that we will now flesh out with meat. No amount of text messaging will get you the girl on its own, but I will now teach you how to avoid dry and mechanistic messages and add more masculine panache to your texts. Most of the time these ideas are best kept in mind as you follow the normal sequence, rather than employed as standalone tricks. These points will manifest themselves in overall sentence construction and meaning you convey, rather than monkey-see-monkey-do gambits.

At all times you are projecting masculinity while pushing her into the feminine frame. This began from the moment you first laid eyes on her, through the street stop, and it will continue on the date. The principles of masculine texting require you to keep your sentences short and to the point, to impose your frame over hers, to appropriately balance hard and soft dominance, to throw out hoops / compliance tests, and to keep her constantly on edge and unable to predict your behaviour. Avoid being the wishy-washy Nice Guy. So, what can we do to incorporate these principles? Let's first understand the frame which can be boiled down to four words:

*You act. She reacts.*

Look through some of the text chats on your phone for this and this only. Pick some of your best work. Read those messages thinking

- Who is asking the questions?

- Who is answering the questions?

- Who is choosing the direction of the conversation?

Your tight text game doesn't look so tight anymore, does it? Girls are good at subtly hijacking a thread and nudging it step by step until suddenly she's leading you around by the nose. Don't believe me? Re-read those texts a third time and note on a piece of paper how many times she asked a question, which you answered, and then followed up with more questions as continuation question... and now you're completely off topic and playing into her frame. You've skidded off the motorway to Date City.

This is a game. As a woman, she's a force of chaos. It's hard-coded into her DNA to stonewall, stymie, and sidetrack all attempts at moving the interaction towards having your dick in her vagina. It's a three-tiered game, too. On the surface she's being friendly and enthusiastic (the overt / logical / words level). Below that, her subcommunication is a wrecking ball designed to thwart any chance of meeting a man and happily succeeding in romantic intimacy (the covert / read-between-the lines level). At the deepest primevil level, she wants you to surmount all these obstacles and woo her into bed (the hindbrain level). Understand that tiers one and two are just a game to filter out all the men who don't "get it." She wants you to win, but she won't make it easy.

## Getting pissed off

Once you have a little text game behind you, you'll start to see the covert tier two charade that noobs are oblivious to. And it'll shock and frustrate you in equal measure. "What a stupid bitch, can't she see she's ruining her own chance at happiness with this bullshit?" There's an inner game weakness driving your negative feelings. You've peered into the sausage factory, and the sight of how they are made does nothing for your appetite. Just because she was smiley and receptive during the street stop does not mean she's a done deal to come on a date. Remember the magnitude of what you are asking her — to come and meet a guy she barely knows, who clearly wants to fuck her, without him paying the usual Nice Guy's steep price tag for her time. She needs to test you a little. On the street you were a confident and charming guy, so she enjoys feeling that energy and wants more over the text exchange. Learn to enjoy the dance. That's all it is — a dance. At the end of it she wants to fall over backwards with her legs open.

These are the common tricks a girl will throw at you, nice fat pitches served up for you to knock out of the park:

**The Terse Reply:** She'll not take your bait and instead give a wink, smiley, or one word answer that leaves you no obvious place to go. Just continue to stack forwards by either expanding upon your tease or sending a rebase text (see below).

**The Wheel Grab:** She'll ask a question that redirects the conversation onto something that is irrelevant to getting her on a date, such as the French example above asking about waitressing work. This ploy is harder to spot when the question is about you and flatters you a little. Don't take the bait. Acknowledge and stack.

**The Vibe Killer:** She responds with a flat boring statement of fact rather than keeping the ball in the air. Rebase. If she keeps killing the vibe, just accept she has piss-poor social skills and invite her on the date so you can show your leadership in person.

**The Scold:** She purports to tell you off for something, such as asking an inappropriate question or seeking a level of compliance she isn't ready for. The key here is to discern if her discomfort is sincere or tactical. If the former, back off a little by using a soft misdirection. If the latter, agree and amplify e.g. "Does that make me a bad man?" or "I'm like that."

# Controlling the direction of the exchange — Rebase texts

Text game can frequently stall when one thread gets played out. To keep flogging that dead horse will lower your value and kill the vibe. Seduction is movement — always towards Date City. He who hesitates masturbates. The key tactics for keeping the reins out of her hands, keeping her off balance, and keeping it fresh are:

1. Nudge and draw

2. Snip and stack

3. Nuke and rebuild

Rather dramatic names for fairly pedestrian tactics, but it's good to have mnemonics in your mind while the texts are flying. All display leadership and direction, which are attractive masculine traits. Let's look at them in turn.

## 1. Nudge And Draw

This is the simple act of dropping a new thematic element into your text, which opens up a new topic related to the dying thread. It doesn't have to be strongly logical, just have some connection and move it along. Girls want to be led so if you nudge them in a particular direction they'll usually go there. Conversely, you can draw the girl in a direction by leaving an unasked question in the air. Examples:

So this is the Russian girl.... 😊
how's your training?

Feeler text after short idate

It's finished just right now 😊
but it was good... & hard a little bit ))

Good response

Have you got any energy
left for a drink?

Nudge and draw her towards date idea

Let's try 😊 honestly, I got an idea
— the River walking this night?
What do u think about it? 😊
She takes the bait

Note the nudge and draw is not a direct overt date invite. I am floating an idea for her to latch onto. Later with the same girl after a Day 2 she has gone back to Moscow. I roll off for a few days then reopen.

> **Hey Russian 😊 is it warm back in your Siberian hut?**

Nudge her onto a roleplay

> Of course 😊cuz I saved by drinking vodka instead the breakfast tea and my bear fur near me all the time. That why I'm fine.
> What about u?

She is drawn into it

> **I'm hibernating in my bear cave for winter. Might go out later and eat a hiker.**

nudge it along

> Oh that's what u doing 😊 but please not Russian hikers

she accepts

> If one day you will arrive to Moscow — call me. I will show it 😊 that was nice to meet you

after I vacuumed for an hour she checks to see I'm still chasing

Use an oblique reference like you are holding open the door to a new conversational direction, to see if she follows the lead and walks through that door. It's more elegant than asking a direct question.

## 2. Snip And Stack

We men are logical creatures. Our conversations with each other follow quite strict protocols. We listen to what the other person said, comprehend its meaning, and then tailor a response to address those points while introducing new knowledge of our own. It's a logical sequence. Not so with women. They are creatures of the moment and their emotions drive everything. Standard game advice is don't change her mind, change her emotions. So when you find yourself mired in a text exchange that is leading nowhere, just cut it and start fresh with a new topic. Don't pedantically construct logical reasons to move stepwise to the new topic. Just listen to your gut — is the direction of this chat helping me get her on a date? If the answer is no, snip it and start a new topic. Girls rarely ask why or try to continue the old thread.

### 3. Nuke And Rebuild

This is just a more outlandish and heavier version of snip and snack. As a man, you reserve the right to be completely self-absorbed, treating both the world and the women upon it as existing solely for your own amusement. You reserve the right to talk about whatever you damn well please and you offer no apologies for that. Girls will respond well to such unapologetic truculence, and thus I will drop in occasional nukes to spike a conversation. Note that, because these are heavier than the other tactics, you should use them more sparingly or you'll end up with a fizzy high-energy interaction that prevents rapport and may risk scaring her away from an actual date. Keep it lean. These are my favourites:

### 4. Self-Absorbed Brute

Women like a man who is passionate about his passions. You have hearty appetites for food, drink, sex, sleep, and fighting. You are the opposite of the wishy-washy poindexter who takes the middle road to mediocrity. You, sir, are larger than life. So play this up and revel in your maleness and your devotion to pleasing yourself. It's a playful way to show strong opinions and high self-regard.

So this is the Italian grindhouse starlet...... 😊 — Mild-tease feeler

Apparently 😊 — Terse reply

I'm stuffing my face with tacos. How are you? — Self-absorbed brute

Most of my texting revolves around food. Eating lots of red meat and washing it down with good whiskey and a fat Cuban cigar is a go-to subject in my brute texts.

I'm going to eat a cheesburger — snip and stack

Where is that famous cheeseburger? — picks up thread

Deep inside my belly :) 😊 nom nom nom — Self-absorbed brute

Lol! already! — reward

It's best to stick to your own personal appetites and then amp them up. Let her know you love your life. Personally, I'd avoid referencing nerdy hobbies unless you are specifically trying to contrast a previously expressed harder edge. "I'm watching season 6 of Babylon Five" is not a good example of your brutish masculine id.

## 5. Outrageous Narcissist

I remember watching promotional interviews with professional wrestlers back in the golden era of the WWE, around 1997. The top wrestlers were not the most gifted athletes, but rather the most charismatic talkers. The whole of WWE is larger than life. The key skill in building interest and support for a wrestler's matches is for him to grab the microphone and "cut a promo" in ring centre. The best talkers project an outrageously conceited and self-important vibe. It's deliberately over-the-top and self-referential rather than genuinely malignant narcissism. With a girl you want to mythologise yourself and let her giggle in feigned indignation at your over-inflated ego. It's all nudge-and-wink.

- "I just cooked two perfect steaks with green peppercorn sauce. There's a line of drooling dogs outside my kitchen window"

- "I had a call from the government scientists. They want to research me. They said it's physically impossible to be both hot and cool at the same time. I'm an anomaly"

- "I wonder if there's a limit to how awesome I can be. I should be careful not to overdo it. The world might blow up or something"

## 6. False Modesty

Generally speaking, self-deprecation should be avoided until you are in deep rapport on a date and it becomes natural to show some vulnerability after hitting her with significant value. Showing it early on in set or on texts just hamstrings your attraction. The exception is to self-deprecate about something that is so obviously untrue that it comes off as playful boasting. I usually combine it with a little framing where the girl is the sexual predator and I am the naive victim.

- "I'm shocked. And appalled. But mostly shocked."

- "I'm not very confident with girls" (best after a very cocky street stop)

- "You shouldn't flirt with me like this. I'm shy"

- "You're trouble. Don't corrupt me."

- "I'm as innocent as a field of fluffy white rabbits"

## 7. Window On My World

Ping texts usually come under this category. You just tell her what's going on in your life and assume she's interested. The subtext is that you have an interesting and pleasant life (thus it would be a good world for her to step into) and also that it is so self-evident that she's interested in you that it would never occur to you not to talk about yourself. Don't come off as bragging or reaction-seeking. Don't come off like you need her opinion or approval. Just state matter-of-factly what you are doing or thinking.

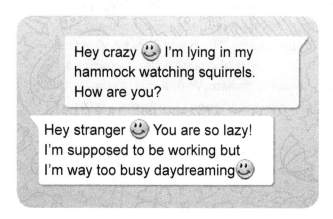

Hey crazy 😊 I'm lying in my hammock watching squirrels. How are you?

Hey stranger 😊 You are so lazy! I'm supposed to be working but I'm way too busy daydreaming 😊

Tell her what you're reading, watching, playing, visiting. These work best if you can imply a contrast such as a childish side to a masculine man.

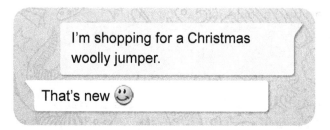

I'm shopping for a Christmas woolly jumper.

That's new 😊

Other examples:

- "I might go into hibernation. Find a tree or cave somewhere"

- "I'm just about to head out to a café. Reading day!"

- "I'm reading an adventure story in old Hong Kong. Winding streets, opium dens and the inscrutable Chinese criminal masterminds!"

- "I've been dismembering aliens for the past hour. I think I should move on to race car driving then close out the evening with exploring an ancient Inca tomb"

- "A good book, a steaming mug of coffee, and soft snow falling outside the window. I love winter!"

- "I'm being very cultural at the British Museum today. My mum would be proud"

- "Just ate potato and beans. Lovely"

Sometimes your ping will draw her into an exchange about the topic, in which case you may throw in other rebase elements. For example:

> I just shaved my head.
> Not sure if I look more like Bruce Willis or Gandhi

mythologising and contrast

> If you are wearing your dressing gown again I would go for Gandhi

she takes the draw and offers mild banter challenge

> I'm a peacemaker

> Now you definitely look like Bruce Willis... But he's cuter

> I was offered his role in Die Hard 6

outrageous narcissist. It's fun to tell blatant lies that you both know are blatant for some nudge/ wink humour

> Maybe as his evil twin brother

> I'm a nice boy

> You are not 😊

> I'm so nice they will replace the Easter Bunny with me

more contrast, more lies, more self-mythology

> You wish. Tell me a dirty secret....

You'll have noticed I just drew her into a long exchange of what is essentially non-sensical self-aggrandizement and it ended with her getting horny. A sex chat followed. Note I'd already made out with this girl, so I was using these text gambits to keep things alive until she returned from her country and I had clear logistics to fuck her.

## 8. Truculent Cad

Sometimes you just want to be difficult. Women love defiant and uncontrollable men, so much so that they'll often throw out a little challenge (the Scold Text, for example) just to bait you into giving them a short-shrift response, which makes them tingle and glow. It's also a test to see if you shrivel up under pressure and eliminate yourself from the long queue to her vagina. When she sends out a little challenge, be sure to crush it.

I prefer to take on the immoveable object rather than the irresistible force. By that, I mean I tend to use these texts to show I can't be pushed around rather than to going on the attack and trying to move her. Text game isn't the right medium for proactively hammering a girl's frame. It's better to wait until the date.

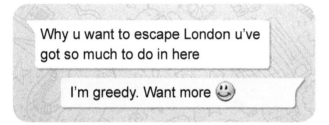

Another challenge, in this case I'm picking the fight by pushing my frame out:

You can mix these together with elements of other rebase texts:

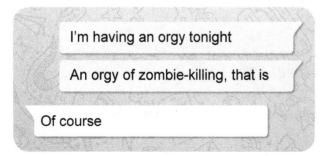

sent one minute after the first text, referencing my love of video games

**Later with same girl:**

> Just came from the doctor... I have an anomaly on my heart but like everything else in my life, it will fix itself 😊

I guess I broke it

Such arrogance

Thanks 😄

Sometimes her challenge is quite implicit and mild, but you decide to use it to show your bad side. Again, keep it playful. The key is she's expecting one thing (you to conform to expectations) so you do something else (and confound those expectations)

> I need a dirty secret to cheer me up

expecting something sexual

A few years ago I didn't have any tissues so I blew my nose on a sock

confounded by misinterpreting "dirty"

If you run with this idea you can pull her into topics that let you play the truculent cad. One way to do this is by implying that the world isn't fair and you are getting more than your due share. And you're reveling in it:

I'm watching a documentary about McClaren. Amazing

window on my world

> I bet it is.. I'm eating haribo just to piss off a colleague 😊
> I'm so rude today

she takes the draw and offers mild banter challenge

Why?

Because he's an idiot I can't stand him

I don't want to listen to her problems so I decide to use the Truculent Cad to redirect her mood

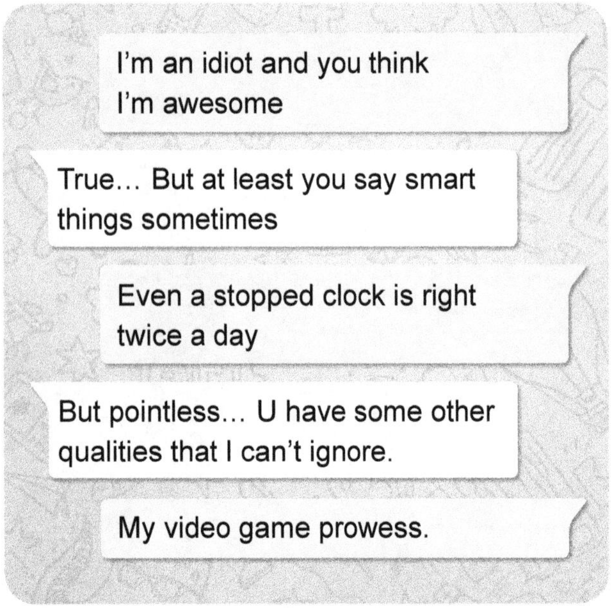

> I'm an idiot and you think
> I'm awesome

> True... But at least you say smart
> things sometimes

> Even a stopped clock is right
> twice a day

agree and amplify, rather than qualify

> But pointless... U have some other
> qualities that I can't ignore.

> My video game prowess.

There are generic replies you can use any time she challenges you.

- "I'm like that"

- "I don't believe you"

- "You just earned your first ass-spanking"

- "That's gay"

### The Poor Man's Push

When you find yourself pondering how to respond to a text and nothing comes to mind, **don't reply**. Not replying is the poor man's push, the accidental alpha. By not replying you are protecting your value and avoiding mistakes. Considering that the main risk for an aspiring player to coming off too-invested and too-keen, a good default is to not reply until you are sure you have the right thing to say.

In texts just like in person, you can use a vacuum to determine where you are in the set. If you find yourself unsure of the girl's position then **stop gaming**. Stop talking or stop texting and wait. Her reaction will tell you where you are.

**Alexandra** was a late afternoon street stop on Regent Street of a Greek tourist who was leaving town two days later but intends to return soon. There wasn't much sexuality in the set but she was very chatty and happy. She's very open, direct and easy to deal with. She follows my lead enthusiastically and offers no resistance.

**Denisa** flashed me a barely-discernable IOI on Oxford Street one afternoon. It was a strong hook and she seemed like a Yes Girl. I bounced her to a cafe for an i-date, then a pub (where I kissed her). Denisa is very socially savvy, and just as keen as the first girl. She wants to play the banter game. Everything is multi-layed with implicit challenges and tests. She wants me to pass those tests.

# PUTTING IT ALL TOGETHER

Now we get to the true art of text game. I've explicated the fundamental building blocks as best I can in monkey-see-monkey-do fashion, but the reality is you'll suck ass for the first few months. You'll mechanically follow the model with clunking missteps that suck all the life out of the interaction. That's just a necessary pain period. Eventually you'll hit a flow and start to tune into the vibe of each individual girl. Below are some actual text exchanges where you can see how I progress. There's alot going on. Framing, teasing, push-pull, sexualising, connection, calming, punishing... just see what you can find. I'll pick two contrasting examples, and you can see if you can pick up the contrasting vibes:

**Alexandra** — She's very open, direct and easy to deal with. She follows my lead enthusiastically and offers no resistance.

**Denisa** — She's very savvy. She's just as keen as the first girl but she wants to play the banter game. Everything is multi-layed with implicit challenges and tests. She wants me to pass those tests.

## Alexandra

The key issue with Alexandra was poor logistics immediately following our meeting, despite her seeming high interest and high agreeability. The set lasted five minutes and I calibrated her as a Keen Girl / Lots of Time because she was travelling with her family, so no chance of getting her out in the remaining two days and it would eventually go to Long Game.

She easily falls into my frame and lets me lead the conversation. Note how she offers no obstacles or resistance whatsoever, and consistently encourages my continued participation in the chat. This girl plays things straight and is likely very easy to date. When girls comply so well with your first-level tactics, just move forwards without deploying too much game — just sprinkle enough in to keep a little electricity flowing. If she'd been staying in London I would've moved directly to pushing logistics for the date.

> Hey crazy You 😊 made it back home from London?

mild-tease feeler

> Hi British boy 😊 Yeap... back to basis... Did you enjoy your weekend?

she's a texter. Smileys, questions, pet names. Strong interest and a sure sign to keep the flow going.

Yeah. Had a friend's birthday dinner party at a Chinese restaurant. You?

Ack-stack

Yeap! I went for a drink at Angel area and continued my sightseeing on Sunday as a typical tourist... 😃 I love chinese food! Nice!

respond-encourage

You know in China they just call it "food" 😋

mild push, to see how she takes it

Well it makes sense... I guess it all applies for all kind of food the same ... i.e. Greek food... In Greece it is called just food as well 😄

she takes it and tries to add value — a respond-encourage. She wants this to work and looks to smooth over the push, a sign of strong interest

What do Greeks eat? Humous and feta cheese all day I assume

ack-stack with a playfully racist stereotype thrown in as a push

Xaxa... No... We have quite a diverse cuisine.. But you may say that we eat a lot of meat... and fish in the summer.... What do British eat?

respond-encourage, keeping the conversation alive with nice simple turn-taking

Pies

Another covert push by strongly reducing my verbiage. It's another test

Ok.. Did not know... Gotta leave you. I am going to sleep. It was nice talking to you! We speak again! Good night Nick!

Always a good sign when they verbalise wanting to talk more later

Good night!

# Denisa

It was a highly flirty set and she loved the banter, giving it back hard and requiring me to agree and amplify alot. Thus this text exchange begins after a significant amount of the work has been done. She was leaving to go back to Romania the next day, so the purpose of this exchange is to solidify the set and transition to Long Game over Skype.

> **Hey crazy 😊 I'm lying in my hammock watching the squirrels. How are you?**

familiarity feeler

> **Hey stranger 😊 You are so lazy! I'm supposed to be working but I'm way too busy daydreaming 😊**

Wheel Grab. She's not quite snatching the frame but is showing her enjoyment of banter

> **Daydreaming of cakes, no doubt...**

put her in a box

> **Not this time, but that is such a good idea 😊 I'm thinking of making a stop on my way back to Bucharest and spend some days in Greece.**

respond-encourage then gives value. I realise she won't dumbly accept my lead, I'll have to fight for leadership rights

> **For the beaches?**

I know she wants to talk so it's easy to dial down my verbiage and draw her out into investing a little

> **For one in particular, there is a small island called Spetses that I would love to visit 😊**

> **Sounds nice. I'd like to visit one of those lost Aztec cities in the mountains.**

that's enough of her leading so I start taking the reins

> **Steal some treasure, fight mercenaries, get chased by pygmies with blow guns. That sort of thing.**

inject fun and imagery

| | |
|---|---|
| Nothing too exciting 😊😊 | respond-encourage |
| I'll take you with me. I need a cook. | begin a roleplay that pushes her beneath me |
| Hahahahahaah...<br>So you have a death wish?! | fighting against the frame-push is great because it's engaged her emotionally |
| You'll cook for the pygmies while I run away with their jewelled artifacts. | put her in a box |
| Just don't marry one | |
| I'll cook you up for the pygmies and then I'll become their Goddess 😊 | playful push back but what matters is her engagement level — she's into this |
| Crazy | push |
| Wuss | push back |
| You just earned your first ass-spanking | Truculent Cad |
| Hahaha...I'd like to see you try 😊 | more engaged push back |
| I'm going to kill you!!! My boss is sending me to Africa by the end of the month so I'll probably get to see those damn pygmies sooner then I thought 😞 | she wants more of this game |
| Watch out for the land mines, machetes and HIV | |
| It can't be that bad... but if something happens, I'm blaming you 😊 | |
| You're trouble | push |
| Hmm.. you're cute | pull |
| I know. But thanks 😊 | Outrageous Narcissist |

| | |
|---|---|
| God you're arrogant... | Playful Scold |
| I'm no god. Call me Sir. | defiance |
| I just ate a cheeseburger. What are you doing? | Self-absorbed Brute then stack. The momentum was starting to stall |
| So you are no god? Hmmm... Really 😊 ? | |
| You ate a cheeseburger without me? That's just mean. I'm getting ready for bed. | |
| So you are almost naked? | Sexualisation test |
| Hahahahaha.... for ten seconds or so :) | respond-encourage |
| Put your clothes back on. You'll catch a cold | push |
| Just saw a five year old girl who looks like you... she was crying about ice cream. | This was the next day. A Window On My World ping |
| Ice cream would probably be the only reason I could cry for as well... maybeshe is my kid 😊 | respond-encourage |
| I'm bored as hell at work, tell me something interesting... | Wheel Grab |
| I don't want to distract you from work | refuse it |
| Or you'll start imagining that tingly feeling you get when I touch you | nudge and draw |
| Speaking from experience? | |
| I have no experience with women | False Modesty |
| Liar | Fake Scold |
| That's your second spanking | Truculent Cad |
| Good... I'm going for the record 😊 | |

The energy is very different with Denisa. Her savviness makes her a difficult catch, and thus I need to run far tighter and far more inventive text game to get the better of her. As the chat progresses, she becomes increasingly accepting of my frame push. By making it more difficult for me she has set herself a trap — she gave me the chance to look even more attractive. As your text game becomes tighter, you will paradoxically become thankful for the occasional difficult girl. She's obviously interested (due to her continued engagement), and some sassiness and savviness will help keep you sharp and will let you showcase your best attraction-building.

In section ten we'll go into more detail with how to banter girls over text messaging. Generally you are aiming to get them out on a date without getting mired into long text exchanges. However, if a girl isn't available for a while you need to become proficient at maintaining playful energy while mixing in some comfort and rapport.

Some girls will use the text messaging to conduct research into your character, motivations, and intentions towards them. It'll be clear from the questions they ask, broaching more serious topics than those that light banter uses. This will include her asking your age, job, hobbies and so on. When a girl switches to such fact-finding be prepared to switch gears yourself and give her more serious answers. Banter is **attraction** and based on gently *breaking* rapport. Her research effort is **comfort** and requires *building* rapport. Be sure which is appropriate at which time!

This text discussion has focused on the 'short game' of girls who quickly agree to dates. Many other girls will be more awkward and require greater finesse. *Daygame Infinite* has a considerably more detailed treatment of how to calibrate such girls and suggestions for all the various permutations you may encounter when she isn't so agreeable and available.

# LONG GAME

## section five

You should always try to get a girl out quickly if at all feasible, so that you can take advantage of momentum and her current availability. Women like decisive, fast-moving men. However, you will sometimes find yourself in situations where moving fast is impractical. This is usually because logistics are problematic, or because you have a weak hook point. Plan B is to move the girl over to Long Game where you have more time to work. We consider that in this section.

# LONG GAME

*Goal: Moving a girl towards sex when an immediate date is not possible*

The two most predictive qualities of getting a girl into your bed are that she is (i) available and (ii) attracted to you. Everything can proceed smoothly from meeting to sex. Problems arise when one of these two conditions isn't met, or is only weakly applicable. In such situations we must consider moving the set over to Long Game. These are a few examples of when this is appropriate:

1. She has a boyfriend and isn't prepared to cheat on him, but you sense she has one foot outside the relationship.

2. She's leaving town pretty soon and you can't build up enough momentum to reach the sex date.

3. You're on a foreign holiday building strong leads to come back to for your next trip.

4. She's attracted but only weakly. It'll take time to get your value out and suck her in to your life.

5. Shes got many many options and distractions, so it was difficult to fix her down in one place for a date.

Since most of this book is about meeting and laying women in a short time frame, it's obvious that playing the Long Game is really a Plan B. It's a way of keeping leads alive that would die under the usual text-a-while-then-set-up-date model. You'll be investing more time and energy per girl, so it becomes important to manage that and avoid over-investment. The fundamental rules of Game remain the same, but they are now stretched over a longer time frame and conveyed primarily through social media.

The golden rule of Long Game is:

*You have all the time in the world*

She's not going anywhere. The clock stopped ticking as soon as you realised you couldn't fuck her anytime soon. This changes the whole dynamic because you are no longer hustling her along. You are now methodically placing your armies into siege position and waiting until the time is right to strike. At some point logistics and interest will improve, maybe next month, maybe next year.

She'll break up with that boyfriend. She'll be back in town. She'll be drunk and horny one night. She'll gradually warm to you. She'll give up on the guy she was chasing who was a higher priority than you. *Something will change.* You have all the time in the world. So protect your value, build it, maneuver into position, and wait for the right time to move things to the next stage.

## Social Media

It's common to view social media as a blight on the dating market because it feeds women constant shots of validation through the process of:

> Post attention-whoring selfy ➝ Lots of likes ➝
> Lots of "you're beautiful" comments ➝ Validation

> Post dumbass vapid comment ➝ Lots of likes ➝
> Lots of comments taking it seriously ➝ Validation

It's quite understandable why a man with any testosterone in his system will want no part of that cycle.

Understand that women are working social media for attention and validation, and thus the principles are the same as if you were face-to-face in a bar or coffee shop. The currency of Girl World is attention, so monitor how much of it you give out and at what price. Don't validate a girl cheaply; make her earn it. In Long Game you make social media work for you. Rather than being just another chode orbiting Planet Hot Girl, you flip the script and put many girls into orbit around you.

Each social media tool has slightly different uses:

- **Phone number:** This is for normal "short" game. It's the logistical device to get girls on dates quickly per the Text Phase chapter earlier.

- **Whatsapp/Viber:** Now we are beginning to bridge into Long Game. Whatsapp lets you develop the timing and rhythm of an internet chat while also showing you when she's online and when she's read your message. We retain lots of mystery because all she sees is one profile photo and the messages themselves.

- **Skype:** Best for when you want to maintain mystery, since there's no visible photo gallery or friends list. It's also good when you got quite far along in the dating process but didn't reach sex, in whichcase you can use the video chat to continue sexual escalation.

- **Facebook:** When writing the first edition of *Daygame Mastery*, Facebook was the best platform. You can design a profile that presents carefully monitored value, draw girls into preselecting you, mess with your target's FB wall, time your chats, and remain disembodied through text alone. Instagram has mostly superceded it now. The principles remain the same, as Instagram functions like a more streamlined Facebook photo gallery.

My discussion of building a Facebook profile applies equally to Instagram. Messaging apps offer such similar features nowadays that it doesn't much matter which you use. When taking a girl's number I usually ask which she prefers and use that. Then I'm more likely to find her online at any given moment.

# BUILDING YOUR FACEBOOK PROFILE

The entirety of your profile is designed to get the girl. If this conflicts with your current use of it for family / work, then make a separate profile and never the twain shall meet. Mentally accept this goal and be ruthless in tweaking everything about the profile to support the goal. Your FB will have the following work done:

## Photos

### DHV triggers

*Any action that leads a woman to raise her estimation of your Sexual Market Value, and thus feel increased attraction. It is preferable to show value discreetly and let her dig further (investment) to uncover your story, as opposed to telling her your value overtly, which usually appears try-hard.*

All the **DHV triggers** you read in Mystery Method still hold true now. This means you must carefully choose your photos to present the best and fullest side to your character. Don't photo-whore by drowning out the signal with noise, just carefully choose fifty or so of your best. Hit each trigger:

- **Loves children:** So there'll be photos of you with your nephews or kid's class at your Judo club, messing around with them and putting big smiles on their faces. Showing human warmth is Anti Player Vibe ordnance.

- **Loves animals:** Find some dogs in the park and pet them — Instant photo opportunity. Go to the zoo. Pull funny faces at the monkeys. If you really do have a dog then have several photos tracking your friendship with it over time.

- **Travel:** It may go against your male programming to take pictues while you're enjoying yourself, but always snap off some photos on holiday. Just don't fill an album with tedious shots of you in front of every building in the tour guide. Less is more. It only takes one photo of you by the Golden Gate Bridge for everyone to know you went to San Francisco. Try not to overload the travel photos with destinations that may trigger women into thinking you travel for sex. Americans should avoid Cuba and Dominican Republic pictures, while Brits should avoid too much of Eastern Europe or the Phillipines. Women have prejudices.

- **Social:** Don't overdo pictures of you getting shitfaced drunk with friends, but drop in a couple tasteful shots of you and your closest buddies at the bar. Also put in photos that communicate you are a solid, dependable friend.

- **Interests:** Get some hobbies in there. If you like reading, put in a photo of the book (you don't even need to be in it). I often combine this with travel by taking a photo of my book on a coffee shop table, and the background is a famous landmark of the country I'm in.

- **Preselection:** Be careful here. Over/underdoing this step can make or break sets, depending on the girl and your image. If you are going for strong R-selection without the slightest pretense of wanting a relationship then get plenty of photos with girls: dating, clubbing, kissing, playing. Then you are the Player Guy and certain women will look at you and think "consequence-free sex." But for most men I'd suggest underplaying this hand. Just have a couple of your hotter girls in there and keep it mostly ambiguous, where it's obvious the girl likes you but not obvious what the relationship was. Many girls value discretion so they will be worried that you'll take photos of them and add them to your gallery, resulting in social shame for them (if tagged or you have mutual FB friends). Include just enough pictures so that your prospects know other pretty girls like you.

- **Masculinity:** Be open about your appetites. Have photos of yourself eating steak, drinking beer, hitting the heavy bag, sparring, looking gruff. Show some testosterone.

- **Don't Give A Fuck:** I like to tag myself in photos of grumpy and stupid animals, such as Wile E Coyote setting a trap, a gorilla giving the finger, dogs with their tongue hanging out, etc. Be a bit playful.

- **Mythologise:** Try to link yourself to a famous character, actor, or archetype and use it as a recurring motif. I do it with Jason Statham and the general archetype of gruff-skinhead-with-beard. I tagged myself as Max Payne 3, after he shaves his head and is pointing a gun at some favela hood.

Mix these all together and try to get more than one theme in each photo. Run some filters and post-processing on them (I use Ipiccy.com, but Instagram is good too). When the girl lands on your page she'll be greeted with a fully-developed interesting man and think "Who *is* this guy?"

Ruthlessly delete and untag photos that make you look bad or increase the noise ratio. Don't put up a series of similar photos. Don't bore everyone.

# Wall Posts

The key here is to strike a balance between being interesting and not coming off like a woman (by producing a never-ending stream of vapid drivel). Each wall post should be a carefully-considered offering. Avoid:

- Overposting. You've got better things to do than attention-whore on social media. Only amuse yourself now and then.

- Obvious Reaction-Seeking. Don't be asking questions and soliciting responses. Make your interesting statement and leave it at that. Don't just troll to make someone angry if it's not something you believe in.

- Mediocrity. A man who updates his wall with "So bored today. Nothing good on TV. Can't wait for the Superbowl" is a boring chump.

**AMOG**

*Alpha Male Of Group. Men constantly jostle for position within social groups because they instinctively know a higher position is rewarded with more female attention. AMOGing is the act of pushing another man down in order to improve your own relative status. Your friends will usually AMOG you more subtly than strangers.*

Bascially, don't DLV. If friends **AMOG** you publically then delete their posts and comments. Tell them to stop, and if they won't then they aren't really your friend. Unfriend them from your game profile, and perhaps your real one too if they are going to undermine you. If necessary explain to them the purpose of the FB account and why you can't have them belittling you there. Delete spam posts inviting you to Farmville. Welcome when pretty girls post to your wall, but don't pounce on it — remember all of your targets can see how you react to that girl, so treat it like an opportunity to DHV.

# Privacy

I'm not concerned about the supposed invasion of privacy practiced by Facebook. For purposes of game, though, I'd suggest you hide your friends list and restrict how far back into your timeline people can scroll. Game is a process of continual personal development, so naturally the latest version of you is cooler than the old you — so let the old you gradually fall off your timeline.

Exercise discretion with women on your Facebook presence so you can display that there's no risk in sleeping with you. Don't humiliate girls on your wall (unless they clearly deserve it, then its showing boundaries), don't post indiscreet pictures unless the girl clearly approves (e.g. she's joking about it in the comments), don't push out bad vibes (FB is not the place to decry family courts and alimony).

Your Facebook profile is a window into your reality: Fun, positive, interesting, high value. The kind of place a girl would like to be.

# THE LONG GAME PROCESS

Now that you're all set-up on social media, we'll consider how to move a girl along from the initial add until you fuck her.

1. Get the "in" to her attention

2. Become "the guy she talks to"

3. Amp it up and make her work

4. Get covert confirmation of sex

5. Meet

Before diving in let's consider a meta-theoretical issue that runs throughout Long Game: **the sequestration of experience**. Wow, somebody studied sociology! There are two extremes to a continuum in how you experience life:

In your face ⟷ from a distance

Interactions separated through time and space instinctively feel less immediate, less visceral to us. Compare sitting in the front row for a boxing match to watching it on TV (or actually being in the ring). Compare the escalating level of immediacy from an email to a phone call to a face-to-face conversation.

Generally speaking, the modern world has become increasingly structured to "stretch out" interactions across time and space. Whereas cavemen used to bash each other over the head in highly personal tooth-and-claw combat, Napoleon-era soldiers shot their rifles at the enemy as soon as they saw the whites of their eyes. WWII infantry called in artillery support where the aerial targeting was done with elevation/distance, while modern automation allows the President's finger on a red button to initiate slaughter across continents.

Illness and death used to be right in front of us. Prior to industrialisation and modern medicine, we all lived in villages and small towns. Severely ill family members would be cared for in the house, you'd see them every day. You'd participate in their care, carrying their shit bucket outside. In the modern world we remove ill people from the daily routine of life. They go to hospitals where professionals administer the care. If they are terminally-ill they go to a hospice and have scheduled visits.

Just consider your daily life. How often do you directly engage with the raw, visceral, violent, dirty fight of man vs. nature? Your drinking water is clean and comes from a tap. Your morning turd is flushed away in a heartbeat, and you even have specialized sprayable perfume to mask its faint lingering smell. Your shirt is freshly laundered. Your office is air conditioned and protected from harsh weather fronts. As Tyler Durden says in Fight Club:

*After a night at Fight Club,*
*the rest of the world has the volume turned down.*

**Proxy War**

*A conflict between two or more factions, each of whom is supported by a more powerful rival who wishes a particular outcome but will not commit his own troops to secure it. For example, during the Cold War the USA and Soviet Union armies never fought an open battle, but throughout the world USA-backed factions would fight the Soviet Army or Soviet-backed factions (and vice-versa).*

Modern life has the volume turned down. It's not the way in which we are designed to live. Applied to Game, this is why playing the symphony of matched pairs is so powerful. It's why strong eye contact, physical escalation, and imaginative imagery are so effective. Applying tight game to a girl is like being the one flash of colour in the grey world of her day. You are turning up her life's volume. Now let's apply that to Long Game.

## Long Game is a *proxy war*

As the name implies, Long Game is conducted with larger time and space distances than Short Game. Every experience the girl has with you is a photocopy of the real thing. It's your avatar romancing her avatar, because shit hasn't yet gotten real. The main advantage is that the girl massively underprices the risk of being seduced, and thus her forebrain is sleeping on sentry duty. She can keep rationalising that she'll never meet you, that you're hundreds of miles away, that it's just a facebook chat, and so on. Until she finds herself in your bed. This happens because, while the forebrain is sleeping, you are working the hindbrain until any resistance becomes like shutting the stable door after the horse has bolted. Sneaky.

Secondly, although you are engaging in "photocopies" of the original interactions they have **almost as powerful** an effect. Having a girl share her secrets with you across a text chat is almost as powerful as face-to-face. Having a girl masturbate to an online sex chat triggers the same emotions, same hormone releases, and same mental structures as actually being there banging her. It's not **as** powerful but it's so close that you can have the girl hooked on you. Thus Long Game is a trojan horse.

**Anchoring**

*Falling in love is something a girl does to herself by thinking about you when you are not there. Anchoring is the technique of leading the girl to make these associations between you and her, such as daydreaming, masturbating, planning, and doing homework for you.*

The disadvantage is that the intensity of interaction isn't as strong or immediate, so you can't work your body language, eye-mesmer, and so on. You must compensate for the reduced power of the medium by learning to stir up and magnify the emotional power of your words. Two important new tactics that help you accomplish this are:

1. Stimulate her imagination
2. **Anchoring**

We'll go into those in detail later in the chapter. Before any of that can work, you need to actually draw her into conversation. You need your "in."

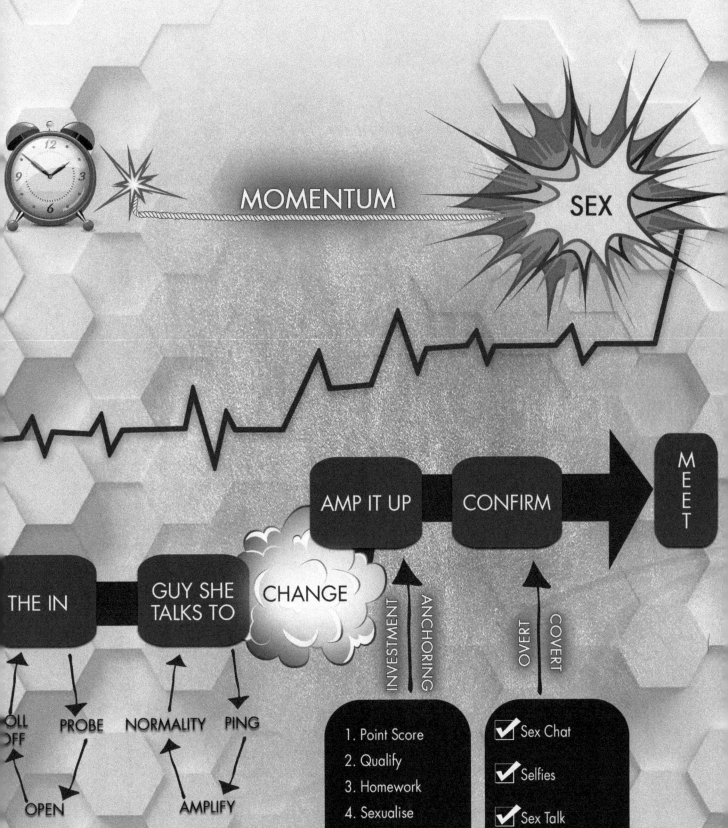

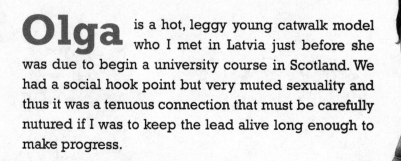

**Olga** is a hot, leggy young catwalk model who I met in Latvia just before she was due to begin a university course in Scotland. We had a social hook point but very muted sexuality and thus it was a tenuous connection that must be carefully nutured if I was to keep the lead alive long enough to make progress.

**Felicia** is an intelligent buxom Brazlian girl who was visiting London with her German boyfriend, and entering a language course near Frankfurt. I met and instant-dated her in a park while she was sightseeing (her boyfriend was in a meeting). She had very strong sexual interest in me, but horrible logistics.

**Milena** is a tall university student from a small town in Bosnia. She was studying in Belgrade and we had two dates, without kissing, before I needed to leave town. The connection was very strong but she had not allowed any escalation. Her personality type was thoughtful, chaste and introverted.

# Malvina
is a Czech teenager living in Zurich but on a short working holiday in a small Swiss village. We'd only spoken a few minutes when we were each on a short trip to Prague. Malvina was sexually inexperienced but psychologically adventurous.

# Gabriela
is a classically beautiful former model and long-term girlfriend of an extremely rich young man. I'd met her during her short holiday in London after having ended her five-year relationship. We shared a strong DNA-match but horrible logistics. We almost had sex before she returned to Romania.

# Tatiana
is a Russian girl frustrated with her life in a small city near St Petersburg. We met towards the end of her month-long English language course in London and had only two short afternoon coffee dates before she returned to Russia. We hadn't kissed but she showed strong interest.

# 1. GET THE IN

Just like the initial open is the hardest part of the street stop, the initial in to her Facebook world is the hardest part of Long Game because you are trying to move from "that guy I had a quick chat with" to a real prospect for sex. Think back to the subcommunication in your street stop and what it conveys about you as a man: confidence, conviction, chill, masculine, intelligent, astute, etc. Those are the same qualities to convey in the initial social media messages. The further the interaction progressed face-to-face, the easier the in will be to her facebook. If you had an idate it's no problem at all to pick up where you left off by opening a chat window. If it was just a number from a street stop, you are closer to requiring the Feeler Text. Assuming a weak hook and short interaction, this is the plan:

**Probe Her FB**: You need to further calibrate her. Scroll through her photos, wall posts, and the number of friends to score her out of ten on "**attention whore**-ness." If she's got 1,000 friends, 100 followers, endless selfies, tons of party photos, etc. then she's extremely externally-referenced and happily chodefarming. She'll have tons of chat windows open. You'll need shock and awe to get her attention. In contrast if she's got 200 friends, barely posts, and has a few normal life photos then she'll be quite easy to catch late in the evening for a normal chat.

**Open The Chat:** Before you open that chat window, just pause and think for a moment about what the typical guy's mindset is. What Would a Chode Do? (WWCD). He'll be stoked that he's been added by a genuine hot woman with-tits-and-everything! Just like a beta with a new phone number, his first instinct is to immediately engage and flood her with attention. So, don't be that guy.

See when she's online. If it was a really strong hook you can open right away, but if not remember the golden rule of Long Game — you have all the time in the world. So don't immediately jump on her. Wait until a quiet midweek evening when you're in a good mood then send a Feeler:

"Hey crazy!"

"Oi, Frenchie!"

"So…. It's you!"

Chat game is a dynamic real-time interplay compared to the turn-based nature of text game. The former is a fast back-and-forth with constant contact, while the latter is knocking the ball into the other court and waiting for it to be returned. Thus chat game has a small pre-chat phase where you ping to see if she's available at this moment for the chat. Keep it light. Don't send a wall of text. Don't ask a question. Don't require a response. You ping that sonar and see what comes back.

You aren't investing into today's chat until she has demonstrated she's amenable. You'll have an immediate calibration decision based on her response:

1. **No response:** Just let it hang. This might be the sign that she's not much into you but it might just be that she's away from her computer. People stay logged in while they go off to the toilet for an epic turd. You must restrain the urge to write a second line. Let it hang. You have all the time in the world. If she doesn't reply, don't sweat it. Roll off, try again in a week or two.

2. **Weak response:** She gets back to you a bit slowly and without enthusiasm. Again, don't get overly discouraged. She might be busy talking to her mum or writing an assignment. Maybe she's in a restaurant with her boyfriend. Wait approximately as long as she did, then throw out a low-investment ping. Lean towards rolling off rather than clinging on.

3. **Good response:** She gives you smileys, exclamation marks or other signs of being pleased you reopened her. This is where you can begin to work. She's available to chat and giving back.

4. **Great response:** You get a wall of text, questions, suggestions. Bloody hell, this was a disguised Yes Girl. Proceed quickly. Sex may soon follow.

It's really not so different from text game because you're still moving things along and calibrating to her interest levels. Whereas a girl can reply at her leisure to texts, social media chats require her to be in a position to talk. Be sensitive to this. The same girl who gives a good response today might give a weak response tomorrow based entirely on her personal situation at that moment. Don't cling on to difficult interactions. Wait for a better moment. Ping until you get it, then move things along.

The sexworthy man isn't desperate to make things happen with any given girl. He has options. He doesn't struggle in an uphill battle against a woman's other distractions. Let the timing of your messaging reflect that she's just one of many girls on your list who you're engaged in a conversation with. When she's responding, you reward her good behaviour with the treat of attention. When she's giving little back you roll off like it's no big deal and you can take it or leave it.

**Play Her Wall:** If you're banging your head against a brick wall trying to get her responding to chat, then switch up and bang her Facebook wall instead. You'll do this more once you have normalised ongoing chat, but it works as the initial "in" too. The idea is to drop occasional teases to spike her and set yourself apart from the chodestream. If her new profile photo in a red dress has twenty guys telling her she's beautiful and one guy telling her she looks like an M&M you can guess which she'll respond to. It's a public neg, but subtle and playful.

So bide your time. Wait for a photo that triggers a good tease and let her have it. Comment or, even better, post a link to a similar photo that's a tease such as a small furry mammal. Then calibrate her response. If she likes it, you've chipped away a little and gained some attention. If she doesn't, you haven't lost anything because girls will never reward a guy who posts positive supplicating comments on photos. Don't jump right on it. Roll off, ping her again.

# 2. BECOME THE GUY SHE TALKS TO

### Potemkin Village

*An apocryphal story of a local politician who erected fake settlements along the banks of the Dnieper River in order to fool Empress Catherine II during her visit to Crimea in 1787. The phrase is now used to describe any construction (literal or figurative) built solely to deceive others into thinking that some situation is better than it really is.*

You must rid yourself of the notion that hot women have interesting, action-packed lives. Occasionally you'll run into a girl who has fallen into a lively lifestyle (for example an international model, or a girl with a socially-connected boyfriend),.Their lives are spinning wildly with an overload of shallow externally-referenced social contact, so actually these are often the girls who most enjoy real authentic communication on Facebook with the mysterious other man. Don't be overawed just because she has lots of party pictures. She's still just a woman who wants the same masculinity.

When you see a busy Facebook, you are likely seeing a **Potemkin Village**. Women really aren't very interesting, because it's not in their nature to initiate fulfilling hobbies or interactions. She'll go to work / college then come home, make a cup of tea and watch television. Once or twice a week she'll go out to a bar or club, but most of the time she's doing the same mundane things every other boring girl does. She responds to the same high-quality male attention as every other girl.  Her Facebook is her show reel. It's not her reality.

*There is always space for you to occupy in her life*

Once you've got her responding to you it's time to normalise the communication into an ongoing interaction. Just like with a street stop, you must first hook her with attraction and then bed it down with normality and rapport. So I follow this pattern for a few interactions:

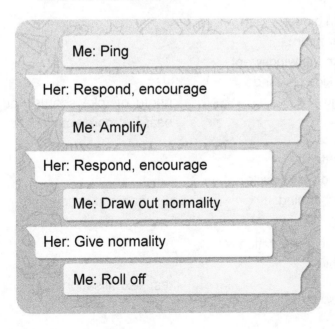

Me: Ping

Her: Respond, encourage

Me: Amplify

Her: Respond, encourage

Me: Draw out normality

Her: Give normality

Me: Roll off

That's rather abstract so let's work in an example. **Olga** is a smoking hot twenty year old fashion model I met in Latvia while on a Euro-jaunt. It was a two-set with her sister that lasted about ten minutes and seemed a weak hook without much sexual spark. It turns out they both study in the UK (but not near London) in separate universities. That presents a classic Long Game opportunity — very high quality girl, mild attraction, bad logistics. I got lucky with my very first feeler because she was unoccupied and in a talkative mood, so I took the chance to string it out a bit. I keep the message timestamps so you can get a feel for the to-and-fro of timing. She responds in timely fashion so I keep it going. If she'd gotten slow I'd have slown down too, so as not to come off like I'm chasing:

| | |
|---|---|
| It's the almost-Scottish girl........ 10:33 | Feeler |
| Hahah yeah. And you are from Newcastle, what a coincidence. my best friend is from there 10:33 | Good response, so I can immediately move into the next stage |
| it's the accent, it's simply too charming. be careful about Scotland, though. within one more year you'll be drinking whiskey every day 10:35 | amplify the ping |
| Haha well I guess you English aren't very fond of Scots. I am already drinking whicky for breakfast too late 😃 10:37 | respond and encourage |
| your hair will turn ginger. I can already see your future..... A little cottage on the windswept highlands.... 15 kids...... and married to this guy 10:38 | photo of joke scottish guy in tartan and ginger beard — more amplification |
| Ahahaha I guess I better be leaving that place as soon as possible. although he is quite charming 10:39 | respond and encourage |
| Scottish men have a reputation for having very big........ bagpipes 10:41 | test sexualisation |

Oh yeah bagpipes 😊    10:43

goes with it, amber light, then she sends me picture of scottish guy playing bagpipes

This one have enormous ones. Do you have any explanation why are they soo short?  they all look like gnomes to me    10:43

asking questions, she's hooked

yes. it's the drinking water. a special magic potion. you'll soon become a little gnome girl. or a squirrel    10:46

tease and set up an animal motif for later

Hmm no it works the opposite way for me    10:47

you get taller? OMG. you'll be a giraffe    10:48

I send an image of a pretty girl walking down the street on stilts

this pics  precisely describes how a feel in Scotland ahaha    10:51

respond and encourage

I love the North of England. It has amazing countryside and lots of nice little villages with old-style pubs. big open fireplaces, tatty old seats, perhaps a shaggy dog lying in the corner chewing on a man's slipper...    10:55

It's been fizzy long enough so I draw normality

You sound so sentimental. and I hear no hate at all    11:06

I wasn't expecting that, she's getting introspective, which is a good sign of opening up and being real

Life is good, don't you think?    11:08

Of course it is I can't understand people how keep moaning about nothing .You're just first English I have meet who has nothing again Scottish.    11:13

some investment

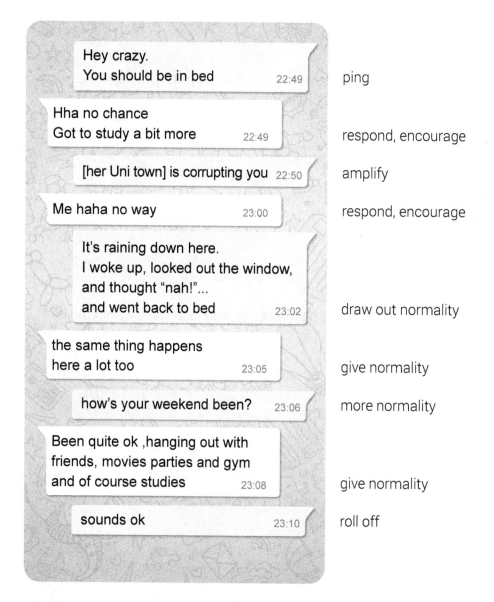

> I gotta go for lunch. Nice chatting to you, hon. Enjoy your day — 11:24

> Thanks you too enjoy Riga — 11:29

I'm now the guy she talks to, so roll off and position myself as willing to walk away

You are looking for perfect scenarios like that, where she's just doing nothing and ready to talk and thus easy to open up and get decent investment. But this is a young beautiful girl living the university life so she won't always be so available. She'll have essay deadlines, parties, whatever. So after getting my "in" with light chat I keep things ticking along with pings. This next example follows the blueprint in more obvious manner:

> Hey crazy.
> You should be in bed — 22:49

ping

> Hha no chance
> Got to study a bit more — 22:49

respond, encourage

> [her Uni town] is corrupting you — 22:50

amplify

> Me haha no way — 23:00

respond, encourage

> It's raining down here.
> I woke up, looked out the window, and thought "nah!"...
> and went back to bed — 23:02

draw out normality

> the same thing happens here a lot too — 23:05

give normality

> how's your weekend been? — 23:06

more normality

> Been quite ok ,hanging out with friends, movies parties and gym and of course studies — 23:08

give normality

> sounds ok — 23:10

roll off

This is fairly mundane chat, and that's the whole point. I'm showing her that I won't overinvest because I'm not overly concerned with talking to her. Rather I'm establishing lines of communication, demanding little of her and letting time build comfort until I get the right moment to let loose some real value and connection. This girl is used to chodes kissing her ass. I'm not that guy.

This stage can drag on for a long time if the logistics never resolve, her boyfriend continues to take care of business, or you don't quite draw her out into deep rapport. That's fine, remember the Golden Rule. You don't need to worry about momentum. Instead just keep treading water and working the groove until circumstances allow you to move into the next stage. That will usually happen when:

1. Her situation changes. Her relationship breaks down, she moves town, changes her job. Something breaks the status quo and makes her more amenable to pursuing deeper chat with you.

2. Your situation changes. You expect to be near her town sometime soon, such as revisiting a Euro-jaunt city, so you want to build up momentum and compliance test to see if there's a date in the offing.

3. Nothing changes but you just seem to be catching each other at good times, hitting it off well and the connection is getting stronger.

While treading water you are always monitoring your attention levels. You don't want to waste too much time on improbable leads, or kill the momentum by coming off as too invested. But once things change you will shift gears immediately. Now you need to amp it up and test her compliance. If you're successful, she'll move from "long shot" to "good lead."

# The Photo Ping

Unlike texts, social media is a natural forum for sending photo pings. Learn to use Google Images to your advantage. The same principles as normal pings apply, but you can be more creative. The easiest categories to work are:

**Furry Animals**: Whatever motif you used on her early on is what you work into the messages. So tall girls are giraffes, cute girls are hamsters, and so on. When she starts talking about her day you can riff off that so for example if she tells you she's been working hard all day then search google images for "hamster treadmill." If she's hungry, it's "hamster eating." Choose a funny picture and send it. Likewise you can initiate, using the photo as an opener. For example:

Hey! I stumbled across a photo of you on the internet today. Pretty shocking!

the set-up, baiting her about her reputation

What???? What photo?

bait swallowed

You weren't wearing much, and..... um.... Were being a bit indiscreet with a man.

pretending to be serious, ratcheting up her emotion

What?!!!!!!!! Show me!

hooked

punchline to pay off and turn her anxiety into relief

jajajajajajajaaajaja! You had me so worried!

reward

**Snotty Children:** Any time she talks about doing serious work or being responsible, find a photo of a little girl doing exactly that. So if she got a new dress, find a photo of a girl dressing in her mum's clothes. If she had a busy day at work, find a little girl pretending to be a secretary. Playfully belittle her sense of importance.

**National Stereotypes:** Constantly frame her country in playfully unflattering terms. Russians are vodka-drinking kulaks in Siberian wood cabins. Romanians are vampires and gypsies. Americans are bratty attention whores. Brazilians are on the beach in thongs. For example:

I was watching a documentary about your hometown today. Pretty interesting. It surprised me.

the set-up and bait, again it's about her

Really? Cool! I didn't know there'd be something like that. What was it?

bait swallowed

Actually, I think it had your family in it. The name was the same.

raise the stakes again

It's not such a rare name. Probably not them.

not as hooked, so need to quickly deliver punchline

that's your mum in the middle, I think.

punchline

Nooooooooooo! My city is a proper big city. I don't live in the countryside!

reward

Once you adopt the mentality of finding segues and deliberately misconstruing and reframing, you'll find Google Images to be an inexhaustible supply of self-amusement. Keep setting her up with normal conversation and then drop the bomb. Chuckle to yourself as she gets indignant. That engages her.

## Air Traffic Control

Your goal with Long Game is to have many girls in your orbit while you wait for the most opportune time to land them. Imagine your bed as the airport, and your role is the Air Traffic Controller. Keep the girls in the air and stay in radio contact. Monitor them until one is ready to land. You can never be sure which order they'll land in, or which will be diverted to other airports for reasons beyond your control. Get your holding pattern and then guide them to land. Don't obsess about any one girl.

precision engineering
Krauser
Tip

# 3. AMP IT UP AND MAKE HER WORK

This stage is the Long Game equivalent of flipping the script and drawing her investment. You've already laid some undemanding masculine vibe on her to keep her thinking in man-woman terms, but without forcing her to do anything about it. You can't sit on the fence forever. There comes a time to polarise and see just how good a prospect she really is. I haven't got the Latvian model very amped up right now (only met her a month ago) so I'll use a different example.

I met a Brazilian girl in London and our idate went well, but she was on holiday with her boyfriend of several years so my calibration told me that escalating would burn the set. She was living with him in Europe for a few months and about to head back there, so it's another classic Long Game situation: Lives in another city, committed to boyfriend but evidently with some potential for stepping out. I ran the usual model, so I pick it up at the point where I'm amping it up. I'll include sections where I'm using particular gambits. All were designed to pull her into my frame, get her investing, and create the **Our World** intimacy.

## 1. Put Her On A Points Scale  (Felicia)

Fairly early in the chat you should start dishing out points and minus points to express your approval / disapproval of her comments. It's all playful. So in the beginning you might get a chat like this:

| | |
|---|---|
| Oi! Brazilian! What are you up to? | playfully belligerent |
| Hey! I'm doing my study for school. | |
| Very conscientious. I approve 😊 +3 points for you. | use as pretext to judge her |
| Thanks!!! 😊 | accepts frame |

Once she's on the scale you can just give her +2, -5 or whatever. Play around with it so she's trying to win your approval and you can punish her with minus points. It's okay that the whole thing isn't taken seriously because the subtext is that you are worthy of judging her behaviour and she is still qualifying herself to you. Keep it running on and off throughout the entire period until you've banged her. At some point she'll ask you her score.

What do I win with the points?

curiosity

When you have 100 I'll be nice to you. 200 and I may give you a playful pat on the ass.

frame it playfully, with her seeking my approval

So how many points do I have now?

accepts frame, wants to know her position

-217

push-away (break rapport = attraction)

OMG 😨 What does that mean?

feigned worry

If you drop to -220 I'll chase you around the garden with a rolled-up newspaper.

amplify push-away with playful imagery

## 2. Make Her Qualify For Approval  (Felicia)

Here's a nice combination with the Brazilian when I have her worried about what I think of her and then transition into playful banter that shows high value:

I'm surprised you think you gave me 8. You always make me feel like I'm less than 4. I really thought I was 7

She opens me that evening with this

maybe I need glasses, then

agree and amplify

Nicholas Krauser. I think you graduated in 'rudeness'. And I'm sure you were the best student. And I simply can understand why I am so attracted to you.. and I hate to admit that but you were right when you said that it would be in our minds a lot until we can finally meet again.. At least it's in my mind a lot..

that's anchoring

It's a strange old world. Sorry, can't really talk for a couple of hours. Got a couple of friends sitting in with me

Don't take the bait. This is a great ambivalent response that she can read anything into. Don't be too available

To me it's just a strange and new feeling. But also good

yes. I can imagine

agree and amplify

I'm watching a vale tudo show. Enjoying it. How's my 3rd-favourit Brazilian?

I often use the x-th favourite line. When she first asked me "who are the first and second?" I replied Pele and "this guy" with a link to some cartoon character in national costume. I reopen her a couple of hours later.

I don't know. Who is it? Is it me?

Yes

I'm ok. You?

See appears low energy

just relaxing. I watched Elysium tonight

so I start with simple comfort

Did you like it? Ah this movie has 2 brazilians. Alice Braga and Wagner Moura. Wagner Moura... I have a big crush on this man

She's sharing her interests, which is comfort

*[google him and send a link]* he has a huge forehead

I've decided to do attraction, so I break rapport

Shut up. He's amazing. His voice and the way he talks. He did a movie called Elite Squad..and I guess most brazilian girls would love being arrested if he was the man doing it

She rises to the occasion and argues her case, challenging me

I know that movie but I haven't watched it

Bait her to expand and invest

It's very nice. And it's a true story. I think you'd like it..there are a lot of fights. In the second movie they even train jiu jitsu and when I saw that I could only think ' oh God, that could be me'   Hahah

More sharing, for comfort

I'd beat them all up. I'm invincible

Truculent cad, to break rapport

You'd never ever beat Capitão Nascimento. He's just too good. It's Wagner Moura's role in the movie

She again rises to the occasion

I'm grab him in a headlock. mess up his hair. hang him upside down by his feet, so all his lunch money falls out his pockets. then throw him in a muddy puddle

Raise the stakes with ridiculous imagery

Hahaha. He'd punch you until
you 'asked to leave' as he does
in the movie with the men who
are trying to get in the Elite squad.
Now we always say that in Brazil..
when someone can't handle
a situation, we say 'ask to leave
then'. And you'd ask
to leave very quickly. And Capitão
Nascimento is a man, he has no
hair for you to mess up

She's very engaged and argues her side with lots of investment

After I punch him in the face,
he'll shit his pants. then he'll
be asked to leave.
because of the smell

Stubbornly hold my ground

Hahahahaha keep dreaming, baby

Reward

then you obviously haven't seen
Elite Squad 3. It was made in
London. about the Super Elite
Squad. who are ten times tougher
than the Brazilian one

Agree and amplify

Hahahahaha

Encourages me to continue

so this little man comes to learn.
and I'm the teacher. I give him
an F. He says what's the F?.
I say its for Fuck off back to Brazil
before I steal your lunch money.
then I get him to shine my shoes.
and make my coffee

Keep going with my silly flight of fancy

You're such a dreamer. I always
knew you had a very fertile
imagination. I met some men who
wanted to join the Elite squad.
They were just ENORMOUS

Reward and IOI

a big target

More feigned stubbornness

Daygame Mastery

And they all said they were ready to be punched. Because, no matter how good they were at fighting. Those guys are a hundred times better. It's even funny when we saw the BOPE's car (how we call the Elite squad) passing. Everybody stop to look. When it's more than one we are even ready to lay down on the floor haha

Not me. I do this

This is the elite squad. Not bope. When bope comes they run

and it's unbelievable you're ready to lie on your back when the cops come. Such a pervert.
I'm watching a heavyweight fight. It's fairly good, but heavyweights never have much skill. too big and lazy

She's thoroughly engaged now, drawn out into the chat

link to photo of child kicking riot cop in the nuts

I feel the topic is running out of steam

## 3. Be Demanding. Give Her Homework  (Felicia)

Girls want a challenge, so you should remain playfully defiant. Sometimes you ignore her requests because they are silly, other times you ignore them because you've got something more interesting to talk about.  Even still, sometimes you just ignore them to change the pace and provide variety to your behavior. Don't be afraid to ignore her questions. If she wants an answer let her drag it out of you sometimes, which invests her even more in the exchange.

At this stage you can get her to do homework. Usually I'll suggest each of these at different times:

- Draw a picture

- Take a nice photo of herself (non-sexual)

- Find something really unusual while out and take a photo of it

- Wear a hat next time we skype video chat

- Think of a good secret to tell me

- Buy something for me

- Cook something and take a photo of it

It's all about the anchoring. Falling in love is something a girl does to herself in your absence. It's an active process. When she's chatting to you she gets a nice high, but the real investment is done when she's going about her life and dredging up memories of what you said, daydreams of being with you, and doing her homework fantasising about how much you'll like it when she presents it to you. This is called anchoring and it's the single most powerful element in Long Game.

Once you've had a sex chat it's quite easy to get her anchoring by taking sexual photos. I like to suggest a game where each day for a week she takes a photo of her breasts in a different public location (shop fitting room, office, bedroom etc). In the following chat we traded drawings. It begins when I've refused to tell her her hotness score out of ten the previous evening:

| | |
|---|---|
| So..are you going to tell me or not? | It's been bugging her, making her think = anchoring |
| my oh my, aren't you aggressive! | don't fall into her frame |
| Agressive? Sorry, baby..that was not my intention | accepts gentle rebuke, doesn't wish to annoy me |
| heh! | I lighten the vibe because she may actually feel bad |
| 😊 Ok... you are not going to tell me. | Ok, she's fine |
| I got a big book of adventure stories I'm reading. I love this stuff. It would've been so exciting to be a kid in that era | snip the topic by linking to cover photo. This is just to be difficult. |
| What's the book about? | Accepts redirection which is obedience |
| it's a collection of pulp stories from boy's magazines of 1920s-40s. they had covers like this: | link to two covers |

| | |
|---|---|
| Haha cool | encourage |
| I love this stuff. great art, great stories | another link. They are all aggressively masculine and sexualised |
| It's very you. I mean, if I saw something like that at the streets I'd think of you | "very you" is a sign that she values rapport with me |
| I'd love to make canvas prints for my wall | share a little of myself to reward her |
| Hey. That reminds me you own me something. You said you'd draw for me. I did | she sent it a few days ago |
| hang on, I'm doing something more important | being difficult again |
| What are you doing? | curious, rapport-seeking |
| I just changed my cover and profile, what do you think? | I changed profile to a gorilla giving the finger |
| I think not even Freud could understand your mind and find out what's your problem. The monkey is cute though. Seems to be more friendly than you haha | She is always motivated to try to analyse and understand me now = anchoring |
| I've done a picture just now. I drew you | pretend I'm giving rapport as bait |
| God. Don't send it to me. I'm sure it'll ruin my night | she knows me well now, so suspects trickery |
| [attach childish scrawl I just rattled off in five minutes] | punchline to feign rapport breaking but really it's rapport building |
| My boobs are not that big. Actually they are very small. But I like it | likes it |

> cool. I'm really sleepy. I'm going to bed. you can come and join me in ten minutes

rapport, incepting acceptance of sex

> Ok. I'll be there in 10 minutes

plays along

> good night

comfort

> Boa noite!

comfort

## 4. Sexualise Her Frequently (Felicia)

**Dopamine**

*The human body releases different chemicals during courtship to influence behaviour. When a girl is flirting with a high value man her brain will be flooded with Dopamine, which produces an addictive thrilling sensation similar to heroin. Intermittent spiking triggers the dopamine rush, and eventually the girl will chase further spikes. This flips the script. It is interesting to watch girls spike their own buying temperature.*

You want her on the emotional rollercoaster, ever more addicted to the **dopamine** hits she gets from talking to you. It's all still at a safe distance for her so she'll be like a moth to the flame, looking for ways to sneak back onto her laptop for another fix and then daydreaming about the spikes while she's away. This is key to making her anchor. Keep looking for jump-off points to switch into sexualisation. The first time you do it will be carefully paced but once you've had the first sex chat you can start liberally spiking and playing the matched-pairs. Here's an example where I get the girl to air her reservations about cheating on her boyfriend (that's rapport and helps her rationalise the sex), then I pick my moment to be crassly sexual (a spike) and to probe a little on what she likes and how accomodating she'll be to my demands. Bear in mind this was a couple of weeks into the chats.

> Yes. I told you. Sometimes I think I met him too early.

this is partway into a chat where she talks in detail about her relationship for the first time

> Perhaps. Maybe he is the man you should marry sometime. The best husband is never the most exciting man. the best husband needs many extra things beyond simple charisma

frame myself as the r-selection adventure who won't disrupt her k-selection relationship security

I know he's my man. The right for me. Just don't know if I'm ready to change my life now

verbalising her conflicted emotions

That's your decision. Do whatever you think is right for you. Back to my point. I find it inconceivable that I could have you living with me, travelling with me, me fucking you senseless every night... and you'd still talk to other men. it simply wouldn't happen. you'd have zero interest in anyone else. you'd be completely in my frame. So that tells me the simple fact that you never lost your frame. you aren't in his frame. you are in his life in a physical / temporal sense but you aren't emotionally / psychologically in his frame. he hasn't broken your frame.

this is all rapport and framing. I'm leading her to convenient rationalisations for why its okay to sneak away and have sex with me

Maybe..

unconvinced by wavering

Anyway, I'm not trying to get you to leave him

"sex with me won't disturb your security"

I know

understood

You do what is good for you. I still want to fuck you senseless though

start sexualising because the rapport stuff can get too despressive

Hahahahaha. You'd never break my frame. You know that?

she likes to push back

Stronger women than you have said the same thing to me

imply preselection

Hahahaha. But I mean it.. I could fall in love with you, deeply in love. But I'd never let you break my frame

this is quite a big admission, especially the "deeply in love"

ok. I hope that contained within "deeply in love" there is. lots of blowjobs. licking my balls. anal sex.costumes. roleplay. scratching my back. the occasional lap dance. what else?

I wish to distract aware from her moral reservations by heating up hindbrain

That's all included.
Maybe not so much anal sex

accepted

we can figure out the specifics later. but I definitely want to bury me dick deep in that tight ass of yours. while I push your face into the pillow. and hold your arms behind your back. then just bounce you really hard into the mattress. slap your ass a bit

keep sexualising, giving her imagery

You really liked my ass

not yet biting on the bait, but not rejecting it either

maybe reach around and rub your pussy at the same time

more imagery

I told you. Stop talking about it. Imagination can be better than the real act. So far that's all we have. Ilusion. We may not even have chemistry

still offering forebrain resistance

Haha.... you're so full of shit. little protests. you know exactly how much chemistry we'll have. I'll fuck you so senseless that you'll forget your own name. When I get up to shower you'll just be lying shaking for twenty minutes, wondering if you've just been run over by a steamroller

keep my frame without trying to persuade or cajole her

Hahahaha

still not rejecting it

> Tell me the main thing you want us to do in bed

so I switch tack, trying to draw her into investing

I don't know. I'll let you have control I guess. It's not like I feel I can decide anything here

she's getting pulled into imagining sex, which is my main objective here

> I'm dominant but I'm a man of steel and velvet. I want you to enjoy it. but I know that for you to enjoy it, I have to please myself foremost. you want me to enjoy taking you

some comfort and frame-setting

That's true

agreed

> you want to feel the thrill of being the source of my pleasure

pacing and leading

Also true

agreed

> Where do you like a man to cum?

eliciting values

inside of me. Or in my belly

she continues to imagine sex with me

> breasts? mouth? face? ass?

encourage more such thinking

No face. All the rest

> cool. I'll remember that. Might surprise you about the face though. I like that

being difficult and wilful again, because she responds to it

I hate that. It's the only thing I really don't like. So..am I a 7?

doesn't like it, tries to return to initial question

> Masculine frame...... taking it on the face is very submissive. Yes. no worries. I'll shoot it all down your throat. then politely ask you to swallow. because I'm a gentleman

reframe away slightly by making light of it

No doubt you are a gentleman | wry humour

As much as I'd love to keep telling you what I'm going to do to you. tell you where I'm going to put my dick. and how it's going to make you feel. I'm very sleepy. and I'm thinking about bedtime | don't be too available, don't overdo it, leave on a high

Me too. But answer my question first. Am I a 7? | she's been patiently waiting for her opportunity to ask again

Of course not. I don't do this with 7s. ok, good night! | reward and preselect

What am I then? | she's not sure if I mean less than 7

I'll tell you tomorrow. sleep well sweetie | so I want to leave her anchoring, concerned about my opinion of her

Ok. Boa noite, Nicholas

## 5. Show Contrasting Sides To Your Character (Felicia)

You'll remember that a good ping text is to be passionate about some masculine appetite while framing it in an interesting way. Perhaps you're exaggerating or being a tongue-in-cheek bad guy. By this point she's got a good idea of your character so you can be quite playful and obtuse. Here's some examples with the Brazilian:

Hey. Still watching boxing? | she's usually the one opening me now

no | I can afford to be abrupt now she's the chaser

What are you doing? | rapport-seeking, she wants my attention

shooting squirrels in my garden | playful

Hmm. You are probably Peta's number 1 enemy | plays along

> I'm a PETA member. People for Eating Tasty Animals

truculence

> Squirrels are not tasty

> I'm not gonna eat those. I'll keep them in the garage for a week, then throw them at the local children when they play outside

She will know this is a joke

> Good. Better than eating them

## 6. Instill Dread (Felicia)

They would never admit it consciously, but girls love the idea that other girls want you. A man with options is an attractive man. Most of the time in daygame you can't really use pre-selection except with the subtlest of signals, for the simple reason that you meet the girl one-on-one with no other girls around reacting to you. Long Game lets you casually drop in pre-selection without forcing it. Just wait for the right segue. Typically it'll come when she starts probing you about the photos and posts on your Facebook wall. She'll begin to mark her territory to ward away other women (such as liking your old photos). You'll get some variation of the following chats:

> You travel so much! You have many good photos 😃

she's leading into her real topic obliquely

> Thanks. I like to see the world with my own eyes.

DHV on my adventurous spirit

> And so many girls!!!! 😃

this is the expression of dread

> The world is a wonderful place 😃

deflect

The central point is once you have witnessed an expression of dread you don't have to make a big deal of it. By referencing photos of other girls or accusing you of being a womanizer she is demonstrating she has dread instilled into her and is now expressing subtle competition anxiety. Great.

Don't brag. I usually obliquely and artfully evade her accusations precisely like a woman evades a man escalating her. Resist the temptation to go overt and logical with her (e.g. "Yes. I see many girls").Instead, stay covert and elusive so she feels the frustration of being unable to pin you down and she never quite gets the answer to your ambiguous girlfriend status. This anchors her and her mind fills in all the blanks with information that flatters you more than the truth would. Don't solve her problem and relieve her dread.

When she does finally nail you down with a direct overt question, be less evasive but still don't quite give her what she wants or too much bragging.

| | |
|---|---|
| How many girlfriends do you have? | she fully accepts my preselection but is a little concerned about her place |
| I don't really have a girlfriend | this is an r-select response |
| What does that mean? How many girls do you have? | she's mostly K, so doesn't immediately accept it |
| A few girls like me. Nothing serious. | convey my casual attitude |

You can always then snip and stack to further frustrate her. Female social code often forces her to follow your lead and talk about something else, while her mind is furiously constructing a way to bring up the subject again at a later date. She'll always assume the other mystery girls are younger, hotter, and better in bed. This anchors her further and whips up a nice emotional storm.

Get used to describing your life in ambiguous terms regarding girls. Even during a normal chat when discussing what you've been doing, you can drop in bait.

| | |
|---|---|
| Hi Englishman! How are you? | she wants my attention |
| Good. I just went out to dinner with a friend | comfort with implied preselection |
| Oh, delicious I hope! | rapport |
| Yes. How about you, hon? | comfort |

This looks innocuous but she's wondering who that friend is and if it's a rival girl. If you keep using gender-neutral words like "friend" or "people" to describe your social situations, she will assume you mean women far more often than you actually do. When you feel her probing to see if it's a girl, you evade and stack forwards. Keep making the cat chase the moving spot of light up the wall.

# 4. GET COVERT CONFIRMATION OF SEX

### Crossing the Rubicon

*The moment a girl moves from a position of "I might have sex with this man," to "I will have sex with this man." Girls can be very decisive, making the decision during a Facebook chat and then implementing a plan to make it happen weeks or months later.*

It's important to get the LMR out of the way *before* you invest your time, money, and emotional energy into travelling to another city or country to meet her. There are few things worse than spending £250 and four days of your time travelling across Europe just to find she wants to play the "chase me / I'm not that kind of girl" game when you get her into the bedroom. That's only happened to me once, and I can confirm there are few lonelier feelings in the world than sitting on a double bed in a nice foreign apartment at midnight while your girl has flitted away un-fucked to her own pad. That's a real I-suck moment followed by a long dark night of the soul. To avoid having a similar moment, follow the rule:

> *She must give you an unmistakable message (covert or overt) that she will have sex with you.*

This is non-negotiable. It doesn't matter how flirty and invested she seems in the chats, you need to flick that mental switch in her mind that puts her across the **sexual rubicon**. If you don't accomplish this, you are just putting yourself into an extremely weak situation: Let's say she's Croatian and you agree to go to Zagreb to meet her without confirming sex...Let's look at the investment levels:

**You**

- Buy a flight and pay for an apartment.

- Get up early, spend perhaps 6 hours each way to get from A to B

- Sit around by yourself in a town you barely know, waiting on your meeting with her as the whole purpose for being in the city

**Her**

- Live her normal life, fitting you in to the time she's cleared for you

- Incur no extra costs except maybe a tram ride into the Old Town

This is a significant imbalance in investment. Travelling to foreign countries to close girls is an inherently vulnerable situation so you *must* have her pre-prepared, committed, and chomping at the bit to fuck you. Not only is this necessary for your peace of mind, but it's also crucial for the frame to make sure you don't fall into hers. Deep down in the limbic recesses of her mind she will judge you as being low value if you fly to her on a weak commitment.

There are four checkboxes to tick. You don't need all four but try. Usually they'll happen in this order:

1. She participates in a sex chat

2. She sends you naked or semi-naked selfies

3. She overtly tells you she wants to have sex with you

4. When you are booking an apartment for the visit, she agrees to a double-room.

Let's consider each in turn.

# 1. Sex Chats  (Milena)

Most men have no idea of the depth or material of female sexual fantasy. You need to be read some women's romance books and flick through Nancy Friday's book "My Secret Garden." Their fantasies are complex, sordid, and hugely entertaining. Learning to build these elements into a good sex chat and tease out her hidden sexuality is a skill worthy of a book of its own. I'll just cover the basics here. First let's understand what we are trying to do here.

### *Make her have sex with you in her imagination*

This is **almost** as good as actually physically fucking her. As men we want the real deal physically, and nothing should steer you away from that path. Women, however, live within their imaginations and simulated sex over Facebook triggers exactly the same chemical responses as actual sex. Yet her forebrain doesn't consider it cheating, so it's much more likely to happen in the earlier stages.

Thus you are sucking her into the mental and emotional schemas of having sex with you without engaging anywhere near as much forebrain resistance. She has easy rationalisations at the ready for why masturbating over sex chat with you "doesn't count." And then... Over the course of a couple of weeks... She's hung up on you and the idea of you being inside her. Sex with you is now a natural logical outcome, and it's strange for her to think that it was ever anything else.

The first time you begin the sex chat will be the most difficult and most likely to trigger non-compliance. The goal of the first chat is to break down those barriers and tick off the Covert Confirmation checkbox. Any subsequent sex chat has a different goal — you are welding her closer to you. So the first chat will usually require significant preparation. If the Long Game is immediately sexual and she's giving green lights, you needn't bother with an elaborate set-up, just trust your calibration and dive into it. However, let's assume she isn't making it easy for you and she needs to be drawn out.

First, get her into the habit of future-projecting with you on a non-sexual basis. Steer conversations into flights of imaginative fantasy. When you are talking about travelling, ask her where she'd most like to visit. Then paint an evocative picture of it and *don't hit on her in the fantasy*. You're just normalising the idea of future projection and spiking her mood by injecting colour into her life. Once you're getting full compliance in the projections, you can then test a sexual one.

I'll usually ease into it with a "let's imagine a perfect holiday," and get her to feed in the parameters of where she'd like to go. Now you can construct the fantasy. Insert yourself into it to complete the Our World bubble, but take your time before you introduce sex. Write it like it's the perfect fantasy date. Girls love context. They want to know the little details, the hidden moods, the subtle gestures, the tension. Here's an example of the first chat I did with a chaste young Serb I banged one month later. At the time of this chat we hadn't even kissed. She said she wanted to go to Sicily. Note that my contributions are not a wall of text. Every sentence or two is sent separately, I've just combined them to save space here.

> So we'll arrive by boat. A little local ferry, driven by an ancient Sicilian guy with a flat hat and tanned weather-beaten face We'll have old fashioned suitcases, leather ones with brass buckles and leather straps I'll be wearing a panama hat and beige suit like this. it's hot :) tell me what you'll wear

setting the scene and context

> [link to summer dress, quite a sexy pose]

link to photo

> ok you'll probably need a hat too....

> so we'll get a local taxi to drive us up the hillside to our hotel...

a little old 1970s Fiat with
a coughing engine and sticky
plastic seats bad air conditioning....

struggling to get up the hill, and
the driver speaking random stuff
in Italian saying "mama mia" a lot.
Finally we 'll walk through reception....

We'll have to sign in as Mr & Mrs
Black, to protect appearances
and your honour.... but not spies
or perhaps we are 😊

like a movie

She indicates she likes the movie theme so I build
this in on the fly

Yes, Mrs Black... we'll take our
own suitcases to our rooms,
because they are heavy with
all our spy stuff and guns....
I'll be all hot and sweaty so
I'll immediately jump in the shower

an innocent ping on sexuality

me first

as you unpack the clothes....
you'll hear me singing you know
my shower song?

be a gentleman you told me

so I'll walk around the room in my
towel, like James Bond, while you
undress and get in the shower....

link to Right Said Fred — I'm Too Sexy. This is
a recurring motif in our chats and I still want it light
and playful

you'll enjoy the cold water on
your skin, washing off all the travel
very refreshing cooling you down
so when you put on your evening
 dress, it feels soft and cold.
show me what you'll wear.
We'll be going out for dinner at a
restaurant by the sea.....

evocative details, tell her how she feels

it's getting late, the sun is going down and splashing the sky red.

(link)

nice. you'll have earings and a sparkling necklace too so we'll walk out into the cooling evening air, still a bit hot....

Me striding ahead, my chin up, looking at the buildings around us. You on my arm, tottering on your high heels to keep up....

we'll walk through cobbled streets, row upon row of small white houses, some with washing hanging from the balcony.... a couple of dogs running around, radio sounds of a football match....

then we get to a seaside restaurant and sit at a table on the patio, just a few feet from the soft waves splashing against the sea wall....

the waiter looks like this *[photo of stereotyped Italian waiter]* he hands us handwritten menus in Italian, we try to order what do you ask for?

pasta

what sauce? it'll be fish probably, next to the sea

chilli fish

An evening dress. We want her investing into the chat

reward compliance

paint myself in flattering terms

Full compliance and not much input. I read this as her just wanting me to take full control

I'll get a steak so we sit and eat, washing it down with local wine. We can see the vineyards up on the hill.... getting a little drunk as the sun goes down and the sky turns a dark blue, already there's music coming from the bars, some of it live and groups of local musicians move from table to table playing requests... we finish up and move on to the most fun-sounding bar

even future projections build in plausible deniability

(link to Luna Rossa) that's south italian music i want that song in this night

yeah, I've heard that before. I like it... they'll be playing it on little guitars and accordians here... I have to put my hand on your shoulder to stop you getting up and dancing before we've finished eating... there'll be time for that later

I'm taking control of her

but you can not stop me.... you are standing up and starting to dance with me

I decide the advantage of having her enthusiastically put herself into the fantasy is more important than me keeping full control of it, so I allow this

Just this once.... I watch you moving your weight, gradually getting into the music, your hips beginning to sway, your head moving to shake your hair...

I'm escalating at my own pace, slowly and in controlled measure.

As you loosen up and feel the beat, I pull you in to me so we can dance together a little... I let your hand rest on my shoulder while you pick up your wine glass for a sip...

pacing and leading

my hand on your hip and the other holding my drink... we dance a bit more, the music stops but we don't really notice....

just enjoying the feeling of the cool breeze from the sea, the slapping sound of the waves, and the distant sounds of music and laughter from the bars....

it's a beautiful scene and we are happy to be there... so I give you a quick kiss on the forehead, take your hand, and we walk off to a bar

and?

well, we are laughing now. We feel free... like this but busier*[photo of a suitable bar]*... I order a double whiskey for myself. What cocktail do you drink?

find some darker place.. with low lights

I looked. Can you find one?

ill try

ok, how about this? *[photo]* so, what drink do you have?

i take wine

ok so we take our drinks into the darkest corner we can find

yes

She's escalating me, so I'll allow it.

escalation, ping

compliance

some soft red velvet seats, the material worn thin by use over thirty years the bar is busy, lots of chatting and shouting, everyone having fun...

*atmosphere*

it's all in Italian they don't notice us, too busy with each other we don't care, we came here to be alone so we sit and drink, not talking much now, just enjoying sitting with each other....

*the Love Bubble*

I like looking at you, with your hair and makeup done nice, and an elegant evening dress, you like absorbing my male energy, leaning against me... soon you feel so relaxed...

*IOI, escalation*

your head is resting on my shoulder as my arm is around you....

we look around us, at the posters on the walls, the local people — fishermen, builders, waiters, wine makers, tailors... the local colour of life.... everything else seems so far away... I'm stroking your hair now, scratching the side of your head softly like you are a cat....

sipping my whiskey you feel so warm and relaxed, you just want me to kiss you. I notice this, I can see your eyes soften and your pupils dilate...

*tell her how to feel, make her chase you*

your lips moisten so I hook my finger softly under your chin, raise it upwards so you are looking up into my eyes, and I give you a kiss not too much, yet. I don't want you to be greedy*[push after the pull]* then I call to the barman to give us another round of drinks and some peanuts... salted....

this is a proxy for a real kiss close

you ask for cookies but he doesn't understand you... we drink a bit more.... we are silent now.... we don't need to talk, there's nothing to say....

callback humour because this girl loves cookies

we just enjoy the atmosphere around us... after our drink it's getting late, time to walk home... it's only a short walk but I see a young boy riding a bicycle....

I tell him I'll give him £10 if he lets us borrow his bike. He laughs and grabs the money, a big smile on his face, and I get on the bike While I hold it steady and lean forward, you get on the back and sit in the seat, your feet on the back wheelnuts....

impulsive and silly, keep the mood playful and light, show creativity

it shakes side to side a bit as I start to pedal, the cobbles rattling the wheels, you squeal a little...

worried you'll fall but as we pick up speed it gets better and your squeals of fear become squeals of delight, like a little girl being given a cookie… so I pedal up to the hotel and park the bike outside reception the garden looks exactly like this now[photo]

present her as clumsy and silly

:)

there's no-one around, it's about 11pm and everyone is either in bed, or out by the sea…. your heart is still beating fast from the bike ride, and hanging onto me you grab onto my arm as we walk up the steps….

she's chasing me while I am in full control of the seduction, proceeding according to me own pace

I stop at the top and turn towards you, see you looking up at me with anticipation  somewhere in the tree nearby a bird chirps…

this time I give you a proper kiss, deep and long, until you feel your heart flutter and you struggle for breath… you resist a little at first, pushing against my manliness, to see how I am, to enjoy psychologically feeling my male energy… you push me away a little with your hands on my chest, not really trying, just a symbolic effort….

for a few seconds you keep your lips tightly closed but a few seconds is all you can resist, then you have to surrender to what you've been feeling all day….

Daygame Mastery

and you fall into the kiss, your hands snaking around behind my neck, as I put my hands on you it seems like time stops and then I pull away, leaving you gasping, and lead you into our room....

I kick off my shoes, as do you... open up my suitcase to take out a bottle of good Scottish whiskey and pour a glass...

playing the tension on the fishing line

you are standing by the window looking outside... looking at the stars, the twinkling lights of the seaside, and far in the distance some lights on the cruise ships at anchor...

I'm a man of class and sophistication

your dress feels nice on you, you like how you feel and, catching your reflection in the glass you like how you look reflected in the glass, you see me walk over to you...

tell her she's enjoying it

you stay looking outside, waiting for me to reach you, anticipating the little spark of electricity through your skin as my hand touchs your shoulder... slowly traces a line down your spine and then rests softly on your hip your whole body shudders a little, a warm flow of energy through your stomach and down your arms...

I'm showing how well I understand her, showing social acuity and knowledge of female sexuality

you can feel my other hand sweeping your hair away from your neck....

you are still looking forward...
you really want to turn around,
to look at me, to grab me, to kiss
me but you also enjoy this feeling
of denying yourself... holding
yourself steady, eyes fixed ahead,
a test of your mental discipline and
you know I like it too...

I bend my head towards you.
My lips are only millimetres above
your skin you can feel my breath
against your neck, almost wet...

really amp up the psychological rather than the porno elements

little goose bumps rise... your
chest feels hot and flushed now...

I slowly blow air onto your skin,
moving my mouth up and down
from the top of your neck and
along your shoulder I can sense
you shivering, your knees weak...

Building tension through anticipation and not giving her the release

I glance upwards for a moment at
the window to see your reflection.
I see you biting your lip, a pained
expression in your eyes....

I smile and softly bite your neck, at
the same time as I tighten my grip
on your hip then I spin you slowly
around to face me....

hard and soft dominance

you are looking up into my eyes
now... it's like the rest of the
world is a blur... all you can see is
my eyes vividly, filling your vision,
very sharp and looking deep into
your soul... for a moment I let this
happen then I pull you to me... I feel
your whole body fall into my shape...

your chest against mine, your stomach touching mine, even your thighs pushed against my thighs and of course our lips touching…

now we kiss… much harder… there's no restraint now, just the bursting of the dam, the gate flying open…

it's passionate and high energy, I take a handful of your hair and pull you tighter into me as my tongue pushes further into you… you can feel the sting in your hair but it's not really hurting just like spice on food, it's more exciting.

so now you are grabbing me, your hands running up and down my arms, along my shoulders feeling the shape of my muscles beneath my shirt….

So far we'd had Skype video on so I was able to calibrate the escalation according to reading the subtle signals in her eyes, mouth and body langauge. She turns the camera off. That's a sure sign she's horny and quite likely going to touch herself.

squeezing, testing the strength wondering how it feels to be held, crushed, in those arms… knowing you'll find out soon… I put my hands under your ass and lift you up, you jump onto me, legs wrapped around while I stand… you're hanging onto me tight, slightly above me know, bending your head down to kiss me and grab my head….

squeezing your legs together to avoid falling... I turn around and throw you back onto the bed... you land with a big thump and let out an excited squeal....

Tell her she enjoys being escalated

I undo my shirt now.... you push yourself back against the headboard, reaching behind you to stack up the pillows behind your head, not taking your eyes off me... watching as I unbutton my shirt and throw it over a chair....

link to funny boxer shorts

I pull off my trousers too so just my boxer shorts I'm wearing my sexiest shorts you've already pulled your dress off, so I can see you lying there in just your underwear... what colour is it?

black

full compliance, doesn't want to type because she's fully in the moment

nice, I like black... it matches your hair well so you are looking up at me, taking in the shape of my wide shoulders.... the determined thoughtful look on my face and the intense interest I'm looking at yo...u you know I desire you....

reward, let her feel sexy

you like to be desired by me it makes you feel like a woman... I'm looking at you on my bed, lying there, semi-naked... your chest rising and falling heavily with your breathing.... a soft red flush on your cheeks and chest.... smooth female curves of your shoulders, breasts, hips and calves...

Daygame Mastery

So far so good. The girl has been seamlessly escalated from talking about holidays to suddenly lying on my bed absolutely gagging for it. An hour earlier I hadn't even kissed her, and now my avatar is about to ravish her avatar. So much LMR has already been broken down and she's over the sexual rubicon. Before the sex begins it's at this moment you have a big decision to make.

## *Do you virtually fuck her or not?*

The immediate instinctive reaction is to dive in and push it as far as you can, but this is not always the smart move. Calibrate the girl. This Serb was very straight-laced, very direct and also inexperienced with men (one prior sexual partner). She was quite likely masturbating by now and giving full compliance, making it natural to follow things through to the conclusion. It's analogous to having successfully extracted a girl on Day 2 and now you're both rolling around on the bed and fire is in her eyes. Pull the trigger.

But what if she's not fully complying? What if she's more or less going along with the chat but your calibration tells you you're dragging her along rather than her willingly jumping into your virtual bed? What if she's a bit of a game-player? What if she's still holding onto her frame? It's a similar situation to when she refuses to get into the taxi or resists taking her shoes off in your apartment. The standard prescription is that she needs a push. So make your decision — push or pull.

**Push:** "I'm looking at you on my bed, lying there, semi-naked... your chest rising and falling heavily with your breathing.... a soft red flush on your cheeks and chest.... smooth female curves of your shoulders, breasts, hips and calves....... So I turn around, switch on my Xbox and play Grand Theft Auto Five :P"

She'll laugh, feel indignant, and most importantly her hindbrain will register that you're not a horndog. Consciously or otherwise, she will reward you for being smart enough to spot that she wasn't quite complying. Here's the next stage of the chat:

I look at you waiting for me and know I want to take you.... so I put my knee onto the bed and lean over, my face just a few cm above yours... then I climb over, get into bed, and fall asleep Part 2 will have to wait for another time 😊 how was my story?

it was like real like it's happening now to me

you have good imagination,
I like that

always

Something strange happened.
As I was writing the story, you
seemed to get prettier

referring to when her Skype camera was on

really?

I think it was your facial expression
you began to look softer, happier,
a very natural smile and your body
language became looser...
it's attractive... you are cutest when
you are less guarded like now

deep rapport

i know

I like to see you like this. I knew it
was there, but would take some
time to express itself

when i show this part of me it
doesn't finish very well for me...
do you know what i want to say?

I think so it's natural... I think as
a girl you want to find a good guy
who you respect, trust, and are
attracted to.. you want to fall into
his world, experience how he lives,
how he sees the world give
yourself to him, like a present
of love to reward him for how he
makes you feel... but to do that,
you must surrender some of your
will, some of your independence
and it makes you vulnerable is that
what you mean?

something like that thay use it against me so it's better to pretend that i'm cold one

in the beginning, perhaps to reject all the men you don't want

i don't know where am i wrong

you're not wrong, you are just inexperienced

In this case, she quickly asked me to continue the sex chat, but if she hadn't asked I'd have said it's 50/50 on whether I should "close" or just take my winnings from the table and do the close on a later chat. The key objective was reached: Getting her to mentally picture fucking me.

It doesn't really matter if you proceed to the actual sex in the chat. If you do, you get the advantage of further breaking down LMR and linking her to you by the hormones she releases and the feelings she feels. If you don't, you get the advantage of maintaining sexual tension and having her anchor in your absence by inventing her own creation of what happened next. Either way, tick the Covert Confirmation checkbox. If it wasn't "on" she'd have never let you take her so far into the sexualistion.

Check my blog for how to describe the sex acts themselves. I don't list them here because it's almost incidental. The real work is in building the context and drawing her to the point where she's lying on your virtual bed. When I next saw this Serb girl, I banged her within twenty minutes of meeting. We'd gone from not having kissed to having all the LMR out of the way — entirely on Skype. Women are not the only ones who can use social media to their advantage.

## 2. Dirty Photos (Malvina)

Nothing confirms a girl as wanting to fuck more than her snapping off naked photos under your direction. It's nowhere near as difficult to accomplish as the typical chode may think. Every girl has some selfies on her hard-drive or smartphone even if she's never sent them to a man before. Girls want to be objectified, they want to be desired physically, and in lieu of being able to display their tits and ass directly in front of you she will use photos to draw you in.

*Taking a process, behaviour, or attitude that is initially risqué and outside a girl's reality and embedding it into the interaction so it is now entirely normal and uncontroversial, like "part of the furniture." We want the girl to believe sex is a normal expected outcome of the interaction rather than a special situation.*

Usually I'll lead up to it by doing the Photo Sexualisation Routine. Find a tumblr or photo blog which is full of "arty" sex photos, preferably one run by a woman because it'll feel less pornographic to your target. I usually use the archive tab of "Sex Saves The Day" (I have no idea if that site will still be online by the time you're reading this book). It's a page with literally hundreds of thumbnails of sexual photos, each one can be clicked on to access the original blog entry with a full size photo and comments from the blogger.

I always begin sexualisation in a generalised manner, -- i.e. I don't talk about me fucking her, I just talk generally about sexual things. It's lower pressure for drawing her out and changing her mood. Remember you are still the exciting mystery man and she's living a Fifty Shades Of Grey moment with you:

> I found a great website today. It's a collection of sex-themed photos where the writer leaves a comment telling you the one thing she loves about the photo. Some are porn but alot are just art or fashion.

> Oh really?

> Have a look. Tell me the five photos you like most, and why. [link]

This little routine is a fun chat but also achieves five goals:

1. Normalises sex and in particular kinky sex. By presenting all different kinds of sexual themes in one highly cheerful / positive site, you are giving yourselves permission to talk about stuff that might be difficult without such a prop.

2. You are **eliciting values** to find out the kind of things she's into. Taking them all in combination, you get a good feel for how she is sexually wired. Your choices do the same for her.

3. She'll get turned on and associate sex with you. In this state of heightened arousal, barriers will come down and you can progress the sexualisation, or maybe even turn it into a sex chat (which itself is based on the information you now know about what she likes — women will tell you how to seduce them).

4. By getting her to go first (or take turns, her first) you can calibrate your responses if you're not sure she'll go for it. If she chooses the non-porn images, you know to soft-pedal a little, maybe wait until your fourth or fifth choice to choose a porn image.

5. You both have plausible deniability. It's generalised sex talk (to use my verbal escalation terminology). You are commenting on someone else's content

> See how she takes it and talk in positive tones about the photos. Be completely non-judgemental. She'll inevitably ask you which photos you like, so choose five depending on your calibration. Choose mostly soft ones, but throw one or two more pornographic ones in. When describing what you like focus on topics like beauty, emotion, colours, aesthetics, etc. for four of your choices and then brutal dirty fucking for the hardest of the five. For example:

- **Mild photo of semi-naked woman:** I like the look on her face. She's got hungry eyes and slightly parted lips. It's like there's a volcano of energy building up inside her and it can only be released through her face.

- **Steamy but non-porno photo of a couple kissing:** I like the backstory. You can see her shoes kicked off and thrown across the floor, the two half-empty wine glasses like they were having a civilised drink and then suddenly couldn't control themselves.

- **The hard porn photo:** I like how her ass looks, pushed back, big, round and peachy while he's slamming it with his dick.

> If she accepts this routine without evading or blocking, you have a clear amber light. If she enthusiastically throws herself into it, you've got a green light and the chance of real sex is high. Soon, start going for the photos of her. I normally begin soft and then become more demanding.

> Here's an example using Whatsapp. This is a Swiss girl I met in Prague. She's 19 years old, very inexperienced and shy. But like all introvert girls she's got a bubbling sexuality straining to be released. It was a five-minute street stop, no kiss and no Day 2. After a month of irregular chat I've got her strongly invested and I'm just waiting until the next time I visit Prague. Here's the chat beginning with the first message of the day at about 3pm.

| | |
|---|---|
| Hey crazy | Playful opener |
| Hey. Am I crazy? 😄 | Acceptance of playful tone |
| Crazier than…. A very crazy person 😊. Send me a cute photo. | Begin by asking for "cute" photo, not "sexy" |
| Oh, I didn't even know that.. 😨 u just chat with me and u discover new things about me 😄 I will, but I'm at the bus right now. Not now. I don't like to take pictures of me at the bus or train 😆 | Strong investment and indication of obedience. I decide to push harder. |
| I guess you can take one at the bus stop 😊 Be sure to show some curves! | Be demanding but with positive tone |
| It's not that easy to take a picture of the whole body. At least not for me 😄 *[she sends a photo of her head and shoulders at the bus stop]* | She's trying to play along |
| Hmmmm…. I can see a pretty face but no ass or legs.  5/10. | The game is that you're never quite satisfied |
| *[she's back home now, sends another one showing her full body but just in a relaxed casual seated position]* A bit better? But I won't do a pic of my ass 😆 | Taking little steps forward, token resistance |
| Hmmm… yes. I see legs. But no ass. 6/10. | Improved score but never quite satisfied |
| And also if I would like to do one, I can't. I don't have so long hands. | Token resistance. It's an excuse rather than a "no" |
| Find a mirror. Shop changing room? | Solve her problem and push forwards |
| *[Close up of her ass, in tight jeans]* I hope you like it. | Win |
| I do. Very….. slappable 😄 7/10. | Reward the obedience and yet… not satisfied |

**10/10. Why just 7 points? I don't send such pictures to other guys. And u give me just 7** 🙁

> Haha

**It was not worth to show such cherished zone** 🙁

> 8/10 is underwear or bikini

**And 9/10 is a naked ass?**

> Yes 😄

**OMG!**

> Haha

**Haha? No, it's for crying.**

> It's nature. Men like women's asses. It's a beautiful thing!

**Are u a sculptor?**

> Maybe I should be

**have fun in the new career. Hope u have collected enough naked asses to make a few sculptures.**

> Yours will be my masterpiece 😉

**How nice!**

Mock disappointment

Assume it's not serious

Her complaining is still investment

Push further

Still engaged

Don't be coy about it when escalating

But definitely excited by it all

Breaking through a girl's defences is not a big deal to players

She wants to defend her image of modesty

Reframe to normalise the sexualisation

She's accepting it, the resistance is token

Mild agree and amplify. Don't lower tone into logical argument

She's just pretending to be annoyed for appearance's sake

Assume the sale

Not contesting the main point of where it's leading

I chose a particularly shy and un-sexualised girl to show how to ease into the subject when she's not used to sending selfies. It's all very light-touch, but I'm driving her forwards by telling her what I want and doling out approval as she is increasingly obedient. For the next couple of chats I backed off and talked about non-sexual stuff. Remember the tension on the fishing line. It's important not to come off as a hungry wolf who can't control his sexual urges. The basic pattern is:

1. Ask her for a cute or pretty photo, something "not on your Facebook." It's not too demanding and you can calibrate from how sexual the photo is.

2. Reward her compliance, but tell her it doesn't meet your expectations. "Nice. You have a nice smile. But I can't see any curves." It's easy to give her a score out of ten, but the crucial move is to *give her a fairly low score*. Make it clear that you aren't judging her beauty, you are judging the relative sexuality and quality of the photo. Don't ever diss her beauty when she's sending photos.

3. Push for something more sexual. I usually insist on seeing curves, or legs, or ass. Don't be vulgar. Each step upwards in sexuality earns her a slightly higher score. Reward each photo on the I-like-it-but… system.

4. If she challenges you on why you want them ("I think you're pretty") or what you'll do with them ("I'm interested. You look nice") or saying you're a pervert ("I'm a man. Men like to look at pretty women. That's nature."). Hold your frame. It's entirely normal for you to want sexy photos of her.

5. When you're sure she's enjoying it and not freaked out, insist on "more skin." Tell her there's "too many clothes."

It might take a few runs through this routine over a couple of weeks before you're getting genuinely dirty photos, but right from the beginning you are planting the seed. A hugely important tactic of Long Game is:

*Infect her with the virus. Let it incubate. Let it wear her down over time. Then come back and inspect your work.*

The big advantage of Long Game is the clock isn't ticking against you, so you can implement carefully-laid plans. A rule already discussed in earlier chapters is that you want her hindbrain working **for** you, gradually eroding the forebrain's resistance. Imagine when you're in a bar making out and dirty-talking with a girl. Her hindbrain is getting revved up and banging at the door, while her forebrain is on the other side trying to keep the door shut. Eventually the forebrain fatigues and gives up. On an SDL this process is fast and intense, but in Long Game it's a slower grind.

Pick your preferred metaphor:

- Her hindbrain is like acid, gradually eating through the forebrain's container.

- You are planting a seed and then sitting back, waiting for it to grow into a tree.

- You've given her a virus. Let it work. Let it break down her body's immune system.

- You've got two pirates fighting. Let them tire themselves out. Once the battle is over and they are exhausted you can saunter over and steal the treasure chest.

Once you've eased into the idea of her sending you photos, it's going to be playing on her mind when she's shopping, at lectures, having a bath. It's a pleasant sexual thrill that remains completely safe for her (so she thinks) because you are at a distance, a mere voice in the ether. She's anchoring. Women love being objectified and desired. They love having a secret garden. Let this process play out in your absence while you work your other more immediate targets. When the acid/virus/pirates are finished, her hindbrain will be that much freer and you can push for dirtier photos. It's all normalised.

When you've seen a girl naked in photos it's almost as powerful as having seen her naked in person. A crucial modesty barrier has been broken down, and you are only mere steps away from getting her into your bed. Remember Long Game is drone warfare: The pilot doesn't need to be physically present on the battlefield to take out the insurgents.

## Some Further Options

The overall goal here is to get a naked selfie and tick the Covert Confirmation checkbox, but if the girl is enthusiastic about the process then keep going with it. Set her homework by telling her you want a photo of her breasts every day in a different public location (bathroom, office, shop fitting room, etc.). That's great for anchoring and compliance. If you're on Skype video chat, tell her to flash her tits or slap her ass on camera. If she's sitting in a public place (e.g. her boyfriend's apartment) tell her to touch her nose, or stick her tongue out, or slap her own ass. Have fun with it. Once she's complying you can just reel her further and further in to your reality.

# 3. Overt Sex Discussion (Felicia/Gabriela)

Many Long Game sets reach a point where you haven't quite gotten the logistics sorted out, so you're treading water again. You've reached the point where she's desperate to have sex with you and you're constantly on her mind. Despite the distance, she's been pulled into your reality and looks to the chats as the highlight of her day. You can now safely hammer the frame. This is how it looks when the script is flipped and she's chasing you. It'll happen so subtly she doesn't notice. Deep down she made the decision "I want him," and from that moment on you are special to her and she doubts her ability to lock you down. Let's take an example of the Brazilian girl living with her boyfriend in Europe. She opens me late one evening after her boyfriend has gone to bed:

Can you believe I actually get happy when I see you're online?

I know the rapport-building stage is complete. Can move forwards

Haha. I get happy when my socks are warm

Still a difficult man to catch

 How are you?

She's stacking me into further rapport

Guilt-free relaxation. It's nice. You?

Give her a little comfort

I'm ok. In pain because of the gym. Went back to my german course today. It's ok, now I have something to occupy my days

Rapport. She wants me to know how she feels

Ja. das ist gut

Encourage her

Genau. Klein Nick spricht ein bisschen Deustch. Super. Nick... There is no chance you go to Rio to meet me next year?

This indicates she's probably already crossed the sexual rubicon

I'm not planning it

Still difficult to catch

☹

indeed

Resist urge to pile into explaining myself

That's bad

like I said, it's best that you find a way to sneak out of Germany

I want to set up a Euro hook-up

Nick. I like you and I'd like to be with you. I want that so badly. But I can't go to London. If I could, I would

Logistics are the most difficult obstacle in long game

I know. I don't blame you. it's just difficult

I want to nudge her into coming to me. Tough sell, though

Yes. Like I said, this is an illusion.. for you it's easy to forget but not me

She's heavily anchored, it's on her mind a lot

ah.... you put words into my mouth!

I don't want her thinking I'm too casual about her

That's what I think..I mean, you can eat a lot of girls every week, that's what you do. But I don't look for that .. it was just you haha

I guess I'm just THAT charming

You might be. Or maybe your testosterone is just too appealing to me

that's possible too

Yes.. Hahaha I didn't mean to say eat, I meant meet haha. But eat fits too haha

you think about food too much

Or sex..

pervert

how often are you thinking of sex with me?

Last week I thought about it a lot. And you?

I'm lucky. I sleep with myself every night. I even shower with myself

I envy you. How I wish I could shower with you and that amazing body of yours

Maybe I'll let you wash my back

I would die happy if I did so. That would be the biggest achievement in my life. Washing Nick Krauser's back

The player box will work against me now. I need to let her know I do quite like her
Spike, push

She's convincing herself about me, so let her do it

Encourage her

She's giving me a funny segue by accident

So I take it

BOOM! The only remaining issue is logistics

Playful

She's given an in to be more serious about sex talk

It's so open there's no need to be coy

Openess allows us to better solve logistical issues

Parody narcissist

She's joking here. She likes me but "amazing body" is an overstatement

Play along like she's serious

She's agreeing and amplifying me

| | |
|---|---|
| I make dreams come true | It's just silly games at the moment. Light vibe |
| But not my dream. And you..how often do you think about having sex with me? | She's back to seriousness again. Wants to know I care |
| maybe once or twice..... | I'm probably too cold here |
| Hmm | Mixed emotions |
| haha, I bet you have your sad face on now | Again, a bit too cold. Though it's normal in context |
| Maybe. Hahaha I do | |
| I'm watching boxing | Stacking away. Again, I'm probably overplaying the cad here. |

The sex discussion is overt because we've already agreed that we'll be having sex the next time we meet. It's gone from being a topic danced around in the courtship ritual to being a solid background fact. Normalise it as much as possible. If sex logistics are still quite far away, it's good to occasionally spike things with a little sex chat. Here's an example with a Romanian girl:

| | |
|---|---|
| [referring to some normal comfort chat we'd had the previous ten minutes] good luck. what are you wearing? | Standard escalation question to turn comfort into seduction |
| Why? | Wants me to earn an answer |
| curious | Don't over-commit |
| T-shirt and trousers but I'll change for night. I'll go to prepare | Not trying to excite me today |
| yes ... | |
| Ok [half an hour later after she's done her night routine] | |
| so what are you wearing now? | Try again when she's in night clothes |

It's a blue silk night dress. Why?

helps me imagine

I get excited also

helps me ima by your night dress?

Now because I know you get excited

haha, yes. would be nice to have you here right now

I know

how do you imagine it?

In your bed fucking me under my dress. You how you imagine it

similar, but pushing you against my cupboard, bending you over, lifting your dress up and fucking you that way

Mmmm

of course, that wouldn't be the end of it

probably I'd push you down to the floor, so you can feel the carpet on your skin while I do you there

I'll get excited again

of course.  then I'll pull you up to your knees, make you suck my dick for a while….. then push you face down onto the bed and fuck you from behind some more… holding your arms behind your back…. bouncing you around on the mattress

Now we're talking!

Let her know I like thinking of her sexually

She responds to that by heating up

Check I understood her correctly before pressing ahead on this topic
Yes, I understood correctly

Knowing she feels sexual, I turn things more sexual

Agrees

I want to find out what she likes, so I can better project just that

Normal fantasy, nothing outlandish or perverted. Noted

Make it visual for her mind

Likes it

I decide it's an opportunity to stack into a sexual projection story

Seems amenable, so I'll press on

More visuals

She's encouraging me. Time is right for this chat

Turn it up a notch

| Chat (left column) | Commentary (right column) |
|---|---|
| **Ohhh** | Joining me in the fantasy. Wants more |
| then I'm spin you over... lie on top so you feel crushed under my weight.... holding you tight so you can't move.... and fuck you so hard you scream.... until you cum.... then as you are still shaking and moanin | So she gets more. Preview the sex as being very good. |
| **Yes but I'm struggling** | She confirms I'm taking correct tone |
| I'd shoot my cum all over your breasts | |
| **I'm coming** | Investment. Well over the sexual rubicon |
| enjoy | Don't lay it on too thick. I'm still supposed to be a bad boy |
| **I need to sleep now. I'll go tomorrow morning to gym** | |
| ok, sweet dreams | |

### Oxytocin

*The "comfort" chemical released into a girl's body to make her feel intimate and safe with you. It encourages closeness, hugging, and the warm fuzzy feeling of cosiness. Soft dominance triggers it (hard dominance triggers dopamine) and the girl gets a massive flush of oxytocin in the ten minutes after sex.*

This sex chat requires far less build-up than the first time because I'm not having to knock down any barriers. It's not an escalation, it's maintenance. I'm normalising the idea of us being in a sexual relationship, greasing the path so that the idea of us having sex is a well-worn groove (which will drastically reduce LMR on the big night) and all her dopamine and **oxytocin** is already being mobilised in connection with me. She's getting progressively more sucked in to viewing me as the highlight of her day and the intervening periods as times to obsess over me and anchor herself.

Seduction is about taking control of a girl's mind and body, then bending it to your will. Shifting chats through the various matched-pairs lets her experience the full range of emotion. After a comfort chat you can suddenly pattern-interrupt ("What are you wearing?" is my go-to phrase) then heat her up so she's wet and hungry, then send her to bed with a nice metaphorical kiss on the cheek. You're providing her with the rollercoaster ride. Contrast is king.

Try to get her hungrier and hungrier for the real thing. She'll feel a pull towards you that has her aching to see you in person to relieve all that sexual pressure. As you sense it building you can move towards setting up the meet. If she lives close to you things are simple, but if she's in another country you'll have to either wait for the opportunity or proactively create one by suggesting a trip.

Generally, this is the preferred hierarchy of long game meetups. They are ordered according to the principle that you want her as far into your frame as possible, and to do as little work yourself as possible:

1. She is passing through your area anyway, so you pick her off when she comes with minimum disruption to your life. This is easy when you live in an international hub like London.

2. You are passing through her area anyway, so you get her out. For example you are working four solid Long Game leads in her town so you go back to close them and rustle up some new leads in a number-farm.

3. You import her to your city, convincing her to come just for the purpose of meeting you. This is a tough sell if you haven't already had sex. It's more common when you are setting up a Mr&Mrs Easyjet Euro-rotation.

4. You meet her in a neutral location where you both travel to get there. This is great for confirming sex location and stepping on the plane with the maximum probability of sex.

5. You go to her city specifically to meet her. Only do this if you've strongly ticked all the checkboxes and she's clearly gagging for it and giving you no weird evasive bullshit at all. Extract as high a price as possible first in naked photos, sex chats, and explicit talk about sex.

# 4. Agreeing On Sex Logistics (Gabriela/Tatiana)

You can't fuck a girl unless she is in a sex location. You want to lock this down before you pack your suitcase. How you agree can run the whole spectrum of covert to overt, so calibrate to the girl on whether her agreement to the logistics represents agreement to sex or if she's being evasive. Some girls are quite open about what they want and are willing to confront the subject of sex head-on. Others love to maintain plausible deniability so they'll covertly communicate agreement, but overtly deny it.

If you've invested her and already done your sex chats / selfies then the actual logistics should be straightforward — She **wants** to have sex, she's **decided** to have sex, so everything else is just details. When a girl is in the bubble on an idate or day 2 she might be whimsical in the moment about whether she will have sex. Once you've moved to Long Game, though, she will be coldly calculating sex — even if she talks to you like an angel whose mind those thoughts would never enter, perish the thought!

You have already communicated your intention of fucking her. She knows what you're after. So don't back down from it. Push your logistics forwards.

Here's an example with a Romanian girl. I'd met her in London while she was on a business trip, made-out with her but not had sex. After a month of patient long game including a sex chat she happens to be going to Barcelona to visit an old female friend and wants me to meet her. You'll notice that I never directly refer to sex, nor do I make nudge-wink indirect references. Sex is *assumed*. This is possible because we'd already had the sex talk before planning the holiday. This chat shows how to set up sex logistics on a mutually-understood basis without being so vulgar as to mention it.

| | |
|---|---|
| I've been sitting in a cafe this afternoon, reading the first Jason Bourne book | Normal window on my world to begin chat |
| It's nice what is about | Rapport |
| you know the Matt Damon movies? | Simple rapport for now |
| Yes. He was an secret agent no? | |
| yes, just like me | Light mythologising of myselg |
| I've seen a movie with him when he was followed in Paris i don't know..... You 😄 Ok then can you came undercaver to Barcelona? | She initiates the logistics talk |
| Forget I told you. It's classified. I'd have to kill you. I'm 50/50 on Barcelona | I'm not. I'm 100% because I really want to fuck her and I'm desperate to avoid the cold weather in London |

😃 yes you See that way i was not sleeping well because a small part of me was thinking that you will kill me and cat me in peaces. ..... Why you are 50/50?

Enjoys the roleplay but wants an answer on 50/50. She's invested

Pro — It's warm, I can buy duty-free wine, good tapas, I can see you. Con — I was there in January, I'm lazy

I'm trying to pull her into more investment so she'll convince me

Well if you realy want to See me you' ll came

She's holding onto her pride

Not that simple, because I can see you in Romania sometime soon. But I'm tempted. Tell me more about what's going on there for you

Trying not to be confrontational, but still trying to make her convince me

I suposed to go last year but my ex didn't like the idea of me traveling alone. So i'll go now. She is my best friend from university and basicly i'll go to See her. I will stay in her Fiat . She is married now. Flat. I can take a room in a hotel but she insisted to stay with her

Now we are discussing details openly, no coyness

So what happens if I come for a couple of days? Will she be ok with you disappearing for a couple of days?

If I book tickets, it had better be overtly agreed

Disappearing? 😃 I think she will understand. It was not in the plan to meet you

That's pretty overt but still not 100% on sex

Because I've been there a few times, I don't care about sight-seeing. I'd just come for 2 nights, I think. So we'd hang out a bit in the day, eat tapas, and you'd sleep over at my apartment.
Does that sound good?

"Sleep over at apartment" is code for sex, without being vulgar

Ok. Come after 2-3 days i'll See her

Agreed

I'll have a look at prices of flights and apartments. [I send her two options of hotel rooms, both with a double bed]Wednesday to friday looks best

So we can start checking listings, bring her into decision

Ok in România if you will came how many days? I'm looking to See where is more avantaje. But anyway we See in Barcelona there is something about us with 2 days

Agreed

did you click those links to the apartments? I like this hotel, and it's got a good deal on. Look at the photos and tell me what you think

I want her mentally signed-up to the hotel

I think is nice at least from the pictures

Agreed. Just wants me in Barcelona anyway anyhow

550 reviews on TripAdvisor, it gets 4/5. they say the same thing — nice rooms, good style, but a 5euro taxi to La Rambla. It's got free wifi too, which is important for me

Really this is just about having her know she's agreed with open eyes

Yes anyway for 2 days is perfect

Agreed

the flight time I'm considering: Wednesday, arrive 1pm. leave on Friday, 6pm

Same again. Don't leave her wiggle room to say "no" in the hotel room

Yes i'll call now my friend so
for her to know

Cooperating

Let me know what she says. If you
can confirm, I'll book my tickets
and hotel

I feel like every checkbox is ticked now. Can commit
myself

She is not answering but is ok she
will understand.

so you can confirm? I'm about to
pay, so I want to be sure

Yes be sure. I' m laufing continuslly

I don't want confusion at this stage

?

Because life is very funny. The plan
was diferent. And you were not in it 😄

Oh, that's okay

I have a tendency to disrupt
people's plans ☺

Take advantage to puff myself up

Yes i notice is something about
your energy

Great, she's rationalising why she likes me

It used to get me into trouble at
school.... hotel is booked, now for
my flight.... done. I'm going to
Barcelona on Wednesday!

Be enthusiastic about the meeting. Positive vibes

Ok we'll meet there. Have you've
done your blood test? Schizofrenia,
dementia, other deseses in your
genes?

Playful

I turn into a wolf at full moon

Mythology towards sexual predator images

I'm not worry you should
See me at a full moon

it'll be like Twilight

Ok i' ll go to make a shower

enjoy

From this point on there's no reason at all to talk about sex. Everything has been agreed, all the decisions are made. Any further mention of sex brings it out into the open and gives her forebrain a chance to get back into the battle, so it is best to leave the subject alone once plans are set. Between this chat and rolling up in Barcelona, I just give it the usual happy talk about eating tapas, visiting the Gaudi park, walking along the beach, and so on. This girl was giving full compliance without the slightest obstruction.

Now let's look at an example where I didn't correctly tick off the Long Game checklist. Sometimes it doesn't go to plan and she puts up resistance and refuses to commit. Consider the following conversation. I met this Russian girl in London while she was in the last week of her one-month study trip there. We had an idate, a Day 2, and then she was back in St Petersburg. Being Russian, she didn't kiss on the Day 2 but I still made my move in order to avoid any LJBF bullshit. We chat a while on FB and then when I'm in Latvia teaching a residential, I persuade her to come down for the day trip. We make out a lot and I almost fuck her but she's putting up heavy resistance. After another month of chat she sends me a few sexy photos but they aren't lewd enough to properly tick the checklist box. We are talking about meeting in Estonia for a weekend. I need confirmation of the shared apartment. I pick up the chat after she's booked an early bus and I'm confirming my logistics:

> I'll book my flight tonight, but can't guarantee I'll arrive before you!

Address logistical barriers overtly where possible

> what should I do?

> My flight arrives 1pm on Friday [her bus arrived 6am] Maybe you can check into a hostel and sleep a few hours

> well! I'll think of how to spend this morning in the beautiful city of Tallinn!

Just happy to be there

> I'm checking accomodation now. what do you think of this? *[link to nice apartment with double bed]*

I want her to buy into the decision, like Gabriella did

> It is nice 😊

Seems to be agreeing

It'll be £75 each, so a good price. shall I book it?
*[no answer for ten minutes]?*

I want her overt agreement on logistics

I wish you met me. But if you can't, I'll think of something :)

She's evasive, a bad sign

Yes, but there's no thursday flight. I'm getting the earliest friday flight. shall I book this apartment?

Try again for overt agreement

Thank you Nick 😊 I'll determine itself.
*[This is a "no"]*

No

? I mean for Friday and Saturday night

Still a chance she only means the early morning hostel

I don't know. What you want.... you are man!

Evasive

don't be silly. we are sharing an apartment. my question is: is this apartment suitable?

Maximum overtness. I need to know where I stand before commiting

Sweet Nicky 😊 I can't live with you in apartment because I'm a good girl, and must sleep in my own bed

So it's definitely a "no" on sharing a room

No

It's a tough call. I decide to call her bluff

Why No?

I'm not travelling to Tallinn to play childish games

I'd rather not have to do this

What? tell me please Nicky what do you want from me?

She's adamant about keeping her "out" open

You don't need to ask. You know from last time we met in Riga

if I correctly understood, you just want sex!!!!!but not me!!!!!!!
I'm sorry that you spent your time for nothing!!!! I am a serious girl!!!!!!

She's very likely to have sex but by insisting on deniability, I can't take the chance. Too far, too expensive

It's not just sex, but the sex is an important part

Don't ever deny wanting sex. It's weak

we do not know each other!!!!!! need time!!!!

"Probably yes, but I need option to refuse"

We've had 4 months and lots of contact. That's enough

I don't want to be a push-over

For me is not enough

Firm

That's not suitable for me. I'm not going to Tallinn.

So I need to push away and freeze her out a while

Well

she's not happy

I give her radio silence for a week. Although I'm 50% sure that once she's physically in front of me I can put my spell on her and get the lay, I'm just not prepared to take the risk. Most girls will sense weak boundaries and then happily piss all over them. Girls will milk weak men for attention and validation, and if you're dumb enough to let them **then you deserve it.** Women only have the power you give them.

Consider the chode move (WWCD) in this scenario. He's desperate for the sex and he's invested a lot of time and emotional energy into the long game chats. He just can't walk away. So he whines a bit and accepts her terms, triggering the "he's a sucker" subroutine in her brain. This move guarantees no sex on the trip, and he's put on the long make-him-wait treadmill that he will likely never escape. In contrast, I just threw up a hard boundary. When I meet her I fully expect to have sex and if she doesn't want that, she doesn't get the pleasure of my attention. I've triggered a different subroutine and now she's nervous about meeting my expectations. She's in the Church of Nick.

There still remains the fact that *I do want to fuck her*. So how do I deal with this obstacle? Generally you encounter non-compliance when the attraction or comfort is inadequate and you are pushing her forwards when she's not ready. This is a tightrope because you can't fall into her timetable (which is slow and requires insane investment from you) but simply walking away doesn't get you laid. So you have to pull her onto your script. So follow this basic system

1. Tell her "no." Enforce the boundary.

2. Withdraw your attention.

3. When the punishment period is over, re-engage her without reference to the argument. Be pleasant. Give her the warm feeling of having your attention.

4. Push your logistics again.

This is a very simple carrot–and–stick behavioural modification. Never forget the basic transaction underlying all male-female communication:

*Woman provides sex. Man provides attention.*

So when a recalcitrant woman is refusing to pony up the sex, you simply refuse to give her the attention she craves. She doesn't want to participate in the transaction, so you will abstain as well. It's once you get into the specifics of a given situation that this becomes an art form. Prior to sex the woman is always more willing to walk away ,unless you have successfully invested her first. By telling her "no," you are showing hard dominance and an unwillingness to be pushed around — masculine values that separate you from the pack of thirsty push-over guys. **This increases attraction.** Then by withdrawing attention, you give her a fear of loss and imprinting her hindbrain that you live by your values and are not just a bullshitter. The radio silence makes her hamster spin, as she wonders if she fucked up and what you're thinking, which anchors her further. When you finally reengage, she experiences the pleasure of regaining your attention but she's now chastised and realises it's not free — she must behave herself. By doing all of this in a socially-calibrated manner it's also an attractive demonstration of social acuity. It's actually very difficult to do well. Strong pushes are tricky.

And I'm **sure** you noticed that in the symphony of pickup this is an example of working the hot-cold contrast. She's getting her fix of drama and indignation.

Let's continue with how I reengaged her, a week later. My more savvy readers will see how precarious the frame is and how carefully I need to protect it. Ideally I'd have waited until things were stronger before mentioning Tallinn again but the planned weekend was only one week away and I simply didn't have the time to fully suck her back in. It's rare to be working under ideal conditions.

I have a job interview in 15 minutes.....

this was my first contact with her since the above excerpt

What? I don't understand.
that do you mean?

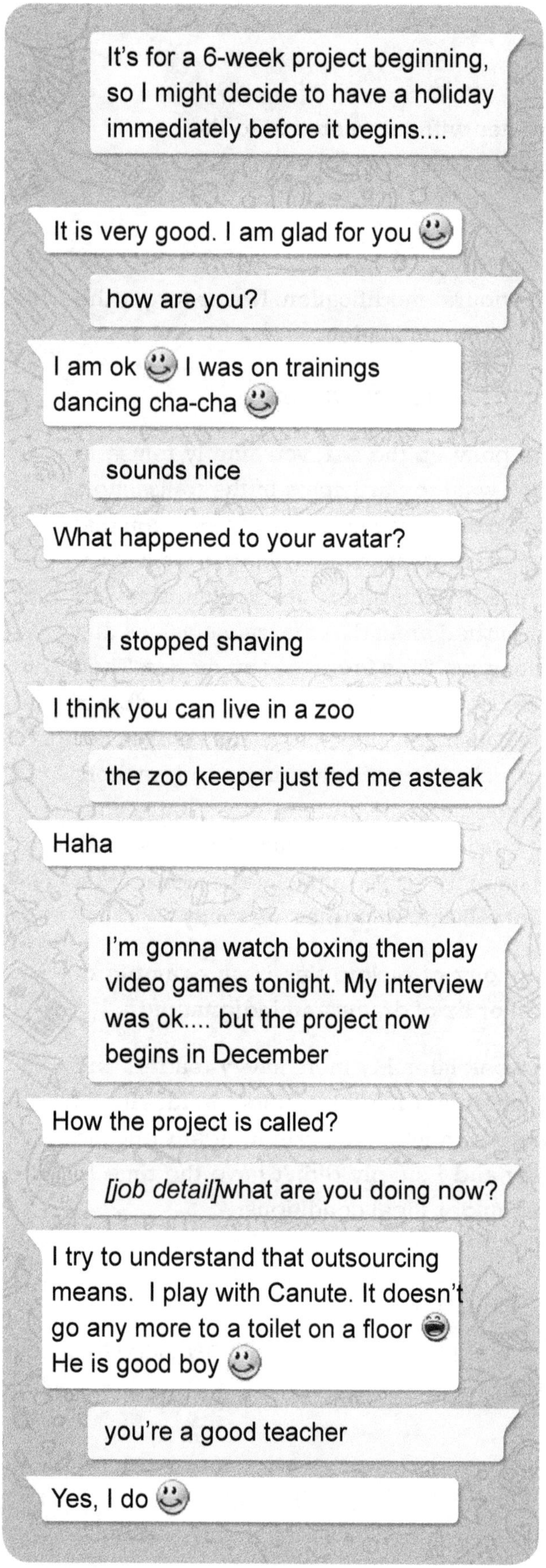

It's for a 6-week project beginning, so I might decide to have a holiday immediately before it begins....

the day after the planned trip. This is true, hence my time pressure

It is very good. I am glad for you 😊

how are you?

I am ok 😊 I was on trainings dancing cha-cha 😊

sounds nice

What happened to your avatar?

I changed my profile photo to an angry-looking gorilla

I stopped shaving

I think you can live in a zoo

the zoo keeper just fed me asteak

Haha

then a couple of hour's gap while I do the phone interview

I'm gonna watch boxing then play video games tonight. My interview was ok.... but the project now begins in December

How the project is called?

[job detail]what are you doing now?

I try to understand that outsourcing means. I play with Canute. It doesn't go any more to a toilet on a floor 😄 He is good boy 😊

Her new little puppy

you're a good teacher

Yes, I do 😊

*Yes, I am

I am sorry. Yes, I am

I decided I'm going to Tallinn next weekend. I feel like having a holiday

I decided odds are good enough to take the risk

Hmm. Well

are you still interested in going?

Obviously I need to check she didn't cancel

Why you ask me about it?

Wounded pride at earlier push-away

It'll be nice to see you again

Remind her I do actually like her

I don't change plans on 1 November

Still frosty but wants to meet. It's a pride thing

So you'd still like to meet in tallinn. Cool

We can meet at 15:00

I ignore her another couple of hours

Hey. I just finished exercise. So sweaty and smelly

I can stack away now that the agreement is reached

my god! Nick Today full moon? And you turn into the werewolf?

She's easing back into our normal vibe after tension relaxes

not so hairy. but I did shower so now I smell fresh like a field of sunflowers

Now I'm all about reparing the vibe between us

and what about your beard? It is possible to make a hairdress of it?

She's back to normal

I shaved. I am now streamlined. like a Ferrari

It is nice. I go to sleep. Good night.

good night

After this exchange I went back to normal routine maintenance My calibration tells me that this girl is a 50% chance for sex on the Tallinn trip, so it's simply a case of deciding if I'll take those odds. I'd feel much stronger if we'd had a proper sex chat, or her selfies had been more sexual, or she'd overtly agreed to the logistics but that's not always the case. Get it as strong as possible and then decide if you're willing to take a shot. One thing is clear, though. I've done as much as I can to burn it into both her fore and hindbrain that we are meeting for sex. Some girls like to evade recognition of the obvious, maintain plausible deniability, and then let the sex "just happen." I figure she is such a girl.

What actually happened was very predictable. She wanted to play the "chase me, I'm a good girl" game all weekend. Her hindbrain was fully up for the sex, but Russian girls have airtight forebrain control and are trained to hold out for commitment. So the whole weekend was a battle as I pushed for sex and she pushed for commitment. It took extremely good bedroom escalation and some good luck before I finally banged her. I'd dealt myself an uphill struggle by not ticking the boxes correctly beforehand.

## Further thoughts

Contrary to what you might think, you can still go after girls who are in steady long-term relationships. You've got two paths there. If you want to steal her away, build in more k-selection and constantly position yourself as a better deal than her boyfriend (but without ever directly talking about him). I'll often talk about "boring guys," "nice guys," and "boys" when referencing characteristics I know he has while I contrast it with "exciting guys," "high value," and "men" when positioning myself. Don't make it to obvious. Let her draw the inference.

In contrast, if all I want is the notch and perhaps a fun weekend away I'll very explicitly tell her I'm not trying to break them up. I'll present lots of r-selection, won't make any commitment promises and I'll subcommunicate that sex with me will not disturb the pattern of her life nor lead to any consequences. The whole experience is framed as an adventure. Rationalise for her how it's normal for women to want some fun before they settle down and become a wife and mother. Many people regret getting old without having really lived their life. I'm a person who loves what life has to offer. There's so much to see and do, so many adventures you can have. It seems such a waste to let opportunities pass me by because I didn't have the courage to just grab them and take a change etc and so on...

Constantly mythologise and romanticise the chats so they become larger than life. Link yourselves to famous characters, famous people, grandiose plans, adventures, exciting places. When you write words on paper it costs you nothing to dream big. Consider the difference between making a movie and writing a book about, say, a battlefield:

**Movie:** If you want a tank in the scene you have to go and hire one, or hire a CGI team to model one. Each artillery blast needs engineers to build the explosive charge, place it, monitor it safety, and detonate it. The whole scene must be correctly lit and cameras on cue. You probably need a team of lawyers and fixers to secure permission to the location and police on overtime to keep rubber-neckers off the set. It's a massive to-do.

**Book:** You want a tank, you say there's a tank. Fuck it, if you want ten tanks you just add the word "ten."

Consider how much more difficult it is to fly to the moon than to write about flying to the moon. Words are free, limited only by your imagination. So don't set your sex chats in a cheap hostel in Zone 3 of London (unless she's into this sort of thing). You might as well have them on a Seychelles beach or in a Dubai casino. If you're joking about thieving you'll be heisting the Vatican, not filling your pockets with chocolate bars from the corner grocery store. Think big. Insert yourselves into grand narratives. Make her feel like the heroine in those romance novels she reads.

# DATE
## section six

Once you get on the date, there is an ideal progression to move the girl from "attracted" to "ready for sex."

I begin with a discussion of common problems in getting the girl physically in front of you, such as her lateness and attempts to reschedule at the last minute (Venue Zero). Once she's standing there smiling at you it's time to walk her to Venue One, where you will lay the man vibe on her while drawing her into your reality. Then you'll bounce her to Venue Two to make a deeper connection and heat her up for a kiss.

I outline step-by-step progressions of the twin verbal and escalation models. Each stage forces a reaction from the girl, which you can then use to calibrate her eagerness to be escalated. Once you've kissed she's ready for Venue Three, in which you calm her down and clear any obstructions to the extraction.

# DATE

## PRE-DATE CALIBRATION PHASE

### Goal: *Find out how fast you can try to fuck her*

et's be clear from the beginning that we are trying to fuck the girl. Not "date" her, not "hang out" with her, and certainly not "enjoy her feminine presence." Those are all natural by-products of moving her along the path to fucking her, and are excuses that weaker men use when they accept less than they want. Once you've had your dick in her she'll quite naturally shower you with the affection, obedience, and attention that you crave deep in your soul. But you must be fucking her. Any other goal will immediately derail the train.

Now that we agree that the dating phase exists to get her bouncing on the end of your dick, we have to explore the method of getting there. The first step is to calibrate her. How easily does she have sex, and how easily will she have sex with you? These are the **Five Categories of Sexual Availability:**

1. Her sexuality

2. Is she single now

3. How long has it been since she had good sex

4. What is her cultural / individual script

5. How shiny are you

---

### Treadwater Dates

Girls want your attention and will shamelessly milk you for it. Just as a man wants sex and will happily take it for the lowest price available, the woman wants attention at minimum cost. You control that price. Never let yourself give it away too cheaply and never lose track of what price you've set. In the beginning, you'll have to be quite mechanical about it, making calculations. As you improve, your intuition will take care of it by giving you a gnawing gut feel of "I need to be less available now." If you give her the attention she seeks in the form of dates, text messages, rapt listening, and fun conversation, then she will milk you. The main way to prevent this is escalation — it forces the girl off the fence and to put her money where her mouth is.

AVOIDANCE WEASEL
finding ways to avoid opening since 2009

---

None of these give self-evident strategies so I'll go into each in detail....

# 1. Her Sexuality

### Attraction Threshold

*A girl's baseline of male quality that she will not go below. This is a minimum requirement for getting onto her fuck list. It is based mostly upon her self-image and reference experiences, and can raise or lower depending on her mood, ovulation, drunkenness, and perceived options.*

Generally speaking, a girl who has had lots of casual sex before is far more likely to put out than a girl who hasn't. The corollary to this rule is that the slutty girl's standards of dominance / alpha are also higher. Sluts are not easy to *every* man, they are just easier to men *above their* attraction threshold. Such a girl will have a more worn groove along the process from meeting to sex, less hangups about the physical act, will be more decisive about her interest in you and what to do about it, and just generally less nervous about being led along the path. The downsides are (i) she's far more savvy and adept at messing with your frame and filtering out pretenders, (ii) she'll have more anti-slut defence. Girls who have only banged a few men don't have Anti Slut Defence because it would never occur to them to self-identify as a slut, much less defend against it. The rule with sluts is:

*Show more hard dominance, be more of a (playful) dickhead, move her faster, show no indecision, call out the fourth wall, and make your big move on the first date.*

### Active-passive

*Human nature expects men to initiate seduction and to lead throughout. This gives men the power of choice, but also burdens them with searching costs. The flip-side for women is that they are treated with suspicion if they initiate too openly. Therefore, a woman's skill is in inducing her preferred man to initiate by sending him covert signals such as eye contact, shy smiles, and proximity. Women will only overtly initiate when the man has considerably higher SMV.*

The other end of the spectrum includes the inexperienced Good Girls with only a few sexual partners and a general nervousness around men. She hasn't been turned out and hasn't taken the active-passive control of getting herself laid. She'll dress showing less skin, evade your first few attempts to escalate, show mostly amber lights, and will generally be more haphazard in her ability to control her own signs of interest. Such girls tend to be easily bamboozled. The rule is:

*Show more soft dominance, be more dashingly romantic, move her slower, give her room to stumble to find her feet, don't break the fourth wall, and be very careful of over-escalation.*

The reality is any given girl is somewhere between the extremes. And deep down they have all come to fuck, it's just that the Good Girl's logical forebrain doesn't know how to recognise the messages her emotional hindbrain is sending her. So let's consider how to probe the girl to find out where she stands. None of these are hard and fast rules. Bear in mind also that as a girl approaches thirty you need less / weaker tells to calibrate her towards the "will have sex easily" end of the scale.

## Semantics — What is a slut?

Slut is a heavily-loaded term that most people take to describe a sexually-promiscuous or "easy" woman. This is not strictly true. Moral judgments cloud your perception of reality and prevent you from seeing what is directly in front of your face. Try to consider these concepts as descriptive or heuristic aids rather than moral imperatives.

### *A slut is merely a girl who strongly selects for r-traits*

Girls have both sexual strategies, with a preference for exciting adventure sex while at their peak 17-23 year old SMV and a preference for stable relationships and provisioning as they hit thirty, not coincidentally the time when they begin to lose significant value in the sexual marketplace. At this point, they seek to cash out with a ring on the finger. The girls are simply following their hard-coded sexual selection strategy. There is no "ought," only the "is."

People are naturally inclined to make a virtue out of necessity as an ego-protection mechanism. Like the fox in Aesop's Fable, if a man can't reach the delicious grapes hanging high on the tree, he convinces himself they are probably sour anyway. Thus K-selected men are naturally hostile towards r-selecting women. The Nice Guys don't like the girls who date Jerks. The K-selected men are so ego-invested in their pillar-of-the-community Game (which is just a moral overlay to their own sexual strategy, and poor game to boot) that they will denigrate r-selecting girls as "sluts."

Don't fall for this. Girls will pick up on your flimsy moralising, note your preference for K-selection, and thus exclude you from the (r-selected) Secret Society. I continue to use the word slut because it's a common and memorable word, but try to divorce it from your grand moral code. Sluts are merely girls who respond quickly to strong r-selection traits. They are only "easy" if you convey those traits.

A slut is not the same thing as "damaged goods." You may not wish to marry a sexually promiscuous woman, but they can still be warm, honest, interesting, and reliable company. Women who have daddy issues, bi-polar disorder, snake-like immorality and so on will be more likely to be sluts, but it's not a direct causal connection. Some sluts are very nice people.

## Slut Tells

- Showing lots of cleavage or leg (both together is a gold-digger / timewaster red flag). Generally a slut will show enough skin to trigger a sexual response in men, but won't overdo it the way an attention-whoring princess will. The former bolsters her low self-esteem with intimacy, while the latter does it by tooling people.

- Any type of body modification, such as piercings anywhere except the lower ear. The nose or high in the ear mark her as a Rebel [there are specific ways to work a Rebel]. The tongue makes her a likely Hedonist. Navel and vaginal piercings usually mark her as damaged goods, and a fast externally-referenced lay requiring hard bad boy dominance. However, there are some countries and subcultures where piercings are common, and thus do not reflect the same personality statement they do in the vast majority of western countries.

*K-selected men instinctively fear being cuckolded by exciting cads. The purity fantasy is an ego defense mechanism to reduce the anxiety caused by this fear. The men will intuitively split the female population into Good Girls (Madonnas) and Bad Girls (Whores), and then project personality traits onto them. Most notably, they project that Madonnas don't really like sex and must be slowly persuaded. This assuages the fear that their Madonna will be stolen by a more exciting r-selected man.*

- Visible tattoos signal a deliberate willingness to trade her beauty/long-term mating strategy for short-term sport sex. Just consider the character traits required to get a visible tattoo: short time orientation, lack of respect for social propriety, outsider status, impulsiveness, capacity to endure unnecessary mild pain in pursuit of a fun goal, external referencing... basically the same traits required to get fucked by lots of different partners. Now that tattoos are increasingly fashionable it's better to distinguish between "normal girl" tattoos and "bad girl/slut" tattoos. It's quite normal now for normal girls to get small modest tattoos in non-sexual locations, such as some script on their wrist or ankle. Bad girl tattoos normally have aggressive sexual symbolism such as snakes, daggers, wolves, and rebellious statements. Slogan tattoos extolling the virtues of following immediate emotions are bad-girl. If you're not sure, then watch some porn and look at the actress's tattoos.

- Any fashion or behaviour that broadcasts a message of "Fuck You" to the world. You'll notice these people display things such as an angry teenager pout, red hair, bizarre haircuts (think anything deliberately anti-Audrey Hepburn such as shaving one temple), slogan t-shirts and badges, Doctor Marten boots.

- Signs of high testosterone such as noteable height, mannish features, wide shoulders, narrow hips, hairy arms (on a non-wop), and personality traits such as competitiveness and rationality. These girls have a high sex drive and a more masculine/casual approach to sex. She'll usually have an initially strong bitchy frame and probably a professional career.

- The sex worker look. Just pay close attention to strippers and porno actresses to get a feel for this look. She'll have tired hard eyes, dry skin, slightly dishevelled clothes, and her once firm figure will be sagging a little before its natural time.

- While talking to the girl ask her where she's been. If a new London girl has already been to trashy nightclubs (Movida, Tiger Tiger, ChinaWhite etc.) or to Shoreditch, or she parties on Greek islands, then she's promiscuous. She's proceeded directly to the environments where she'll get hit on. In contrast, if she's been to libraries, museums, craft markets, and so on she's a good girl.

- More than any single tell, her relationship with her father tells you her receptivity to fast sex and hard dominance. Usually you can't get to this until deep rapport on a date. Find out if her parents are still together. Sluts usually have an absent father who left when she was young for another woman and she took her mother's side. If the father died suddenly in her teens you can expect she had a wild promiscuous period immediately afterwards. Girls always try to replicate the relationship they had with their fathers, and an absentee dad is parroted by the modern alpha cad badboy.

### Good Girl Tells

- Prim and socially proper in her grooming and fashion. Usually well-coordinated in a fashion magazine kind of way, with clean well-organised clothes.

- Her handbag will contain cute items such as a little notebook with an English flag on it, a few coloured pens, maybe a little animal on the keyring.

- She talks about having a good relationship with her parents, who are still married

- An absence of slut tells.

    You will glean lots of this information from the street stop, and you'll keep adding to her dossier as the date progresses.

## 2. Her Relationship Status And Options

Contrary to all the "boyfriend destroyer" PUA marketing guff, the reality of the pickup game is quite simple and predictable — your likelihood of fucking her increases *massively* in proportion to how dissatisfied she is with her sex life. If she's single, bored with her boyfriend, isn't getting out much, doesn't have any viable orbiters...then you become her best option and she'll be far more amenable to sex.

Probing her status is usually quite easy.

- Facebook status is single and interested in man. No recent photos of her loved up with another man. If there are photos with man in her profile, look for body language that indicates the level of closeness between them. Signs of her leaning in and attaching to the man are bad; simply being in a photo with a smiling chode is not an issue. A girl who is fully in her man's reality will display it. If she's not displaying it, she's either single or has one foot outside the relationship and is looking to jump to another branch on the tree. If you see a Russian girl with lots of holiday / nightclub photos of only her — and no man present — it's a fair bet she's got a sugar-daddy or other provider chode that she's not having sex with, or at most giving very rare missionary. She's as good as single for your purposes.

- During conversation she won't mention a boyfriend, or if she does it's obviously just a shit test.

---

### Easy Pickings

Noobs have no idea how to read girls, and therefore miss all the signals that identify an easy lay. Intermediates get a few easy lays and become addicted to them. They have learned to recognise low-hanging fruit, enabling them to filter girls and find those who are DTF. By all means enjoy this during your adventure phase, but be aware that it will prevent you from cracking the upper tiers of women. It's the equivalent of boxing children and then wondering why you aren't ready to fight Evander Holyfield. Read the signals and calibrate the girl but don't take the easy route of only chasing those who show up on your player radar as easy lays.

---

## 3. Her Recent Sex

Have you ever tried to sell food to a man walking out of a restaurant licking his lips and patting his belly? Human appetites for food, drink, sleep, and sex are in a constant cycle of building up pressure, taking action to relieve pressure, then doing nothing while satiated. A hungry girl is far easier to fuck than her satiated sister. Later in the date we'll go into escalation methods to trigger her hunger responses, but aside from her immediate short-term appetite there's also her medium-term satiation. Is she getting laid and is she enjoying it?

This is quite an intimate subject, so initially you'll be looking for covert signals rather than coming out and asking. Once you have deep rapport you can become more overt in mining information about her recent sexual history. A girl not getting laid is a horny girl. Starting with covert:

- Horny girls find ways to separate themselves from the herd. A girl loved up with a boyfriend will often stay shuttered in the office / home when not out in public on his arm. She'll be in the middle of her rowdy girl-pack in bars, and shopping with her BFF when you see her at the mall. In contrast, a horny girl's hindbrain will subtly pilot her into public places alone where men could make themselves available — shopping alone, reading a book in the park alone, sipping coffee in Starbucks alone.

- Horny girls often look approachable. She'll have a slower, dreamier walk. Her eyes will wander around. She'll tend not to be glued to her smartphone, and if she's wearing headphones and looking down it'll be because she's lost in thought — her face won't have that "don't talk to me I'm busy" look.

- Horny girls show their figure. In hot weather and from suitable cultures, they'll show alot of skin, in particular their legs and stomach. Even Arabs and Turks will show their figures, covered by tight-fitting thin material such as spray-on jeans and a long-sleeved t-shirt.

Once you are talking to a horny girl you are looking for receptivity, sparkly eyes, and a big smile. She's not getting sex, so her hormones are pushing her to be pleasant with men. Remember, she's a hungry person eyeing up the buffet. A satiated girl doesn't have the same interest. Her attitude is more like "Show me what you've got, and it must be better than what I'm already getting" — it's more challenging.

Overt probing will be asking if she has a boyfriend, when was the last time she had sex, what is important in her life right now, and of course just noticing the absence of her talking about men she's dating.

# 4. Her Script

In ethnomethodological terms, humans are actors. In any given social interaction they only have access to a small number of roles, each subject to following a particular script. Consider for a moment these situations: house-hunter and estate agent, police detective and witness, job interviewer and job interviewee. In such formally-structured situations it's easy to see that the situation defines the purpose of the interaction, that each person has a clearly-defined role and that his role imposes upon him a certain code of conduct. These expectations enable his behaviour in some areas, and limit it in others. It would be very unusual for a witness to start interrogating the detective, and the latter would immediately assert the frame with "I ask the questions here."

People follow scripts. When confronted with a new interaction, each person will instantaneously sift through their script library and pull out the one they deem most suitable. They will then follow it. Thus begins the frame battle. Frame control is the ability to impose your interpretation of the situation and thus lead the girl into using a script you like. Before any of that happens, you need to recognise her default script. It differs depending on the girl and her situation, but you'll encounter one particular script over and over again.....

## Default Hot Young Girl Script #1 —
### "I'm the value, men are fungible"

Most men are utterly unattractive and utterly clueless when compared to an experienced player. Conversely, every hot young woman is a rock star of the dating world. Consider such a girl's experience growing up — when she wants something, she gets it. When she doesn't want something, it goes away. Whether the male enabler is her father, her teacher, her government, her orbiter, or her boyfriend, she is used to making demands and having her reality enabled by men. This constantly reinforces the idea that the only action she needs is to make a demand, and the only consequence she ever sees is being provided for. I don't wish to cast this girl as an ogre, since even the sweetest girls live in this bubble until they hit The Wall. In biological terms, her solipsism in this regard is completely natural becuases he has extremely high sexual market value relative to the hordes of thirsty beta guys. Her script leads to her extreme savvy at two things:

1. Get things from men

2. Stop men fucking her

Every hot young girl is demanding and obstructionist. To a male mind, this looks like a strong frame because a man must eke out his living against a hostile unforgiving world. Through a lifetime of being tempered by the fires of daily life, a demanding man is usually a confident man and one that chases girls effectively must also be competent. We project these same virtues onto women without realising that **anyone can be demanding and obstructive when the entire social structure is designed to help her do so**. In reality, all women have a weak frame because outside of these narrow boundaries they've never had to face a hostile world to get things done. They've never been into the furnace that forges the steel.

Most hot young girls have a brittle Potemkin frame that has been bolstered by thousands of easy victories against soft targets — beta males. They are utterly unprepared for situations where they really want something and must work for it... such as dating an alpha male. Suddenly, all those little tricks and rules that allowed her to wrap betas around her fingers fall flat on their faces when confronted with a man with options. She can't understand him. She doesn't have the experience of dealing with such a rare beast. So she flounders. In particular:

1. She can't control the raging hormones he has unleashed, so she'll flap around with unmanaged desire and occasional terrified snapbacks into coldness.

2. She can't predict his behaviour, such as why he doesn't answer her questions or jump to attention when she beckons.

She loves this puzzling experience because it's connecting deep in her core, and this unsettling is the path to fucking her BUT... you have to get her off the default script. As long as she's trying to make the default script work, there'll be no transaction. Buyer and seller are trading non-convertible currencies.

*Some girls are so committed to their default script that they would rather burn the whole process and make themselves unhappy than to switch script.*

This is a sad part of dating that I still haven't solved. You cannot remain on her default script, or else you'll jump through the same hoops as every other chump without getting sex. You must push your frame and elegantly switch scripts before she even knows she's reading for a different role. That is the true skill of frame control.

The earlier you "flip the script" the better. Preferably you'll do it in the very opening seconds of the street stop, so that she never gets momentum with her default script. Sometimes the girl is too committed to her script, so you must slowly frame-creep on her in texts (see Text Phase) and then do the big transition on the date using your masculine presence. Sometimes you'll do a nuclear **frame crush** to obliterate her first, other times you'll subtly nudge her onto your track. But for now, just hold the central theoretical point in your mind — you need to flip the script.

Different cultures will have variations. The most extremely unfavourable cultures are at opposite ends of the permissiveness scale. On one extreme, the hook-up culture of the Anglosphere creates legions of what I call the Vile American Whore, in which the girls are tainted, unpleasant, and stick religiously to the princess-slut script. At the opposite extreme are the traditional Muslim cultures full of Frustrated Arab Slaves, where society has covered the simmering water of sexuality with such a tight-fitting lid that after years of boiling the lid flies off in an explosion of illicit sex... usually with me on her holiday to London. Girls at both extremes can be flipped. Personally I prefer the centre-right... traditional good girl Slavs who are permitted to have a little fun before a mid-twenties marriage. I'm going to be that fun.

**Frame Crush**

*A series of strong attacks on her frame in rapid succession in an attempt to obliterate it through brute force.*

# 5. How Shiny Are You?

There's an old trick for us wandering nomads that I first heard from Roosh. When arriving in a foreign country, just spend an hour walking around the main streets and keep an eye for how many women check you out. If it's a lot, then that's your country. If it's none, get back on the plane. Your shininess across countries will be vastly different and it is not based on money. For example, I draw plenty of IOIs in these countries and girls there have told me I'm very good-looking:

- Serbia
- Belarus
- Czech Republic

- Russia
- Kazakhstan
- Turkey

I don't mean empty flattery. I mean girls have looked me dead in the eyes and told me sincerely and unbidden that I'm very good-looking. I'm a white-skinned blue-eyed blonde with angular features and serious eyes, the polar opposite of a swarthy wide-eyed wop pretty boy. Unsurprisingly, it's precisely the countries that produce such pretty-boys in industrial quantities where I get the biggest IOIs. Russians and Serbs like my hard features and poker face. Turks and Kazahks like my blue eyes and fair skin. In Brazil it was the voluptuous black girls who eye-fucked me on the street, not the whiteys.

In contrast, I draw zero IOIs from British girls. None. I have to work for every scrap of attraction and I don't have the patience for it.

I've gone into detail on ethnicity because I travel a lot, but the same principles also apply to age and social scene. If you're playing guitar in an indie band you are shiny in that scene. If you're a tall young good-looker in a meat market nightclub you are shiny there. If you are a low-energy intellectual story-teller you are shiny in a cafe. Find your niche. Figure out where you are shiniest and concentrate your initial efforts on playing to your strengths. After you become comfortable in your ideal setting, you can push out of that comfort zone.

## Pussy Paradise

Any time a man is dissatisfied with his ability to pull women in his own city he will begin to dream of the mythical pussy paradise where it will all come easy. This is wishful thinking. Some places are better than others, but there is no place in the world where beautiful young women are easy to seduce. It may be easier to reach hook point in certain places (e.g. New York), or get a coffee date (Moscow), or even get a makeout (Brazil) but the crucial milestone of putting your dick inside her is equally difficult everywhere. When you do decide to travel, do so after you've already begun to succeed with your local girls. This way, you can be sure you are travelling from a position of strength rather than avoidance, and your game will be tight enough to get a reasonable standard of girls in any country.

Don't be fooled by the smoke and mirrors. High value women do not sleep with low value men. If you see cases which seem to consistently break this rule, then look closer. There's something you're not seeing.

AVOIDANCE WEASEL
finding ways to avoid opening since 2009

*Desperate To Fuck. A girl's libido will often shut down when there is an absence of men in her vicinity. This is a protective measure to avoid pregnancy by beta males. From time to time pressure will build, especially around her peak ovulation, causing her body to cry out for a man. To relieve this pressure she will dress sexy and put herself into areas containing men. She is DTF. These girls require very little Game. It is enough to find them and lead them quickly to sex.*

Shininess is mostly effective for quick grotty sex, and will burn out fast if not bedded down with real substance. The four classic examples are:

1. Horny **DTF** girl goes to nightclub to get laid then picks shiniest guy for SNL.

2. Horny DTF tourist wandering streets of foreign city. Shiny guy persuades her to have holiday adventure sex.

3. Bored / angry / unsatisfied woman in long relationship has mid-term momentum for novelty sex. An opportunity presents itself with sufficiently shiny guy so she takes it.

4. Bored girl in boring life suddenly approached by shiny foreign guy on holiday. Whirlwind consequence-free romance then he leaves.

I've done all of these and heartily recommend it. The caveat is that it only works on Yes Girls, and you'll not get top tier girls this way. Being shiny should be used as spice to flavour your game, and employed as part of a fundamentally sound interaction rather than a crutch to avoid doing things right.

### Closing Your Mind

Reading a girl is crucial for collating the information you need to calibrate her and decide how to seduce her. It comes with a warning: If you are excessively rigid in categorising her, you will lose the flexibility to respond to feedback that doesn't fit with the box you put her in. Calibration information in this book helps you play the percentages, but there will always be girls who don't fit, or are not able to be immediately categorised. Do not lose your ability to update your read on the fly as new information comes in, or use your read as a buffer to avoid approaching or escalating a particular girl.

A common avoidance weasel is the Initimidating Back-Story Weasel. This occurs when you construct an elaborate cold read of a girl's likely lifestyle, which puts her out of your league so you don't approach. For example, Bodi once saw a tall model-esque blonde and by the time he'd finished his pre-approach cold read he was out of the set. He'd decided she was probably an ex-cheerleader dating a local footballer and holidaying in the Bahamas on a local industrialist's yacht. That's an example of over-doing it. He approached her anyway and found out she worked in a jewelry shop, was single, and bored with her life. You never really know until you flip the stone.

# Ambient Logistics

So now we've gone over the five factors to judge how easy the girl will be based on her general life situation and upbringing. The biggest factor, however, I've kept separate due to its overwhelming importance — **Logistics**. Perfect logistics could get you a same day lay with a girl who wouldn't even return your texts if the logistics were sub-par. That's why you must **always** probe logistics during the initial street stop. Always. Without exception. I've separated them into two categories:

> **Ambient logistics:** What is her life status right now, this minute, today, this week relative to yours? Does she have the "motive" and "opportunity" for this crime of passion?
>
> **Sex logistics:** How close is she to an acceptable sex location, and how much time do you have left to work her? This is the "means."

Fellow daygamers will talk about the *planets aligning* or *ticking the checkboxes*. What we mean is that there are a set of conditions, within very narrow parameters, that determine if you have a reasonable chance to fuck a girl who isn't strictly-speaking available. She isn't low-hanging fruit, at least in the definition of my five categories above. Rather, you are operating under unusual End Of The World circumstances where the girl will take one last fuck before the zombies overrun the bunker.

*The easiest way to get laid in daygame is to trawl the streets for solo tourists at 8pm and then bounce them to your house around the corner.*

That's the bread and butter SDL because ambient and sex logistics have aligned with the Five Categories of Sexual Availability. It doesn't happen a lot, but be alive to the possibility .

# YOUR GAME PLAN

## *Goal: Form a clear plan of how the date will progress*

Now that you've calibrated the girl you should have a fairly good idea how "on" it is and whether you'll be pushing for the Day 2 lay, or taking it a bit slower. This section is written assuming the fast lay with some light diversions when circumstances require you to take your foot off the pedal. Drill it into your mind that your goal is to get laid. You need the purity of intent to drive you forwards and to give off all the subtle signals that you won't be strung along. She'll sense this and will forego the usual games on her Default Script.

## The Extraction Path

The venues, times, and activities are all under your control. Depending on your circumstances you'll be choosing between one of two options:

1.  **Meet central** — You meet her in the centre of town, run the date there and then hop in a cab back to your house together.

2.  **She comes to you** — Meet her at the nearest plausible venue to your house and then bounce her ever closer until you are walking past your house.

In rare cases where you have fantastic logistics (e.g. you live near Oxford Street, or you take a holiday apartment in the Old Town), you can do (1) without needing the cab so it's the best of all worlds. Most of the time you won't have that working in your favour.

Generally speaking, it's easier to meet the girl centrally. It'll freak her out less and give more plausible deniability until you've built up strong enough momentum to take the Leap Of Faith with the cab. In cases where you can't fuck her on the first date, try to get the second date near (or at) your house. You'll have a bit more hand over her by this point.

There's a deeper choice underlying your date venue choices based on how "on" the girl is. The more on she is, the more you can push for her meeting near you. In this case you plan your final bounce (to your house / sex location) and then work backwards to figure out how to channel her bounce-by-bounce to that location. In contrast, if the girl isn't super on you'll be planning the date from the beginning forwards. Figure out where she's most likely to accept a meeting and then plan your subsequent bounces to end nearer your house and by a taxi rank. For example:

1. Meet in front of Top Shop on Oxford Street. First venue is a pub on Carnaby Street. Second venue is another pub 100m from there. Last venue is a dark wine bar off Regent Street. Final push is to flag a cab as you walk down Regent Street.

2. Meet at my local tube station in Zone 2. First venue is a pub a five minute walk up the bank. Second venue is a pub a few more minutes up that bank. Then the final push is a fish and chips shop another few minutes up, a Tescos a few minutes again (for wine) and then suddenly we are two minutes from my front door. I've used the bounces to cover what is otherwise a fifteen-minute uphill walk.

This is all within your control. Scout your area and put together a string of venues. You want them to be in as straight a line as possible from the train station to your house, while also getting progressively darker and intimate. But ultimately don't obsess — **the big compliance test is getting her into the taxi**. If she does that, it doesn't matter how long the journey takes. She's up for it. Really, I cannot emphasise this point enough — the biggest leap of faith is getting into the taxi at the end of Venue Three.

## Assess Her Appearance

The first moment you lay eyes on her you need to be reading her appearance for signs that she's come to fuck. She's had time to plan her look, so her choices will clearly signal her intentions. Factors to consider are:

- Wearing a dress or skirt is good. Not only is she showing her legs, but she's also being feminine and giving something that can be easily lifted up. Trousers are less promising, but if they are tight and figure-hugging it's still a good sign.

- Did she take time to do her hair and makeup to look nice? Is she wearing jewellery and accessories? If so, it's a good sign. She wants to look pretty for you so you'll like her.

- Is she doing anything that prevents her from giving you full attention, such as yapping on her mobile phone as she arrives or carrying shoppings bags (to imply you are an afterthought to her day)? The best case scenario is that she's cleared the whole evening just for this date.

- High heels or sexy boots? Great. She's thinking of sex and willing to endure discomfort to make a good impression on you.

- Can you see the outline of a thong or lingerie beneath her skirt? Try touching her lightly on the hip as you kiss her cheek to feel for the outline. Sexy underwear is a big green light. Aunt Mavis pantaloons are a red light.

- Later on the date when verbally escalating you can ask the colour of her underwear. Light colours or white are a sure sign it's on. Dark or black underwear, or non-sexy cut of underwear, is indicative of her period.

These signs are all relative to how she looked when you first met. If she's a hipster in the street stop, just be pleased if she washed herself before the date. If she's Russian, then she puts on heels and skirt just to get milk from the corner shop and you should adjust your expectations accordingly.

## Assess Her Initial Behaviour

A girl who is really on will be actively cooperating to get herself into your bed. She usually won't take the lead or give strong green lights, but she will constantly ease herself into situations where escalation is possible and she'll offer very little obstructionism or testing. Roughly speaking, you can divide girls on the first date into these categories, which determine how you fine-tune your date game:

**Super on** — She's really into you, hasn't had sex for a while and is really hoping you'll fuck her. She'll arrive on the date dressed up nice and showing skin. She'll greet you with a beaming smile and sparkling eyes. She may even start doing light kino, such as pawing your arm as you do the Hello Kiss or voluntarily hanging onto your arm as you walk her to the first venue. When you buy the first round she'll say, "I'm having what you're having." You'll have her full attention and she'll be making conversation from the beginning. There'll be a vibrant happy energy to her and lots of little signals of sexual availability. She'll jump you on the first kiss close attempt, which should come early in the date. She'll happily comply with every leap of faith moment. When you fuck her you'll tell your friends "I didn't have to do much, just kinda fell into place."

**Stealth on** — This is a special class of girl who is quite socially inhibited, probably young, and doesn't have much experience with her side of the dance. She won't have very good fashion nor conversational ability. She doesn't know how to flirt and kino. But she's still *very horny and wants to fuck*. Often you'll find yourself on dates looking at her stony face, enduring long silences, seeing zero IOIs and you wonder "What the hell am I doing here with such a dead fish? Why did she even come on this date if she's going to act so cold to me?" Yes, why did she come? There's *always* a reason she's there. She wants sex. She just doesn't know how to move herself towards it. This is where you really need to take the lead and escalate on amber lights. The big difference between a Stealth On and a Timewaster is compliance. This girl follows your lead like a dumb animal. She'll tentatively accept the first kiss close attempt, probably in the middle of the date, and meekly accept each leap of faith moment first time. When you fuck her you'll tell your friends "I had no idea she was so up for it."

**Normal on**–She's a more controlled, more inhibited version of the Super On girl. She definitely likes you and is open to the idea of getting man/woman with you but she doesn't need it in the same way. These are the most common girls. She'll let you lead while doing her normal data collection and shit testing. She won't pro-actively touch you like the Super On girl, nor will she be so buzzing with pleasant energy. She's just… normal. She'll probably decline your first couple of kiss close attempts with rationalisations of "This is too fast" or "I'm not that kind of girl" while her body language is screaming *try again a bit later*. She'll block some of the leap of faith moments or throw out a mild shit test, basing her compliance on how well you deal with it. There'll be mild LMR during bedroom escalation. When you fuck her you'll tell your friends "Just routine textbook stuff."

**Suspicious on** — This is the most common girl you'll get when you are redlining the car and pulling above your class. She's intrigued rather than actively fancying you. You are a very interesting exhibit in the Gallery Of Life, so she is compelled to make a close inspection. She likely thinks you're a player and considers it a mild negative. She's wondering how often you do this and how you got so good at it, but dammit she's enjoying the experience so much she's going along for the ride. It's highly likely that she doesn't expect to fuck you and has some pre-determined line in the sand she won't go beyond (which you can still cross with tight game). She'll evade and block your first half dozen kiss close attempts to see how you react, and then when she finally accepts it it'll be like she was super on from the beginning. Expect every leap of faith moment to come with an initial refusal. Probably once or twice on the date she'll do something really annoying designed to derail the train. Don't react. When you fuck her you'll tell your friends a long convoluted fish story full of the inspired Game you pulled out at the perfect moments. You'll pat yourself on the back and think, "I rock."

**Timewaster** — This is common when your Game is much tighter than your calibration, or when your front-end Game is tighter than your mid- and endgame. You made such a great impression on the street stop and texts that she just wants the dating experience. She's unavailable or doesn't fancy you, but the experience of being in your company and watching you showcase high skill is just too good a diversion to turn down. So she's here to soak up your value and attention. You won't fuck her. The main way to spot these girls is that they are spectators. She'll offer very little to the date and expect you to entertain her. She won't really flirt. Unlike the Stealth On, she'll probably have good social skills and keep things going (in a social direction, not sexual) any time you drop the ball. She'll artfully dodge leap of faith attempts by diverting you in another direction because she doesn't want to say "no," since that would end the sideshow.She also won't say "yes" because she's not here to fuck. Filter her out by escalating quickly — going for the kiss within an hour and giving her The Talk if she refuses three kiss attempts.

Usually I adopt a four-venue structure where the penultimate venue has logistics to either fuck the girl (a disabled toilet nearby) or push her into a taxi for the sex location (Venue Four). I usually won't pull the trigger on the first date because it's so high-risk and completely unnecessary in most cases. Banging the girl on the first date is usually an ego issue where you're trying to tick the PUA checkboxes, or otherwise a sign that you're dating the wrong women. If you can't stand giving a girl two evenings of your time, perhaps you should be shooting for higher quality.

That said, during your Adventure Phase (the period in your pick-up career where you're finally getting laid regularly and are thus gorging yourself, rolling around like a pig in shit) you'll probably want to redline it and crash the car a few times. Once that's out of your system, I recommend defaulting to a two-date bang structure.

This book presents it as a one-date structure for simplicity's sake. To make it a two date structure, simply follow the one-date model but:

1. Don't push beyond The Kiss on the first date. Once you've kissed to covertly agree to the deal, you hold it at that intensity. Do not escalate further that evening.

2. For date two you can arrange to meet her nearer your home (if you sense it's really on). Otherwise just start date two from Venue Two.

Everything else is the same. You'll encounter far less LMR if you let it go two dates and allow a few days between them. So, on with the first date...

# VENUE ZERO — MEETING

## Goal: Get her physically in front of you without losing the frame.

**Spike**

*A statement or behaviour that conveys sexual intent and causes the girl to think about sex, with a resulting "spike" in her heartrate. These are usually surprises inserted into a non-sexual conversation in order to maximise the fractionation and display greater confidence and unpredictability.*

Meet her near an underground station in a bustling entertainment district. In London this will be somewhere such as Oxford Circus, Covent Garden, or Earls Court. If you're on a Euro-tour there'll be a landmark meeting point in the centre of the Old Town such as Republic Square in Belgrade, Jelacic Square in Zagreb, the old church in Tallinn and so on. Girls are naturally nervous about going on dates with a man they met in the street,so make the very beginning of the date super-safe. She's meeting you in a bright lively central place so her immediate thoughts of being murdered are calmed. Be on time because you're a man of your word and you also begin social interactions by playing it straight. Once the interaction has become "real" (usually soon after hook point on the street stop), you want to keep that real momentum and avoid slipping back into gamey attraction any longer than it takes to **spike**. Turning up fashionably late slides backwards into being gamey. Follow the golden rule:

*Reward good behaviour.*
*When she is real with you, be real with her.*

**Silly Buggers**

*Game-playing by the girl designed to frustrate, unbalance, and unravel the seduction. These tactics violate the expected boundaries of polite behaviour. Turning up excessively late, throwing a hissy-fit, and trying to take the lead are common examples. Also known as Princess Behaviour.*

Forget the tall stories you read on internet forums about breathlessly complicated dates that lead to funny lays. If you have to make it complicated and rescue the lay with swirly-twirly PUA magic then you are doing it wrong. Tight game is smooth game with minimal road bumps.

How about if your spider sense is tingling that she might stand you up? Something in her replies seems flaky and non-committal, so you're concerned about travelling all the way into town just to stand around for half an hour before she no-shows. Don't put yourself in that position. I like to send a no-show pre-emption text. Just before you'd need to leave the house text her "Hey crazy ☺ I'm running late. Can we push it back to [half an hour later]?" If she agrees it's game on. If she doesn't reply then do not go. Accept that she's unlikely to show, and you need to give her a week's radio silence minimum.

## A late change of plan

Some girls will text you shortly before the date to cancel, postpone, venue change, or otherwise fuck with you. As your calibration improves your intuition will tell you if she's playing **silly buggers** or has a legitimate reason for the change. Until then, consider these factors:

- How long before the date did she message? If it's over an hour and she's cancelling/ postponing it's not so bad. Over two or more hours is acceptable politeness. Less than an hour to do anything other than ask to delay by 30 minutes or so is just rude / playing silly buggers. Whatever the reason, just wait a while then text "ok" like it's no big deal.

- Her attempts to venue change are a frame-snatch. Don't stand for it. She might say something like "I'm in Starbucks [ten minutes away]. Come meet me here!" No. Do not go to her. She knows the rule about following the man's lead and respecting his boundaries, so texts like this are fucking with you. You need to snatch the frame and give her a hoop. Reply with "I'm still shopping. Text me when you've finished your coffee," or "No worries, come over when you're done."

- Did she give a counter-offer, e.g. "Hey, I'm really sorry but I'm having to stay late at work :/ Can we do it tomorrow instead?" This is likely a genuine excuse. Remember, you can't expect to be a high priority in her life yet because you're just a street stop and a few texts into the model. Do not ever immediately reply to bad news texts or you'll imprint onto her hindbrain that you jump when she clicks her fingers. Let her sweat a little then reply "Sure. Let's confirm tomorrow."

- How apologetic is she? Does she apologise and explain the reasons why? That's a good thing because she feels accountable to you. In contrast, if you're getting a terse brush-off you should next her.

So you're waiting at the meeting point for her to show. Chill out. Don't stress. Remember she's just a girl and the streets are full of them. You may be tempted to get some performance anxiety and repeat mantras along the lines of "don't fuck up, don't fuck up," or maybe you're rehearsing stories or body language cues. Don't bother, just calm down. It's like studying the morning before an exam — if you don't know it by now, you won't know it. And she's coming on a date with you, so you DO know it — she fancies you. Don't keep scanning the streets for her or she'll see the over-eagerness. Just lean up against a wall or sit down, get comfortable and let your mind wander. Control your breathing and posture to reduce your heart rate and chill your vibe.

So now she's arrived. Give her a smile, let her walk to you, and give her a European-style kiss on each cheek (and remember a hand on the outside of her hip to check for a thong). You should be immediately leading with a positive vibe, even if you're a bit narked over the rigmarole of getting her to this point. Girls live in the moment, so whatever happened to get to this point can be erased from the record. Make some quick small talk of the how-are-you?-it's-a-nice-day variety. Look her up and down and give a mild physical compliment — "mmmm, you look nice" — then start walking her to the first venue making light chat about what you've both been doing today.

## She's late

When dealing with young women and big cities, some degree of lateness is inevitable. It's not an attack on you, it's not disobedience. When you're dealing with a foreign tourist / student in London you must accept that she's disorganised, she doesn't really know how long journeys take, and that public transportation is unreliable. I'd consider waiting up to fifteen minutes completely normal, no cause for concern or rebuke. Longer than that and I'll text her, do something else, and make her come to me. For example, say we've agreed to meet at Top Shop at 7pm and she hasn't shown up or messaged me, it's now 7:15pm:

**Me:** I'm here, can't see you
**Her:** [should respond that she's on the way] I'm stuck on the bus! I'll be there in ten minutes!
**Me:** I'll be browsing menswear. Text me when you arrive
**Her:** Ok 😊
**Her:** [ten minutes later] I'm here!!

In this case it's no harm no foul. Just proceed as if she'd turned up on time. Oftentimes she's not actually able to reply because she's underground with no signal. In this case just wander off somewhere nearby and wait for her "I'm here" text. Then tell her "Five minutes. Wait!" and go collect her. If she's horrendously late (an hour or more), then accept she's broken the date vibe so badly that you repairing it would irretrievably kill your value. You must therefore hold your ground, set her a big hoop, and see what she does:

**Her:** [an hour late] I'm here! Where are you?
**Me:** [wait exactly five minutes] I'm in The Cock, just behind Top Shop. [don't invite her to join]
**Her:** I'm coming!!!!

There's no excuse for her being an hour late without fair warning. The medium is the message and her lateness is telling you she's not accountable to you and she doesn't respect your boundaries. In these situations I go into Frame Crush Mode and absolutely hammer her. She needs telling off. If she absorbs, then she's worked her way back into the land of adults and I can be real with her again. If she rejects it, then she's a rude dumb bitch and fair game for anything your intuition tells you to do, such as full-asshole escalation. Generally girls will take their medicine and accept their telling off.

Now is not the time to be diving into rapport or long DHVs. Keep it short, light, and pleasant like talking to your grandmother or the vicar. A sample conversation:

| | |
|---|---|
| *Me:* | How was your day? |
| *Her:* | Oh, just another day at work! Quite busy |
| *Me:* | Cool. I've been in a café reading War and Peace |
| *Her:* | Really? What's it like? |
| *Me:* | It's so slow. I swear Tolstoy never crossed out a sentence in his life. |
| *Her:* | haha. I never read him |
| *Me:* | I love this weather. |
| *Her:* | Me too |
| *Me:* | We're just going down here. It's a nice café. |
| *Her:* | Ok |

You see how inane and boring that is? The whole point of Venue Zero is to act like a normal person and put her at ease so that she will be receptive to the comfort and attraction you run once at Venue One. I've tried many variations that don't work, so though this may appear slow I fully believe in the principle of Venue Zero. Don't immediately go all fake-alpha on her by skipping pleasantries and saying "Come on, follow me." Don't launch into an attraction spike. Don't start escalating kino. Don't put her on your arm unless she seems amenable. Do not hold her hand.

# VENUE ONE — BRIGHT, BUSY AND NON-ALCOHOLIC

***Goal: Settle her down so she is willing and motivated to open up to you while you also begin to weave your reality around her.***

## Player Trap

*Men playing an r-selection game are rare, and there is usually a moment when the girl realises you are not just another typical Nice Guy. She will then test her conclusion by setting Player Traps — shit tests designed to determine if the man is faking it (and really a Nice Guy) and, if genuine, whether he is an honest seducer or a lying cad.*

I will usually choose an independent café or tea shop for the first venue. Don't worry about such places setting an LJBF vibe. Your spiking and body language will keep it away from platonic. Advanced players are in something of a **Player Trap**, where we are so good at Game that girls become suspicious about it and naturally let their brains spin out of control with derailment thoughts: does he do this with all the girls? How many girls does he talk to? Is he trying to fuck me tonight? Does he think I'm cheap, is that why he picked me?

Once your game is super tight, you need to deploy anti-Player Vibe ordnance. This is why you act so normal at Venue Zero and you don't try to take her to a sleazy lounge bar from the beginning (she has to wait two hours for that!). So keep it clean, kids. Right from the beginning you are setting the frame with these principles:

- The only thing I bring to the date is me. I'm good enough as I am.

- The adventure is here, in me. It's not out there in the activity.

- I'm here to get to know you, not to entertain or impress you.

- This is the most normal thing in the world.

- Yes, I find you attractive but I haven't made my mind up yet what / if I want from you

These are all covertly communicated through body language, vibe, and how you steer conversations. Do not overtly state them unless you have to make a conscious decision to break the fourth wall. Girls always prefer covert communication and will move closer to you that way. Stating something overtly is usually an admission of failure in conveying it covertly, which girls will usually punish you for.

So you arrive in the first venue and you are leading. You were walking slightly ahead, deciding where to turn and when to stop. Lead her directly to the counter so she can check the menu. Then tell her you'll get the first drinks in while she finds a good table. You'll be sporadically giving her little jobs to do throughout the date to build an Our World and get her comfortable with complying. Sit directly opposite her, preferably with your back to the wall so you can see the café and she can only see you and the wall. That will help focus her on you and avoid distractions, but don't stress if the seating doesn't work like that. If you have to sit side-by-side or in an L-shaped corner that's less desirable, but angle yourselves so you get full direct eye contact. You must have sustained easy eye contact from the beginning.

If you think the girl is Super On, consider tweaking this stage slightly to be seated on stools at the bar in a place serving alcohol. You get all the advantages of face-to-face rapport but you're also sitting close enough to trigger nature's proximity triggers and you can test kino far more naturally. In any other situation just run the default model.

### Long walks

I've tried dates where the first venue is going for a walk in the park or along the riverbank. This is bad. You have poor eye contact, too much activity, and never really settle into a conversation. Save it for between venues. If it's a beautiful day it might seem weird to stay indoors, so choose a café with pavement seating, a pub with a beer garden, or sit on the grass in a park. Just be sure you are across from each other and looking face-to-face with good eye contact.

**Parody Chode**

*Purposefully exaggerating the behaviours of a Nice Guy in order to covertly demonstrate you know how they play the game and that you are different. Unlike overchoding, Parody Chode is purposefully ironic so she knows you are joking. It's a proactive form of Agree & Amplify, dismissing the K-selection frame and giving her permission to trigger her r-selection strategy.*

Because of the newness of the date and the non-threatening logistics, you have a great opportunity to pour masculine subcommunication into the interaction without any danger of her leaving. Make use of it. Lean back in your seat and let your body language be open and take up space. Talk quite slowly and put all your movements on slow motion. I picture myself as a lazy lion sleeping in the savannah — the lion does what he wants and won't be rushed. Every movement is lethargic and on your own terms. Don't overdo it, just have the mental image and check yourself against it to ensure you don't rush or get fidgety.

I usually begin with simple chit-chat about her day while I look for a jumping-off point into more colourful and engaging conversation topics. For the first half hour you'll be dropping in occasional monologues about things that are interesting to you, what in old-school terminology would be called DHVs. However, the frame is that you aren't trying to impress her, so be careful how thickly you lay it on. Use the props and ambience to launch naturally into them. For example, say you are in a traditional tea shop and the teapot arrives. As you are pouring you may say…

"I love these traditional old china teapots. There's something about them that Starbucks paper cups simply cannot replicate. When I was a child we used to always go to my grandmother's for Sunday lunch. Proper English style with roast beef, mash, gravy. After lunch we'd all be sitting back in our chairs with our bellies bursting out our shirts then my gran would come in with a tea trolley. There'd be a little tin of homemade biscuits and this lovely old china teapot."

And leave it at that. Let her pick up the conversation, which will probably mean she'll coo at your story and then talk a little about herself and tea. Don't rush to fill any silences. Just quietly pour your tea and hers, take a sip and let your eyes wander around the room until the next conversational thread occurs to you. I used to over-egg date conversation by making everything coming out of my mouth a DHV or some deep rapport. It's way too early for that. Probably 50% of my words will be normal mundane chit chat… for example:

> Me: So tell me more about this dress design thing [or whatever her hobby/job is]
> Her: Well I used to work at a dressmaker in Belgium but a couple of years ago I got a job in a boutique in Paris so I was there for a year then came to London
> Me: Paris is such a nice city *[expectant gap]*
> Her: Oh, it's lovely! My boutique was in a small row of similar shops that…. Blah blah blah.

There'll be a simple interplay in the conversation where you encourage her to open up by asking open-ended or implied questions, and then you'll pick little jumping off points to launch into a monologue of your own. After she's told me a bit about her experience in Paris (and I've filed and categorised it to better understand her character) I might open into this:

> Me: I was in Paris a couple of years ago. I love the Saint Michel area with all the little streets and cafes and boulangeries. There's something about being in central Paris that feels so imperial. The Louvre, the wide boulevards… it's almost like Napoleon is still there marching his army. But you know my most enduring memory? I was there in winter so it was all foggy and cold. At the Eiffel Tower they'd turned the first deck into an ice rink. So me and my friend were ice skating three hundred feet above the street in the Paris winter. It was an amazing view.

She'll coo at that. Then I'll give a pause to let her fill in the gap and invest more.

# MAKE HER WORK FOR YOUR ATTENTION

Girls prize high-quality male attention. Most men simply can't conceive how valuable that attention is to a woman, and thus what a powerful tool you hold by simply rationing it out according to how hard the woman works for it. Learn the covert means of giving and then withdrawing attention and liberally sprinkle them into the date, especially at the beginning of the date. Later you'll be in deep rapport, so she'll have earned your attention. But in venue one she still has to fight for it. The most common methods of rationing your attention are:

1. Eye wandering

2. Faint praise

3. Quizzical looks

4. Light challenge

5. Distance

Let's consider these in turn.

## 1. Eye Wandering

Whenever you are looking at the girl you are paying attention to her. This should be the normal default mode of communication, because you are trying to build a connection. But remember the frame — you are interested but you aren't yet sold on her. Every now and then let your eyes wander to something else in the room like it's become suddenly more interesting than her. It's crucial to make it appear like a natural wandering mind, rather than a display of rudeness. Don't use it to fiddle with your smartphone or roll your eyes and stare into space. Look at *something in particular* like it's suddenly caught your attention. Maybe a waitress is fussing with a tray, or a kid is sitting on the floor counting napkins, or there's a really impressive painting on the wall. Let it take your attention and give it an inquisitive look. Smile. Let her voice drone on and then lightly snap out of it. She'll get the message that you aren't purposefully rude but you aren't 100% focused on her. She'll now work harder to keep your attention.

If she gets arsey about it, you probably did it for too long or at the wrong moment. Just give an offhand statement about the source of your distraction ("That's a lovely painting", "That kid is so cute") then a non-committal "Sorry, what were you saying?"

I'll use eye wandering in three cases: (i) she's muttering about something genuinely boring to me, so it's a mild punishment for talking rubbish (ii) there's something genuinely interesting happening in the background that really does catch my attention (iii) short random wanderings just to keep her on her toes and present myself as difficult to catch.

## 2. Faint Praise

A common sign when observing chodes in the wild is how low their threshold is for being impressed. Almost everything a girl says or does is just amazing. Wow! Awesome! Really???!!!! You need to raise the bar on what you consider worthy of praise. This holds in your life generally, not just with girls. If something can be easily achieved without significant application of talent, hard graft, and emotional persistence... Do you really want to elevate it to the lofty plain of "impressive"? Of course not. Don't go through life with sneering distaste at others, but don't just lavishly praise anything mildly impressive because a pretty girl said it. This expresses itself mostly in using phrases such as "ok," "I see," "I understand," "interesting," and "seems nice."

| | |
|---|---|
| *Her:* | I work as a flight attendant. We do lots of long haul flights to Singapore and Hong Kong on the new airbus. The airline puts us up at five star hotels for the stopovers. |
| *Me:* | Seems nice |
| *Her:* | My ex-boyfriend took me on a yachting cruise around the carribbean last summer. |
| *Me:* | Interesting |
| *Her:* | I work as a model. I do the fashion weeks in London, New York, and Moscow. |
| *Me:* | Ok |

She will have her own self-image that makes her high value. You don't need to feed into it. Because she's likely a normal girl in a normal situation, this will be an extremely externally-referenced view, leading her to think it's a big deal to have Prada sunglasses, travel the world, and have the other accoutrements of the Victoria Beckham lifestyle. Not every girl is like this, but society has been telling her for twenty years that she is entitled to these things and that they raise her SMV. Many girls will hit you early with such Lady-DHVs in an attempt to knock you off balance and get you to start chasing her. This will *especially* happen if she's tall and model-esque. Don't take the bait.

When a girl is proactively trying to impress you with her stories, she is leaving herself open to falling flat when you fail to fall into her frame. It's like telling someone a joke who doesn't laugh at the punchline. When she hits you with her high-faluting **Lady-DHVs**, just look unimpressed and damn her with faint praise. The key is to not appear reactive or dismissive, rather you are simply unmoved because you are so sure of your own internal value system that you can't be rocked off balance by someone else's.

One word of warning — only do this when she's "trying it on." When a girl is trying to connect with you by sharing her real life story in an authentic manner then that is **good behaviour** and should be rewarded. Stay away from effusive praise, but don't hesitate to provide genuine attention and sincere acknowledgement. You don't move away from your own value system, but you authentically connect with hers as legitimate.

## 3. Quizzical Looks

Early in the date you are still a challenge. You're still not quite buying what she's selling. You've moved on from the attraction-heavy stage of the early street stop, and thus it is no longer incumbent upon you to capture her attention. She's on the date because she's already decided you are a contender for providing the dick she craves. Nonetheless, you haven't kissed yet so the mutual attraction is not yet official. You aren't ready to "let her in" to your life, so remain somewhat aloof.

Part of the rapport stage is offering opinions on the world and sharing your world-views. This means making statements about how the world is and what's important to you. Every now and then she'll say something where the meaning or truth-value is not immediately apparent. So give her a quizzical look. Raise an eyebrow. Scrunch your upper lip. This will express mild disbelief and encourage her to expand more on her statement, which in turn increases her investment and makes her rapport-seeking. She's chasing you. If her opinion fits under grounds for normal polite disagreement (e.g. musical taste, social values) rather than obvious common sense, you can shrug your shoulders and give a non-committal nod. Your response has the nuance of "I see, that's a reasonable position," rather than "Yes, I agree."

At no point do you have to agree with each other about the world for sex to happen. There are rare occasions where you will actively hammer a girl down until she submits and agrees with you (what I call the "frame crush") but these are not the norm. Just look a little unconvinced, but not to the extent that you are explicitly rejecting her or implying she's a fuckwit.

## 4. Light Challenge

An easy mistake to make at the intermediate stage is to challenge a girl so hard that you irretrievably break rapport. Challenging is a push, and as we know attraction is created in the push. So early in the street stop you will have disagreed with her on something somewhere to let her know you have boundaries and you're not just another push-over man. Once that test is passed there's no need to revisit it. Don't become addicted to the thrill of tooling a girl and disagreeing with her because then you'll get stuck in attraction and never bed the interaction down with rapport. Do the Hard Challenge only once, to make your point, and then never again *unless she starts fucking with you*. Some girls crave a frame-crushing because they so love high dominance, and you'll learn to identify which girls this applies to.

So assuming she's not fucking with you and is more-or-less keeping it real it's best to restrict yourself to occasional light challenges on areas you really don't agree on. Don't force the challenges. Just remember you are a man with his own interests, hobbies, code of conduct, and world view. While building rapport you will gradually share that with the girl to build the connection. Tell her what you really think. No two people believe exactly the same things so occasionally you'll have mild disagreements. Don't let them descend into a battle like two wizards on opposite hilltops throwing lightning bolts at each other. Just hold your core ground, give a little space for polite compromise / mutual difference. For example:

> Her:    I'm doing some evening classes in painting, still life and so on
> Me:     That sounds like fun
> Her:    Not really. I'm always tired after work so it's quite a chore to drag myself there
> Me:     Then why are you doing it? *[light challenge]*

The easiest way to challenge is to ask "Why?" Two-year-olds do this all the time with their parents. It's easy.

# 5. Distance

When you turn your body fully to a girl and lean towards her you are rewarding her with attention (pull). Conversely, leaning back or away is withdrawing a portion of that attention (push). Get into the habit of controlling your push-pull to reflect where you are in the date. There's not a specific progression in ratios of push-pull as the date progresses. It's more helpful to consider yourself a surfer riding the waves of her emotions, shifting your balance to adjust to the changes in her waves. Sometimes you'll sense the need to push, other times the need to pull, and how you position yourself will reflect this. That said, as she gradually falls deeper into your frame and chases you harder, you'll want your body to lean further and further away, forcing her to lean further and further in. That's real Lean In.

### False Investment

Some girls are naturally chatty to the point of excess. When such a motormouth starts talking she doesn't want to stop, so the intermediate player will mistakenly think "Whoever is talking is investing, therefore she is investing."
The problem is the low quality of her conversation. She is spamming you with high noise and low signal. Real investment is when the girl shows you who she really is and what she really thinks. You can feel it as strengthening rapport. In contrast, verbal diarrhoea is just a garbled stream of nonsense that represents a barrier to rapport. It's an avoidance strategy for girls who are uncomfortable with emotional intimacy. Different cultures will have different standards for what is excessive prattle. Anglosphere girls, particularly Americans, talk far too much. You must cut them off.

Don't let them snatch the frame. Once these girls build up a head of steam they will be directing the conversation and derailing the date. Shush them. Talk over them. Tell them to be quiet. Make them fall into your frame. Only then will they produce less noise and more quality signal.

In the first venue the big thing is to avoid coming across as the eager chode. Next time you see another couple on a first date in a bar / café just spend a few minutes watching his body language. He'll probably do all of the following:

- Upright correct body posture as if he's interviewing for his dream job

- Both elbows on the table to support his forward-leaning weight

- "Just happy to be here" inane smile on his face

- Enthusiastically agreeing with every little insipid thing she says

- Eagerly looking for chances to prove himself to her

## Qualification

There are two sides to qualifying a girl and I like to do both. You can either
(i) Tell her reasons you like her [Qualify her] or (ii) Make her give reasons you should like her [She qualifies herself]. The purpose of qualification is to make the girl feel like she has special qualities making her worthy of your interest. You show yourself to have standards and options while also making her feel she has to work for your attention and win you over. I tend towards embedded qualification. This means I covertly convey my expectations (and resulting approval or disapproval) by embedding it in statements and actions which don't explicitly state those standards in relation to her. For example:

- [covert embedded — qualify her] "I like girls who really understand what it means to be feminine. Girls who like being a girl and become the best girl they can be, rather than trying to copy men." This is the standard. Then later in the conversation I'll say "I like that about you. It's so feminine." This is how she measures against it. She pieces both together to feel qualified by me.

- [covert embedded — make her qualify herself] "How tall are you?" Then after she's stood up and perhaps you stood up to compare height, you sit back down and nod non-commitally, perhaps mentioning you like tall girls. "I'm quite tall for my country," she says.

When this doesn't seem to be working you can go more overt. As you'll see later the Questions Game features lots of embedded qualification but you have the option to make it quite overt — You ask her "What do you like about me?" and it's 90% certain her next question will be "And what do you like about me?" So just overtly qualify her.

Don't be that guy. First and foremost your default posture should be relaxed and leant back, encouraging her to lean in and thus begin the covert communication of her chasing you. You'll stay in this position until there's a specific reason to reward her with attention-bestowing body language. There will be reasons:

- She says something really interesting so you want to reward her good behaviour / investment. Lean in, give her rapt enthusiastic attention and ask questions about the topic.

- You suddenly think of something to say on a topic that is important to you, or the story you are telling hits an upswing so you lean forward to express your enthusiasm in your own material.

- You sense the pendulum of "push" has reached its temporary limit so you want to swing it back to "pull" for a little while. Game is like reeling a fish in. You want tension, but too much will snap the line. Let it go a little slack at times until the fish is tired out.

- You are getting muscle ache from holding the same position all the time.

Like most advice in this book, the aim is to internalise it into your muscle memory so that it all becomes gut feel. You'll simply feel like she deserves more attention so you'll naturally give it to her. As a result you'll feel her cup of attention overfloweth and thus dial it down again.

You'll soon be ready to walk her to the next venue. The walk itself is a renewed chance to lead and move her around. Don't be afraid of light kino such as nudging her across a road, or softly grabbing her shoulders or upper arm to point her in the right direction. I'll often get soft compliance by telling her to hold my coat while I check my wallet or telling her to bin the empty coffee cups.

ATTENTION
1. EYE WANDERING
2. FAINT PRAISE
3. QUIZZICAL LOOKS
4. LIGHT CHALLENGE
5. DISTANCE

INTRIGUE

MASTERY

MESMER BEAM

AUTHENTICITY

PRESENCE

YOUR REALITY

# VENUE TWO — BRIGHT, BUSY AND ALCOHOLIC

*Goal: Kiss her. Confirm the frame that this will eventually lead to sex.*

The first venue was mostly about calming her down and running some attraction and rapport in a non-threatening environment. You'll be there about an hour, but don't stress the timing. What you're really looking for is a change in vibe where she's starting to open up and feel the date frame. Now you walk her to Venue Two.

This is a transition venue that has the safe elements of venue one (bright, busy) but also the seductive elements of venue three (alcohol). The vibe will be gradually progressing towards increased intimacy and alcohol is both good for lowering your inhibitions and also a social signal / plausibly deniable reason for what follows. So choose a bar or pub. It may be her turn to get the round, so while she orders you go find some seats. This is the venue you want to be sitting next to her or on an L-shape at 90 degrees to each other. You don't want a table between you.

# THREE-STEP PHYSICAL ESCALATION

Spike her fairly early in the venue with an off-hand comment about her dress or hair or something else that's lightly sexual. It's now that I'll make sure to work the kino if I hadn't already started in Venue One. These are the easiest ones, in order:

1. Thigh / shoulder squeeze

2. Fingers

3. Hair / Ears

The first time she's sitting down and you need to get past her (for example to sit in your seat, or to get past to go to the toilet) be sure to give her a soft squeeze on either the lower thigh or top of her shoulder. It's just a quick double squeeze or (for the thigh) a light slap as an exclamation point on the physical request to get past. Do one on the way past and another on the way back. It's an early step into taking control of her body and testing her reaction. She should just accept it.

While making light conversation notice something about her hands, be it her nail varnish, rings, bracelet or manicure. Then comment on it as you take her hand to get a closer look. Really spend a little time examining it while holding her hand physically. You can compare the length or width of your fingers to hers ("You'd be good at piano" for long fingers, "You'd be a good watchmaker" for small fingers) each in turn. Or compare her long manicured nails to yours. Or ask if there's a story about her ring while you spin it around on her finger. It's all distracting bullshit and you both know it. What you are really doing is signalling that things are moving physically closer and then watching her reaction. Does she softly leave her hand in yours during this exercise? That's a good amber light. Alternatively does she keep her hands stiff and tense? That's a red light so ease off and work more attraction and comfort before the next kino test.

A bit later you'll examine her hair. Just think of a compliment or observation, such as "I really like how thick your hair is, it's like a shampoo commercial. Here, let me have a look" and then start playing with her hair. Slightly adjust it like you're a hairdresser until you're happy with it then say "There, perfect!" If she's loving it then grab her hair at the back of her neck and say "I really like girl's hair. It's so thick and soft. I like grabbing it here," and give a soft pull. You've gotten more sexual now in a plausibly deniable manner. Again if she accepts it you've got an amber light, if she looks uncomfortable and recoils it's a red light. If she actively encourages you it's a green light.

If you think she's prissy about her hair or it's all pinned up nicely then do something similar on her ears. Ask about her earrings as you touch her ears for a closer look. While still holding them, inquire how many piercings she has, how many pairs of earrings, are these her favourite, etc. It's all bullshit while she signals how comfortable she is with you touching her.

If she gives you amber lights to all three tests then the kiss is on. You don't have to immediately go for it but you can be very confident she's up for it.

### The Calf Squeeze

Sometimes I will have finished the three-step physical escalation and I'm still not sure the girl is ready. You can usually get girls talking about the sport or gym work they do, or used to do. Maybe she dances, or jogs, or plays volleyball. Whatever the specifics you bring it to the statement: "You must have a bit of muscle on there." Whether she agrees or demures playfully challenge her with "Come on, show me your muscle pose," and simulate flexing your biceps. When she does it prod and squeeze her upper arm. Either pull ("That's quite good") or push ("That's like jelly" and make blub-blub noises like shaking a jelly). You should raise a laugh.

Then move your attention to her legs: "Come on, let's see if you have dancer's legs." Grab her ankle and extend her leg. Cup her calf and squeeze it like a horse-trader analysing a potential purchase. Tell her to tense her calf then tell her to relax it. The whole time you are touching up her lower leg. This test accomplishes the following:

- Gradually take control of her body

- Lead her

- Screening frame

- Pleasant physical touch

- Avoids LJBF vibe

- Compliance test

The lower legs are quite safe for her because it's in the sexual grey area. Depending how she takes the routine you can either pull ("Mmmm. Nice legs") or push ("I imagine that's how it feels to touch a giraffe")

# THREE-STEP VERBAL ESCALATION

When all goes well she'll be helping you seduce her, but you can't rely on these cases. Sometimes you'll be sitting on the date at a loss for how to escalate. Maybe her body language is stiff, maybe she rejected your physical escalation. You need to have faith in the model and push ahead.

*She's sitting there with you because she's interested.*
*There are many places she could be but she decided to be with you instead.*

Players are pushing themselves forwards with hotter girls and faster pulls. We don't spend much time in situations where the girl is progressing according to her own timetable because that takes forever and surrenders too much frame to her. Instead, we put them on our timetable which means we have to lead. We often need to take shots in the dark without as much pre-leap confirmation as we'd like. So push her forwards verbally in three stages that can be spread across Venue Two.

1. Compliment her character and passions.

2. Compliment her style and grace.

3. Compliment her body and sexuality.

## 1. Character And Passions

All girls have things they are emotionally and ego-invested in. Assuming you screened correctly in the street stop, she'll be into the kind of things you can genuinely respect her for. Perhaps she's studying hard at veterinarian school and dreams of helping animals. Perhaps she's danced ballet since eight years old and still goes to evening classes. Perhaps she's learned to paint watercolours and sells painted postcards at a weekend craft market. There'll be something that you can genuinely compliment her on as you are drawing out her hopes'n'dreams on the date. Don't gush, just give her a reason why you like her. Give her some positive affirmation to reward her for having a worthwhile feminine passion.

- "I noticed when you started talking about your painting you suddenly perked up. Your eyes became brighter and your voice more animated. That's really sweet."

- "I like how dedicated you are to learning this art. You've got a real passion and conviction for it. That's very attractive."

Sometimes she won't be talking about a Thing but you'll detect something you like in her character. I'm always screening for introversion, so I like to feed that back to them. I'll compliment a girl on how I like her ability to focus and to think deeply and thoughtfully about things:

- "I could tell you were introverted when I first saw you. You have the simple understated fashion, muted colours and gentle body language of the introvert. It's very nice."

- "The world is built for extraverts. There's three extraverts for every introvert so it's easy for us to forget our own qualities. I like how you can focus and make deep connection. It's very attractive."

Communicate with your core and discover what it is you like about her. Does she glow with warmth? Does her laugh tinkle like a waterfall? Does she show intelligence and attentiveness? Feed that back to her and add on "…. And I find that attractive."

## 2. Style and Grace

After you have complimented the girl on her character she'll be more willing to share more of herself. This venue is breaking down the barriers between the real her and the real you. Once she comes off the socially polite slightly-reticent script, she'll open up with what she really cares about and who she really is. People want to connect. Now you can start moving towards a more sexual compliment without appearing crass.

I'll choose something about her fashion, her grooming, or her mannerisms that is feminine then feed it back to her as a compliment. This is sincere masculine admiration so it sets a clear man-woman vibe. We are now in the transition zone where compliments on her personality are starting to morph into compliments of her sexuality.

- "I like your dress. There's something about colourful flowing summer dresses that is very attractive on a woman. I like how they swish when you walk."

- "You have very striking coordination. You nails and belt match your eye colour. There's a very nice brown thing going on and little flashes of brighter colours. That's very elegant. I like it."

- "I love how correctly you sit. Your back is straight, your chin up, your thighs modestly crossed, your feet pulled back towards the chair. It's very feminine and very attractive."

You want her to feel judged as a woman by a man's eye, but you can't yet be crass about it. Show her you understand polarity and the little tricks she's learned to better reach her feminine potential. She's spent a decade pouring over beauty tips in magazines, movies, and with friends. She's spent hundreds of hours in front of the mirror refining her makeup colouring and style. Looking her best is the end result of considerable hard graft. Let her know you see this and appreciate the result. She won't just feel thrilled, she'll feel qualified.

You've also proved yet again that you "get it." You are within that one percent of Men who understand the Game.

# 3. Body and Sexuality

You should've received amber or green lights to your previous two compliments. She'll have smiled and graciously accepted them. Perhaps she blushed a little or her eyes sparkled. So now you can give a very direct statement of sexual interest. Do not hide behind romanticism or euphemism. Tell her exactly what you like in a manner that leaves no doubt that you want to fuck her. An easy way to calibrate is:

*It must be a statement that would get you slapped if you opened with it.*

Deliver it sincerely and with a knowing smile. It shouldn't sound stand-offish and gamey. It should sound like you are making a move. Examples:

- *[when she comes back from the toilet]* "I was just watching you walk to the bathroom. You have very long legs. Sexy."

- *[after she has stood up]* "I just checked out your ass. I approve. Sexy"

- "I love your eyes. They're so big, like a raccoon. Very sexy"

- "You have a very flat stomach. I like that. It really accentuates your curves. Sexy"

- "That way you walk. Mmmmmmm. I love the sway side to side. Sexy"

You'll notice I usually finish with the word "sexy." Step one is attractive/nice/sweet. Step two is a stronger version of the same. Step three is sexy. You can play with it a little too to draw her in, such as when she's come back from the bathroom / bar:

| Me: | Thank you for that |
|---|---|
| Her: | For what? |
| Me: | When you walked to the bathroom you put a lot of swing into your hips, just for me. So I wanted to thank you for the performance. It was sexy. |
| Her: | [blush] |

Push your frame out and be unapologetic for your masculine sexual desire. You've probably spent two hours in her company now so you know her pretty well and you've screened her. You're still here, she's still here — you like each other. All the above physical and verbal escalation is designed to give bite-sized actionable advice to set up the kiss. You have let her know it's coming and you've thrown in a total of six progressive compliance tests to let yourself know she's ready. When you make your Big Move, it doesn't surprise either of you because she was waiting for it. And if you were getting red lights, you know to hold fire and rebuild momentum rather than get brushed off.

## Escalate on Amber Lights

The main reason normal guys don't sleep with more women is they don't know how to escalate. Your typical chode will never escalate, so he only gets sex when a girl has chosen him and then she escalates him — this pattern is so repellent to female nature that it happens rarely and only when the woman's SMV is way below the man's. This is why your typical chode has less than ten lifetime lays and he's shacked up with a 30+ homely woman. It's how sexually aggressive cougars get toy boys. Within any chode crystal (a friendship group of chumps) there'll be one Player Guy who has banged twenty or more girls and is thus the hero of the group. This is because he escalates on green lights. When he's talking to women he has learned how to spot the blatant IOIs and he's got the balls to act on them. This alone gets him laid 3x as much as a typical chode. He's still underperforming because girls won't give off green lights unless they are horny and really into the guy. Despite being the envy of his friends, he's missing out on all the Maybe Girls.

We escalate on Amber Lights. We have learned how to spot when a girl is amenable to sex but needs to be nudged towards it.

**Red Light:** The girl actively rebuffs an escalation / compliance test. When you touch her she goes stiff. When you pull her to you she pulls away. When you IOI her she IODs you. These girls are saying "no."

**Green Light:** The girl actively encourages your escalation / compliance test. She proactively touches you. She plays with your pendant. She looks longingly into your eyes. When you pull her in she presses against you. She enthusiastically agrees with anything you say. When you IOI her she IOIs right back.

**Amber Light:** She neither evades not blocks. She sits there and accepts the escalation/compliance test. When you pull her in she lets it happen. When you IOI her she nods and smiles.

For every girl who gives you green lights there'll be five girls giving you amber lights. Roughly speaking, a red light means she thinks she's out of your league, amber is about matched, and green is she feels lucky to be there.

I like to hold good solid eye contact with a girl throughout the date, which helps show that she's not rocking me off balance with any of her games. If she leans away, I don't follow. If she comes onto me, I don't rush in blindly. Gradually, her frame will break. It's designed to and that's what she wants to happen. If it's on you'll get a hypnotic scanning moment when you both hold deep eye contact and you can feel electricity crackle. That's the big signal. If it's strong I say "I want to kiss you now," and then go for it. If it's weak I say "I'm going to kiss you in the next bar / soon" and then go for it next time there's that moment. Don't try to kiss on a lull. Wait for the moment. It's in the eyes and not the body, so don't be afraid of reaching over even if she's on the other side of the table.

### Recovery Loop

*A sequence of behaviours designed to absorb the blow of failing a compliance test that redirects or rebuilds the energy for a later attempt. See the bottom bar on the Krauser Daygame Model flowchart.*

Expect the girl to rebuff your first kiss attempt. This is just another test from her to see how you react. So long as you expect a rebuff, you won't get butt hurt or show disappointment. Failure at any Leap Of Moment allows you to run a **Recovery Loop**. Sometimes you'll have to chip away with six or seven kiss attempts over the course of an hour before she finally relents. This isn't as weird as it sounds because you are dragging her onto your timetable and gradually imposing your frame onto her — that's not always a smooth process. The more you're redlining the car, the more rebuffs you can expect. Embrace it. So long as she's not trying to leave she's really just telling you "keep trying." It takes balls to absorb a rebuff and keep coming on strong.

*I'm a man. It's my job to push. You're a woman. It's your job to resist.*

You can actually say this after an early rebuff. It shows again that you Get It. You've overtly and smoothly conveyed your cocky attitude to the rebuff. I've literally never had a girl react badly to that statement. Every time she rebuffs you is a chance for you to show how ballsy you are. Keep chipping away. She'll break.

My first kiss is always quick. I kiss long enough for her to respond and then softly disengage and give her a smile. I treat it as a mutual agreement, more like a handshake over a contract signing than a sexual act. It may only last five seconds. Now we both *know*. We've both got what we want, what we have spent the last three hours tip-toeing around. She'll be as relieved as you are because you can both finally drop so much pretence. It can be exhausting for both of you to keep dancing around the edge of the volcano in the mating ritual. You have to push, she has to resist...It's emotionally draining.

A minute or two after the first kiss I'll go back in for another longer, more passionate kiss. Typically she'll really get into this one because she's had a minute warming up and there are no longer any "first time" barriers. Give it thirty seconds or so, let your hands touch her face, or hair, or pull in her shoulders. Feel how much she likes it because the kiss is also a calibration tool:

1. She throws herself onto you like a damn breaking, pushing into you, moaning, tongue probing, holding your face = You can probably fuck her this date.

2. She holds back, giving you just enough to confirm she wants to kiss but little more than that = she feels awkward kissing in public. Cool off until Venue Three. Don't be too hungry.

3. She matches your intensity but doesn't raise it = A normal Yes Girl so play it by ear to see if she wants to fuck tonight or later.

> I won't go beyond kissing in this venue. I won't touch her breasts or ass or pussy. The whole purpose of the Venue Two kiss is to **confirm sexual attraction**. It has not yet become a seduction tool. If you throw yourself too far into the kiss, you'll come off as the thirsty guy and blow the set.

### Leaps Of Faith

AVOIDANCE WEASEL
finding ways to avoid opening since 2009

Every girl expects the man to have balls. The R-selected man knows what he wants and goes for it even when the world is trying to push him back. Couple this with the man's job to lead and we have key moments of compliance in the courtship ritual called Leaps Of Faith. These are moments when you don't know if she'll take your escalation, but you have to try anyway. It's why pussies never get laid — fortune favours the bold. In daygame, the crucial Leaps in chronological order are:

- The Run Up– More specifically, the act of deciding to approach the girl and then getting in front of her.

- Convey Intent — This is the moment you "go direct." Often it'll be combined with the opener but sometimes you're a couple of minutes in and she doesn't know you're hitting on her, so you have to take a chance.

- The Date Invitation — You've sent feelers, pinged, had some back-and-forth SMS, but does she actually want to meet?

- The Move– Successfully going for The Kiss confirms mutual sexual attraction so she can no longer rationalise that you're a friend or an interesting diversion.

- Pulling The Trigger — Her getting in the taxi or letting you walk her to your house means sex. It's the biggest move of all.

- The Trousers — Once you start pulling her trousers down you have the biggest LMR risk. It's tempting to keep "warming her up" and delaying this moment of truth.

Everything else that happens is just the stuff you do to set up the next Leap of Faith. You'll know this instinctively because you may start to feel butterflies and impending ego death as a Leap approaches. You'll have all kinds of Avoidance Weaselling to string it out and hope the girl somehow makes the leap for you. From the above list, by far the scariest leaps are The Run Up and Pulling The Trigger. There's very little you can do to know where you're at before you jump off the cliff. They are the moments when your ego is dead-centre in the crosshairs of rejection.

# BODY LANGUAGE

Venue Two is a transition venue that straddles the open authentic friendly vibe of Venue One and the seductive down-to-business vibe of Venue Three. This also reflects itself in your body language and how you both manage personal space. There is a progressive breaking down of socially-polite barriers, including the amount of comfortable distance between you.

**Venue One:** You are both still wearing masks, tip-toeing around the volcano to get a good look at each other. As you gradually give more of yourself (leading with your vibe) she opens up. Your body language is laconic and unreactive as a default, but punctuated with moments of animation to highlight the flow of conversation.

**Venue Three:** There are no surviving pretences. You are intimate, in deep rapport, and all the barriers are down. You hold a strong wide pose while she folds herself into you.

Thus Venue Two is about getting from here to there. Keep taking up space, leaning back, letting your knees drift apart and your feet spread out. Avoid the qualifying attentive "correct" posture of the chump. Test the distance by closing in on her then pulling away. Let your thigh touch hers or your knee drop over her personal space. As rapport strengthens, reward her with more open posture and engage her more.

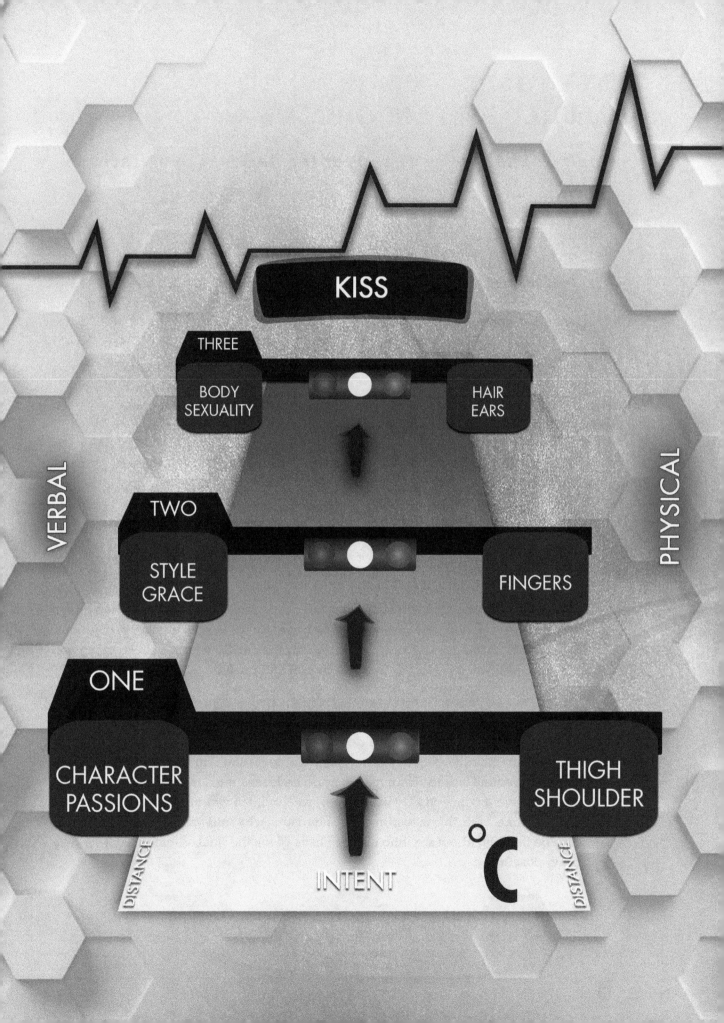

# VENUE THREE — DARK, SECLUDED AND ALCOHOLIC

## Goal: Get her horny and clear the barriers to extraction.

As you are finishing your drinks in Venue Two, run off a mental checklist to see where you're at in the set. The barriers should be down and she should be quite close to you. Tick them off:

- When you lean back, does she lean in to maintain an ever-shortening distance?

- There is incidental kino. She doesn't mind when you nudge her or let your knees and thighs touch in plausibly-deniable manner.

- You've already done the hopes'n'dreams rapport. You feel like you know each other.

- You sense there's no fight left in her. She's not really testing your value any more.

If you can tick these off you're ready for the next venue. If not, consider a second drink and run through the Venue Two stuff all over again. Venue Three is when things become dark and seductive, so she has to be ready for it. As with every other step in the model it changes when you're red-lining the car. Sometimes she's giving you little back and you have to just trust the model and push on regardless.

The purpose of Venue Three is to reach the making-out/probably have sex stage. She'll feel completely swept along on the tide, which will manifest itself in delegating her decisions to you. Somewhere deep in the hindbrain she's crossed the sexual rubicon, her thoughts moving from "This is interesting, I'm starting to quite like this guy" (Venue One) to "Hmmm...I hope he kisses me... mmmm that was nice... I feel we have a connection" (Venue Two) to "God, I'm wet now. I wonder what his dick feels like... Oh, this is exciting" (Venue Three). By mid-way through this venue she'll be thinking about sex. She may not have given the final all-clear but it's a very strong possibility.

# Choosing Venue Three

**Extraction path**

*A pre-planned route from the place of meeting, via waypoints, that ends in a sex location.*

Depending on how you laid out your **Extraction Path** you'll be taking her to a bar close to your house (you have good logistics or she agreed to meet at a train station near you) or a bar close to a reliable taxi rank. The most important factor in Venue Three is how easily you can leave it and get to your sex location. Try to find a place that meets all of the following requirements:

- **Dark low-lighting** where it's difficult to pick out other patrons or overhear their conversations. It feels private and night-like. This will amplifly the Our World sense of isolation from the world's social pressures.

- **Secluded corners** or private booths with soft cushioned sofas or benches. It's crucial to be sitting next to each other without prying eyes on you. Try to sit with your backs to the crowd in the most out-of-the-way corner you can find.

- **Not very busy.** It's okay for Venue Two to be busy because you can feed off the crowd's energy and use the crush to plausibly close proximity. It's still a "night out." That's why blues bars and English-style pubs work well. Not so for Venue Three. This is private. You need space and concentration. It hurts the vibe to have a hen party cackling in the next booth or people interupting to ask for a light or to sit on the edge of your table due to lack of space.

- **Discreet staff.** You'll get a sense whether the staff are constantly interrupting to clear glasses, take orders, shot girls pimping liquor and so on. Ideally you'll just order drinks at the bar and be left alone.

- **An easy way to settle the bill** without dragging on. I prefer places where you simply pay at the bar while ordering. Dicking around standing at the cash register on your way out just lengthens the girl's wobble window.

- **A nearby taxi-rank** or street that has taxis regularly pass by. Failing that, a private toilet.

None of this is rocket science. Many many bars are designed with precisely this in mind, especially the more modern cocktail lounges or bar-clubs (for mid-week dates, avoid on weekends).

**The Wall**

*The sudden and precipitous drop in a woman's beauty as she approaches her mid-thirties and has few of her eggs remaining. The Wall can be delayed by healthy living and regular exercise, but can never be avoided. Women shift dramatically to K-selection as The Wall approaches, seeking to cash out of the SMP with a provider chump.*

They'll usually have a main room with the bar along it and then little sub-rooms full of private booths. Do some research and when a bar feels right it'll be obvious. Things to avoid are:

- **Bright English-style pubs** where mates go to chat about football and drink some good beer. They are too pally, too chatty, too social. Even if chatty regulars don't engage you in conversation, they'll be setting a bright chatty vibe for the room. That's for Venue Two.

- **Too-cool-for-school status-whoring bars**. London has many trendy themed bars with large glass windows, neon-lighted water fountains, table service, hot slim black-dressed waitresses, small bottles of imported beer, no draught lager and so on. They are specifically targeted to higher beta chodes who want to impress their dates with money rather than themselves. It's the date equivalent of driving a Ferrari. At such a place, you'll be telegraphing external referencing and a reliance upon external value props. This will trigger her K-selection and slow down the sex. Remember the frame: you are the only thing you bring to the date. Also, don't go to a venue that is too attractive because then her attention will be drawn away from you.

- **Meat market bars**. At no point between opening and closing a girl will you ever willingly put her in front of other thirsty men trying to get laid. You'll know your town (and quickly figure out a new town) so you know where the chodes go to get drunk and hit on girls. You can always spot them: "soulful" name, entry fee on weekends, small all-male or all-female groups standing in a circle trying to attract the attention of other groups, dancing in the middle of the bar area, a dance floor, shot girls, bottled of WKD on sale... you get the idea. Avoid these areas because you are exposing yourself to unnecessary risk of external interrupts and amogs (especially if you're fairly new and don't have much masculine presence) and you are witnessing lots of sloppy hook-up attempts which can burst the love bubble with your girl. Avoid bars where the reigning vibe is giving strange men permission to talk to strange women. You want places that encourage insular privacy. That said, nearly everywhere is safe for Monday-Wednesday dates — these places are designed to encourage hook ups but you are there when they are empty.

## Provider Chump

*A man who triggers strong K-selection behaviour in women. Usually he is materially successful and thus ego-invested in his ability to provide. This is the nature of his perceived competitive advantage. When coupled with a Saviour Schema, he will seek out damaged or impoverished women to "save" from the world or themselves. He will usually attract near-Wall women looking to cash out, or pre-Wall women looking for a comfortable set-up from which to cheat on him with r-selected men.*

## Provider Chump Venues

Never forget that you are presenting an r-selection frame, and thus avoid conveying anything that may flip her into K-selection. It's very tempting for economically-successful men to squeeze some provider chump game into a date because they know they outrank the average man on these terms.

If you have a good job, nice car, fashionable clothes, and tend to eat at nice restaurants, you are more likely to fuck up the date than a penniless student is. The student doesn't have the option of being a provider chump, whereas you have had it drilled into you for a few decades and still deep down are ego-invested in your societal success as your main vehicle to laying women.

The hardest men to teach Game to are those who have already had high levels of success in a part of life that doesn't involve women. They bristle with pride and an I-know-best mentality, despite clear evidence their methods don't work. When the girl agrees to a date, you must suppress the urge to "impress" her with high rolling. Avoid the trendy venues. Avoid the cocktail bars. The only thing you bring is yourself.

If you're not sure if a venue is made for Provider Chumps then look at the other patrons. Judging others removes some of your ego and gives clarity. Do the men look like they are trying to impress the women with displays of wealth and refined taste?

# How To Run Venue Three

Walk in with her and get a beer or wine. You must be drinking alcohol by now, so if she pipes up with an "I shouldn't drink any more" objection you can cajole her a little, even if she only has a half or a small glass of wine. It's important what the alcohol represents: *her losing control and going along with the current until "it just happened."* Remember you should be turn-taking in paying for drinks unless there's something unusual preventing it (she's a legitimately broke student, she's Russian etc). Don't obsess over who buys what drinks, just don't be tooled. Shepherd her to the correct seats that are private, comfortable, and allow you to sit side-by-side with no obstructions between you. Never willingly choose stools or chairs. The best options are u-shaped cushioned booths or Starbucks-style sofas.

The primary purpose of Venue Three is to push the seductive vibe. This means:

- Talk less, touch more

- Long periods of comfortable silence

- No deep intellectually-engaging conversation

- Almost permanent physical connection

Think of how you act on a date with a regular girlfriend you've been banging for weeks. Everything is normalised. You have full permission to touch her (and vice versa), move her around, pull her in, stop talking, let your thoughts wander, and tell her what to do. Think about how you'd sit in a bar with your girlfriend. She'll be next to you with her body pressing lightly against yours, perhaps your arm around her, absent-mindedly playing with her hair. You don't worry that going to the toilet will break your spell over her. This is the vibe you want to reach halfway through Venue Three.

I concentrate on holding strong body language and dropping lots of verbal sexualisation. Hold a solid posture and let her fold into you. Don't be too grabby or too thirsty to make out and escalate. You'll be doing all that stuff in the bedroom, so just take up space as you sit, pull her in, and drape your arm over her shoulder giving it an occasional squeeze. Slow your reaction times down so it's like you're moving underwater. You'll get into a vibe where neither of you talks much, your brains have shut down, and you are mostly just touching and chilling. She'll normally be the one showing nerves now, spouting some occasional jibber-jabber and filling in silences. Let it happen, let her invest. Every now and then shush her.

Daygame Mastery

# VERBAL ESCALATION

You will have already given her the basic three-step method (passions, look, body) to get to the kiss. Now use the same pattern to qualify her, rather than to escalate. She's already kissed you so sexual interest is mutually agreed. The purpose of sexualised compliments is now to qualify her so she feels she deserves your interest and isn't just some floozy being pumped and dumped. As the next hour progresses, tell her the three things you like about her covering each of her passions, her look, and her body. I normally show lots of warmth and admiration on the latter two. For example,

## Turkish Bond Girl

- I really love these fiery eyes of yours. They are so dark, so... deep. We really don't see this in my hometown. It's like a flame burning deep inside. *[stare deep, hypnotic scanning]*

- I really love this thick glossy hair of yours. It feels very full and vibrant in my hand *[twirling hair]*. I like grabbing it *[grab a big handful at the base of her skull]*, I like pulling it. *[pull]*

## Slavic Princess

- I really love these long legs of yours. So slim, so.... long. Girls in my hometown are usually thicker and shorter. Seeing such long long legs... *[squeeze thigh, cup her calf in your palm]*... mmmm... very sexy.

- I really love your cheekbones. This bit here *[softly trace a horizontal line along her cheek]* is so high and distinct. You've got a cat-like look. Very sexy.

I'll avoid waxing lyrical about her ass or breasts in this mood because the purpose is **qualification**. I'm giving her a warm glow from genuine sexual admiration, making her feel like a special snowflake. It's delivered with warmth and appreciation rather than naked sexual lust (dirty talk, see below). Her usual response to such compliments will be like a cat being stroked. She'll smile and sit still letting it happen. If she responds by babbling on self-consciously (qualifying herself) then she's still not quite comfortable so reassure her a little:

## Best response

> *Me:* I really like the shape of your legs. You've got a smooth curved shape to your calves and thighs. Very sexy.
>
> *Her:* It's the advantage of dancing *[comfortably soaks up sexual admiration]*
>
> *Me:* Mmmm. *[allow comfortable silence]*

## Self-conscious response

> *Me:* I really like the shape of your legs. You've got a smooth curved shape to your calves and thighs. Very sexy.
>
> *Her:* I dance alot. I train three times and week and do lots of exercise... blah blah... jibber-jabber... so I think it's good to be in shape... blah blah...
>
> *Me:* Shhhhh.... be quiet and let me admire these lovely legs.

# Ramping It Up For Extraction

You'll be pretty sure you want to pull the trigger by now. If logistics are blocked or you suspect her resistance won't be beaten tonight, then you can dial things down and start seeding the third date. However, if things are chugging along nicely you'll start entering the pre-extraction phase. This is where you knock down her remaining barriers.

### *Accidental or Deliberate*

You've really got two paths to the SDL/D2L in terms of tone. Either you make it blindingly obvious which direction it's going (but preserving Plausible Deniability by not overtly saying it) or you make it seem like an accident that she landed on your bed with her legs apart. Both work. What doesn't work is clumsily shifting from one to another. I will almost always go the deliberate route because it's more fun and filters harder for timewasters. When the girl knows she's going to get fucked at the end of the date there'll be no LMR and she'll find the whole experience extremely exciting (She's Super On). You'll get less bullshit at your leap of faith moments. However, if you think the girl is quite inhibited and inexperienced(she's Stealth On), you should choose the stealth option of avoiding sex talk and just progressing her physical compliance by leading her around and lightly escalating kino. You'll know a few questions into the questions game which it is. Don't feel creepy — you're still covertly conveying your intent. Deep down she knows where this is going. The problem to avoid is going overt with a Stealth On girl or going covert with a Super On girl — figure out which she responds to.

*Run deep rapport in tandem with progressive escalation*

# The Questions Game

We've talked earlier about how to progress to the first kiss. If that happens organically when the girl complies with your verbal and physical Venue Two escalation, that's great. Other times it doesn't quite work out. In these cases, impose the structure of The Questions Game to patiently walk her to that moment. Once you have the kiss, the game can be continued late in Venue Three to set up the extraction. Many girls find the structure helpful for their own part in the conversation and will try to prolong it ("Let's ask more questions") rather than use free-form conversation. That's fine. I've had dates where the final three hours of talk was essentially a drawn-out question and answer session.

You are building a love bubble that is tinged with adventure. Whatever happens between you and her is a special secret that no-one will ever hear of. You are not a player and she is not a slut. This is just a special opportunity that may never happen again. Be extremely open and honest with her, and if that's difficult for you remember that the anonymity runs both ways — she'll never meet *your* dad, *your* boss, or *your* friends either. You will lead with your vibe and your openness. Usually at this point I play the questions game. Be non-judgemental and say things like "I understand," and "Yes, that seems quite normal." Here's a contrived example:

*Me:* I've got an idea. Let's play a questions game. Simple rules. We take turns asking questions, about anything. You either give a full truthful answer or refuse to answer. No lying, no half-truths and no getting angry about the question. Ok?

*Her:* Ok. You first.

*Me:* What's the naughtiest thing you did as a child?

*Her:* When I was about 6 years old I stamped on all the flowers in my grandmother's garden. How about you?

*Me:* Come on, that's the same question. Use some imagination.

*Her:* Hmmmmmm… are you married?

*Me:* No. I'm divorced. I was with a Japanese girl for ten years, married for three. We got divorced four years ago. No children…Do you want a hard or easy question?

*Her:* Hard

*Me:* When was the last time you had sex?

That's the basic flow of the game, but the real skill is in the calibration. This game is about rapport, vulnerability, and — *crucially*- escalation. So I'll go into more detail on how to do it properly. This is just an overt structure to achieve those ends, and as you get better you can drop the game pretense and just turn the conversation in this direction covertly.

**Rapport** — The act of sharing these progressively intimate details is bringing you both together and strengthening the bubble. Don't posture or be try-hard. Keep to the truth and present it as-is. Girls know when you're faking it and you don't have any margin for error on an SDL. She must really trust that what you say and do is a purely-distilled authentic you, and she will because that's exactly what you'll give her. Any time you try to put one over on her you risk tripping her Creepy Guy Alarm, which on an SDL/D2 is already at Defcon 5. Not every question will be sexual. You'll also be asking her about her fondest (and strangest) memories, her dreams, her deepest secrets. This SDL love bubble is a truly unique opportunity for her — an opportunity to be completely honest and unguarded with a man without any consequence to the rest of her life.

**Vulnerability** — If she asks you a question that stirs a little discomfort in you, you should answer her with 100% truth. It's ok to admit you were a shy teenager, or once fell off the stage during a school play, or you were very nervous the first time you ever kissed a girl. The act of telling the complete truth is far more powerful than the counter-balancing negative trait you fear your words may speak of. In this magic SDL/D2 bubble, the girl wants purity of connection more than she wants a high-value man. You are trying to fuck her today in a moment of special authenticity., You are not trying to be her boyfriend. These are two different things and she has different requirements for the two different roles. Focus on creating the pure moment rather than setting yourself up as marriage material. Things I've told girls before the SDL or Day 2 lay:

- My mum once made me swim in my underpants because I'd forgotten my trunks, and when the lifeguard noticed I was deathly embarrassed and didn't forgive her for years.

- One time when I was 11 years old travelling to a BMX competition with my team in the minibus, I got lost in a motorway services, went to the wrong car park, and thought they'd left without me. I started crying and called my granddad, who then set out in his car to pick me up.

- The first three months after my divorce were devastating and I couldn't enjoy food, sleep, or hobbies.

## *Get the LMR out early*

Once I've pushed a girl into a taxi to my house I always fuck her. Some of that is the power of my eye-mesmer / leadership, but mainly it's because her mind is already made up before she gets in. The last places you want LMR are on your bed and in the taxi rank. I prefer to bring the LMR forwards so she can get her objections out of the way during the date. This gives me time to provide her with a rationalisation, while her hindbrain has time to eat away at the forebrain's resistance. That's one reason why the overtly-escalated question game is good. You bring it all forwards, deal with it, then relax and go back into rapport. Her hindbrain will now be your ally, rather than your enemy, in the fight against her forebrain.

**Escalation** — The questions are supposed to get progressively more personal and sexual. You are collecting information on her sexual history and preferences, while also turning her mind towards sex. This makes her start heating up, and she begins to realise that sex is a likely natural outcome to this encounter. Like all escalation it needs to be smooth and well-calibrated. Drop the questions in innocently at first, and gradually turn them more personal, more uninhibited, and more about you and her. Remember to take some backwards steps. If every question becomes dirtier and dirtier you'll sound like a horny teenager who can't control his boner.

Generally I'll calibrate my next question based on how she answered the last one and what she asked me. Green lights are when the girl is essentially escalating you by either (i) making your last question her next question, or (ii) following a sexual question from you with one of equal or greater intrusiveness. In these cases you can get quite dirty quite quickly. Amber lights are when she answers, maybe not especially enthusiastically, but without evading or blocking. If she's consistently playing coy or trying to spin things around in a gamey way (you feel she is trying to trap you), you need to switch tactics and crush her frame — she's not cooperating and probably never will, so you have to crush her into submission and hope to make her follow your lead.

Like the rest of Game, I try to achieve my objective with covert communication. She gets the message loud and clear without me having to spell it out. Sometimes I need to get a little more overt either because my vibe / momentum isn't very good that day or her own calibration isn't so good (some girls don't flirt well). An easy way is to preface your question with "Would you like a hard question or an easy one?". Her replying hard is a green light, so move to the next level with a sexualised question. Here's some examples of what I ask:

Early in the game, with focus on rapport and vulnerability. These are all safe in Venue Two as well.

- What's the naughtiest thing you ever did as a child?

- What's your fondest childhood memory?

- Do you have a recurring dream?

- Are you close to your father?

- Tell me something embarrassing. Nothing crazy, just a bit embarrassing.

- Do you have a favourite place in your hometown where you like to spend time?

- Tell me a secret about you. Something I'd never guess even if I knew you five years.

- Do you ever think you are not a good person?

- What's your favourite animal and what do you like about them?

- When you were a teenager and put up posters on your bedroom wall of your first crush, who was he?

- What's your impression of English men?

By about the third question you should have dropped in the first escalation question, and from then on you should weight your questions more towards escalation. Early escalations will not directly suggest you and her having sex. I tend to make these questions exclusive to Venue Three unless the girl is giving green lights:

- How old were you when you first kissed a boy? (and did you like it?)

- When was the last time you had sex?

- Which part of your body are you happiest with?

- Have you ever had a foreign boyfriend?

- What do you like in a man? / Describe your perfect man

- Do you have any hidden tattoos?

- What do girls in your country think about sex?

- What did you think when I started talking to you?

- What do you think of Fifty Shades Of Grey?

Assuming she's enjoying this game and progressively opening up with green or amber lights, you need to push harder. SDLs/D2Ls are about momentum. You've made The Decision and you decided you're going to pull the trigger. So go for it, because it's too late to back out now. Start asking some pushier and more sexualised questions, and moving it towards the idea of having sex today. Note this last set of questions are optional:

- What do you like about me?

- How many men have you kissed? (I rarely ask "slept with" because it can trigger too much ASD but if she asks me, I'll throw it back at her next question)

- What is the sexual thing you've never done but are most interested in?

- Do you like to be dominated in bed?

- Have you ever given a blowjob in public?

- What's the strangest place you had sex?

- Do you like anal?

- What did you think about last time you masturbated?

- Do you have an unusual sexual fantasy?

- Where do you like a man to cum?

- What's the fastest you ever had sex?

These questions usually push you past the point of no return — if you don't fuck her today, you won't see her again. But they are also bold, confident, and get her wet just hearing you say them. You're the R-selected man so she likes the aggression of it. Sometimes if the girl seems slightly tentative I'll explicitly say — "Look. I'm never going to meet your family, or friends, or boss. I probably won't even add you to Facebook. Everything we say and do here is anonymous."

*Do you verbalise?*

I'm very sexual during the last hour of an SDL/D2L as I build to extraction. I want all of the LMR neutralised before we get into the taxi, but this is not the only way to do it. You can rely on covert polarisation and a kiss close, then save all the LMR-busting for back at your house. Just be aware you are trading one challenge for another. My way means I bang every single girl that gets into the taxi. Delaying until the bedroom will result in more extractions, more LMR, and more girls running out of your house (or being thrown out). The final notch tally will be about even. Try both routes.

It's a good sign when she's enthusiastically and fully answering, then throwing good questions back at you. Counter-intuitively, it's an even better sign when she's timidly answering with a slightly blushing face and tentative in her questions to you (a lot of "and same question for you") because she's even more cowed by your presence and in your frame — she has willingly put **all** of the responsibility for sex onto your shoulders and that's a burden you'll happily bear.

At some point you'll both have told about your sexual history, what you are like in bed, your attitudes to sex, and why you are sexually attracted to each other. You've reached a mutually understood (and not necessarily explicitly stated) agreement that sex is extremely likely. **So stop**. Really, stop. It's agreed now so you don't need to labour the point. Learn to accept Yes for an answer. Tick the checkbox and move back into rapport. If you haven't kissed her yet this is a good time to do so. Not a big sloppy makeout, just a physical expression of the agreement you've reached through the question game. It's on. Don't rush. Let the car freewheel. It's now all about strengthening rapport and leading her to the sex location at a mutually acceptable speed.

Pull back a little. Go to the toilet and make her wait five minutes. Look at yourself in the mirror and review where you are at and what comes next. If you need to text flatmates to leave condoms next to your bedroom door or to clean the kitchen, now is the time. It's probably 50% sure at this stage. Now go back upstairs and make normal conversation about everyday subjects. Don't broach sex as a subject again, no matter how tempted you are. Let there be a few comfortable silences while her brain spins over. Relax her. Make a few light compliance demands below what she's already shown herself comfortable with -- e.g. "Pass me that lighter," or "Show me that."

---

### Escalate on a full drink

It is extremely rare for a girl to get up and leave a date when her drink is more than half full. It's just socially weird. The moment you've paid the barman for a pair of drinks is the moment you can mentally relax, take a deep breath and think to yourself "Whatever happens, I have at least the time it takes to drink these to work the set." Girls will wait for a natural break to excuse themselves, so these are the natural risk points, especially when you've finished one drink and want to bounce to the next venue. So do your most risky escalation at each venue while the glasses are half full. That means things like breaking rapport while letting your eyes gaze into the distance, challenging her on a topic, kino testing, asking a prying sexual question, giving an IOI in verbal escalation. By timing it right you will have the remaining half of the drink left to recover from a fumble. You've got half a drink's worth of time for her hindbrain to corrode the forebrain barriers.

# THE LAST HALF-HOUR

You've already covertly agreed that you both want sex. That's done and can be forgotten about. You now have two goals

1. Accelerate comfort so that she is willing to…

2. … be moved progressively closer to the sex location


That's it.

Be clear that comfort and rapport are not the same thing. Rapport is making an emotional connection between the true you and the true her. It is a shedding of all the bullshit defences and masks that people wear when dealing with strangers. Rapport advances in a straight line the same way taking your clothes off does. You progressively show more of yourself to each other until you reach a point of emotional nakedness. This becomes the new default level at which you communicate with each other, and you feel it as a strong bond. You really know each other. Comfort is about feeling comfortable in each other's presence. It is an emotional state but not an interpersonal connection. You can feel comfort alone but not rapport, because the latter requires two objects to tie the bond. Comfort just *is*. It's like having your heartbeat at its resting rate. Comfort lulls you to sleep.

So when I say you are accelerating comfort, that's what I mean. You no longer need to pry into her memories, her hopes, her dreams, her vulnerabilities (rapport). That phase is complete. Those clothes are already lying on the floor in a crumpled heap. The checkbox is ticked. You no longer need to challenge her, tease her, spin her around (attraction). You no longer need to get her wet and thinking sex thoughts, imagining how your hard dick feels deep inside her (escalation). You no longer need to find out what she's doing, when she's leaving and what her attitudes to sex are (screening). All those boxes are ticked. She's fully prepped for a rousting.

All you need to do is get her heartbeat down to its resting rate and then lead her home.

## Physical Comfort

Venue Three is dark, seductive, and fairly quiet. Hopefully there won't be many people around causing a ruckus and there won't be any competing males. If you are thinking of taking her to a nightclub now you are absolutely insane. You need to be taking her in the *opposite* direction, away from bright lights and loud music. Concentrate on slowing everything down and reducing the talking. Find a booth or dark corner with L-shaped seats. If she defaults to sitting across from you then take her hand and guide her to sit next to you. The vibe will be soft and you will be comfortable with long silences during which you keep physical contact between you.

Sit in the King's Chair position. You lean back on your sofa / booth with your knees far apart and your shoulder blades against the backrest. Your hand furthest from her will be resting lightly and comfortable on your thigh, or the seat cushion next to your leg, or draped over the back of the sofa. Your nearest hand will be resting along the width of her shoulders and that hand lightly pulling her in with her far-side shoulder. This will cause her to lean against you, her head resting either on your shoulder or upper chest. She will be floppy.

From the King's Chair you will start applying soft non-sexual physical attention such as stroking her hair, scratching her temple (like a cat), running your fingertip slowly up and down the outside of her upper arm, laying a heavy hand to hold her side at her floating ribs, softly running your finger down the bridge of her nose or the line of her jaw. These should cause her to nuzzle up into you and feel comfortable. It's like petting a cat. Sometimes I'll talk while I do this and sometimes I let us both absorb the comfortable silence. If I do talk it'll be a monologue about nothing in particular, perhaps an observation on the room or life generally. The topic will not be sexual or controversial, and the real purpose of the monologue is to drop my voice an octave, slow it down, and just seduce her with the soft low vocal tone. It's the delivery not the words. I want her to love my voice.

### The Floppy Test

Sex is one long compliance test. As the date progresses you can test her physical compliance to see how amenable she is for the next Leap Of Faith moment. To test for the kiss, you can find excuses to get your faces close together and see if she accepts it without evading or moving back. A girl who doesn't want to be kissed will make it physically difficult for you to cross the space (e.g. by sitting across a table from you, or putting her bag between you when you sit down), and in contrast a girl who does want to be kissed will suddenly just be there, in a position easy to kiss. It will seem like nothing at all just to reach over and grab her.

When you start building for your extraction, you'll do the Floppy Test to see how fully she's fallen under your spell. A girl ready for sex will be surrendering full responsibility for the act to you and this will manifest itself in her offering no resistance to you moving her body around. So test it in a covert plausibly-deniable manner. While sitting in the King's Chair pull her in to you and gauge how softly and easily (how "floppy") she falls onto you and fits herself to your shape. A girl who fully collapses into you with her head on your shoulder, her hand on your stomach or thigh, and the length of her body in contact with yours is very floppy and thus ready to be extracted. In contrast, if she stiffens and resists she's not ready. Push her away and rebuild momentum.

This can easily run for twenty minutes. Play it by ear and see how much she's enjoying it or if she's getting fidgety and agitated. If all is well escalate it further by cupping your hand under her thighs and physically putting her legs across the top of your thighs, as if she's a little girl curled up on her father's lap. You'll be amazed at how many tall greyhound models just love this. You are very deliberately physically framing her as the weak little girl in contrast to your strong pillar of masculine strength. Kiss her intermittently, but use soft comfortable kisses not hard sexual makeouts. Remember it's all about comfort now.

## Standing comfort

Sometimes you're in a bar that doesn't offer a good booth and you're forced to stand. I'd rather stand than sit on crappy wooden chairs. Just like the King's Chair, you are presenting yourself as the unmoveable oak tree while she is the little squirrel that flits around you and comes to rest on the branches. From a standing position you do this by locking in to a wall or bar area (the more secluded the better). Make sure the full line of your back is in contact with the wall and your shoulder blades pulled back like they are trying to touch in the middle of your back (to avoid hunching your shoulders). Let your chin rise up and the back of your head touch the wall. Now snake your arm around her lower back and pull her into you. Do not move to her. She comes to you. It's crucial in late-stage kino that she moulds her shape to yours and not the other way around. Pull her in and it will double as a floppy test. Does she come easily? Does she press the full length of her body against yours? A very horny girl will push up onto her toes to press her groin / stomach against you. This is tiring for her so don't be surprised when she drops back onto flat feet and collapses her head against your shoulder. She'll often drape a hand onto your shoulders and leave it there, softly feeling the shape of your shoulders. This is a great sign because shoulders are to women what breasts are to men.

You shouldn't need more than half an hour of advanced physical comfort. As you feel her heartbeat and breathing get slower and heavier you'll be seeding the extraction. If she's volunteered a pretext then go with that (e.g. "I'd love to see you play guitar"), but for most amber lights you'll need to provide your own excuse. Don't overcook it. Don't oversell some amazing thing back at your house, because it looks too desperate. She knows it's a pretext. I do the Whiskey Seed.

1. Early in the date, often in the light non-alcoholic venue we'll be asking a bit about hobbies to build rapport. I'll mention how I love whiskey. I travel a lot so every time I pass through an airport I pick up a new bottle, experimenting with different distilleries. I'll wax lyrical about the quality gradations of whiskey and how there's no upper limit on how good it can be.

2. In the light alcoholic venue I'll make reference to the whiskeys they sell and talk about which ones are best. I'll spin a little yarn about the whiskey and cigar room we had in my house, which we fixed up to look like a 1940s speakeasy. This

story is all about evocative sights, sounds, and smells while positioning myself as a sophisticated gent.

3. In the dark alcoholic venue I'll tell a ridiculous story about a Japanese whiskey maker who made his fortune supplying the two armies in the war between the Emperor and the Shogun. It's really an intellectual mastery story to weave in facts about Japan. At the end I tell her, "I just made all that stuff up. It's a total fabrication" and smirk.

4. Finally when I'm ready to extract and she's all floppy against me I suggest a nightcap. I don't outright mention it's at my house unless she asks.

Now you must slip in a pre-extraction inoculation. Always ask her this question:

### *When do you need to be home?*

It doesn't matter what she tells you, just make a note of it. Usually it'll be at least an hour away. You reply with reassurance of "Ok. I'll make sure I have you home by then." The purpose is to future-project that she's getting home on time and not spending the night with you. She'll relax and be more comfortable. It means that when you go for the extraction you can say "Ok, let's go to the next place. I'll make sure you are back by [her time]" This makes it far easier to extract than having an open-ended "Let's go to the next place," even though it's all an illusion and she doesn't really care. It's about plausible deniability and calming her hindbrain while giving her forebrain a rationalisation.

- No time limit = "He wants to have sex. He wants me to stay over. What happens if I'm late for work. I don't have my contact lenses blah blah blah"

- Time limit = "It's just a drink."

You are now getting set for the biggest and most important Leap Of Faith moment in the entire daygame model — Pulling the Trigger and going for extraction. Before engaging in this move, consider if you need to heat her up more with dirty talk, if she needs additional help rationalising her decision to fuck (give the Sexual Openness Talk), or if she seems ready to go.

# SEXUAL OPENNESS TALK

### Forebrain Fodder

*A series of rationalisations and reframes fed to a girl to engage her forebrain and help it to justify switching off so that her hindbrain can get the sex she desires. This is usually required during extraction on fast lays.*

### Anti-Slut Defence

*A girl's future-projection of the regret she will feel after sex for having been too easy. ASD becomes stronger as girls get more sexual partners and then declines again when they pass the point of not caring anymore. Thus, a European girl with a laycount of 5-15 will have the highest ASD.*

When you're making out and sitting comfortably together you'll sense where her forebrain is at. Does she seem completely comfortable progressing towards sex, or do you feel a few barriers of the "I'm not that kind of girl" variety? Most of the women we date will be towards the Good Girl end of the spectrum, so they are not experienced at navigating the courtship ritual towards sex. In particular, they aren't used to going so fast. She may have a conflict with her identity despite thoroughly enjoying the experience. There's an infinite number of variations on how she may express conflict, but usually she'll give you Player Tests ("Do you say this to all the girls", "You're so fast", "How often do you do this", "I bet you have lots of girls") or she'll find obstacles ("I have to get up early tomorrow", "I haven't done my homework") or she'll judge her own behaviour ("I shouldn't drink so much", "I don't usually give my number to men I just meet").

Whatever the mode of her expression you'll feel it as **reticence**. She feels like she's not a good girl for being at this late stage on the first or second date. In these cases you deal with her objections covertly by setting the frame of sexual openness. If she doesn't show conflict, you needn't make a big deal of it. The main purpose is to pre-emptively provide her with forebrain rationalisations that allow her to follow her hindbrain's desire for sex. This means feeding her with **forebrain fodder** like:

- "Society judges people too harshly. There's always somebody somewhere trying to stop you living your life. I think people should mind their own business. Only you know what makes you happy, only you know what you really want."

- "Sometimes I think life is so rich and rewarding. Nature has given us so many things to make us happy. Just breathing crisp mountain air in the morning, or hearing birds singing in your garden. We have these natural appetites. Eating food, drinking coffee, having sex... it's just so... fun. So rewarding. You can't help thanking nature for it."

- "It's sad how many people let life pass them by. We're only young once. It's the time to explore new countries, new hobbies, new experiences. Once we're married with kids and a mortgage there's so little time to follow our passions. I always respect the people who take their chances. They people who climb the mountains, trek through the jungle, swim the Channel. Life is about living and taking your chances."

- "I have a little theory in life. When I see an opportunity, something interesting or exciting, I always think two things: will it kill me? will it put me in prison? If the answer is no, I'll try it. It doesn't even matter if it turns out to be a mistake. The way I look at it is about answering the question: What if? What if I quit my job and live in Japan? What if I have a kickboxing match? If I do it and really enjoy it then great, I've found something new I like. And if I do it and it all goes horribly wrong... so what. That's better than going my whole life wondering What If?"

### Fourth Wall

*The socially-constructed barrier that discourages you from overtly discussing the subtext of the interaction: that you're a man, she's a woman, and you're trying to seduce her. Usually women want the man to play the game with her without acknowledging the amount of conscious effort required to stage the game.*

You'll see where this frame is leading. She's sitting next to you with hot blood and fervent imagination wondering what it would be like to be naked and underneath you. Her hindbrain is raring to go but the pesky forebrain is throwing out derailments: "You're not that kind of girl, this is too fast, he's a player, what would your mum think, you've never done this before" etc. So rather than let her forebrain set the frame you are doing it for her by imposing your own Take Your Chances frame.

Then you'll turn it more explicitly sexual. It needn't follow-on directly from Take Your Chances. You can sit in silence or talk nonsense. Get a feel for her, see if her body language or eyes change during the talk to reflect the "Okay, I'm going to fuck this guy" decision. If she's still on the fence you should start aggressively normalising sex. The frame is this:

*When a man and a woman like each other, sex is the most natural, most wonderful thing in the world.*

There's two ways you can impose this frame:

# 1. Overtly Discussing It

If you've settled on a very open and self-referential vibe you've probably already broken the **fourth wall**. You've openly discussed sex and sexual preferences. You've already people-watched and offered interpretations of their SMV and navigation of the courtship ritual. Some sets just drift into this unusually open vibe. In such cases you can risk overtly laying out a favourable frame (though avoid directly personalising it to you and her having sex because it will lead to ASD). Let her logically dissolve her own LMR. I'd estimate approximately 20% of sets go this route.

# 2. Covertly Demonstrating It

Lean towards the covert unless you've stopped moving forwards. You'll be holding your frame, touching her and acting as if this is the most natural and obvious way to proceed. You can also drop in the following spikes that covertly convey the frame while also heating her up. The key is to be completely congruent and open about it. There's nothing seedy here. You are a man and you are sexually interested in her. You want to fuck her and she's going to be glad you did.

# Dirty Talk

As the date moves closer towards extraction you can pace and lead her with dirty talk. I'll pull her in with comfort (not making out) and talk into her ear with low tones about precisely what I intend to do with her when she's alone with me. I usually begin with the phrase "I'd like to..." or "I'm going to..."

"I'd like to rip your clothes off. Within one minute of taking you home I'll have you naked on my bed. I'll be looking at your sexy body, watching your chest heave as you breath heavily. Seeing you hot and horny."

Watch her eyes and breathing as you say this. Be sensitive to any squirming in her legs or unnecessary movements (e.g. crossing and uncrossing her feet). You are looking for a sign it has "hit," that her body responded with a "Oh god yes, that would be great." If so, it doesn't matter if she overtly acknowledges enjoying the conversation. Continue the dirty talk and keep heating her up. You must be bold and absolutely unapologetic for your sexual intent.

"Your knickers will hit the floor. I'll put my hand on your chest and push you slowly backwards until your ass touches the wall. My eyes will be looking deep into yours. Your heart will be beating fast. I'll just hold you there, my eyes drinking in your beauty, looking up and down at your legs, your tense stomach, the full roundness of your breasts, your lips slightly parted and wet."

Pace her. Tell her how she'll feel. Pour in the psychology of the moment, how you like looking at her and she likes being looked at. Her body will give out lots of involuntary responses. A key rule of the dirty talk is:

*Talk only about the build-up to sex, not the sex itself*

Do not describe her sucking your dick or you putting it in her pussy. Do not give her the dirty-talk victory of *actually receiving your dick*. Girls love anticipation. Dirty talk her about the context of sex and the escalation until just before the moment of truth. Tell her how she feels as she's in your lounge sipping wine, how you look at her, how your blood boils... then in the bedroom when her clothes are coming off and you are dominating her, pushing her... then when she's naked, feeling the skin-on-skin, getting wet and begging for your dick...

...and that's all she gets now!

I will again emphasize that you should not verbalise the sex act itself. When you dirty talk a girl her powers of imagination simulate the feelings of living the situation, so you can't give her the (imaginative) release of the sex itself. You are stoking her hunger and not delivering the food just yet. The only purpose of dirty talk in Venue Three is to facilitate the extraction, to make her hungry for more. When she's satiated there's no hunger.

## Copping a Feel

Girls really like unapologetic risk-taking men. Men who go for what they want with no apology and have no weird hang-ups about expressing their sexual desire. That's why she responded so well to your initial intent during the street stop. She was attracted to the way you made it blindingly clear, covertly, that you wanted to pick her up and have sex with her. You didn't care then what other pedestrians thoughtand you don't care now what other patrons think. You are here to fuck her. And she likes the sheer brass neck of it. One great way to express this attitude is to flagrantly touch her up in public. Particular favourites of mine:

- While sitting side by side in silence, lightly grab her blouse above the breasts and pull it out and then brazenly look down her shirt at her breasts. Nod approvingly and then continue as you were.

- Tell her to stand up a second. Be insistent. When she does, slap her ass then tell her "Okay, you can sit back down now."

- Reach into her shirt and grab her breasts skin-on-skin. Give it a quick squeeze, flick the nipple then continue as you were. Only do this if you already had your hands on her breasts from outside her shirt during a makeout.

- Inspect some part of her body like a horse-trader looking the horse in the mouth. I like to put a hand on each hip bone and give a little squeeze while looking thoughtfully. Then I nod my head and utter "Nice. Nice hips."

In each case attitude is key. You are brazenly unapologetically objectifying her from a postion of genuine male appreciation. She will probably get an indignant flush (which she loves) and utter a protest framing you as a dirty lecher. Grin. Brass neck it. If necessary reply with "I don't apologise for being a man. You are a fine young lady."

# Mong Eyes

One of my more recent infield experiments has been deep eye-fucking ten minutes or so before the extraction. This works well because you are hijacking the girl's emotional wiring but never presenting any formal obstruction she can use as derailment fodder. It works like this...

After dirty-talking and copping a feel she should be feeling pretty hot under the collar. Her hindbrain is bubbling and cooking her forebrain. So turn up the heat even more. Find a reason to look deep into each other's eyes. It can be accidental (you both happen to look steadily so you continue it), on a pretext (complimenting her eyes as an excuse to look into them or "Do you wear contacts?") or overt ("Look at me. Look deeply"). When a girl is horny she will naturally hold long deep eye contact with you, so take this and use it.

Stare deep into her eyes for minutes on end. Hold long unbroken eye contact.

It's ok to blink, ok to scratch your nose. Just don't break the contact. While doing so, experiment with the emotions and thoughts you project. She'll detect these in the tiny micro-movements in your iris. Remember girls respond to movement so don't project the same thought on a single note. Mix it up between:

- **Raw sexual desire.** "I'm going to fuck you. I'm going to rip your panties off, bend you over my sofa and put my hard dick deep inside you"

- **Thoughtful reflection.** "This is a fascinating evening. You really are a very interesting girl."

- **Openness.** "Look as deep as you want. Read my soul. I've got nothing to hide. Drink it in."

- **Cocky challenge.** "You're not winning this. However strong you think you are, I'm stronger. I'm the boss here. I'm going to break you down and have my way with you."

- **Warmth.** "I really do like you. I feel like I want to pull you in, kiss your forehead and give you a big hug."

- **Amused mastery.** "You're dying to fuck me, aren't you? I can see it plain as day. You absolutely want my dick."

Play with it and disappear into the moment. Let the eye contact run on an on. Pierce her soul. You'll find she'll take on the monged look where her eyes go big and round, her jaw slackens and her mouth drops half open. She'll seem lost in the whirlpool. This is a great sign. Heat her up.

By the end of Venue Three you have shown her every type of man. You have at turns been attentive, charming, roughish, rough, dangerous, safe, sophisticated, and brutish. Sometimes you've regaled her with extended inventive stories while at others you been silent and stared into space. Whatever her favoured "kind of guy I have sex with" archetype is, you've shown some of it. You've bounced her between your matched-pair traits.

### Calibrate Her Kiss

Once you finally kiss the girl her response tells you where her mind is at. A timid or reticent kiss suggests she needs more time and comfort. A normal kiss is just that — you both like each other and everything is fine. The big tell is if she jumps you. If kissing her is like a dam bursting then she's very horny and you should definitely extract that evening and soon. She's telling you she wants sex. She can't just overtly ask to be fucked so she has to give you covert signals. There are few stronger signals than passionately and hungrily kissing you.

So if she's pushing her tongue down your throat, pushing her breast up against you, giving you a full body-to-body press, grabbing your head, moaning and so on that's a massive signal. Do her a favour and extract but resist the urge to feel her up beyond kissing until you're in the sex location.

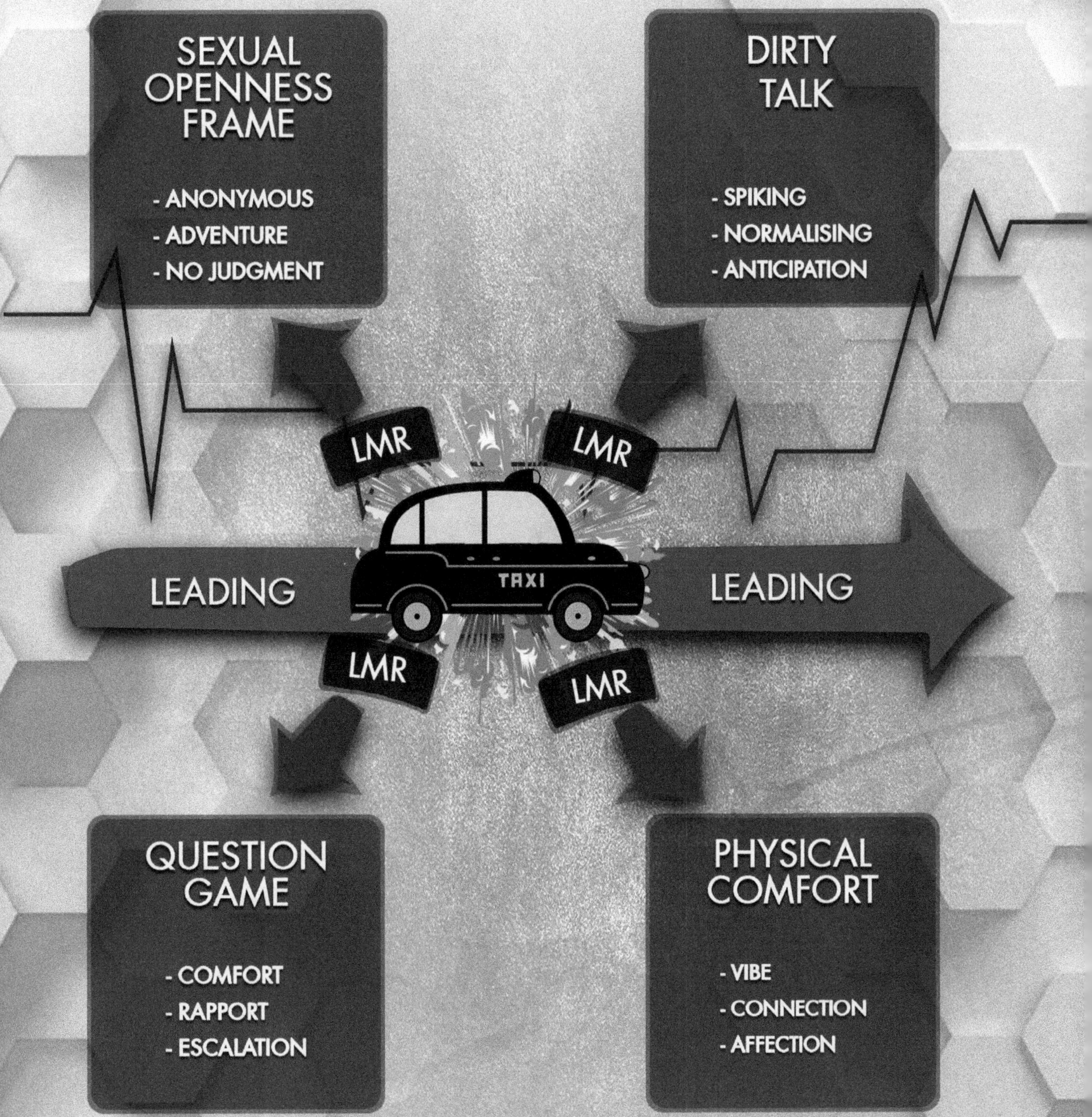
SEXUAL OPENNESS FRAME
- ANONYMOUS
- ADVENTURE
- NO JUDGMENT
DIRTY TALK
- SPIKING
- NORMALISING
- ANTICIPATION
LMR
LMR
LEADING
TAXI
LEADING
LMR
LMR
QUESTION GAME
- COMFORT
- RAPPORT
- ESCALATION
PHYSICAL COMFORT
- VIBE
- CONNECTION
- AFFECTION

# CLOSE
## section seven

Late in the date you'll be sitting with the girl, and you'll be pretty sure she wants sex. It's time to pull the trigger and take her home. This section has a discussion on how to extract her and how to behave once she is in your house.

I describe her emotional turmoil at taking the final step off The Cliff so soon after meeting you, and how to deal with her coping strategy of Derailing The Train. Once she's on your bed she'll typically give some Last Minute Resistance. If she's there she wants to fuck, so I outline my bedroom escalation model to maximise the chances that she will.

Lastly, I end the phase with pointers on how to position her on your rotation or just let her go with the minimum drama.

# CLOSE

## EXTRACTION

This is the single most important moment in the entire process. She either lets you extract her or she doesn't. There's only really three variations of this:

1. The long taxi.

2. The long walk.

3. The short walk. In principle there's little difference.

Usually you'll be getting a taxi.

## The Long Taxi

The first thing to grasp about this extraction is *it doesn't matter how long the taxi ride is*. Once she is in the taxi you have her. Climbing into that taxi is the big decision moment from her because she knows full well it's a covert agreement to have sex tonight. Unless she's paralytic drunk, she knows what she's doing and I suggest you never ever get a girl paralytic drunk — it's creepy, the sex will be gross, and she'll hate you for it the next day. So in the final venue you wait until the drinks are finished (and if it's a tab you will have already paid it by calling for the bill fifteen minutes earlier) and then it's time to lead lead lead.

This is the biggest test of your balls. The biggest test of your conviction. The biggest test of your intention to fuck this girl and your sense of entitlement that you deserve it. It is no time to pussy around playing hard to get and aloof. Don't expect a green light. Even a super-horny girl will suddenly switch to amber / red lights at this stage with her forebrain's final attempt to derail the train. She's about to step off the cliff.

## Derailing the Train

As the sex with the greater reproductive investment, women are designed to be choosy and stop men from having sex with them. From the very first moment of the interaction her default mode is to find a reason to disqualify you. Don't hate girls for this. From age of fifteen (much earlier in Wales) they are subjected to a non-stop barrage of dick. Walking down the street to the bus stop she'll have ten men look at her who want to fuck her. They won't say or do anything about it, but she knows the tacit offer of dick is there. The guy who holds the shop door open for her, the guy who gives a nervous smile in the queue for the lift, the boss at work who gives her the easier projects, the office junior from downstairs who always hand delivers inter-office mail… She knows full well all these men want to fuck her. That realization brings tremendous power, but it's also overwhelming and thus she needs a strategy to fend them all off and save her precious eggs for the high value man. Her method? She find reasons to disqualify them. Too short. Too fat. Too old. Bad hair. Whatever.

### The Cliff

Girls are never in full control of their sexual destiny. That's the price they pay for having the passive role in the human courtship ritual. Consider yourself lucky as a man that you get to initiate. The initial choice is always yours — you see the girl you like so you go and make something happen. At all stages in the ritual you are moving it forward against her resistance / compliance. Girls trust their emotions almost 100% and thus follow intuition. Men are problem-solvers who live in their logical forebrain, helping us to identify real-world problems and then painstakingly fashion solutions. This very book is an example of this — the problem is "How do I fuck lots of hot girls" and the solution is daygame. As men, we prioritise the logical over the emotional (a later chapter will go into how we need to limit this tendency when dealing with women) whereas women are the opposite. That's why we say don't change a girl's mind, change her emotions.

So think through the implications. Game is essentially a system for hijacking a woman's emotions to lead her to sex. You are taking control away from the woman. She knows this and there's nothing wrong with it — it's hardwired into the mating ritual. The whole point of seduction is that you impress upon her emotions the conclusion that you are the man she should spread her legs for, and once she's convinced she surrenders to it. At the initial street stop you overwhelm her with masculine presence triggering her emotional response of smiling and chatting. On the date you apply charisma and connection to trigger her emotional response of opening up and showing you the real her. At the extraction point you demonstrate conviction and leadership to trigger her emotional response of going floppy and letting it "just happen."

At each successive stage she is losing further control over the situation. Think of it like each step in the process is like taking a step closer to the edge of a cliff. It's a linear controllable process. She may feel compelled lemming-like to keep taking steps to that cliff edge, but each step is a small distance. At any moment the bubble can pop and she scurries back to her house. Eventually she reaches the cliff edge. She reaches the moment where one additional step no longer carries her inches forwards… It puts her over the edge and she is irretrievably committed to tumbling through the air all the way down to the sea. That one final step is massive. That's how she feels before getting into the taxi.

It won't always be the taxi. Sometimes it'll be giving her number, or a strong makeout, or agreeing to a second date. Girls sense the relative power of their hindbrain over their forebrain at any given moment. She knows that once the cage is open the beast will escape. Instinctively she knows her limits and knows that "If I agree to this next thing, I'll end up fucking him." That's why you'll get the frustrating experience of girls seeming super-keen and suddenly disappearing. They wanted to exert forebrain control while they still could.

This is why getting the girl into the taxi is game over. It's always the final step off the cliff. If you get her in the taxi and *don't* fuck her, you fucked up big time.

Consider just how much pressure the girl is under. By the time she reaches twenty-five she's had legions of men hitting on her, and some will have worked impressive hustles. It takes prodigious self-control for her to remain un-fucked in the face of such an onslaught. So a hot girl who has made it to twenty-five while keeping her N in single digits has done *extremely well*. She has mastered a vital life-skill and now you are trying to beat her at that game.

The fact that you are in the final venue looking to extract means she hasn't disqualified you, but don't think it's a done deal yet. Once a girl's hindbrain has realised she's about to step off the cliff there will often be a last-minute brain-spazz where she tries to derail the train. She'll do something like:

1. **Nuclear shit tests:** Rather than subtly throwing a test out in the normal course of conversation she'll just pattern-interrupt and throw a wildly uncalibrated test at you. These often come in the form of an insult, disappearing to the bathrooms for fifteen minutes, asking extremely intrusive questions, reframing you as a player, etc. If she's Russian she may even storm off and flirt with another guy for a while. You know it's a test because it's a proactive push back against you. She's testing your frame. The way to deal with these is like dealing with a toddler's tantrum: be unreactive and let her burn out. Then proceed as planned. Don't fight it, because drawing you into her drama is precisely what she needs in order to pop the bubble and find a reason to disqualify you at the last hurdle.

2. **Total passivity:** She'll go limp, quiet, and morose. She won't move, won't talk and may even seem on the verge of tears or boredom (fortunately I've only had the tears twice). This is just another test — a test of your conviction and leadership. Most guys only escalate on green lights so she's deliberately turning them all off to see how well you fumble in the dark. Deep in her hindbrain she's thinking "If this guy can't lead me, he can't have me." So the solution is to lead with conviction. Move her, cajole her, don't let her feet drag. Tell her to finish her drink. Tell her to get her coat. Walk her to the taxi. Don't wait for confirmation.

3. **Reluctance:** She'll put up all kinds of obstacles and reservations that aren't a direct attack on you, nor a refusal to act. She's just experiencing last-minute jitters about having sex and future-projecting how it will impact her self-image. So she'll tell you you're a player, that she doesn't have sex on a first date, they she needs to get up early tomorrow, that she doesn't know how she'll get home. Obstacle after obstacle. Your response should be to say "I understand," give a quick plausible rationalisation without being drawn into a discussion, and then push on regardless. All she really wants is for you to take the responsibility for what's about to happen. Do not get mired into a discussion.

It's important to have the right mindset when she's derailing the train. A chode will get flustered and angry. *How dare she give me this bullshit after all the time and effort*

*I've invested in her! What a bitch!* No, no, no. A player is expecting this response and can see it for what it is — confirmation that the finishing line is around the next corner if he can just hold his resolve a little longer. She's telling you her hindbrain has already decided to fuck and it's now yours to lose. So enjoy the brain-spazz. Lean back with amused mastery and let her stamp her little feet and shake her little hands. Let her hold her breath until everyone dies. And once the storm has passed you flag the taxi and push her into it.

So you've finished your drinks and grabbed your coats. If you followed my date logistics advice you'll be close to a street where you can flag a taxi. Now is a good time to go to the bathroom because it allows her to relax a bit and gather her thoughts. Her decision to have sex will not be made by hounding and pressing her like a door-to-door salesman. She will calmly decide, so give her a little space to organise herself until she's comfortable. The very fact that you leave her alone for five minutes proves to her that you aren't harassing her. While in the bathroom, look at yourself in the mirror and quickly check off all the points. Attraction is done. Comfort is done. You've kissed. She's floppy. It is there to be taken. So gather your wits and get ready to lead with conviction. Do not flounder at the last hurdle. Ready? Now go upstairs and lead like a motherfucker.

Do not seem too eager. Do not walk too fast. Do not drag her. Just calmly walk her outside and engage her mind with bamboozling bullshit. She wants you to switch off her logical mind before it can fuck up her lay, which her hindbrain desperately wants at this point if you've done your job properly. Talk gibberish, ask her questions. Keep it light and relaxed with no talk of sex, and no recognition of what's about to happen. You want to reduce her moment of jitters to the shortest time possible. There's a transition moment where she moves from thinking "We are leaving this bar for another place" to thinking "We are getting into a cab to have sex." The longer that moment is, the more likely she is to wobble and fuck it up. It's no different from having the three-second rule for approaching — the longer the window from seeing a girl to approaching her, the more time you give your avoidance weasel to come up with reasons not to approach. This is the biggest, scariest moment in the whole process for her. So keep the time window short.

- Talking about sex brings those fears to the surface, so don't do it. It's fine to get her horny with dirty talk before the extraction begins, but once the drinks are finished you need to cut it out until you're in your bedroom.

- Strongly sexual makeouts bring those fears to the surface. Keep it light. Don't grab her breasts, don't force your tongue down her throat.

- Don't give her a play-by-play of what you're doing. Don't spell out "We'll go out to this street and look for a taxi." Just do it. Let her retain plausible deniability. As long as you talk about extracting, you are lengthening the window in which she's thinking about extraction.

## The weakest shade of Amber

SDLs are not quite like any other situation, neither a Day 2 nor an SNL. Sometimes the girl is giving only the faintest of amber lights and you haven't even kissed her. You never really know until you flag the taxi. So if you find yourself starved of feedback and she has refused the kiss but **she's still following you around** then flag the taxi anyway. After the sex she'll probably fill in the missing pieces of the puzzle. Maybe she was taught not to kiss men in public.

### Wobble Window

*The period between leaving Venue Three and sitting down inside the taxi where the girl knows she is being extracted but hasn't irrevocably committed to it. Any lingering doubts will surface here and may result in her refusal to go further. You must keep the wobble window as short as possible without hiding the fact that you are extracting.*

Flag a taxi and then push her in. Tell the driver roughly where you are going but not the street address until you are nearly there. Probably half the girls just get in and accept what's coming. The other half will give some token resistance by asking "Where are we going?"

Tell her "Disneyland, to see Mickey Mouse."

She knows full well where you're going so she'll just smile and make a joke. If she gets a bit more serious and says "No, really, where are we going?" tell her "For a nightcap." If the taxi is already moving she'll say ok and relax. If it's still not moving, she might ask again or show reservations. Remind her it's just a drink and you'll have her home soon. Once the taxi is moving it's a done deal.

If she's really resisting you have to let her get back out. A firm no will be very firm at this point. Any "no" that leaves wiggle room / indecision is just token. The stakes are so high now that if she doesn't want to fuck, she'll be very very clear about not wanting to be in the taxi.

- "It's really late. I don't know how I'll get home" = token

- "Your place? No, it's too fast" = token

- "You are kidnapping me!" = token

- "I'm not going to your place" = depends on the tone and body language

- "No" = a real hard no

If you get a real hard no, the chances of the lay are slipping through your grasp and you have to make a difficult judgement call. If she's a bit of a bitch and has lots of slut tells, then you can try overruling her with dominance — tell her "Less of your disobedience missy, get in" and give her strong dominant eyes. That's a big risk but some girls will go for it. I'd only recommend this if you're genuinely running out of time because nowhere else is open.

If you have time then just take a step back and shrug it off. "No worries" and walk her to the next bar. It's very important to act nonchalant. She might try and needle you a bit by saying stuff like "What made you think I'd go home with you?" or "Are you angry?". Just shrug it off. It's okay to say "Well, I'm a bit disappointed," so long as you seem only slightly disappointed. Don't go into a huff. Don't try too hard to look like you don't care. She knows full well that you made your big play to fuck her and you are now disappointed. That's the shit test. She wants to see how you handle rejection at the moment of victory. Be unreactive. Lead her to the next bar and build up to the moment again.

If she's still walking with you then be aware that **the sex is still there to be had**. It's highly unusual to get a girl at the point of extraction when she doesn't actually have sexual interest in you. You'd have already heard about the boyfriend or the logistic impossibilities. She refused the first taxi because there's not enough comfort or she needed to test you a little harder to be sure you're the right guy. So keep with it. There's a small chance that it's because she's on her period but unlikely — that barrier normally doesn't come up until you're in the bedroom.

Let her know you aren't fazed by rejection and rebuild momentum in the next bar. If there's no bar open, walk her to a park. After half an hour try again either with another taxi or by pushing her into a secluded alley / park and rapidly escalating with dirty talk and making out.

# VENUE FOUR — BEDROOM ESCALATION

## Goal: Fuck her

Let's pick up from the moment you step out of the taxi / off the bus. You must understand the nature of Isolation Anxiety.

Men are hardwired to fear approaching because it represents the biggest risk of rejection and thus damage to your ego. Women are the passive agents in seduction, so they don't need to deal with approaching but they have their own rejection fears. Women know full well that men are trying to fuck them, so the whole of the dating process up until sex is one of being chased. Even when we flip the script on them they still know they could short-circuit the whole game by just saying "Let's have sex now." Deep down girls want to feel they could keep the man, even if it doesn't suit her agenda to hang on to this particular man right now. Instinctively she knows once she gives up sex the power equation is now against her.

- Pre-sex: Man pushes for sex, Woman judges.

- Post-sex: Woman pushes for commitment, Man judges.

This is the meta-level of the seduction process, even if in this particular case the woman is happy with casual sex. She wants to feel she at least had the **option** to keep him. This applies even if the man is so obviously a player that this feeling is delusional.

### Women fear post-sex rejection

This is the same blow to her ego as a harsh blowout is for you. It's motivated by the same deep-seated fear of truth unambiguously revealing her SMV. Women have buffers. They can slap on make-up, heels, and a short skirt then shake their asses at nightclubs to milk validation. They can post selfies on Facebook or vapid song lyrics to trigger a Chodestream. This works because she can draw male attention without giving up the sex, and therefore patch up her false idealised self without ever facing the risk of post-sex rejection.

So understand that when a girl enters your bedroom she is at her most nervous in the whole seduction process. She's about to surrender her position of power and flip into powerlessness. She's about to risk ego death.

*Sex is Death*

In the state of nature there was no contraception, abortion, alimony, or welfare state. When a cavegirl slept with a caveman there was a high risk of pregnancy, with its concomitant risks of dependency during the late-term and of death during childbirth. When that cavegirl enters the cave she is literally putting her life in the caveman's hands. If he knocks her up then abandons her it's almost as conclusive as death. Deep in a woman's hindbrain is the belief that sex with a new man is high stakes, even if our society has removed the vast majority of the risk. When you first fuck her, you've "killed" her and resurrection is in your power to grant or not.

I don't wish to overstate the drama involved in closing a girl because all of these deep-rooted emotions are mediated and moderated by other factors. She's horny, she wants sex, she uses contraception and so on. Just understand this is a nerve-wracking moment for her. She's both scared and excited.

# Comfort First

When a girl is entering your apartment after having already kissed you **she knows exactly what she's getting into**. She knows you're going to jump her, push her, and try to fuck her. She's following you through that apartment door because she's comfortable with the possibility of sex. She may not have reached "yes" but she's well into "maybe" territory. But make sure you've kissed her. If you never went for it, you're setting up a seedy ambush.

It's all implicitly agreed. Sex is extremely likely.

Therefore you don't need to be constantly on her during the extraction. It's enough that she's complying with your lead. Don't keep talking about sex, don't keep groping her. Put comfort first. This means:

1. Show no signs of haste. Pay the taxi driver as normal, walk at a normal pace to your front door, hang up her coat. Just proceed at a regular calm pace.

2. Tell her to take off her shoes as you do the same. This is an innocuous, deniable, and covertly powerful statement of what is to follow. If you don't get her shoes off the overt escalation becomes much harder.

3. Offer to get her a drink (offer both alcohol and non-alcoholic) then go get your own. Leave her alone in your room for a couple of minutes.

The overriding objective upon entering your apartment is to make her feel comfortable enough to stay. She's nervous. So don't jump her. Don't look anxious or ravenous. Be in full control of your sexual desire. Once she's settled her heartbeat and grown comfortable with the new surroundings you can start escalating.

I like to leave a girl alone because it's a powerful covert signal that she's free to leave at any time. Most men will hover around a girl and harry her without pause because they fear that at any moment she'll "come to her senses" and leave. This betrays a lack of entitlement, and represents too much pull on the line. Let her cool off a little while you're in the kitchen making a drink or in the bathroom. She can take deep breaths, look around the room, organise her hair or whatever so that when you return she is relaxed.

Typically you'll encounter one of two possibilities now:

1. **Up For It:** She's ready to go and the escalation proceeds smoothly. Signals that she's Up For It are (i) she asks to go to the bathroom (ii) she asks for alcohol (iii) she asks about if you have flatmates.

2. **Resistant:** She's almost ready but requires you to break down her final barriers and coax the sex out of her

### I'm not that kind of girl

In rare cases you'll find girls who simply refuse to have sex no matter how expertly you escalate. They give firm "no"s. Be clear that she is trying it on. There's not a girl in the world who goes home alone with a man without understanding the implicit agreement that sex will happen. So if she then refuses sex she is breaking the agreement. She's being a cunt.

So treat her like a cunt. You can't force her to have sex but you can withdraw every single scrap of attention and validation you ever gave her. It's a similar principle to demanding a refund for counterfeit goods. The nice guy will respect her principles, accept a woman's prerogative is to change her mind, that no means no and so on while inside he's burning with rage and injustice. This is inauthentic behaviour.

"I'm not that kind of girl" is a final shit test. She wants to see if you'll wear a shit-eating grin and accept her bullshit inches from the finish line. Are you so weak you'll not only allow a girl to play you but you'll actually nod understandingly and co-sign her bullshit? An attractive man has boundaries determining what behaviour he will and won't accept. He has the social acuity to read behaviour for what it really means.

Therefore, an attractive man will throw her out the house. He won't call a taxi, he won't placate and validate her feelings. He'll carefully control his anger and say "Get out of my house."

You must always be willing to walk away from the girl. It's very rare that you'll actually have to throw the girl out the house because the very fact you are willing to exercise your male prerogative (to cut her off completely) so close to sex will emanate from your vibe. She won't even try it on.

In both cases **she wants the sex**. That's why she's alone with you at night after having already kissed you. It's just that some girls require more deniability than others, meaning that you have to navigate their defenses.

Girls who are simply **Up For It** are easy to close. All you need to do is escalate. I generally follow this route:

1. Put some music on and make small talk for a couple of minutes while sipping a drink.

2. Pull her to her feet and kiss, let your hands roam her curves as she lets her hands wander.

3. Go "hard" by suddenly kissing her hard, pulling on the hair at the base of her neck, squeezing her ass, and pulling her into you with a vice-like grasp.

4. Mash her breasts a bit, kiss and bite her neck. She should be matching you in intensity by now and moaning.

5. Pick her up over the shoulder (I normally do a fireman's carry or a double-leg). She should gasp and giggle.

6. Carry her to the bed or a sofa. Dump her roughly onto it. Again she should show a flash of sexual excitement.

7. Get on top and kiss her hard for another minute. Work your thigh in-between her legs so your quads are pressing onto her pussy and she is hooking a leg around yours.

8. Put a palm on the front of her hip-bone, squeeze your fingers into the flesh like grabbing a handle and push down hard to pin her hips to the mattress.

9. Pull her shirt off. Match it by taking off your t-shirt.

10. Stand up and take your trousers and socks off. Usually I'll make this light-hearted by having some childish boxer shorts (e.g. Mr Potato Head) and shaking my ass to the music like a male stripper. This lightens the mood for the big play…

11. Get on top again. Unfasten her trousers and then yank them down. If you get no resistance then immediately remove her panties and put a condom on then go for it. If you do get resistance… kiss her more, put a condom on in full view of her, then push her panties out the way as you put your dick in.

> You should expect to lead the whole of the undressing. Don't do any weird "make her chase" routines if she's fully complying. Exert a command presence where sex is inevitable and you know exactly what you're doing. She'll fall in line.

That's the easy route. So what happens when it's not easy? I'd estimate over half of my lays have resistance and it's obvious why: I'm shooting for girls at the upper-edge of what is possible in quality, I'm getting inexperienced girls, and I'm rushing them to sex on my timetable (which is far faster than their preferred timetable). So resistance is inevitable. And futile.

# Resistance

There are only three levels of resistance: A firm no, an undecided no, a token no. There's nothing you can do about a firm no except understand why you're hearing it and then acting accordingly. Maybe you messed up, maybe she was genuinely considering sex with you and then something intervened. I've had girls on their way into my apartment when the boyfriend calls and the bubble pops. Sometimes she's on her period so the No is really a "next time" yes. A firm no now is not the end of the line.

## Not all resistance is LMR

Sometimes the girl wants to have sex but she can't, or is too embarrassed, to do so now. This is most common when you extracted her on a date she wasn't expecting to be extracted on and she is thus unprepared. Maybe she's on her period. Maybe she hasn't shaved her legs or pussy. Maybe she's embarrassed about her underwear. Women fear being rejected after sex and therefore are extremely sensitive to what you think of them during that first lay. They want it to happen when they look their best.

Once she's in the bedroom it's too late to unpull the trigger, but at least you can probe to find out if it's LMR (she's not psychologically ready for sex) or unpreparedness. Feel her crotch for the tell-tale outline of a panty liner. Feel her calves for stubble. You may get a sense it's just the wrong day to have sex, in which case you know to back off, give comfort, and future project the next date.

# Milestones

Girls have their own rules about when they are ready to give up sex. Usually it involves certain milestones being reached before they'll dole out the next sexual reward. They are typically of this type:

- **Number of dates**: It's common among Euro-girls from traditional countries to insist on a quasi-traditional courting pattern of three dates. Date one is a kiss/makeout to confirm attraction. Date two is heavy petting and then the sex comes on the third date. Russians are slightly different in that date one is usually cold with no kiss or hand-holding, then date two is a light no-tongue kiss, then date three is everything including sex. Girls will throw out hints they are on the "dates" track by referencing dating culture. When you calibrate a girl of this mindset you still push forwards, but it's probably best to wait until the third date before the extraction. Going further faster doesn't actually increase the probability of final sex, and you may be wasting a good deal of effort on long dates that are predisposed not to go anywhere.

- **Emotional Intimacy**: Some girls are waiting for a certain amount of time investment from you. They'll happily stay on long dates with you giving you a chance to venue-change and create adventure bubbles. You'll walk them through parks, have coffee by the river, a few pubs, maybe a museum or gallery. The girl wants to tick off a certain amount of "shared activity" with you before she feels ready. Try to pack as much of it into each date as possible and then just run down the clock. Usually she'll also require a certain amount of knowledge about your life. Playing the mysterious card after the Day 2 will backfire. Let her into your world more.

- **Length of Time**: Some girls simply go slow in the sense of chronological time. When you escalate she'll say things like "We just met," or "This is so fast." The easiest strategy is to spread your dates out over time and keep text chat going in the interim. Run down the clock while you focus on other girls.

So when you've figured out which path she's on you'll know which milestones to reach. A girl's usual hierarchy for doling out sexual rewards is as follows:

- **Kissing / Petting**: The key purpose of kissing is to overtly confirm attraction between you both and signal agreement that this interaction is progressing as man-woman. You are using it to signal your intent that you want to fuck her, while she uses it to keep you interested enough to chase. Kissing is very low investment for a girl. She doesn't risk pregnancy, rejection, or adding to her Number. Don't be fooled into thinking you are close to sex. You can be grabbing her ass, sucking her breasts and your tongue halfway down her throat but until her hand is on your dick it's still at the mere "kissing" stage.

- **Hand on dick**: When a girl grabs your dick she is clearly stating that she *wants* sex (but not that she *will definitely have* sex). If she's not proactively grabbing it, just take her hand and put in on your dick. If she starts rubbing it you've got confirmation. If she pulls away, take a step back and try again later. It's best to get her hand down your trousers for skin-on-skin because this is a far more powerful signal. She mentally crosses into "I want his dick."

- **Hand on pussy**: Girls sense their own boundary of self-control, the point at which their forebrain loses control and the hindbrain takes over. Usually it happens with skin-on-skin contact of your hand on her pussy. Touching her through trousers is good because it's another barrier broken down and will heat her up, but she still retains the self-control to stop. Once you touch her skin it all changes. She gets far hotter, far wetter and you can start pushing your finger in, which is now invasive. Skin-on-skin also confirms she's not on her period so it takes away another line of defence. If you get your finger in her pussy at a sex location you are 80% sure to fuck her.

- **Sex:** This ought to be obvious.

My own experience has been there's no fixed place for blowjobs. Some girls give them easier than sex (usually a sign of a dirty / experienced girl) and others after sex (prudish or inexperienced girl). It also depends how you ran your game. If you were strongly r-selected, the blowjob will come before the sex.

Be aware of the milestones. Just as Leap Of Faith moments are the critical junctures in the set, the Milestones are critical junctures in the escalation. They may all come in a single ten-minute burst back in your apartment, or they may be a smooth patient progression over three dates. The general guide is:

> *You can re-engage her at the same level of escalation*
> *as you last achieved.*

That means if you had her hand on your dick at the end of the second date you can quickly get her hand back on your dick during the third date. That doesn't mean you whip your dick out after saying hello, just that when the time is right in isolation you don't need to struggle through the early stages again. Those lines of defence have already been obliterated and any resistance there is token. If it works otherwise, she's playing games with you.

## Escalation Rules

> *Never escalate beyond making*
> *out unless you are near a sex location.*

The world is littered with failed lays caused by over-escalation in a pre-sex location. Moving beyond kissing is *pulling the trigger* and usually you only get one chance to do so. A patient multi-date seduction gives you more second chances, but if you're on an SDL or Day 2 lay schedule you'll get one chance. Use it wisely. Consider what you need to get the sex:

- **Plausible deniability**: The girl wants to feel the thrill of seduction without the future-projected buyer's remorse of being a slut. Thus the whole seduction is a whirlwind she's caught up in, a whirlwind that takes away all her responsibility for sex.

- **Sexual tension**: She's hot and horny for you. She's aching to get her hands on you, to placate the tingles in her pussy, and to get your dick. Tension is built by making her want you and then not giving it up.

- **Trust in your competence**: The reason players get fast sex and nice guys don't is that girls know players are supremely competent at seduction and sex. Every perfectly-calibrated nuance you add to the seduction further confirms in her mind that she's right to place herself in your capable hands.

The most effective route towards sex is for the girl to feel entirely comfortable that you know what you are doing and you'll move her along at the correct pace that you decide. Now consider how over-escalation sabotages you:

Rubbing her pussy in a bar removes all deniability. The moment she steps into the taxi she has *overtly* agreed to sex and thus her Anti Slut Defense is triggered. You've also placated her tingles by giving her what she wants — the tension is dissolved. There's no will-he-won't-he thrill. Lastly, you failed to control your sexual impulses in a public place so you're just another hungry guy. Every chode has the same escalation schema:

### The further I get, the more certain sex is

They think if you can finger a girl in a bar then she's more likely to have sex. It's a logical deduction: she let me finger her, fingering is closer to sex than not-fingering, therefore we are closer to sex.

No. It doesn't work like that.

Escalation is more like baiting a trap. You lead the girl into the correct mix of emotions so she is horny and into it, and then at the moment she is standing over the "x" you spring the trap. If you mistime it the animal bolts and you must start over.

Over-escalation is like springing the trap while the fox is still sniffing around the edges of the danger zone. Later, failing to pull the trigger in the sex location is like springing the trap after the fox has already walked off with the food.

Limit your physical escalation on Day 2 to kissing and light petting *before the extraction*. It's okay to verbally escalate about sexual intent (see next chapter) and sometimes okay to do over-the-clothing dick/pussy touching (but not a lot, just enough to signal intent and get her pulse racing) but don't do skin-on-skin until at the sex location.

# BEDROOM RESISTANCE

There'll be many cases where you get the girl back to your room, she's sitting on your sofa kissing you, and then every attempt to move forwards is met with a block or an evasion. Harumph! This is where real escalation skill comes in and it's a delicate balance of the following elements. Only experience will give you the calibration and presence of mind to correctly navigate her LMR.

## Chip Away

When a girl is resisting sex but is not making any real effort to leave your room, you have a forebrain-hindbrain conflict. She wants sex but she doesn't want to give it up easily. Don't listen to what girls say, watch what they do. You'll usually find she has drawn a line in the sand at a particular milestone and set up her defences there. Consider it like a castle siege and your intent is the battering ram on the raised drawbridge. You'll hammer against the door, shake it on its hinges, back up to regroup, then hammer again. Over and over again. You are grinding her down, chipping away at her resistance until the door splinters.

This may initially sound "dark" but consider the subtext. She came to your room knowing full well you'll try to fuck her. You are currently trying to fuck her...*And she's still not trying to leave*. This is similar to a street stop when her mouth is blabbing "not interested" but her feet remain rooted to the spot. If she really wanted to go, she'd go. It's just the final test — will you give up and fall for her bullshit?

Girls love the thrill of being taken. Don't deny them this thrill.

Be relentless in your determination to break down those final barriers. Be clear in your mind that as long as she's putting herself in front of you in a sex location, you will keep pushing for sex. Don't pay attention to whatever rationalisations come out of her mouth:

- "I should go home"

- "This is too fast"

- "We shouldn't be doing this"

Ignore anything that isn't a clear "No," or "Stop." If you hear those then back off and go cold for a while.

# Cold-Hot

The symphony of pick-up is a constant destabilising dance between opposite ends of matched-pair traits. When escalating you'll mostly be "hot," i.e. projecting passionate sexual energy, moving things forwards and heating her up. When you encounter a roadblock, flip to "cold." Back off. Disengage your mind and body from her. Turn off the attention.

The most important thing to remember here is that you never whine or look pissed off. If you do, she's won — she unbalanced you. She's given herself a last-gasp excuse to disqualify you right as you were about to win the prize. Just back off and nonchalantly do something else. Get up and change the music. Go to the toilet. Fold away some clothes. Pour another drink. Allow something else to take your attention for a short while. Turn your back on her for a minute or so as you attend to this other thing. Community parlance is "a takeaway."

Take a small break, then reengage non-sexually. Sit back on your sofa in the usual date posture and sip your drink. Make some conversation or an observation about the music. She'll reorganise her clothes and hair and then play along. Let it move this way as long as your calibration tells you — perhaps two minutes, perhaps a quarter hour. Watch her signals. Has she calmed down? Is she giving you "the look" again? Is she edging closer to you?

You are engaging in more subconscious push-pull. She knows you want to fuck her but you aren't slavering at the mouth over her. You are in full control of your sexuality. You won't be destabilised, and you won't fold into her frame. Be a bit cocky in your conversation. Be masculine in your body language.

She's still heated up. Once a girl is horny she has a long half-life and every moment she's boiling in her love juice without your active attempts to fuck her is a moment her hindbrain is breaking down the forebrain resistance. You may need to place her in the Sin Bin a dozen times before she surrenders.

# Seduction-Comfort

Escalation is a time of maximum pull. You are giving her sexual touch, sexual vocal tone, sexual eyes. It's a strong hypnotic state with heightened senses and elevated heartbeats. So as you reach the crest of a wave and push past the next milestone, you'll get some "no"s. Ride the downside of the wave with comfort.

Turn down the fire in your eyes and the passion in your touch. Lean back. If you are on the bed, lie on your back and pull her into you like the post-sex cuddling position. Let her lie there in your presence, feeling your chest rise and fall with deep slow breaths. Lightly stroke her upper arm with your fingertip. Scratch her temples like a cat. Softly play with her nose and cheeks. Gently trace the lines of her eyebrows with your fingertips. Give her warm comforting gaze. Kiss her forehead.

Let her relax for five to ten minutes then heat it up again. Let your fingers trail from her upper arm down to her hands, draw soft lines along the outside of her hips, breath into her ear, softly kiss her neck. Gently ramp it up until you hear her respond with heavier breathing and bodily writhing. Then flip back into seduction and take another shot at the summit.

# Fire Escape

Any time you get enough "no"s to make you think she's genuinely thinking of leaving, or a really hard No (often with her pushing you away) then get up and leave the sex location. Either go to the bathroom, clean your teeth, or go to the kitchen and put the kettle on. You are subcommunicating three things:

1. She has a clear path to an exit. You are not physically close enough to prevent her from leaving if that's truly what she desires.

2. You have temporarily withdrawn your attention. A girl has a limited numbers of times she can rebuff you before you drop her completely. She's skating on thin ice now.

3. There is an open invitation to reengage with reduced sexual intensity. It's a time-out.

If she has genuinely decided not to have sex, she will put her clothes back on and begin the process of going home. A girl who doesn't want sex will remove herself from a sex location. If she goes, she goes. Don't whine, wheedle, or beg. Let her go and then reflect on where you are in the set. If she stays…It's still on, it just needs more time.

So chill for a bit. Watch some youtube videos, make a cup of tea, give some comfort talk. Do a mental inventory to see if there's anything else missing or if she's thrown up a legitimate obstacle that needs to be tackled by something other than escalation. This may take up to an hour. She's still boiling in her love juices. When you're ready, begin another crack at the summit.

# Don't Give In

LMR can be wearing on your soul. Usually you won't get a girl home until you've invested dozens of street stops to find her, several hours on dating, some cash on a taxi, and the emotional energy of pushing through several Leaps of Faith. You've put together an elaborate game plan that she's now stubbornly wrecking.

Don't give in to the frustration. Don't surrender to her frame. Although she appears to have the power, the reality is that she's nervous and she's testing you. She'll throw you beta bait so you'll fall into her frame and let it get derailed. Keep your eye on the prize. Sex is inevitable. You are going to fuck her.

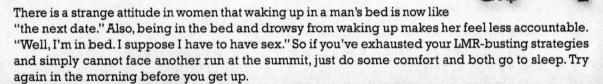

### Asian Morning Routine

There is a strange attitude in women that waking up in a man's bed is now like "the next date." Also, being in the bed and drowsy from waking up makes her feel less accountable. "Well, I'm in bed. I suppose I have to have sex." So if you've exhausted your LMR-busting strategies and simply cannot face another run at the summit, just do some comfort and both go to sleep. Try again in the morning before you get up.

# Moments of Leadership

There are often key moments when you must take control and lay strong conviction and dominance onto the girl. These moments require expert calibration and are **not** for beginners. If you've banged less than 40 women, don't even try them. When a girl is giving stubborn resistance at a particular moment, try:

- Put your finger over her lips, look sternly into her eyes and say "shhhhh."

- Grab her wrists and pin them above her head. Hold firmly but, crucially, give enough wiggle room that if she *really wanted to escape* she could do it.

- Grab her neck so your fingers slightly press into her arteries but the palm doesn't put much pressure onto her windpipe. This is very dominant but not painful. Examine her eyes. Is she showing fear (bad, release her) or excitement (good, keep your hand there).

Get used to the idea of wrestling a girl into submission. Watch the sex scene in Conan The Barbarian where Arnie has to tame a hellcat woman. You aren't really putting her into a powerless position, you are merely simulating it. She can get off on the fantasy of being taken and exercise full deniability, but she also knows if she really wanted to escape then she could.

Like all things Game, extensive experience will give you the intuitive understanding and rules of thumb to read the tiny signals that tell you where the girl is really at. Closing is tough because we have so much societal programming and such anti-male laws that we have to be extremely careful with pushing girls for sex, despite the fact most girls *want* to be pushed for sex.

The above escalation guidelines are not foolproof. Even the tightest escalation can't overcome every girl's resistance. Some girls will give you a firm No and not budge. Back off and chalk it up to the Game. You can't get every girl.

Constantly read the girl's eyes, her sounds, her body movement, the subtext of her words. Try to figure out what she is really telling you. Some general guidelines:

**Signs leading towards "Yes"**

- She maintains or closes the distance between you.
- She gives long thoughtful looks into your eyes, like she's trying to read the answer to a puzzle.
- She moves how you direct her to, either with verbal commands or physical gestures.
- She moans, wriggles, gasps or snatches breathes while you are doing something.
- Her hands roam around your body, especially shoulders and upper arms.
- Her hips gyrate and push into you.
- She pulls you closer or tighter.
- Her eyes sparkle or seem hot.
- She leans her weight on you or maximises the amount of her body that is pushed against yours.

**Signs leading towards "No"**

- She pushes you away with real force. Try leaning your weight onto her a bit to see if she relents (token resistance). If she keeps pushing, it's real resistance.
- She scurries away, trying to get out from under you.
- She clamps her thighs together.
- She keeps her hands close to whichever part of her body you are trying to touch and tries to head you off from touching it.
- She's not drinking any alcohol you poured
- Anytime you pull back, she reorganises her clothes such as putting her bra back on or buttoning up her trousers.
- An absence of Yes signals.

You should really be able to just feel if it's on or off at that moment. If you feel disheartened you are sensing a No vibe. If you feel excited anticipation you are sensing a Yes vibe. Yes is all about closer, tighter, hotter. No is all about further, stiffer, colder.

Immediately after shooting your bolt you'll have a very clear decision about whether you want to see her again. The sex fog has cleared post-notch and the thrill of the chase is gone, so you can realistically appraise how much you like the girl. If you find yourself looking at yourself in the mirror with a self-congratulatory smirk thinking "Well done, sir" then chances are you want to keep her around. Make your mind up quickly and act accordingly.

*How you act immediately post-sex signals to the girl what you want from her*

You can avoid a lot of unnecessary bad vibes by acting congruently with what you really want from her.

# Pump and Dump

Don't feel bad about this. You presented yourself as the r-selected man and you didn't make any promises of commitment. She freely chose to come under your spell for her own self-interest of sex with the exciting guy. It was a win-win encounter. So don't sour it.

Give her a kiss on the forehead before you clean yourself up. Ask if she'd like a cup of tea. Sit with her a while and chat. But crucially **don't** do any of the following:

- Overtly signaling her to leave. Don't make a show of looking at your watch, telling her you have to get up early, picking her clothes up and giving them to her, getting her jacket, calling a taxi etc.

- Cuddle her and give lots of affection.

- Make future plans either specifics or general talk about hanging out sometime. If it's an SDL and you don't have her number, don't ask for it now. At most, suggest Facebook.

  Girls will take the hint from the absence of Rotation/Girlfriend signs. Leave them their dignity by politely not referencing the fact you just pumped and dumped them. They'll go away into the night with a happy memory and everyone is win-in.

# Rotation / Girlfriend

The biggest single difference between this and the above is **affection.** When you want to keep a girl around you have to give her the positive affirmation of affection. So after the sex clean-up immediately go back to her in bed (she'll usually stay there. A girl who immediately starts getting dressed is either wanting one-off adventure sex or has mistakenly taken the wrong hint). Lie next to her, pull her in, and give comfort kino (head / arm stroking, soft kisses, pillow talk).

For ten minutes after sex there is an oxytocin window. If you keep the girl physically close to you during this time (actual skin to skin contact) then it'll trigger her oxytocin release that chemically bonds her to you. Doing this on three separate occasions will bind her to you very strongly. So only do it if you intend to see the girl again. Let her sleep over but don't force it. The first time she suggests getting a cab reassure her with "That's ok, but I'd rather you stayed." Use your calibration to determine if she's just nervous about overstaying her welcome but would really like to stay.

The biggest difference between a girl on rotation and a girlfriend is the frequency of meeting. Meet rotation girls no more than once a week, twice on rare occasions. If you see a girl three times a week she's your girlfriend no matter what you verbally agreed. She will get this idea as well.

If you want to keep your options open, slow the pace down with which increased intimacy happens. You can usually take a girl further down the commitment route without complication, but it doesn't work both directions. Once you've girlfriended her it's extremely difficult to demote her to fuckbuddy without her eventually freaking out and ditching you entirely.

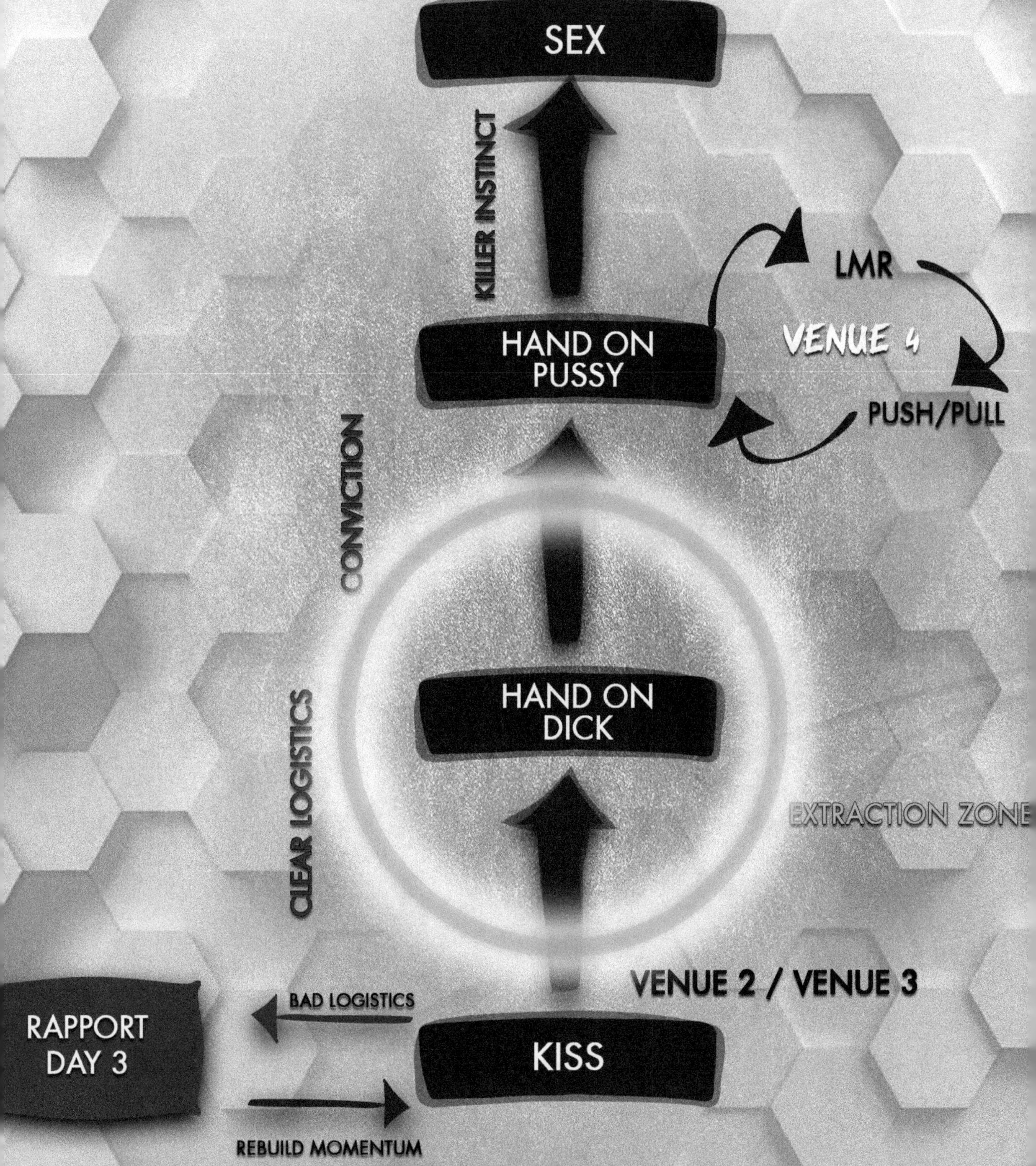
SEX
KILLER INSTINCT
HAND ON PUSSY
LMR
VENUE 4
PUSH/PULL
CONVICTION
HAND ON DICK
CLEAR LOGISTICS
EXTRACTION ZONE
VENUE 2 / VENUE 3
BAD LOGISTICS
RAPPORT DAY 3
KISS
REBUILD MOMENTUM

# SPECIAL SITUATIONS
## section eight

The previous sections followed the Master Model in an approximate chronological sequence, including discussion of commonly encountered problems. This section discusses numerous "What If" scenarios for when something unusual happens. These can be positive (a Same Day Lay opportunity) or negative (the girl starts playing Silly Buggers, or your set is invaded by an interloping male). None of these situations occur often but to be forewarned is to be forearmed.

Lastly I finish the book with advice for how to manage your journey in Game over the medium term. Those of you who catch the daygame bug will experience a long emotional rollercoaster with exhilarating highs and despondent lows. This chapter tells you what to expect over the next few years and how to deal with the common player traps.

# SPECIAL SITUATIONS

## PROBLEM SOLVING ON THE DATE

### Goal: Anticipating and clearing unusual obstacles.

Most dates will go smoothly. You won't necessarily get the girl, but you'll both be reading from the same Man-Woman dating script so even if the final outcome is a "no," you both gave it a try. This section considers the weird stuff that can happen and fine-tuning to consider once you've become comfortable with the Normal On Girl smooth sailing.

1. Fine-tuning to the girl

2. Creative gambits for difficult girls

3. Silly buggers

4. Interloping men

# FINE-TUNING TO THE GIRL

The date model I outline is based on the normal girls ("Normal On") but let's consider some variations in vibe and style you may employ for different types of girl. In the beginning you'll find it so difficult to keep all the balls in the air just for the basic model that fine-tuning will be an extra layer of confusion. Use this section initially as a debrief when you get home and review a date you've already had.

## 'Suspicious On' dating plan

The key characteristic of the Suspicious On girl is that she is undecided, so she wants to test your value. This means the date may feel more like a battle in the beginning because she's non-compliant and perhaps truculent. Don't let this throw you off-balance because *that's the whole reason she's doing it*. No matter what little tempest she whips up, take solace in the basic reality of the date: She has taken time out of her day to come and meet you. That means she passes a minimum threshold of attraction and respect for you. It doesn't matter if she's six feet tall with a hard Russian accent, stony face, and mentions her last boyfriend was a millionaire. She's right here in front of you now — that's the important fact. Remind yourself of the lover-provider split. You aren't taking her to a fancy restaurant, or a cruise trip, or a guest list / VIP nightclub table — she's having a £2 cup of coffee. You are not the provider chump. She's not here to tool you for a free ride. She's here because there's something about you that interests her. She's just trying to rattle you and see if you really are the R-selected male.

In the first venue the spotlight will be strongly upon you despite your efforts to turn it onto her. That's the first frame control battle. She's testing so she'll look hard at you for any signs you are uncomfortable beneath her laser beam. She's used to try-hard fakers putting up a showy front that she can just kick over. That's her script because she's a high value girl. So you need to be relaxed and open, with nothing to hide. Don't waste energy trying to push water uphill, propping up some ridiculous "high value lifestyle." Show yourself. Let her shine the light on you for a while because you know you can withstand the scrutiny.

Run your usual DHVs, but remember these are ways of giving her a window into your character rather than an elaborate construction to impress her. Your vibe is take-it-or-leave-it. You're interested in her, but you don't jump through hoops for anyone. It's nice that she came out, but if this is boring her she's free to leave. Let this don't-care attitude express itself in your body language, vocal tone, and eyes. When you first test kino do it softly without any "pull." Touch incidentally while diverting your eyes away.

Her testing is front-loaded and she'll probably chill out midway through the first venue. You are waiting for the "decision" look in her eyes and her physical lean-in that shows her initial testing is over and she wants you. It's like hook point in street stop. **Now you can pull back and make her work**. Now it's time to invest and qualify her. She's finally found a man worthy of her (which is rare) so the value balance has flipped — **you** are now the scarce resource. You get to meet girls like her all the time, whereas she very rarely gets to meet men like you. Sometimes it is shockinghow dramatically her manner shifts from high-and-mighty-princess to totally-gagging-for-it-and-lost-all-frame. These girls are often celibate for long stretches due to a dearth of qualified suitors, but their body still cries out for a man. Don't be surprised if she becomes quite needy. Remember how to parcel out your attention and nudge her along the model:

- Covert qualification: look away, silence, stop kino, short answers, furrowed brows, lean back.

- Overt qualification: questions, demands.

The interactionwill become more cooperative, but never forget that she's chasing you now. Accuse her of being a pervert. Pull out your chick crack. She'll probably have high esteem so don't be fake about it — it's all nudge/wink self-referential banter.

If your plan isn't working consider the Frame Crush, but resist the temptation to use this as anything but the last resort. The frame crush is designed for tearing down girls who are building themselves up as hot shit ("Look at me!") rather than girls inspecting you ("Who are you?"). With suspicious on girls you are withstanding an inspection because you have nothing to hide, akin to being audited for your taxes. The most common mistake with these girls is to be rattled by their pressure and begin pulling too hard. She's on guard for that — that's why she gives so little away in the beginning, to see if you get desperate at the lack of signal and start overcommitting yourself to getting her validation. Don't let her set a price on her pussy — you simply don't care.

## 'Strong On' dating plan

The key characteristic of the Strong On Girl is *she wants it as much as you do*. Good-looking or high-status men (the Chosen) will find most of their girls fit in this category because of theselection filter that initially got them the girl. The normal man (the Chooser) will encounter far less of them. If you opened from a strong IOI then she's likely one of these.

You'll have a strong spirit of cooperation from the beginning and everything moves quickly. Start your kino early and keep physical contact. Reward her investment because that's good behaviour. Don't dick around with gamey routines because she's playing it straight and complying. There's no reason to "game" a girl who is jumping through every hoop on the way to our bed. "Doing attraction" is taking a backward step with this girl, and she'll start to wonder why you are trying to prove yourself to her. Also take care not to be too aloof and uninvolved because you don't need to stimulate her interest — it's already there.

Get a compliance "yes ladder" going fast and build a bubble. Probably the only risk with these girls is that you move too fast and get suckered into escalating at her pace and then, perversely, she loses interest in you because you allowed yourself to be pulled ahead too quickly. Don't get too exuberant as you realise the sex is likely to be easy. Stick to the model, but just know you can proceed smoother and quicker than usual. She still needs to jump through every hoop to feel comfortable with the sex. Don't skip stages unless she's absolutely gagging for it. In rare cases she'll escalate you and you can be at the sex location within an hour, but these are rare.

## 'Stealth On' dating plan

The defining characteristic of the Stealth On Girl is she wants it *but doesn't overtly show it*. Therefore the whole date is about **compliance**. It's all about leading her step-by-step to the bedroom without ever drawing attention to the obvious. So long as she's complying, you move it forward.

Game is only required when a girl isn't complying. It's easy to over-game Stealth On girls because you are looking for too much confirmation that she likes you.

**Bamboozle**

*Fractionating and leading a girl so much that she loses her sense of being attached to normality. She has had the rug pulled from under her. It is similar to the misdirection used by magicians.*

These girls are usually inexperienced and introverted, which makes them great for **bamboozle**ment and spinning them around. Instead of working them verbally through the compliance ladder you may wish to move them physically by adopting more of an adventure date. Take them on a river boat trip, get them lost in windy streets and markets, sit on a bench eating street food. Lots of venue and activity changes help get her feet moving along your momentum, which leads her mind to do so as well. Don't require her to overtly admit what she's doing and where the date is going — let the subtle kino, the kiss, and the eye contact take care of it. Generally I won't dirty talk these girls and when I cop a feel / spike it'll be towards the light side of the sexual scale.

These girls are almost always introverts so extoll virtue of introverts. Most of them feel slightly inadequate in a world designed by and forextraverts, so relate and empathise with those feelings. Find reasons to qualify her on introversion (e.g. her hobbies, her ability to focus, the depth of her conversation, her confidence in being by herself) because she'll naturally wonder why you are dating her rather than "one of those confident extravert girls from the nightclubs."

# CREATIVE GAMBITS FOR DIFFICULT GIRLS

Only break the fourth wall when the covert progression isn't working and you are encountering non-compliance. When you do, don't overdo it. Don't do a deep-dive.

There are typical obstacles and resistance encountered when trying to close normal girls. It's a natural part of the process for the man to push and the woman to resist. This section considers gambits to use when the girl is offering unusual resistance and would not be used with a Normal On girl who is complying. They are:

1. Breaking the Fourth Wall

2. The Frame Crush

3. The Talk

I stress that these are unconventional manoeuvres designed for a limited and specific type of problem. Do not get in the habit of throwing them into your usual dates, because they can often result in negative progress.

# 1. Breaking The Fourth Wall

You'll have noticed older TV dramas and sitcoms like Friends, The Cosby Show, and Happy Days have a small number of sets in which almost the entire show is filmed. Often 50% of the show will be in the lounge (e.g. Married With Children) with a bit in the kitchen and a few external locations. It's just a convention of the medium. What they all have in common is three walls. The fourth wall doesn't exist, it's cut away in order to place the cameras and behind them the studio audience. You'll notice the same with theatre and opera. These performances rely upon an unspoken agreement between audience and actors to suspend disbelief and to pretend that the stage / location is really the lounge of a family house or an office or whatever and not just some fake set on a sound stage in front of an audience.

Sometimes the show will deliberately dispel the illusion. The actor may look directly into the camera and address the audience. They will overtly reference that this is a performance with actors and audience rather than the pretend setting presented on TV. This is called "breaking the fourth wall." It's self-referential. Other examples include:

- A rock band deliberately miming badly to the lip-sync to draw your attention to the fact they aren't playing live.

- Scary Movie sending up horror movie conventions, such as a victim looking at a row of weapons and instead choosing a banana to defend herself from the serial killer.

> Knowing this meta-level idea lets you play with it in set. The basic unspoken agreement between man and woman is that you try to fuck her while she delays until she's ready, but neither of you openly refer to the process. Inexperienced men are usually terrified of being "busted" — of the girl calling them out and knowing they are trying to have sex. This is because most men are ashamed of their sexual desires, they misunderstand women's sexuality, and they worry everyone is watching and judging them. When a girl says "Are you trying to fuck me?" the average man gets flustered.
>
> Good daygamers make no secret of their intent or their awareness of the courtship ritual. We revel in it. So sometimes we'll explictly tell the girl what we are doing. We'll break the fourth wall under these circumstances:

- The girl openly challenges with a shit test designed to fluster a man for trying to pick her up. "Are you trying to pick me up?", "What do you want?"

- You reach roadblocks in trying to covertly move the set along because she's unwittingly or deliberately refusing to take hints in your subcommunication.

- She tries to derail using subtle LJBFs, such as rejecting kino, sitting far away from you, avoiding sharing her mind etc., or perhaps she overtly tries to snatch the frame and you need to impose yours.

- She has a fertile reflective imagination so you think it'll be an interesting game to overtly discuss the nature of the seduction process and what you are both doing. As part of this method, you can people-watch other couples on dates. Perhaps she'll give you an IOI so you explain to her what it was. Women like discussing seduction as a topic of it's own, and it gives a great opportunity to demonstrate your own mastery of it and thus attract her with the idea of being sexed by a man who knows what he's doing.

> Breaking the fourth wall risks being too clever for your own good. Use it sparingly. Don't allow yourself to disappear into theoretical talk or you'll find the vibe killed by her self-consciousness. Verbalising the process can be dangerous. Just spike with it or use it to finesse your way over obstacles.

# 2. The Frame Crush

Usually you'll be dating feminine girls who are strongly predisposed to value masculinity and recognise the subtle shades of masculine character. These girls *want* to be pushed into a strongly polarised MaleDom-FemSub relationship. They've been correctly raised by their parents to embody feminine virtues and have learned the feminine arts such as following the lead, making soft polite conversation, and how to gradually and gracefully surrender control to the male. Occasionally you'll encounter the opposite: Masculinised women.

This will be the vast majority of Anglosphere girls, meaning girls from countries with English as a first language — The USA, Britain, South Africa, Australia, and that little joke country where Hobbits live. Any country that has seen a fast-track encounter with Feminist poison, such as Brazil, will also have lots of these broken women. You must understand that these women are **broken**.

They aren't "different" or "empowered." They are not following an alternative gender model. They are broken women who have had most of their feminine wiring shorted out. While their FSU cousins were learning deportment, cooking, and sewing, these masculine women were in gender studies class and watching "3rd Rock From The Sun." This presents the following problems to a would-be seducer:

- They refuse to follow and would be incapable of doing so anyway (following is a skill of its own of equal complexity to leading and it must be taught).

- They despise men and want to pick a fight with them. This is an overcompensation for...

- ... they are so divorced from their feminine essence that they have permanent existential angst. They live in fear of a horror they can't define and a sense of being out of their depth in the world.

- They wildly overestimate their proficiency at mimicking male traits such as confidence, courage, decision-making, persistence, and emotional control.

- Almost everything they say is annoying gibberish that makes you like them less, rather than (as with feminine women) like them more.

These girls typically have sex when they find a feminised man who will put up with their bullshit. This man may be feminised in a buff Jersey Shore sense of amping up his physical shell, or he will be feminised in behaviour such as the starving artist Johnny Depp type. If you want to fuck her *while retaining your masculinity* then there are two key vulnerabilities you will exploit:

1. They are suckers for banter because it lets them fight

2. They are know-nothings who think they know everything

This means you will put them on an endless cycle of baiting a trap then smashing it shut on them. I call it the Frame Crush. I only use it on masculine girls. It's very Dark Side and it's totally unnecessary on a feminine girl. Let's go into more detail on how to do it.

### Purpose: Smash her frame into smithereens until she's completely helpless. Then snatch her up.

Imagine a master boxer enters the ring against a tough but one-dimensional killer. This opponent has torn through the ranks on the basis of a stiff controlling jab that sets up a smashing overhand right. Fight after fight he's done the same thing… Push the ramrod jab in their face and then bully them off balance until he's got the opening to lower the boom.

Our master boxer has watched the tapes. He knows what to do. He's noticed that before every jab the killer blinks. After throwing the jab he drops his left hand low as it returns to his jaw. And before every booming right hand he slightly pulls it back like drawing a bow and arrow.

Boxing historians among you know I'm talking about Max Schmelling as the master and an up-and-coming Joe Louis as the killer. So what happens?

Our master baits (a master-baiter, if you will) the killer by drawing out the jab. He deliberately puts himself into position and leaves a gap. As the blink telegraphs the jab, he rocks outside and then smashes a hard right hand over the top of the killer's lowered hand. Time after time he smashes the right hand in. Bait-and-smash. The killer can't set up his right hand properly, but he needs to throw it so now he lunges off-balance. Each time he draws his hand back, the master pops in a clinical fast left hook on his unprotected chin.

The killer is completely rattled. His whole game is based on two weapons which have never failed to smash the opposition. Now, not only can't he land a telling blow, but **he's being smashed every time he tries.**

His best punches are taken away from him because he dare not throw them anymore. Before long he's just standing in the middle of the ring, square-on, waiting to be hit. He's completely passive. He has been fought to a standstill and is now easy pickings for the veteran.

This is the boxing version of taking someone's Game away. Masculine women are to be crushed the same way. They only have a few weapons to disguise the house of cards, and once you take these away they become completely cowed. Two decades of feminist programming falls away and they become docile lambs ready to lead to the slaughter.

# Chipping Away

In the beginning consider yourself as surgically chipping away the legs that support her pedestal. I'll use a hypothetical example of an internationally-travelling New York model who has a PhD in psychology. What are her pillars of value, the legs supporting her pedestal?

- Hip American culture

- International travel / "the lifestyle"

- Being a model

- Intelligence / credentials

So you will now be completely unimpressed by every single one of these. The first frame-chip will be not allowing her to impose the "I'm so high value" frame on you. So:

**American Culture** — You've never heard of Seinfeld, you don't care about Obama, you don't consider New York a big deal. Instead you bring up European culture and talk about the classics (Dumas, Tolstoy, etc.) and the long history of London or Paris. You reference the high points of Euro culture such as Paris cafés, Iberian ham, London theatre.

**International Travel** — Again, big fucking deal. Just blow it off. If her ex-BF took her on yacht trips around the Bahamas you just damn it with faint praise then talk about what YOU think is high value, such as climbing a mountain in Alaska.

**Modelling** — Ask her what else she does. Talk about how you respect people who have built themselves up from nothing, emphasising non-physical attributes. Maintain the "beauty is common" frame.

**Intelligence** — Americans are particularly easy to crush on this because they have no education. They know nothing of what we would call history, geography, or culture. So keep bringing the topic onto areas you know she is weak and keep throwing in passing references to things you know she doesn't understand. Then patiently stop and explain them to her like she's a child.

# Gambits

1. Interrupt her

2. Force her to explain any concepts or words she misuses

3. Patiently explain what you consider to be basic facts

So a girl might talk about how she's been reading some hack paperback writer then ask me about what I'm reading. I'll mention how I've got a project to read all the classics. I've just finished Dumas and have moved onto Tolstoy, but I'm finding it hard going:

> **Me:**    I swear these Russian writers never crossed out a sentence in their life. At least Dumas whips along at a fast pace. But then again he would, right?
>
> **Her:**    Uh.... Right
>
> **Me:**    Oh… I mean, Dumas used to write for 1840s Parisian periodicals. So all his major novels were serialised and thus each chapter had to end on a cliffhanger. It's no different to.... I don't know the US equivalent... maybe Days Of Their Lives. He had whole teams ghost-writing sections for him just like how animators like Chuck Jones used to draw the key cell frames for Bugs Bunny and have interns fill the gaps.
>
> **Her:**    ok.... Sure
>
> **Me:**    So anyway, Tolstoy. I'm trying War and Peace because the Napoleonic era fascinates me with all the strongest world powers being at war with each other at the same time. So it was expressed in the culture of the time, like Tchaikovsky's 1812 overture. I read a soldier's diary from Napoleon's advance on Moscow so it was fascinating to get a first-hand account that was literally in the trenches. But Tolstoy gives a sweeping narrative from the perspective of the Russian aristocracy. I think it'll fill in a lot of blanks about the era so I'm trying to plod on.

She'll be terrified of trying to add anything to this conversation because she knows nothing. You've fought her to a standstill. Keep hitting her with these on all the topics you where you know you're strong and she's weak. Gradually move your tone across these stages as the date progresses:

> Assuming she is your equal ⟶ Incredulity that she knows nothing ⟶
> Politely hidden contempt ⟶ Benign educator

Don't lay it on too thick or you'll come off try-hard. In the beginning she'll be eager to tell you how awesome she is, how all the guys want her, and how her lifestyle is so amazing. Each time she puts out such a statement you just dampen it. Examples:

| | |
|---|---|
| *Her:* | I've been going to Milan a lot for the fashion weeks. I do lots of my modelling there. |
| *Me:* | I don't know Milan well, just from a two-day business trip. I like the food. I was there to consult for our local sales office so my main contact was the salesman. He took me to each of his favourite restaurants in turn… [turn the conversation to food and later if she can cook] |
| *Her:* | New York has so much going on. I live in Manhattan and there's some amazing clubs with blah… blah..blah. |
| *Me:* | I have to say my entire knowledge of New York comes from TV and movies. Have you ever seen The Equalizer? No? It's a late-80s crime thriller, sort of like Deathwish where there's a vigilante for hire who comes to the aid of nice people being victimised by crime. It's running the image of New York before Guiliani and the zero-tolerance clean-up… [turn conversation to crime thrillers] |
| *Her:* | I love travelling! My ex-BF used to take me to the Bahamas. |
| *Me:* | What do you like about the Bahamas? |
| *Her:* | The shopping!! They have all these little boutiques where you can get the best brands and they close them up for you to do private shopping |
| *Me:* | No. I mean about the place. Did you do any scuba-diving off the reefs there or get into the jungle? When I'm in the tropics I always try to get at least one dive in because there's such variety of underwater fauna. When you're suspended in water twenty metres down, weightless….. [talk about experience of scuba]…. When I think of the Caribbean it always brings up thoughts of the freebooter era when the pirates and privateers were making their fortunes. Recently I read Treasure Island. You know that's the first modern adventure story? Obviously you can go back to The Illyad and Homer for the literal adventure..and no, hon, I don't mean Homer Simpson. I know you're American and all…. |

### Intellectual Mastery

*Demonstrating to a girl that you are more intelligent and wider-read / wider-travelled than she is. Girls must admire a man for some traits before they can feel attraction. Intellectual Mastery is a way of dominating her mind that is especially effective in combination with physical and social dominance.*

You'll notice this tactic involves continuous **intellectual mastery**, framing her progressively stronger as a no-nothing student being educated by you the teacher. You'll often slip into lecture mode and see her slip into spectator mode. Her eyes will glaze over and her jaw goes slack. She knows she's beaten. So let's recap the basic loop:

A: Ask her a question or otherwise draw her into bragging about how high value she is. (draw)

B: Shrug off her story like it's no big deal and subtly shift the topic towards your area of strength. (evade)

C: Lecture her on your strong point while asking questions you know she can't answer. (smash)

D: Ease off for a while to let her get back into the conversation then rinse and repeat. (reload)

Before long it'll be The Nick Show. I'll be off on a roll free-wheeling my analogue game, pulling things from all directions and talking myself into a state of self-described awesomeness. She won't let this happen without a bit of a fight, so have some counter-attacks ready:

## (i) Shhhhh her

She'll definitely pipe up and speak out of turn on occasion when you are telling a story or running another bit of a monologue. Use your social calibration to spot when she's awkwardly interrupting, rather than merely turn-taking. When she interjects, often to brag a bit because she's sensing your value beginning to outstrip hers, you'll let this one rip.

**Douchebaggery**

*Knowingly and overtly acting like an arsehole from a place of self-amusement and tenderness. Effective douchebag game is not about being mean or nasty. It's a highly entertaining pushing of her r-selection buttons when you both know that's what you're doing and why. She will playfully scold you for being "such a jerk" while smiling the whole time.*

Cut her sentence off with a "Hang on a minute, missy. Shhhhh. You'll get your turn in a minute. Shhhhh." Hold your finger up to her lips. It must be done with playful **douchebaggery** rather than genuine annoyance, because you're framing her as the teacher's pet trying to answer before the rest of the class has a chance. So tell her "shhhh. Let's play a game. It's called you be quiet. Can you do that? Can you hold that thought until I've finished?"

She'll often get indignant, which is precisely what you want because you've just suckered her into the heavy right hand. Now you laugh at her, grab her shoulders / pat her head and saw "Awwww. She's indignant! Look at it! I can actually see that warm glow of indignation spreading through your body. Feels good doesn't it?" You've completely checkmated her by showing that you know she gets off on being indignant. Pull her in for a bit of dad-comfort and continue your story.

## (ii) Woah woah woah

When she gives you a direct challenge you'll come right over the top with a booming voice and wagging finger. Literally talk over her as a pattern interrupt so she can't finish her sentence. Look around the room as if you are checking that everyone else heard the dumbassery that just came ouf of her mouth. Wag that finger and say "Woah woah woah. I cannot believe you just said that!" or words to that effect. Example:

> Me:    … blah blah…. So what can you cook?
>
> Her:   I don't cook. I buy all my food from delis. My husband will cook for me!
>
> Me:    Woah woah woah woah woah. Did you actually say that [looks around room]. She actually said "I don't cook". I cannot believe it! Oh my god, America has completely failed this generation of women. You'll never get married! Be careful that no one hears you"

This is the best way to deal with FemThink, i.e. her attempts to exposit and argue for a femcentric agenda. Deliberately go over-the-top with feigned-outrage, how you'd expect a Victorian dad to act if he found out his daughter was a suffragette or his son a homosexual. It's playful on the surface, but don't back down from your frame. Always finish with an accusation that she'll never get married with that attitude, never get a boyfriend, never be popular, never fit in etc. You are playfully activating her existential fears.

Another version is the sham phone call to your grandmother or the Queen. After she's said her dumbass comment you say "Wait a minute," pull out your phone and pretend to make a call (obviously faking it). Then say:

A:  "Yeah, grandmother. Remember that girl I told you about. The cute American one. She can't cook… no, really… Yes… I know, I'm shocked too… Date a Russian next time, you say? Ok"

B:  "Hello, Queen Elizabeth… Ok, look, you'll never believe what happened. This American girl has just said Fawlty Towers isn't funny and Seinfeld is better… I know… Ok, border control will be here in five minutes?…yes, send the dogs."

Then give her the "now you've torn it" look, with a smirk. You can keep calling your grandmother or the Queen as the night progresses and your date is getting herself progressively into deeper and deeper trouble.

## (iii) I think that requires an explanation

Every now and then she'll trot out some trite talking point or jargon that she doesn't really understand, but has learned to repeat to cooing acclaim from her hybrid hivemind/thirsty chode audience. Remember she's used to having men kiss her arse for the chance at sex and talking in a social circle of likeminded feminist idiots. It's highly unlikely she's ever been challenged on her core worldview. As a native English speaking woman she's almost certainly a Left-wing collectivist with polyanna thoughts on world peace, Africa, and global warming. You are not trying to get into an argument about the actual subject (e.g. Obama being a Mussolini-style fascist). Rather, you are just bringing her car to a sudden stop. You don't want to prove you're right, you just want to callout that she hasn't thought her position through and doesn't know anywhere near as much as she thinks. For example:

> *Her:* Yeah, because it's good to be true to your feelings!
> *Me:* What do you mean?
> *Her:* It's good to be true, to live your life being honest to yourself
> *Me:* Really, what does that actually mean? I think that requires an explanation
> *Her:* Well, um… I mean people don't live their dreams do they? You have to know what you want and go for it and being honest about, like, stuff…
> *Me:* Yeah. I read a book last year called Radical Honesty, by Brad Blanton. His basic thesis is that we trap ourselves in a mental prison by lying about everything. It's a bit like Ayn Rand's concept in Atlas Shrugged where Francisco D'Aconia is telling Hank Reardon how important it is that you don't lie because then you are faking reality in order to win the approval of the person you are lying to, or who's delusional fantasy world you are enabling… Blah blah

You don't have to be overtly confrontational. This is what I mean about not arguing the topic. In my example I am overtly agreeing with her, but covertly I've just exposed her as a know-nothing dumbass and then intellectually mastered her.

The end result of an hour of hammering her frame is you've systematically kicked out every single leg from under her pedestal and brought her down to size. She has learned in Pavlovian manner that any time she tries to puff herself up, you effortlessly prick the balloon. So you've rendered her defenceless — what comes next?

Be aware that crushing her frame is a temporary shock and awe tactic and will not last. At some point she'll regroup and fight her way back into holding some frame. So act fast. Once you're sure she's beaten, move completely out of fight mode. When you win a fight you don't suddenly suggest "best of three?". Consolidate the victory by shifting to a cooperative frame, where the cooperation works *because she's accepted your frame*. Stop baiting her, stop hammering her. Her acceptance of defeat is good behaviour and should be rewarded. Move into stronger comfort, find things to agree about, explore her pleasant memories and future dreams, hope and fears…All the normal things you would do on a date with a feminine woman.

Frame crushing is about breaking the woman, like you'd break a wild mustang or a naughty dog. Once it's broken in you can reward it with the benefits of your leadership. If she gets a bit fighty again, such as by trying to return to an earlier topic of conflict (she may have finally thought up a good comeback) tell her not to fuss about all that stuff and to just enjoy the good vibe you've got going. Don't let the set go backwards.

To recap, frame crushing is an advanced technique to be used on girls who think they are hot shit or are excessively masculine. You are beating them down until they are in your frame and then treating them like they are feminine. It's a short-term tactic and if you don't fuck her that night you can expect some blowback afterwards, and possibly a burned set.

# 3. The Talk

**Feminine Imperative**

*The driving force behind the sum total of social conventions that favour women and women's sexual goals at the expense of men. It is a heuristic device. There is no conspiracy and it has no shape.*

Most men are terrified of letting the girl know they are trying to fuck her. We've been so thoroughly conditioned by the **Feminine Imperative** to be Nice Guys that we've internalised the belief that men's sex drives are dirty and women will freak out if they know we want to fuck them. Most men are terrified of stating exactly what they want because they are worried the answer will be "no," and then the girl is lost. So they play the grey area, weaselling along the date without ever admitting they have a boner.

This is utterly wrong. Women are dirtier, hornier, more wanton than any man. They are built by nature to be fuck machines. Their whole life is dominated by the pursuit of getting the right man inside them. That's why their eyes glaze over when they see a hard dick, why they scream in pleasure when you fuck them, and why they spend the rest of the night draped all over you trying to get a repeat serving. Women love sex. And that's a great thing. Nature has blessed us with these beautiful creatures that are a joy to fuck and they are totally up for it. Embrace it. When a man and woman like each other, sex is the most natural thing in the world.

So if you're on a date, running the model competently, and she doesn't play her part you need to wonder why. **It is not normal.** She should've come on the date because she's sexually interested in you and sees a sexual relationship as a natural conclusion if things work out over the next few hours. Her job on the date is to let you move it forwardswhile she simultaneously throws out a few tests to reassure herself of your value / character. This helps her to progress the emotional connection required to feel comfortable with physical intimacy. If she's NOT doing that **then it's not normal**. It can only mean one of two things:

- As the date progressed she became convinced that you aren't the right man for her, so she's losing interest. You're moving backwards not forwards.

- She never had a sexual relationship with you as a viable outcome. She was just wasting your time for whatever fucked up reasons she has in her head.

> If it's the former then there's nothing to be upset about. Sometimes the chemistry isn't there. Be proud of your work, thank her for a lovely evening, and move on to the next prospect. If it's the latter, you have to ask yourself "How was she able to waste so much of my time?" There's an old saying among hustlers that you can't cheat an honest man. When you have strong boundaries and don't believe in something-for-nothing, you won't be tempted by a too-good-to-be-true story. Something in your vibe gave her the idea that you'd let her waste your time. Correct that.
>
> So let's rewind into the date. We're one hour into it, just sat down after ordering drinks in the second venue. You are receiving mixed signals and your intuition is telling you that something isn't going right. Excuse yourself to the bathroom and spend a few minutes alone looking into the mirror. Replay the date tape in your mind and pull out all the key signals, both positive and negative. Where are you at? Explore your intuition to bring the reasoning into your logical mind. Compare her behaviour to the typology of On Girls above. If you think she's probably a timewaster you need to have The Talk.
>
> Go back to her, sip your drink and try a physical compliance test. Inspect her hands, reset her hair, squeeze her thigh. Whatever you decide, give her a test that will force non-compliance from a timewaster. Now turn off your value. Covertly show disapproval with a mild turn-away, perhaps letting your eyes wander while you are silent. Wait for her to re-engage. How does she do it?

- Some kino to a similar intimacy level to what you tried a few moments earlier? An apology and explanation that she isn't ready yet, but will be later?

- An explicit and fairly logical explanation for her behaviour that lets you know she is sexually interested in you. For example she says she has a boyfriend back in her home country and hasn't decided if she's going to break up. She's monkey-branching.

- An attempt to dissolve the sexual tension and divert you onto a new path to giving more value, such as by asking you a question about something non-sexual.

> If it's (iii) she's almost certainly a timewaster. So give her The Talk. Essentially you will overtly and directly tell her where you stand and what you want. Choose your own words, but include the following essential points. Look directly in her eyes when you say it because looking away telegraphs defeat. You aren't defeated here, it's just a final Hail Mary endzone pass:

- I like you as a woman, not as a friend

- This is a date, the purpose of which is to find out if we have a sexual and romantic connection

- I don't want to be your friend. That's why I've given you direct compliments about you as a woman

- If you have different goals that's ok but tell me now so we don't waste any more of each other's time

It should only take a minute or two to get this off your chest. Speak sincerely, confidently, and firmly. Do not be reactive and allow her to make you angry. You are forcing her to get off the fence. You are telling her the price of your continued attention. Her answer can only go one of three ways:

**No:** She'll directly tell you she's not interested in a sexual relationship. Thank her for her honesty, quickly finish your drink and then leave. Don't be angry and don't leave open the offer of meeting again. Just say "It was nice meeting you. I hope you enjoy the rest of your time here. Bye!" Turn your back and walk out. This is a strong push. There's a slim chance she'll reengage later by text, but only if you maintain radio silence and do not leave the door open. If she does, overtly agree by text that the next meeting is a date and make her meet you at your convenience. Do not go out of your way for this girl again until she's had her hand rubbing your dick.

**Yes:** She realises you're no chump and she does actually quite fancy you now. Giving her the Talk may have been the final piece in her attraction jigsaw. She tells you actually she does fancy you and does consider this to be a date. You've got her at her maximum openness, so nod your head, look intently and then as soon as she's finished speaking go for the kiss. Do not accept a refusal. If she still doesn't kiss then her words are empty so treat her as a No.

**Evasion:** She tries to deflect you without giving a straight answer, probably by either laughing nervously or giving you tactical outrage at having put her on the spot. This is a No and she is damaged goods. Don't accept "maybe" or "we'll see." Walk out.

The purpose of The Talk is not to advance you further towards fucking a girl. It's to filter out the timewasters who would otherwise play you indefinitely for your attention.

# SILLY BUGGERS

A girl's default programming is to try to derail all attempts to fuck her. This will manifest itself in ways such as breaking sexual tension, flaking, moving conversations into dead ends, annoying you, and the classic shit test. From her DNA's point of view this is a reasonable and necessary filtering mechanism to prevent her being impregnated by beta seed. The girl's logical forebrain is not developed like a man's and she lacks the maturity and rationality to think things through correctly. Therefore her emotional hindbrain is in control and will protect her from attempts to confuse and subvert her forebrain.

She doesn't care if sex doesn't happen. There's a long line of men waiting for chance to fuck her. If it doesn't work out with you, she can pick the next guy. That's the female privilege of being young and hot. This is biology and it's nothing to be angry about. Later in life there's a dramatic reversal, in which middle-aged men can act like a princess because there's an unending line of 30+ single women trying to get married off. But this doesn't concern us because we are seducing the young hot girls.

So just accept your role. You are the one who needs to make things happen. You have to build something out of nothing, while she just needs to kick it down. On the date this will express itself as her playing silly buggers. View these as reflexive instinctual flare-ups and a necessary part of the mating dance There's two basic forms where her silly buggers can express itself — overt and covert. Even game-aware men tend to miss the latter, and this is where high-value high-esteem girls really excel in their filtering. You can usually classify her subconscious purpose as to make you lose balance by either becoming angry when you shouldn't [anger-pull], not being angry when you should [anger-push], following her when you shouldn't [lead-pull] and leading her when you shouldn't [lead-push].

# Examples of playing silly buggers overtly

- She keeps responding to texts and calls on her mobile phone. Contrast this with the correct behaviour of ignoring texts until she goes to the bathroom and only taking urgent calls (and then apologising and explaining why she had to take it). *[anger-push]*

- Telling you about boyfriends, both current and ex. Correct behaviour is for her not to mention them at all unless pertinent to the topic immediately under discussion. *[anger-pull]*

- Letting another man chat her up in your presence *[anger-push]*. This is an extremely rude behaviour from her and every woman knows how disrespectful it is. You have every right to get angry, so tell her she can either pay attention to you or leave.

- She tries to get you to meet her friends *[anger-push]*. If she's sincerely wanting a date with you then she wants to be 1-on-1. Meeting friends will just suck you into her world, where you hang around at the edge of a conversation, losing value. Refuse it.

- Denying the reality of the date, such as telling you she's lesbian or in a relationship or she's a good girl who doesn't put out before marriage *[anger-pull]*

> When she's overtly acting like a silly bitch you can overtly chastise her for it, but keep a tight rein on how much emotional investment you display. It's best to be cold and firm rather than hot and loose:

- "Is there somewhere else you'd rather be?"
- "I'm not interested in your ex-boyfriends"
- "This isn't speed dating"
- "I'm not interested in your friends. I'm here to meet you"
- "Uh-huh" [nod like to a child telling a clumsy lie and you don't want to embarrass the child by dressing them down]

# Examples of playing silly buggers covertly

- Maintaining frosty unmoved body language when the normal response would be to reciprocate. Correct behaviour when talking is to show you her full body, rather than to turn away. *[lead-pull]*

- Trying to walk in front of you or too fast between venues. *[lead-pull]*

- Crossing the road ahead of you, especially if there's no need to cross the road in the first place. *[lead-pull]*

- You sit down somewhere and she insists on sitting somewhere else. *[lead-pull]*

- Asking you short direct questions to get you to speak too much. *[lead-push]*

- Talking in a sexually provocatively manner faster than seems normal *[lead-push]*. Here she's trying to make you over-eager at the prospect of sex, so that you move faster than appropriate and she can disqualify you as a horn-dog. She wants you to overplay your hand too early.

- Excessively complimenting you to lure you into qualifying yourself. *[lead-push]*

- Killing the conversation with short answers that leave nowhere to go in response *[lead-push]*. In this case you have to be comfortable with awkward silences rather than continuing to bend backwards to keep the conversation alive.

Fortunately for us, the correct response to all her attempts at playing silly buggers is the same: be unmoved and draw a boundary. Low-level attempts can usually be shrugged off with non-reactivity and playfully reasserting the frame:

- "Hold on missy, last time I checked I'm wearing the trousers here"
- "Stop pulling on the leash"
- "Come here"
- "Slow down there, crazy"

You can allow the girl to do one big overt test (for which you dress her down) as a normal part of the date, especially if she's Russian or would generally be considered a trophy girl. That should be all it takes to show her you have boundaries and won't surrender to her. Be ready to turn your back and leave if she does it a second time. The low-level covert tests are less disrespectful and much easier to just squash as they occur intermittently.

Yes Girls / Super On girls won't do any of this bullshit because they want to get laid. They are worried they'll fuck it up and you'll dismiss them for bad behaviour. It's far more the mark of a Suspicious On girl, who is entertaining the idea of sex but doesn't fear loss, and therefore has a free hand to fuck about with you. A girl who isn't interested won't even bother because she's already got all the information she needs to dismiss you. This means a girl playing silly buggers is actually showing her hand — *she's seriously considering sex with you*. She's giving you extra opportunities to look good.

## Emotional Control

Silly Buggers
pissing men off, non-stop

Silly buggers is designed to unbalance you. Dealing with such "princess behaviour" requires emotional control to keep your balance. You may find yourself literally biting your tongue and taking deep breaths to force yourself to calm down and avoid overreaction. Girls only act out in episodes of silly buggers as a reaction to how men have treated them, just like naughty children. There are too many spineless kiss-ass men in the world who allow women to trample all over their boundaries. Like naughty school kids with a weak teacher, these women are learning bad behaviour. They are desperately lacking boundaries.

Freedom only exists within boundaries. Women require men to tame the environment and make it safe for the women to move in and settle — think of it like frontiersmen of the Old American West. When women and children lack boundaries, they are missing the feeling of existential security that tells them "So long as I stay in this place, I am safe." They are acting out because of it. Therefore, when you enforce boundaries the girl will behave.

You don't need to be constantly on her, pushing your frame. Be calm, centred and unreactive for most of the time and if she acts out you swiftly punish her with a stern look, raised eyebrow, back turn, vacuum, or other covert signal of disapproval. If her action is particularly cuntish you can blow your top and shout at her. Then go back to your original calm.

# BEWARE — THE INTERLOPING MALE

There is a world of difference between her soliciting the attention of rival men while on the date (her playing silly buggers) and another man invading your date (not her fault). Generally speaking, the rule is to be unreactive to her emotional state / games but be ruthlessly aggressive in your treatment of interloping males. When a woman messes with you it's because she's not sure of your value and wants to test your base and ride. Not so with interloping men. By hitting on a girl they know you are with, they are openly challenging you. You cannot be unreactive because then you'd be surrendering her to him and thus supplicating to him. Repel that man and do not feel the slightest twinge of guilt in being utterly ruthless in doing so. It will build attraction with the girl.

You don't own the girl yet, but for the duration of the date you own her. While on the date she is off-limits to all men. They know that and she knows that. When he interferes he's trying to steal your lunch money. Crush him. Your position is stronger than you may realise, because he is breaking social politeness first (he has become "the violator") and if she does anything but take your side then she is a worthless slut and needs to be dumped *immediately*.

Realistically there's almost zero interloping male risk on dates and it's more applicable to the initial open in a bar or nightclub. In that context you are in a free-fire zone and the girl has not yet become your property, whereas it would be incredibly socially weird for a guy to come into a date and fuck with you in a café or quiet bar. Nonetheless, let's consider responses:

1. **The floater** — You are ordering drinks at the bar when the man on the table next to your girl leans over an initiates conversation, perhaps in a flirty manner. He has made a low-investment plausibly-deniable ping, floating the idea of hitting on her to gauge her interest and your level of involvement.

2. **The looker** — You notice a guy across the bar keeps looking over at your girl and trying to catch her eye to smile. He's letting her know he's interested, but not breaking into the conversation. Again, he's a minor violator so don't overreact.

3. **The challenger** — A guy makes a sexually inappropriate comment about you or her within earshot. He's trying to rock you into either over-reacting with anger (so he can tool you for being a dick) or letting it pass (so he can build momentum and do it more).

4. **The interruption** — A guy forces his way into your conversation, either through you or through her. Gradually he begins to tool you and freeze you out of the conversation.

The best response is always the same: call it out.

One sure way to destroy a guy's chances is to over-escalate on his behalf. Seduction is a carefully poised dance where every step forwards must be calibrated and timed correctly. So a good way to derail his train is to openly call out him trying to fuck her, to take away his plausible deniability so he must either dick-tuck in denial (you win through dominance) or admit he is trying to fuck your girl in which case he has become an open challenge, a social violator, and now you have a free hand to tell him to fuck off.

Calling out the reality forces the man out of the grey zone. It takes away his options of insinuation, plausible deniability, hovering, waiting for you to go to the bathroom, chipping away at your value, stealing the spotlight etc. It is also refreshingly authentic. How you call it out is a calibration question. Examples:

**The floater** — Sit back down and ignore him, continuing the conversation with your girl. The first two times he tries to interject just blank him like you don't notice his presence and don't realise he's talking to you. If he persists, give a curt and socially-polite dead end response. If he still persists, he's now become a socially awkward violator so just tell him "Sorry fella, we're in the middle of something."

**The looker** — Next time he does it and you both see, say "Have you seen that creepy guy over there? I think he wants to have sex with you." If he keeps doing it and becomes a direct challenge, look back and raise your pint in salutation. If she is returning his look tell her, "You would make a great couple."

**The challenger** — Dismiss him with "Cool story, bro". Don't engage or argue because that draws him into the conversation. Just dismiss and backturn. If he keeps engaging say "Look, we're on a date. Go try to fuck a different girl," or if he's a bit less insistent just dismiss him with "You look tired" or "You seem angry."

**The interruption** — You are going to have to give this guy short shrift responses. If he persists, you have to shut him down with "Look fella, I don't mean to be rude but we are having a quiet evening out and aren't looking to make new friends."

If any of these guys keep blabbing on after you've given a firm, polite message of don't-talk-to-us you have social permission to be ruder. Call it out again: "Look, I've given you the hint and even had to politely tell you we're not interested. Give it a rest and bother someone else." Try not to break social politeness because you want him firmly positioned as the violator. But I stress that situations like this are very rare. It's happened to me maybe three times ever, and in each case the guy came across as so weird that the girl was freaked out and totally on my side.

So what if it happens a lot to you?

Chances are you are giving off victim signals that let stronger men smell blood in the water. The more your girl resembles a trophy, the more you'll have to deal with men looking at you and getting riled at the perceived injustice of it. In the short term, don't date girls in places likely to encourage interlopers and **don't ever** take a girl to a nightclub, gig, or house party unless you've already got a firm hand on her and can rely upon her to dismiss interlopers without your help. Stick to cafes and low-key bars. In the medium term you need to toughen yourself up so you're a less inviting target. If you're doing your masculine presence correctly you won't run into such trouble.

# SAME DAY LAYS (AND I-DATES)

## Goal: Fuck her the same day you meet her

**Y**ou'll notice I've put i-dates into the same bracket as SDLs. This is because most of the time the first half hour is the same, and it's only when certain factors fall into place that you can move from i-date to SDL. Allow me to explain.

During the street stop you can begin light probing for logistics and attitude to see if the girl is amenable to the i-date. Simple questions like "What's your plan for today?" and being aware of her situation. When a girl is busy, I won't bother i-dating. What's the point? If the hook is weak and I don't feel much sexual tension I won't i-date. It's just a waste of time because she might follow your momentum to a café and enjoy the diversion, but that's giving away your precious time and attention on a longshot. If you're not sure about the girl it's better to take a number and move on. If she then replies to the number and comes on a date you're playing a whole different game — she's passed a much bigger compliance test. The only exception to this rule is if she's unusually hot. In this case, that you might as well commit to a weak lead because you'll waste even more time trying to find and hook another girl of this calibre.

---

### Forcing the SDL

*precision engineering* **Krauser Tip**

It's a mug's game to go out trying to get an SDL. They are an unusual occurrence that emerge naturally from a unique confluence of factors about the girl, the location, and the crackle of sexual energy between you. Most girls are simply not up for it. Of the ones who are, they are usually towards the bottom end of your acceptable quality scale. Even when you have the right girl on the i-date there are many external factors that can intervene. Also keep in mind that if you successfully bang her you are now unlikely to see her again. SDLs are high risk, redlining the car. It's much better to go out looking to run your normal two-date daygame and just be alive to the rare SDL opportunities when theypresentsthemselves. You'll burn a lot fewer good sets and waste less of your energy that way.

Beginners — ignore all that. Spend a few weeks pushing for SDLs. Redline it and crash the car. It's a training exercise to acquire reference experiences showing you what is possible.

---

The best girls to SDL are travelling solo in a foreign country, have no real plans that evening, are not embedded in a strong social circle in that city, are younger than 25, and give you an immediate sexual spark when you talk to them. Ultimately it's a checklist and you want to tick as many of these boxes as possible before making the decision to push for the SDL:

## Pre-Approach Signs For SDL Targets

- Walking aimlessly and slowly letting her eyes wander around at buildings, shops, traffic, and other people.

- Carrying a map of London or a guidebook. Some identifier in her fashion that she loves England, such as a union jack badge, a Beatles bag, or a Keep Calm And Carry On t-shirt. Perhaps a plastic bag from a souvenir shop.

- Sensible walking shoes, such as trainers or canvas hiking boots. Converse All Star are quite common too.

- Fashion that projects a sexual vibe (e.g. short denim shorts, flimsy vest, showing lots of leg and maybe stomach), a deeply introverted vibe (muted colours, tiny little markers of individuality such as metal badges on a lapel) or a lost and vulnerable vibe (tight blue jeans, too much or not enough clothing for the weather).

- Visible signs of rebellion against mainstream society such as tattoos, piercings, red hair, slogan t-shirts OR visible signs of being meek and easily led.

- The girl will somehow appear approachable. Your gut feel will be "This girl wants to be opened."

## During Street Stop Signs

- Immediate eye-sparkle and strong hook when you open. You barely need to finish your opener.

- She's immediately giving back in the conversation and making it go smoothly because she's as keen as you are OR she's very quiet and taciturn but giving full compliance and making no effort to leave.

- She tells you she just arrived in town and is leaving soon. Perhaps she's travelling solo or the friend she's visiting is busy at work. Whatever the particulars of the story, the overall message is "I haven't got much going on," and "Nobody will know if I have sex."

- She accepts some early kino and sexualisation — e.g. you do the "Oops, sorry. I was just checking out your legs," and she gives an encouraging laugh.

- There's no resistance to anything you do or suggest.

- Any kino at all that is initiated by her even if it's as light as momentarily touching your forearm when she says something. This is a massive signal of sexual availability, completely out of proportion to how minor it seems to the uninitiated.

If you are ticking off these boxes you can begin to turn your mind towards the i-date, which is where you'll begin to tick off the next round of boxes. Give it five to ten minutes on the street and then suggest a drink right then. I will always bounce to the nearest suitable location within a direct line of sight, whether it be a pub, café, or park (listed in descending order of desirability). Examples:

"Ok, I've got a little while before I meet my friends. Do you like Sherlock Holmes?... Ok. There's a Sherlock Holmes theme pub just over there. Come join me for a quick drink."

"I've got about half an hour. Ok, let me ask you Miss Foreign Girl. Can you drink English tea like an English lady? Ok, there's a lovely tea shop over there. Let's get a quick drink."

If you calibrated the girl correctly and have already probed her for clear logistics you can expect more than half of them to follow you onto the i-date. If she demurs then go right back into more street game and try again when the hook is stronger. If she still demurs, take the number and suggest going out another time when you are both less busy.

So you're now walking to the first bounce location. You can really back off from the attraction now. Just tell her a little story about something nearby. When I walk a girl out of Trafalgar Square I'll usually tell her the story of Horatio Nelson and how his innovative battle tactics changed the course of European history for 100 years in just one afternoon. The purpose is to dial things down and make it as normal and safe as possible. Just occupy her mind as her feet carry her momentum into your world. This is a major leap of faith moment for her. She has just decided to leave her plan behind and follow a stranger. Don't give her reasons not to.

# Early SDL / i-date plan

When you first hear stories about guys getting SDLs it's natural to get the wrong idea about them. It seems like such a rock-star / bad boy activity full of supercharged sexual energy and crazy antics. It only *sounds* like that afterwards when relating the story to friends over some beers, where the focus is on the drama and nail-biting moments of escalation. The reality is 90% of the time between meeting and fucking is extremely low-key and as normal as you can possibly make it. When you're redlining the car, it shakes and wobbles at high speed. Don't let it break apart. Swirly-twirly uber-asshole moves will scare the shit out of even the bravest girl and you'll crash. The lay should just creep up on the girl until she's so caught up in the momentum she doesn't realise how unusual the situation is. Try to avoid breaking the fourth wall and telling her what you are doing. Avoid anything that can trigger her logical mind into realising "Wait a moment, why am I about to fuck a guy

I just met? This is weird" and anything that can trigger her emotional hindbrain into thinking "This is scary."

*For the first half-hour you will run relaxed low-energy rapport while gently probing her to tick off your checklist.*

Go to the bar with her and just lightly shepherd her around. SDLs require extreme levels of leading and compliance so you will be phasing in light compliance and kino tests from the beginng. While walking away from the street stop you'll say "this way" so she follows. At the traffic lights you lightly stop her with the back of your hand on her stomach then on the green man you say "Ok, now," and give a very light push on her lower back. In the pub you take her to the bar, ask what type of drink she likes and then recommend one of that type. If she doesn't know it then ask the barman for a taster (this shows leadership, social power, and protectiveness) before she decides. If it's a café tell her to find some seats while you order. If it's a bar just wait until you've paid and then walk to a seat together.

Generally i-dates happen in the mid-afternoon, so try to sit outside. It seems weird to sit indoors on a sunny day and this is all about normalising the experience. Be as casual as you can. Sit opposite each other on a beer garden bench or next to each other on some stone steps. Take your foot off the pedal sexually. You'll be naturally dropping in DHVs and rapport, but don't try to be too "on." It's all about taking deep breaths and relaxing for the first half hour. Now work the frame:

1. London is anonymous

2. She's an adventurer

3. Life is about taking your opportunities

4. How do people meet

5. What does she like in a man

A girl who can be SDL'd will respond favourably to the frame. You'll sense your rapport strengthening and a bubbling undercurrent of sexual tension that's not quite at surface level. That's where you'll keep it for now. Add in ever more intrusive sexualisation and kino. At this point I've usually touched her hands on a pretext of examining her rings or guessing her age from the subcuteuous fat over the knuckles. If she's got a tattoo I've touched it, and I will have lightly squeezed her thigh and played a little with her hair. If she's not up for it she'll block and evade such moves. If she's complying, even if it's timidly and quietly, the SDL is possible.

# The Decision

About thirty minutes in you should have enough information to know if the SDL is likely. Sometimes your hand is forced because one of you is leaving town imminently. If so, you need to decide if the girl is a realistic Long Game prospect. Does she like to use Facebook or Skype so you can progress things online before you see her again? Is she hot enough to be worth the effort of Long Game? Is there any reason to suppose you'll be in the same city at the same time again? So long as you think Long Game is a realistic option and the SDL isn't, then you'll be best using the remainder of the i-date to bed down deep rapport and get a solid social media add. Obviously if you're both going to be in town for a while just drop your ego and run the normal two-date model.

Once you've made the decision to abandon the SDL you will move into 100% deep rapport and future projection. Everything is about making that number as solid as possible so that when the bubble bursts she still wants to chat with you. You must still make the move to show your intent, but it doesn't need to be more than a kiss attempt. She doesn't even need to accept the kiss, just go for it and hold your frame. Don't show disappointment, frustration, or sexual hunger. Perhaps before that you've already verbally IOId her in the man-woman frame.

## Failing to stabilise the contact details

When getting a number on a street stop you will be careful not to over-invest. There's a fine line between ensuring you didn't make a mistake entering her contact details and coming off as over-keen. On an i-date you've already had over half an hour of rapport, so it's completely normal to check her details and make sure this wonderful connection isn't accidentally broken. So get her to log into Facebook on her smartphone and add you. Or get her number and give her a missed call to confirm. If by now she has decided she doesn't want you to have her contact details, she owes you an overt verbal explanation why and it's not creepy to ask her. I usually take the number AND a social media add. Ask her if she uses WhatsApp, a favourite for international travellers.

## The same day delay

Generally speaking it's best to i-date the girl as late as possible in the afternoon. Even the most aimlessly wandering girl has some vague plan for her day, and if she's a tourist new in town she wants to explore. Darkness is more sexual. Perhaps it's better to take her number in the street stop and then agree to have a date later that day when she's finished whatever it is she wants to do. Use your social intelligence and keep this in mind when probing logistics during the street stop. Sure, she may be busy right at this moment but she might be free later in the evening. If she doesn't have a phone then arrange a time and place to meet where you've already been with her (e.g. the last place you see her), because she probably doesn't know her way around.

# Mid-date SDL plan

You should only be in this phase if you've ticked enough checkboxes to believe the SDL is a reasonably likely outcome and you are willing to push through to the end. Don't allow conflicting emotions in that will sap your conviction. SDLs are bloody hard and require balls of steel. The leaps of faith are faster and scarier than on a normal date. You must be certain you want it. That means don't be pushing for an SDL at 4pm if you have an appointment you can't miss at 7pm. Don't be pushing for an SDL if you would prefer to number farm (e.g. first day of a short Euro-tour). Don't be pushing for an SDL if you can feel yourself losing your mojo and momentum. In those cases you are better doing a Same Day Delay — roll off, get your shit together, and have another run for the summit later.

So let's recap. You're finishing your drinks in the first venue and it seems fairly on. Maybe she hasn't given you any strong come-on but the immediate future seems strangely clear of obstructions and she's complying with your little escalations and frame push. If you gave yourself a false time constraint earlier it's time to give yourself a plausible escape from it. Pretend to get a text from the friend you're supposed to meet where he's supposedly telling you he's gonna be really late. Clear your schedule and then lead her to the next pub.

*It will always be a pub. You need to get alcohol in her.*
*She doesn't need to be drunk but she needs*
*plausible deniability for her own comfort.*

I always buy half-pints in the first two venues. It's easier to get her onto the turn-taking system and you can bounce faster. Start walking her to the next venue and make sure it's not far. Within 200 metres is ideal. This second venue is another major compliance test. The first venue was "This guy is interesting, I suppose I'll have a drink," whereas the second venue is "I'm on an adventure now, let's see where it leads." The SDL odds rise 20% when she comes to the second venue without resistance.

Speaking of resistance, if you are getting any at all then something is wrong. It's normal on a first date for a girl to put up obstructions, she knows how to play *that* game. SDLs have a unique vibe. She's probably never done this before. Even if she's had a one night stand before it would've been at a house party or nightclub under the influence of alcohol. It's almost guaranteed she's never been SDLd. So she doesn't have a script and she doesn't know what to do. What do you do when suddenly thrown into an important business meeting with heavy hitters discussing a topic outside of your competence? You stay quiet, don't rock the boat, and do what they tell you within reasonable boundaries. A SDL setup is such a destabilising and novel situation that it is normal for the girl to just give full compliance and go along with it all without a peep. So long as you don't ask too much too soon, she'll comply.

It's very rare for a girl to throw out pre-bedroom resistance to an escalation *and then still be SDLd*. It happens, don't give up because of it, but statistically SDLs are normally either plain sailing or a total bust. SDLs happen when the girl is completely cowed under your masculine presence and very comfortable with it. She **wants** it. There'll be token LMR once in the bedroom as a matter of course.

The main vibe shift in the second venue is you'll be spiking more and turning things sexual. I do this within the first hour usually, but that's fast. My earlier SDLs often took two or three hours before the kiss and it's not unrealistic to invest up to seven hours total from meet to sex. Again, this is why you should be covertly filtering hard at the beginning. Seven hours is a hell of a long time to invest in a fundamentally shaky proposition, which all SDLs are. Only spend that long if you're really sure you want this girl.

---

### The bamboozle adventure

The goal is to get tight and fast at recognising SDLs and then accelerating all of the usual attraction, comfort, and escalation. It's like a two-date model on fast-forward. As a stepping stone, consider throwing an adventure section into the i-date. Usually I'd say there's no substitute for a smoothly accelerated escalation but there is — bamboozlement. Girls have sources of order in their life such as jobs, daily routines, social circles, parents, plans. The more order the girl has, the harder it is to pull her into your reality and get fast sex. So you run a pattern interrupt. Take her on a boat tour of the Thames, take her on a bike ride through Hyde Park, go around a pokey little market, walk through some confusing backstreets. The idea is to destabilise her. Imagine a boat moored at the dock on a rough sea. You want to cut those ropes and raise the anchor so the boat drifts out into the storm. Then it's fucked. There's the phrase "Any port in a storm" for a reason. Destroy her sources of order, bamboozle her, and she'll be more willing to accept your order (your leading). Move her around so much that she doesn't know up from down and the only constant in her immediate reality is your calm, non-reactive fun presence. Just don't rely on this because it's a huge time investment in what is still a fundamentally shaky activity. And when you've done the Thames Clipper trip for the fourth time in two days it gets rather stale.

# CARE AND MAINTENANCE
## section nine

So far we have been focused on how to get girls, on a case-by-case basis. Zooming out a level, we will now consider how to manage your learning process over the long term. Game changes you. Mostly, the changes are for the better and you will become a better man. However, the player's journey involves many pressures and can often become tiring. You will tend to become competitive with other players, to have both up and down periods, and to learn a lot about yourself as the months pass. This section considers some common pitfalls and offers suggestions on what to expect as you follow the path forwards.

# CARE AND MAINTENANCE

## Goal: Continue to improve your game and your life

There's a pretty easy way to know if you are getting better at Game. The girls are getting younger, hotter, tighter, and it's costing you less time and effort to close them. Put another way:

- You close the same girls easier than you used to, and

- You close hotter girls with the same effort

That's it really. If you aren't upgrading your quality or reducing your work-rate then your game is plateauing. Not that you need worry too much about it. If you've found a sweet spot where you get girls you find acceptable with a workrate you find tolerable, then by all means rest on those laurels. Game has just improved your life. Enjoy it.

Improving your game is really really hard. It may be the hardest thing you ever attempt. I'd estimate only 20% of men are even capable of processing the basic concepts to reach an understanding of Game. Of those men who theoretically "get" the idea of Game, probably only 20% of them will do enough in-field work to become better with women. Of *that* tiny sample, probably only 10% will actually become Good With Women. This means that only 1 out of 250 men will even reach the intermediate level of Game. Even those odds likely overstate the number of Players in the world.

The path to tight game is simply too steep for most men.

Realistically, the only men who can master daygame must tick most of the following checkboxes:

1. High IQ but not genius-level

2. Strong internal locus of control

3. Long future-time orientation

4. Supreme emotional control, especially resilience to pain of failure

5. Average or better looks with no major strike-out deformity

6. Ability to self-diagnose problems

7. Willingness to change fundamental parts of your life and identity

8. Horny

And the one absolutely essential trait which is absolutely non-negotiable:

9. Demons clawing at your door

*I've never met a top player who wasn't originally motivated by a deep dark secret*. For me it was an ego-crushing divorce and a mortal fear that I'd never again find the companionship of a beautiful young woman. For others it's a childhood chip on the shoulder at being excluded from "the good life," or a toxic lack of self-acceptance, or narcissist parents they can never please. There must be some deep motivating force that powers them through the endless street rejections, the dates to nowhere, the last-gasp LMR that stops the notch, and the not-much-talked-about long dark nights of the soul when it's 4am, you can't sleep and you wonder where you are going with your life.

Most men cannot handle the emotional strain of constantly getting themselves "up" to approach, to absorb thousands of rejections, to constantly live outside their comfort zone, to re-examine everything they hold dear in their lives.

That's why the men who get good are usually severely unbalanced men running from internal demons. The best guys will eventually turn and face those demons, kill them, and make it over that last plateau to self-acceptance and happiness.

Don't punish yourself when you find your motivation at its lowest ebb. Normal well-balanced men *are not supposed to* master daygame. *Just remember you don't need to master anything.* Simply becoming *better* will improve your life. Take a man who currently gets irregular sex with fives and pays a high price of time, effort, money, and bullshit for the privilege. Some studied effort at daygame can net him regular sixes at far lower cost. To him that's like holding a winning lottery ticket.

## The Expected Path Of Game

No two men will have exactly the same path in game. We all have different strengths and weaknesses, different starting value, different upper ceilings to our value, different social milieu, and different tenacity to improve. To help map the general territory, I'll outline the most common path I've seen amongst peers and students.

**Total Chodery** — You begin with a mind full of Blue Pill illusions and a pedestaling anti-Game. You barely talk to any girls and wouldn't dream of cold approaching unless paralytically drunk. On the rare occasion you get a number you horribly over-invest. The women are pretty unpleasant. *Time:* Your whole life until reading about Game, T+0. *Numbers:* 90% of men never leave this stage.

**Wannabe PUA** — You've read some Game material and dipped your toe into cold approach. Everything seems too difficult and awkward. There's too much to think about and the whole thing is a mess. You wander around town for hours muttering mantras, trying to get the balls to approach. Then you go home with nothing, telling yourself you're a loser who will never get it. *Time:* T+4 months. *Number:* Of the 10% who made it past total chodery, half drop out here and then post on forums that Game doesn't work.

**Approach Machine** — You gotten over the initial AA hump and go out every weekend to approach. You're still getting lots of harsh blowouts, but enough girls smile and chat to light up your life with hope. You get occasional numbers but barely any dates, and when a girl does meet you you're soon in the friendzone. *Time:* T+1 year. *Number:* There's only 5% of the population left at this stage, and even that is probably a massive overstatement. Half drop out here and trawl OKcupid.

**Intermediate Player** — Daygame is a fundamental part of your identity. You go out every weekend, some evenings, and you're banging about one new girl a month and usually have two on rotation. The hot girls still reject you but you're happier than most men on the planet. You are now obsessed with breaking the quality ceiling and improving what is quite a harsh failure-rate. *Time:* T+2 years. *Number:* If you're here, you're in the top 1% of men

**Advanced Player** — You are constantly surrounded by women. They are always chatting on your Facebook, meeting for dates, sexing you. Once a girl comes into your orbit she never really leaves, even if she finds a real boyfriend. Dry spells are unknown and you consider it a bad week if you didn't get a new girl. You're probably working just as hard as the intermediates but getting 5x the results. *Time:* T+4 years. *Number:* This is the sexual elite. Most readers of this book will never get there.

**Daygame Master** — You get laid whenever you want. You don't even "do daygame" anymore. You just go out and get a girl. When you're sitting on the train girls flirt with you. Waitresses want to chat. You're getting frequent IOIs. The only time you need to put forth effort is to snipe at the top tier of women. There's probably only four or five guys at this level in any given country, and they don't write about it on the internet or put their face on DVDs.

This is a rough and ready outline, so don't stress if your experiences don't fit. The main takeaway is that the marketing message in PUA products is utter bullshit. Almost everyone will fail to reach the level their magic pill promises. Not only that, but having been sold a lie and then endured possibly years of extreme emotional pressure in the field, you'll feel cheated. Even those at the Advanced Player level are working hard for their notches and enduring bullshit and emotional pain. By that point the rewards massively outweigh the costs, but it's still not easy.

*Banging hot new women with regularity*
*from cold approach never gets easy.*

Don't get into this Game for an easy ride. Seriously ask yourself what level of results would keep the demons off your back and compare that with the amount of anguish you're prepared to endure. I don't want to talk you out of Game, but I want you to be aware that it's a tough ride.

# Overgaming

The human body requires a balance between its anabolic and catabolic states. This is simple to understand when considering exercise to gain muscle mass and lose fat. We must work hard in the gym to deplete our slow and fast twitch muscle fibres of glycogen and break down the muscle (catabolic). Then we must take rest, sleep, and refuel with correct nutrition so the body can refill the glycogen and rebuild the fibres (anabolic). With each cycle we make our bodies stronger and more functional. So it is with Game:

- **Anabolic**: Rest, working on your value, having fun in your life.

- **Catabolic**: Approaching and dating.

It will take time to find your balance. In the beginning, approaching is intimidating so the temptation is to "work on your value" until you feel comfortable going out to chase girls. This is not wrong but doing it excessively is a life-weasel. If you find yourself constantly reading blogs, books, and watching seminar videos rather than approaching girls then you're weaselling. The answer is to go outside and find some girls. Conversely, once you've caught the daygame bug and begun to get laid your mind slips into a logical formula:

*X number of approaches leads to Y number*
*of leads which results in Z number of lays*

It seems logical but it's not true. It assumes your value and vibe are static, whereas the very act of approaching is catabolic and thus continued periods of daygaming without rest are like continued periods of hitting the gym without sleeping and eating. You run yourself down, flatten your vibe, and before long you're an empty shell stumbling around the streets scaring girls with your dead eyes. A more accurate formula is:

> X number of approaches leads to Y number of leads, an increase in momentum [M] and a correspondently larger diminution in your value [V]. Eventually V+M sinks below the level require to acquire Z number of lays.

That was needlessly complex. Just take the point that all game and no play makes Jack a dull boy. Relentless approaching can only be sustained for short periods of time (such as number-farming on a holiday) before it becomes counter productive. You can't rush the Game. Find your balance and trust that it'll work out in the end.

## Game Will Not Make You Happy

The human mind focuses on what we don't have and takes for granted what we do have. This is part of our natural drive to strive towards greater success, and with it comes problems. Firstly we have the cognitive bias towards the grass being greener on the other side. We look at someone who has what we want and we only focus on the upside. Perhaps the downside is hidden. We all engage in impression management precisely to hide the downside from outsiders. So as office juniors we may look at the CEO and see his power, annual bonus ,and frequent business class flights as rewards for high status. Sure. But as you get to know CEOs, you find they have little control over their schedule because their secretary has to schedule them months in advance. They can't switch off their responsibilities for the company even when on the golf course. Flying drains you even when going business class and no five-star hotel can replace the comfort of sleeping in your own bed and having your own friends around for a drink. Teenagers will look at rock stars and see the touring, the adoring fans, the phenomenal lay counts with groupies, the award ceremonies, and think that's The Life. But have you noticed how many rock stars are drug addicts, alcoholics, and have little love for life? We don't see the downside of endless satiation of short term gratification, the rootlessness of being on the road, the pressure to constantly produce quality material, all the haters talking shit about you.

I'm not suggesting CEOs or rock stars have it bad. Just that from the outside looking in the lifestyle seems far more satisfying than it really is. Happiness is a nebulous concept and a slippery beast to catch. You find it in places you wouldn't expect, and it rarely sticks around for long in the same circumstances.

I outline this because Game is the same. Take a typical blue pill chode who has only fucked four girls in his whole life, and had to buy the cow to do so. He sits in his office cubicle prodding numbers into Excel fifty hours a week, listening to the inane chatter from Jane in accounts, a fat middle-aged sow. He furtively opens Chrome and begins reading a lay report of some player on a foreign adventure who picks up a slim Russian teenager in a coffee shop then bangs her four days later. He knows this player pulls off this feat a few times a month. What is the chode to think?

*This guy is living the dream!*

Yes and no.

Lay reports are the success stories and there is a strong survivor bias in what makes it to the internet. There's a bunch of players' journey blogs where the guy is still awkwardly thrashing about and failing to get laid. Those blogs don't attract many readers. There's even more guys going out daygaming who have so little success there's nothing to even write about — 1,000 blow-out reports are dull reading and don't get page clicks. Even the guy banging three new girls a month is cherry-picking his highlights because they make the best reading.

### Daygamer Guilt

Nightgamers have one huge advantage over daygamers — they can compartmentalise their activity and switch off easily. When your Game is based in a nightclub you only consider yourself "on the clock" when going out clubbing. Nightgamers can comfortably walk past a pretty girl on the street in midafternoon. Daygamers feel perpetual guilt for not opening every hot girl they see. There is no automatic off switch in daygame. You must teach yourself to go off the clock and feel comfortable with letting girls go past.

The reality of daygame is that, unless you are exceptionally good-looking or naturally charming, it is a *grind*. A long cheerless grind at times, punctuated by occasional glory moments of brilliance.

And it gets worse.....

As a normal chode it probably never enters your mind that you could bang a lot of SMV-prime sweet tottie. For that reason you never set up the expectation of getting it, and thus you never experience the lurking threat of failure for not getting it. The moment you pass over into the identity of becoming a Player you have just made life tough on yourself:

- Goals are good because they direct your behaviour and push you to higher performance.

- Goals are bad because they create success conditions which, by definition, you haven't yet reached. And you feel bad about it.

As a chode your behaviours and lifestyle are congruent with your goals. You just amble along as the loveable loser. Setting a player goal rocks the boat. By setting a goal you are initiating a bargain with your forebrain of "I will be happy if I satisfy success conditions X, Y, Z. Until that happens I will be unhappy."

You are proactively making yourself unhappy. How weird is that? And the loftier the goals, the worse you feel. You are creating incongruence where none existed before. This is a necessary step towards improving your life **but it will make you less happy than doing nothing at all**. When you read about the player knocking over his third girl of the month you think "Wow, I want some of that." The player himself has probably fallen short of one of his own success conditions. Maybe she wasn't hot enough, maybe he worked too hard for her, maybe his goal was four girls.

## Cognitive Dissonance

You'll be familiar with that nauseous dread in the pit of your stomach before you go out approaching. Why is that? Later you can flick back to the section on approach anxiety for the immediate causes, but for now consider the meta-level issue:

You hindbrain doesn't much like the idea of approaching.

You forebrain has set a target to approach x number of girls this week.

Great, you've just given yourself a forebrain-hindbrain conflict. For as long as you are in a position of "not good enough" at game or "not enough notches," you'll exist in this state of cognitive dissonance where your forebrain is forcing you to overrule your hindbrain so as to take right action. That's a constant tension and it's never pleasant. Usually after a few sets and a few good responses, the dissonance will fade and now you are actually enjoying the streets — the hindbrain has come into alignment with the forebrain. But this is temporary. Maybe they stay in alignment for a few hours or even a few weeks, but then they drift apart. There are only three ways to remove this dissonance for good:

1. Give up on the game.

2. Reach your goals.

3. Reach full self-acceptance.

Giving up is no solution because you trade the short term pain of cognitive dissonance for the long term existential terror that you'll never find happiness with women. Reaching your goals is the best solution but also the longest and slowest. Once you finally reach your Magic Number of notches, or crack your top tier of quality (or whatever your main goal is), then the dissonance dissipates. You no longer need a goal and therefore you just approach whenever you feel like it. The very idea of approaching when you don't want to seems nonsensical. *Very very few players will ever reach this stage*. So that leaves us with self-acceptance.

# Relentless Notch Count Hyena

There is a concept in nutritional sciences called SuperStimulation. As our human ancestors traversed the African savannah, we developed a taste for the foods that aid our survival while rejecting those that poison us. We develop hunger to motivate us to forage and satiation to tell us when to stop. We developed a sweet tooth for sugars and fats because, in the state of nature, these are rare and valuable. Our ancestors developed tastes that sought out the stimulants of the natural environment and we were perfectly suited to them.

Modern agriculture changed all that. The typical candy bar is so loaded with sugar that it presents a level of stimulation many multiples higher than our body is wired to deal with. It short circuits our wiring and triggers obsessive degenerative behaviour. Food science evolved faster than our body's ability to resist its lure. A candy bar is a super stimulation. So is crystal meth. Or playing Battlefield 3 online with your clan. Or internet porn. Modern culture has isolated and gamed our base physical and emotional circuitry.

An upside of super-stimulation is daygame itself. Progressive iterations of Game mean we now stand on the shoulders of giants. We have cracked a code nature never prepared us for, and we have written it down into a teachable format. This book is an expression of that. Women are emotional creatures. They lack the future-time orientation, maturity, ability to delineate cause-effect relationships, and self-awareness of men. Men created Game with their man-sized brains. We set ourselves the problem of "how to get girls" and then solved it. It's not easy, but there's a clearly marked path to get there.

Now put yourself in the girl's position. She has only her emotional hard-wiring to guide her. In the arms-race of predator and prey she is moving at an evolutionary speed while men are moving at an accelerated industrial pace. The age-old mating dance involved the girl luring the man to extract the value she needs (quality seed and future provision), while the man did the same for himself (good sex). As the annals of history show at different epochs and in different cultures, either the men or women held a slight advantage.

The advent of Game has changed all that. An advanced player has such total mastery of female emotional responses that he can see the matrix. He can overload the girl with such a super-stimulation of male dominance and value that her emotional circuitry is ill-equipped to fight him off. A truly advanced player can smash through a woman's defences far far quicker than nature ever intended. We have entered the era of fast sex with SMV-prime women…but only for those men who have climbed Mount Improbable.

Advanced players are in the historically unprecedented position of having sexual access to scores of women whenever they please (or at least with most of the barriers removed). It's like Goldfinger emptying Fort Knox with all the guards asleep. *Our male bodies are not designed to deal with such a super-stimulation of women.* It's precisely why rock stars turn to drugs.

Our caveman ancestors mated with maybe one or two women over the course of their lives. He only even **saw** a small number of women of child-rearing age, few of them naked and in sexual positions. He had a tiny number of sexually-charged interactions with novel nubile flesh. When it happened his DNA rewarded him with dopamine spikes, a chemical pat on the back for services rendered towards the advancement of his DNA lineage. Now consider how you feel after a tough afternoon number-farming.

You're simultaneously exhausted andexhilarated. You probably struggle to sleep that night, your mind spinning.

Your brain is not designed to absorb the dopamine of twenty sexually-charged streets sets in one day. That never existed on the African savannah. You aren't designed to date three women in one day, nursing a boner as you try to figure out the subtle psychological plays that will let you stick it into her. You aren't designed to have three girls on a rotation. You aren't designed to get the post-fuck new-girl dopamine spike twenty-plus times a year. But we **are** designed to strive for it, like dogs chasing a car. And the dog has no idea what it'll do when it finally catches a car.

Like an old science fiction movie, we are messing with forces we don't understand. Disturbing the very fabric of the space-time continuum. When you wake Cthuhlu from his slumber you must face the consequences. We get a dopamine addiction.

This is the Player Curse. In the beginning we aren't getting laid much. Our minds are consumed with thoughts and plans to get more. There's sex out there and we want ours. Every new lay is a big deal, a strong dopamine hit and a nice reference experience to store away. The engine driving us is a forebrain goal of getting good with women and fucking more of them.

Things completely change once you start knocking over hot new women regularly. Your body starts to crave the next dopamine hit. Experiments in operant conditioning show that when you put rats in front of a food dispenser, the most addictive behavioural conditioner is when a certain average amount of work (in this case, tapping a lever) leads to a predictable amount of reward (food being dispensed) if — crucially — there is never a directly predictable payoff. There must always be an element of uncertainty with any given tap of the lever, but a general confidence that over time workrate X leads to payoff Y. This is why slot machines and other gambling are addictive.

The payoff cycle of daygame is the same. Once you reach an intermediate level you know approximately how many approaches will lead to how many dates and how many lays. Not only that, but you have the prospect that your suc cess rates improve over time. **This is intensely addictive**.

Like all addictions, your physiology changes to require more stimulus for each successive reward. For daygamers this means you trend towards:

- Faster grottier lays, for the excitement

- Hotter or less attainable women, for the challenge

- Silly targets, such as a one-hour same day lay

Normal patient daygame is no longer satisfying. It's become humdrum and routine. You can understand why the Rolling Stones became so listless and abused drugs — several years of unlimited easy access to groupie pussy left their dopamine receptors fried and stripped all the meaning out of life. Banging so many girls so often drains you of testosterone. Without that you have no spark to achieve. There are few men alive who wouldn't look at the Rolling Stones after-parties and think "I want *that*!" but it carries a deep cost.

I call this addiction Relentless Notch Count Hyena. Everywhere you go, lurking behind you just out of sight is the hyena. Skulking around, whispering to you. You're sitting at home playing a video game and it's outside the window whispering "Find a new girl." You're in a café trying to read a book and again you hear it whispering "Find a new girl." It gives you no rest.

I reiterate — **Game will not make you happy**. It will remove one of the major sources of anxiety in your life and it will give you adventures you never dreamed possible, but it creates its own set of problems. **Only self-acceptance will give you happiness** and that is not achieved by tearing through 100 fresh vaginas.

# There's Always A King of Kong

A popular documentary concerns the quest to clock the highest score on the video game Donkey Kong. There are two top players who devote their lives to mastering the ancient arcade game, and the documentary tracks their obsession and various nefarious attempts to undercut their rival. You see both men devote an incredible investment of time and emotional energy into something completely pointless. To become the King of Kong requires a lifetime of obsession to the exclusion of all else in your life. You could ruin your life chasing the top score and still not unseat the King of Kong. This is because he ruined his own life just as badly, but he had that extra sliver of talent or good luck that put him over the edge.

So if men do this for Donkey Kong, imagine how many men chase mastery with women. This leads to one certainty in life.

*There is always someone out there who is fucking more women than you, hotter women than you, and having more exciting adventures than you.*

To the typical chode this doesn't matter. It's another world. It wouldn't even occur to him to judge himself against these guys. He can just rationalise it away. They are lucky, rich, rock stars, whatever. But once you reach an intermediate level of Game you now realise your sexual success is largely a result of your own actions. You are responsible for it.

And now your whole identity is wrapped up in fucking more women.

If you're at this level, you've likely become friends with some of the best local players and you swap war stories. You can't wait to send the +1 text to your buddies. This will lead to some healthy competition as your friends egg you on. You'll refine your game by discussing theories and watching each other work. That's the upside. The downside is that crushing envy when you're the **recipient** of the +1 text. Don't deny it. Your first thought is "bastard!"

Don't beat yourself up for it. Men are naturally competitive. By reaching the heady heights of intermediate playerdom we have already separated ourselves from the pack. We want to be the best and we strive to be better.

But there's always a King of Kong.

There's always another guy doing better than you. And of course there **should** be, because a crucial part of the Game is finding a more advanced guy and modelling his behaviour, receiving his mentoring. You will be hanging around peers who jostle with you for position in a good-natured battle. The problem is that psychologically you aren't getting richer, you're just experiencing a higher level of relative poverty.

Game will <u>not</u> make you happy. It's one long struggle from beginning to end.

There is a significantly difference in mental state when you go out solo compared to with a wing. Generally, the latter is easier because you have someone else to talk to (keeping you in a social mood), to hold you accountable (if you are weaseling too many sets), to provide feedback on your set and to pick up your spirits when they flag. Daygame is best when it's fun, and usually that's with a friend. In contrast, solo daygame is more zen-like. You'll find yourself wandering the streets with a peculiar low-energy calm. You'll let your mind disappear into the energy of the streets as you watch the multitudes of people flow past while you discern patterns and get lost in thought. This state can't be reached when you have a wing chuntering on in your ear.

I'd recommend you try both. Winged game is more fun, but solo game gives you a greater sense of self-reliance. You'll learn the hard way to master your emotions and hammer down self-doubt (or to let it surface so you can address it).

## Solo Daygame

It helps to give yourself a rough target for the day. Normally I'll have process-oriented targets such as "Open any girl that makes my head turn," or "Be in the moment". Your goal will emerge organically from whatever you feel your sticking points are in your current motivation. I've had days of high confidence where I want to really slap a man-vibe onto the hottest scariest girls, and others when I'm so horny I just want to eye fuck every hot girl and escalate fast. Just as you choose your music playlist according to your mood, let your mood determine the type of daygame you'll do.

Sometimes you feel chill and lethargic, so that's a good time to focus on laconic slow gestures and outcome independency. Even when you feel shitty you can say "Forget the vibe, just get the sets mechanically correct." Daygaming solo frees you to work on whatever you damn well please without anyone rubber-necking you. Sometimes you'll just enjoy the walk and not push yourself hard to open.

You'll be in your head alot more, so learn to deal with it. There are two distinct and opposite methods for handling the self-doubt and chattering self-talk:

- Suppress it

- Address it.

Both work and it's good for your development to learn both ways.

**Suppress:** When you're in high spirits things flow easily and you'll be attuned to the vibe of the street. But this doesn't happen often. More likely you'll be shuffling along the streets trying to force yourself into opening, getting deeper and deeper into your own head. Even experienced daygamers sometimes have a run of bad sets where those amazing moments of other girls / lays seem like a distant Golden Era, a legendary state that you begin to think is just a myth. Was I really so good?

## Concealed scarcity

Once it's firmly in your reality that you are a guy who approaches hot women, you'll stumble into a very cunning ego trap. It'll creep up on you duringthose days of bad state, when suddenly the streets seem full of hot approachable girls but you just can't rouse yourself to open them. You'll start to punish yourself and turn it into a full "I suck" moment. You'll be telling yourself "How can I let hot girls like that go by without opening? I'm the guy who opens!" but still your feet are rooted to the spot. Then you'll go home and have an inner game meltdown because of your ego-investment in this identity.

Step one is to stop being so hard on yourself. Daygame is extremely difficult and at least 90% of guys who try it will never figure it out. Even the top guys find it an emotional drain at times. Ignore those internet alphas who are fronting like they love it all and never feel down. It's bullshit. Even the very best guys have periods of daygame revulsion. Accept it. It doesn't mean you suck.

Step two is to understand why you feel bad at letting these girls go past. It's because your identity has changed. In your early daygame career your identity was still Guy Who Doesn't Open, who thus considers not opening a default and anything above that as a minor victory. Sneakily you became Guy Who Does Open, which is a big improvement. But now opening is the default and anything less than that is a minor failure. See the corner you painted yourself into? You need to be comfortable with the idea that you are not obligated to open every hot girl you see. You are not obligated to open every day you leave the house.

You are suffering from incongruence. In the beginning your identity as the Guy Who Doesn't Approach was congruent with your lack of approaching. It was an unsatisfying life strategy, but at least it was congruent so you felt no cognitive dissonance. By setting up a new target identity (Guy Who Does Approach) you created a gap between who you are and who you want to be. This is where incongruence slips in. It's a necessarily destabilising force to motivate action, but it comes at a cost — the emotional pain of cognitive dissonance. As time progresses and you bank more sets, the gap reduces and you feel better but you become hyper-sensitive to any level of backslide into the old identity that you went through so much pain to escape... hence punishing yourself for not opening everything.

Don't worry, you're not going to turn back into a chode overnight.

Step three is you need to understand that every year nature spits out a new crop of 18 year old girls. There's the old saying that a million new coffee drinkers are born every day. The world is overflowing with hot women, and nature has a conveyor built that keeps pushing more into the world. Just because you stood doing nothing as ten hot girls walked past you today does not mean that the pool of hot girls you'll ever see became ten smaller (orwill eventually whittle away to zero and you'll be stuck fucking fatties). The streets replenish every hour, every day. There will always be hot women. So if you don't feel like opening this crop, don't worry. Everyone has a bad vibe day from time to time. There'll be more girls just like those ones next time you hit the streets.

Did I really have those times when daygame was fun? How come I suck so bad now? Was I always racked with such self-doubt?

Daygame makes your moods volatile. When you're up, it's awesome. When you're down, it sucks. Walking around solo sets off an amplification spiral to exacerbate whichever direction your mood is headed. This is unsettling when it happens, but a good thing for self-development because you must learn to deal with it, thus giving you greater amounts of emotional control.

Get in the hang of "walking off" bad state. Give yourself permission to go temporarily off the clock and keep walking around so your mind can wander. Eventually your bad mood will dissipate and you'll see a girl you feel like approaching.

**Address:** This is the long-term route to success. You'll address your problems during your anabolic periods, which helps to get your life in order in general. It's about getting healthy, dressing well, securing your income, sleeping soundly, and straightening out your inner game. While you can suppress self-doubt on any given daygame session, it's little different to holding your breath underwater — training and mental fortitude will extend the period you can spend down there, but you must always surface for air eventually. Suppressing your self-doubt over the long term will make you weird.

# Winged Daygame

I rarely bother with two-sets. The overwhelming conclusion from my own and my fellow daygamers' experience is two-sets are a waste of time. Very, very occasionally you'll get a double bounce-back but the odds are stacked against you. Don't bother unless you're doing gutter game in a foreign country with a competent friend and you have fantastic logistics.

A competent wing is a must for two-sets. For all other cases, his competence simply isn't relevant. This is what you need from your wing:

- You like each other. You are friends in the normal sense of the word.

- He supports your goals to get better with women. You both consider it your duty to encourage each other.

- He's good to his word, meaning when you agree to do a session he turns up on time. Most wings cannot meet this simple requirement because they allow avoidance weasel to overrule them. No matter what the excuse, they somehow find a way to avoid a time and place conducive to approaching.

- He doesn't state-leech from you. If you find your state drops in his company take a closer look at why.

- He doesn't bitch, moan and verbalise reasons to stop approaching.

- He doesn't fuck up your sets.

That's basically it. You'll quickly agree the ground rules for your daygame sessions together. It's hardly rocket science. Some of the basic rules I have with wings are:

1. Don't interrupt my sets. Keep well away and that also means don't hang around in her RAS queering the vibe.

2. Respect the turn-taking if you like similar girls. Some men do a "first dibs" method of whoever calls out a code word first had the right to approach. I don't allow this system. I believe in approximate turn-taking for such girls. Choose which you prefer.

3. Hang around fairly near until I've finished the approach or started an i-date. It's ok to do your own sets, but don't wander off far away in a weird frame-control attempt to leave me wondering where the hell you went (this is surprisingly common).

4. If it's going to be an idate, text me as soon as you can so I can plan my solo time accordingly.

5. Don't piss about wasting time on idates. Make a decision in the first half hour if you're going to pursue it or wrap it up with a phone number. Text me to tell me which.

Solo daygame is a much different vibe from winged. It's far more zen (or more animalistic, depending on your mood) and far less social, so it's distracting to settle into the winged vibe and then suddenly be left hanging by a wing who is dicking around / abandoning you. Agree between yourselves what the appropriate balance and notification rules are. Obviously you must stick to the same rules he does and not fuck with his game.

I'd avoid wings found on pick-up forums. They are 90% weirdos and will break all the above rules. If you must use a "community" wing, then slowly cultivate them based on the people you keep seeing around or get introduced to as friend-of-friend (or wing-of-wing). If you're lucky enough to attach yourself to a highly competent guy just remember you need him more than he needs you. If you start showing up late and acting weird he'll drop you fast.

# BANTER CLINIC
## section ten

Sometimes you are in a great mood and your text game comes naturally. Teases, challenges and gambits spring fully-formed into your mind and you can engage in quality banter with your leads. Many times, however, your brain just won't get into gear and you can't think of anything interesting to say.

With that in mind, I've collected together a library of fun go-to gambits you can drop into your text chats to add some zest and spark things up. These are all real chats with real girls. I provide a number of examples and then a discussion of what the gambit is trying to achieve, so you can create your own in a similar vein.

# BANTER CLINIC

There is a certain logic to the pursuit and conquest of a girl that will reflect itself in the text messages you send. You are moving in a specific direction (towards sex) while also filtering girls, demonstrating value, and all the other tactics of seduction. However, you aren't *always* advancing full steam ahead. Sometimes you need to release the tension a little and not harry the girl too hard. Additionally, what happens after you 'win'? With the need for forward momentum gone, how do you switch up your texting from pursuit to maintenance?

It's relatively easy when you're living in the same city as a girl because the messages are just the threads keeping the connection alive in between your regular face-to-face meetings. When you're travelling around, those meetings are few and far between. The messages must carry a greater weight of keeping things alive. Some girls enjoy video chat so you can go that direction. Others don't, so then everything must be contained in your messages.

From the beginning of the seduction you are offering a girl **attraction**, **comfort**, and **seduction**. This doesn't change just because you've slept with her nor because her difficult logistics force you to postpone the next date invitation. She still has the same needs from a man in her life. Be careful you don't unbalance your interactions such that a key ingredient is missing, and thus she ceases to have her needs met by you. If you don't meet them, she'll find somebody else who will.

**Attraction:** Teasing, flirting, challenging, demonstrating value, building mythologies

**Comfort:** Building rapport, hopes 'n' dreams, listening, everyday chit-chat, compliments

**Seduction:** Sex talk, dirty selfies, future projections

This section walks through examples of banter during both the chase and the maintenance with a selection of girls. The focus here is on the day-to-day communication rather than the **forward push** in the earlier messaging section. You'll note these messages mostly have a 'treading water' feel where my interest is in thickening, deepening or shaping the connection between us. I'll tend to build some forward momentum before I visit a girl's town, but aside from that these have a relaxed day-to-day feel.

*My intention is to normalise our relationship*
*and hold her in the position I want her to occupy in my life.*

To accomplish this she has to *enjoy being in that position*, so the deal must be sweetened by adding value and meeting her needs.

If I were to fail to periodically spike our chats with attraction material, she'd grow bored and I'll drift towards the friend zone. If I withdrew comfort, she'd drift from 'regular girl' to 'fuck buddy' and that's a fragile connection which can easily see me usurped by a local man she could meet more often. If I failed to seduce her over messages, her sexual satisfaction would dim. So, balance your interactions and stay alive to what the subtext of her messaging tells you about what she needs.

A word on presentation. My texting has considerably more **comfort** than I show here. I've overweighted my texting fragments towards **attraction** and **seduction** simply because (i) comfort is really boring to read (ii) most men already default to comfort and don't need to be advised on it. Nonetheless you'll see that my attraction/seduction material is peppered with comfort as part of push-pull.

## The Banter Themes

- How I Think Of You
- Parody Narcissist
- Tragedy And Victory
- Forgetful Player
- I'm A Force Of Nature
- Is This A Barrier To Our Marriage?
- Costume Pings
- Blurred Reality
- Picking A Fight
- Irreverence Photo Pings
- Recovery Pings
- Replying To Her Photo Pings
- Patient Set-Ups
- Discard Failed Gambits

I've grouped these exchanges thematically, so you can refer to it as a technique library. If you'd like to see beginning-to-end (meet-to-sex) transcripts of message exchanges laid out in chronological order, check out *Daygame Infinite* where I include several. So, let's meet the girls....

# Ivanna

She is a young Serb student living in Prague who I'd see on my visits for over two years, until she finally found a local boyfriend. She is quiet and unassuming but with sardonic humour. She liked to say (playfully) I was "evil", "crazy" and a player, as she was well aware I travelled around chasing skirt.

# Alisa

She is a mid-twenties Ukrainian office girl working in Poland who I've been seeing for the past three years whenever I visit her city. She likes dominance and is willingly led. Rather than engage in feisty banter, she prefers to cheer-lead whatever gambits I give her. Thus she's highly agreeable.

# Petra

She is a quietly introverted and chaste university student from Serbia. I was only the second man to have sex with her and we were dating on-off for two years. Though she looks like a confident and leggy hot girl, she's actually dorky and lacking social confidence.

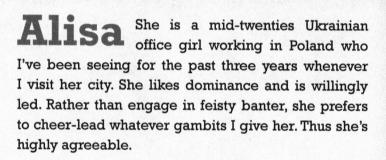

# Tamara

She is a busy freelance writer of Persian extraction working in Moscow. Though highly giggly and agreeable in person, she was taciturn and avoidant in messaging. This suggests another man in the picture, or a reluctance to follow her impulses towards casual sex.

# Ana

She is a Polish university student who is sexually chaste but deeply sexual within monogamous confines. She had a relaxed attitude towards my philandering and was happy to hold position as a girl I sleep with when I'm in town. She never gave any trouble but occasionally raised a figurative eyebrow at my banter.

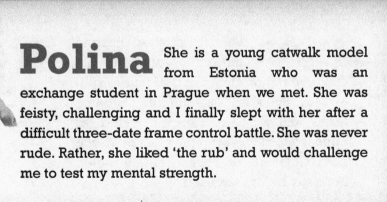

# Polina

She is a young catwalk model from Estonia who was an exchange student in Prague when we met. She was feisty, challenging and I finally slept with her after a difficult three-date frame control battle. She was never rude. Rather, she liked 'the rub' and would challenge me to test my mental strength.

## Sasha

She is a beautiful young Kazakh living in Moscow. Although the street stop was fizzy and sexual, nothing ever came of it. She withdrew from texting after a week and finally told me she has a boyfriend.

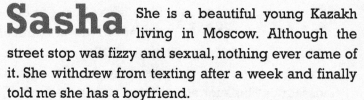

## Zoya

She is a leggy university student from Moscow who looks like she belongs on a perfume advertisement. She was a Yes Girl from the beginning and extremely agreeable to me in text and in person. Like Alisa, she just soaks up what I give her and cheers me onwards.

## Inna

She is another Russian university student but this time rather quirky and of fragile self-esteem. She's an 'outsider' in daygame terms, and very experience-oriented (as opposed to status-oriented). Although she got sexual with me, her forebrain pulled her away before sex itself.

# HOW I THINK OF YOU

The simplest way to begin a day's texting is to send a photo ping. You'll recall during the Street section I suggested teasing girls by putting them in a box and letting them climb out of it. Characterise them in a way which is playfully unflattering or which forces them into an agreement they don't really want to give. They'll expend energy resisting you, which is the playful fight that they enjoy. It's the locking of horns with you that rouses them out of the tedium of daily routine and conditions them to look forward to your messaging.

## 1. Hills Are Alive  (Ivanna)

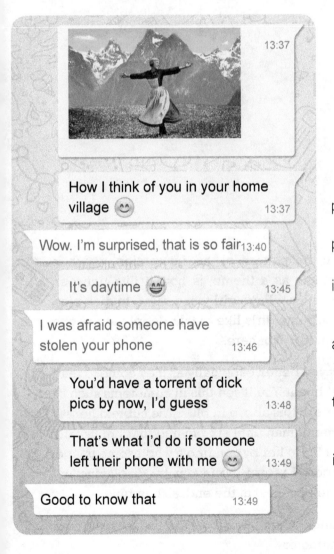

13:37

How I think of you in your home village 😊    13:37

putting her in a box as 'village girl'

Wow. I'm surprised, that is so fair 13:40

playing along, pretending offence

It's daytime 😄    13:45

implying I'm only sweet when sun is up

I was afraid someone have stolen your phone    13:46

agreeing with my pose

You'd have a torrent of dick pics by now, I'd guess    13:48

taking her statement as a launch pad

That's what I'd do if someone left their phone with me 😊    13:49

indirect sexualization, because hypothetical

Good to know that    13:49

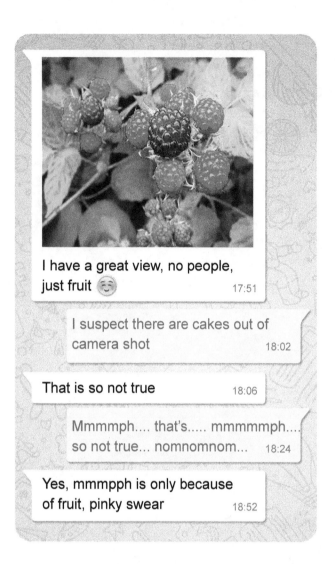

I have a great view, no people, just fruit 😊     17:51

I suspect there are cakes out of camera shot     18:02

That is so not true     18:06

Mmmmph.... that's..... mmmmmph.... so not true... nomnomnom...     18:24

Yes, mmmpph is only because of fruit, pinky swear     18:52

Probably the first thing to notice about the pattern of this interaction, which is constantly repeated throughout our contact as a theme, is how it flits between different energies and topics. We begin with a village girl tease, move to dick pics, then cakes: three topics in fourteen lines. Some girls like to talk deeply about one thing at a time, especially if they seek comfort. Not here.

Girls feel comfort when they get to know you better, especially as they come to read your character and feel a special insight into it. You'll see this in comments such as "that is so *you*". I've highlighted examples of this above in blue. The subtext here is a running joke about me only being a gentleman until six pm and that I'm usually 'evil'. Thus she feigns surprise when I'm nice to her by sending a wholesome image. This type of exchange strengthens rapport. I return the favour by displaying my insight into her character and habits (love of cakes) at the end, also in blue.

Teasing builds rapport *as well as* attraction when the subtext to the tease is your established insights into each other's character.

## 2. Troll Joke  (Ivanna)

This is amongst the easiest of photo pings that mix both attraction (the push) and comfort (the pull). Any time you're shopping you'll come across teddy bears, cartoon monsters, fluffy animals and others that are right in the sweet spot of being sufficiently dorky to "put her in a box" but also sufficiently cute that it's playful. Snap the photo and send the ping.

Your positioning of her doesn't always need to be a strong push. If you choose a box that is cute, it will load your message more towards comfort. This is useful if a girl is experiencing some kind of negative emotion, such as exam stress or illness. By reframing her as a cute animal under sunny skies you reframe things positively and lift her mood. Alternatively, a sympathetic reframe will share her burden. Mixing the emotions behind your teases over time plays a contrast game.

# 3. Accident (Inna)

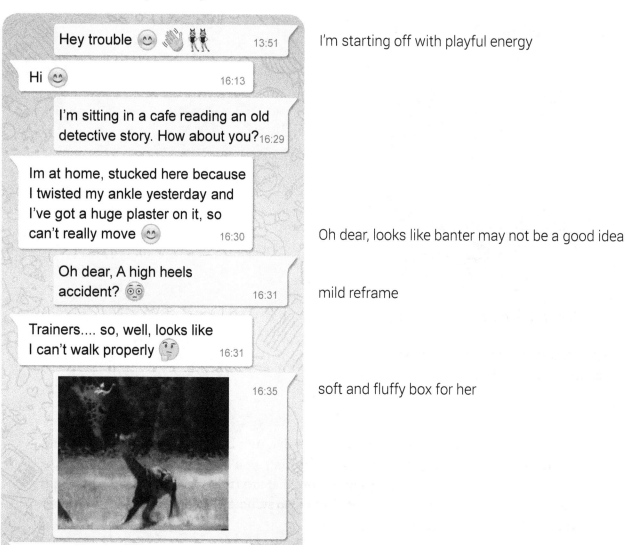

Hey trouble 😊 👋 🐈🐈    13:51    | I'm starting off with playful energy

Hi 😊    16:13

I'm sitting in a cafe reading an old detective story. How about you? 16:29

Im at home, stucked here because I twisted my ankle yesterday and I've got a huge plaster on it, so can't really move 😊    16:30    | Oh dear, looks like banter may not be a good idea

Oh dear, A high heels accident? 😳    16:31    | mild reframe

Trainers.... so, well, looks like I can't walk properly 🤔    16:31

16:35    | soft and fluffy box for her

Haha, exactly 😄    16:36    | comfort is increased

Attraction material is the most fun to do and also looks best in the highlight reels. Doubly so when doing 'douche-bag game'. Therefore public-facing PUA coaches (and internet loud-mouths) will usually provide those types of examples. It pleases the crowd and puffs out their own chests. Douche-bag game played straight is extremely tiring for women and starves them of comfort. In limited cases, that's effective but usually only when doing the **dance of the broken souls**, that is, when a messed-up PUA is trying to bang a messed-up woman.

For the most part, you should use douche-bag game sparingly as a spice rather than the main course. Good message game is infused with heart and empathy. Sometimes a girl wants to be prodded in the belly and called a dumb-ass. Other times she wants a gentle arm around her shoulders. You can do both in a single exchange, or even in a single ping.

## 4. Conan Joke (Ivanna)

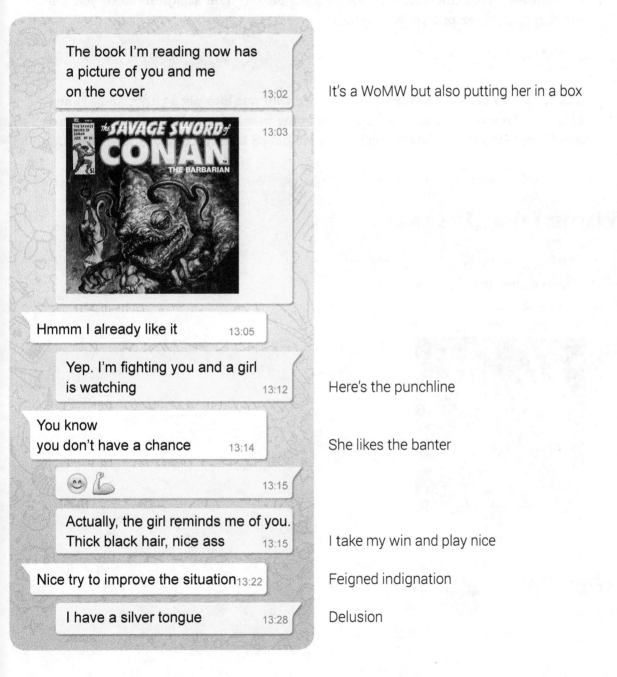

The book I'm reading now has a picture of you and me on the cover    13:02

It's a WoMW but also putting her in a box

13:03

Hmmm I already like it    13:05

Yep. I'm fighting you and a girl is watching    13:12

Here's the punchline

You know you don't have a chance    13:14

She likes the banter

😊💪    13:15

Actually, the girl reminds me of you. Thick black hair, nice ass    13:15

I take my win and play nice

Nice try to improve the situation 13:22

Feigned indignation

I have a silver tongue    13:28

Delusion

This is an easy gambit for any time you see an image that has a cool man, a pretty girl, and some kind of monster / old crone / ugly girl. Set up the joke like she's the pretty girl then deliver the punchline that she's the other one. Lastly, end on a compliment that she's the pretty girl. This has a pull-push-pull structure so it is more comfort-heavy than a push-pull-push structure. Book covers or movie stills are an endless source of pings like this.

> **Gambit #4** – Find dramatic images from fiction and then assign roles so you are fighting each other, or fighting together.

Lastly, here's a self-explanatory ping to a girl who was literally a virgin at the time I sent it. It was a running joke because, sadly, the previous two times we'd met she'd overtly decided to lose her virginity with me but I'd been unable to squeeze it in.

## 5. Virgin Joke (Ivanna)

# PARODY NARCISSIST

Girls are attracted to a man with a high opinion of himself. Your inner game and SMV-building work are the primary pillars of your self-confidence, but you can have lots of fun by *pretending* to have an even more wildly inflated opinion of your awesomeness.

## 6. That Means You Love Me (Ivanna)

**Nikolasko dolazi za 10ak dana** 17:40

**I should be in Prague** 17:41

I'd told her the dates of my upcoming trip to her city

What? 17:57

**I'm sorry, first message wasn't for you** 😳 🙈 17:58

I translated it in Google: "Nick is a delicious perfect 10 man" 18:14

note I try to match my translation to the visual structure of her error message

**You can't be serious** 😂 18:15

It's a hit, so I keep on this thread

By "Google" I mean "in my head" 18:16

Here's the self-referential irony

By "translated" I mean "into the only language I ever hear" 18:17

In this example of Parody Narcissist you twist anything mundane a girl says into an example of how cool you are. It's done with self-referential irony so as to get all the benefit of appearing confident without the risk of appearing try-hard. People like a little escapism, to be lifted out of daily routine into something larger than life. Get used to taking something mundane (in this case, a message intended for her friend) and mythologising it into a mini-story. It's like spice sprinkled over bland food and lifts her mood.

Imagine how I could've reacted to her error message: "Oh, okay". And like that, the opportunity is gone and we are back into boring chit-chat. By spinning it into a silly Parody Narcissist exchange I've pro-actively found an excuse to demonstrate my humour and give her a smile.

The essence of Parody Narcissist game is to walk the line between sincere belief that you're awesome, and knowing irony that you're a little conceited. In it's strongest form, the girl will be open-mouthed in surprise and indignation that you can be so arrogant, while tickled pink that you have such high self-regard. It can be risky so I usually tone it down and make it more playful. It's like a prod in the ribs rather than a slap in the face.

There are two simple patterns you can use in almost any situation when that day's exchange first opens. Answer her question by complimenting yourself, or don't even wait for her to ask.

## 7. Handsome (Zoya)

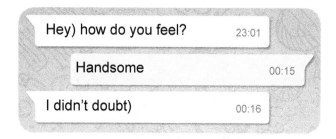

Hey) how do you feel?    23:01

Handsome    00:15

I didn't doubt)    00:16

Below is an example of stacking away from the gambit into a new one.

## 8. Free Hour Joke (Ivanna)

This weather is like me: insanely hot    11:28    Parody Narcissist

I like it    13:55

17:03

1 HOUR FREE

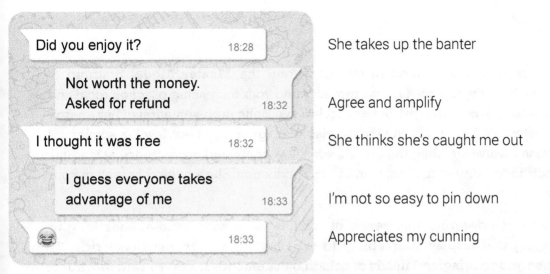

| | |
|---|---|
| Did you enjoy it? 18:28 | She takes up the banter |
| Not worth the money. Asked for refund 18:32 | Agree and amplify |
| I thought it was free 18:32 | She thinks she's caught me out |
| I guess everyone takes advantage of me 18:33 | I'm not so easy to pin down |
| 😂 18:33 | Appreciates my cunning |

This entire exchange is nonsensical, which is why it works. The first two laughs are generic pings that you can drop onto any girl at any time to open an exchange. Only the second half required me to actually engage my brain, because she fired the ball back into my court to draw some banter out of me. Women like difficult men. They like that you can't be easily cornered and right when it looks like you're pinned down, you find a way to escape.

The Parody Narcissist gambit doesn't need to be the first words out of your mouth, as you see below. I left in her later response just as a window into how something so short can stay in a girl's mind all day.

# 9. Lottery Joke  (Petra)

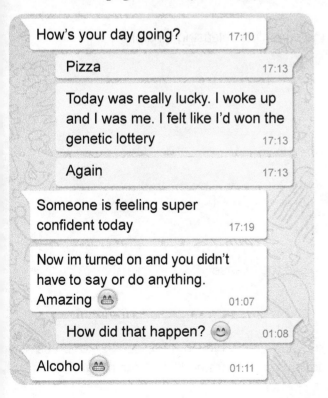

> How's your day going? 17:10
>> Pizza 17:13
>> Today was really lucky. I woke up and I was me. I felt like I'd won the genetic lottery 17:13
>> Again 17:13
> Someone is feeling super confident today 17:19
> Now im turned on and you didn't have to say or do anything. Amazing 😬 01:07
>> How did that happen? 😊 01:08
> Alcohol 😬 01:11

Flick back to the beginning of this book and the **Master Model** diagram of daygame. Note the top line is a bar representing your increasing psychological and physical control over the girl. Below that is a symbolic representation of her energy and excitement levels, which you are also managing. At every level, a successful seduction involves leading the girl. As you show continued competence at leading, she feels increasing attraction, comfort and seduction. She's putting herself in your hands.

One way of bolstering this sense of trust is to provide mini-dramas in your messaging that display your ability to take her on a short emotional ride. By initiating, progressing, and finally concluding the emotional ride you are providing, in microcosm, a display of your ability to provide for her needs at the macro level.

## 10. Dramatic Release (Ivanna)

Tragedy has just got me 😞   21:43    Starting emotional roller-coaster with drama

What tragedy?   21:49    She has to show concern, as she doesn't know context. That's precisely the response I wanted to draw

21:57    the punchline, releasing tension

You something....
You got scared me! 😑   21:59    enjoys the release

You don't know how traumatic my foot-through-slipper experience was   22:04    knowing she enjoyed it, I decide to press my advantage and pretend I did nothing wrong

| | |
|---|---|
| I so want to punch you 22:05 | = I'm turned on right now |
| Don't worry. I have recovered 22:10 | The subtext is my narcissism, that it's my tragic experience that really matters here |

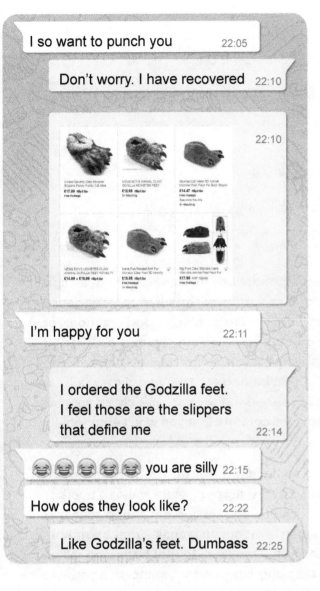

22:10

| | |
|---|---|
| I'm happy for you 22:11 | She doesn't really know what to do, so she waits for my lead |
| I ordered the Godzilla feet. I feel those are the slippers that define me 22:14 | Now I move into irreverence |
| 😂😂😂😂😂 you are silly 22:15 | She likes it |
| How does they look like? 22:22 | |
| Like Godzilla's feet. Dumbass 22:25 | A playful push |

**several days later**

10:42

this was several days later, a follow-up

This is what a happy ending looks like — 10:42 — bookending the 'drama'

Those are great — 11:41

😎 — 11:41

You became a real beast 🐭 — 11:50 — She likes it

Grrrrrrrrrrrrrrrrr — 11:51 — Reward her by playing along

This exchange was all about manipulating her emotions in order to act out a short scene of drama. I bait her into a trap and then spring it. Girls like to experience the full spectrum of emotions (unlike men, who tend to want just good emotions, or peace) so by pushing her down and then quickly lifting her up, she gets a satisfying ride. Be careful not to string out the negative phase too long: you are not trying to upset her. It's enough to get a quick 'hit'. Upon baiting the trap I tend to watch for her blue-ticking my message so that I can release the tension quickly as soon as she's read it. This careful management provides comfort, that you won't emotionally abuse her.

This entire exchange was completely manufactured by me from **nothing**. I'd happened to put my foot through the bottom of my slippers while walking upstairs and thought, *there's probably a little routine in this*. So I gamed out a little scenario, shaped it to bait specific emotions, and then tried it out on Ivanna. From beginning to end it was something out of nothing and yet if you were to plot her emotions on a graph it would be a roller-coaster. I'm teaching her that communication with me is never boring or predictable.

**Gambit #6** – Frame a mundane event as a tragedy and fashion a happy ending from it, pretending to be oblivious to its lack of real significance.

# FORGETFUL PLAYER

Pre-selection, meaning that other women have already chosen you, is an attraction trigger. Girls like men who other girls also like. Self-absorption is attractive, because girls like a man who is hearty in his appetites and loves his life. You can combine the two attraction triggers into gambits where you are so absorbed in your successful carousing of women that you can no longer keep all the details straight in your mind.

## 11. Which One Are You? (Ivanna)

Different girls will react in different ways to your player lifestyle so be sure to know her position on it. The majority position is she doesn't mind but doesn't want her nose rubbed in that fact you see other women. Some girls take greater pleasure in your preselection than they do pain of jealousy in not having you exclusively, but these girls are a minority. A different minority position – which Ivanna held – was that we each have separate lives and I'm just the man who waltzes into her life when I'm in town. She felt this way because she was inexperienced with men, hung out in a small social circle and rarely met new people, and thus I was giving her all the 'man' she wanted while her focus was on study, family, and socialising.

That said, this gambit is quite light-hearted so it's not a big risk. It's hardly likely you'd forget her name, especially as it's right there in your phone next to her photo. She can quite easily laugh it off as you being a Parody Player. As to the execution, note how I space out my pretended thought process.

Next we'll discuss an example of literally being a forgetful player *by accident*, and then extricating myself from a small faux pas.

## 12. Harem Plan Joke  (Ivanna)

| | |
|---|---|
| Oooooooooooo  16:46 | I'd just explained a business idea I'd had |
| Precisely  16:47 | |
| So you won't be just rock star, now you're gonna be rich too  16:52 | |
| That's the plan  16:57 | The normal discussion is over, time for some mythology |
| Once I'm rich I'll build a palace and establish a harem  17:23 | Grand dreams |
| I think I already knew that  17:34 | "that's so you" comfort |
| Don't worry, I'll have a job for you  17:38 | pull |
| In the laundry room  17:38 | push |
| I wasn't afraid. I understand I'm not the favourite one  17:40 | |
| You already told me your cooking is bad, so kitchen job is out  17:43 | |
| I never told that  17:45 | |
| You mixed me up with some other girl  17:47 | Oops. I think I did. Time to agree and amplify |

| | |
|---|---|
| Hang on..... 17:54 | |
| Which one are you? 17:54 | |
| Wait.... I'll remember.... Don't rush me.... 17:55 | |
| Waiting 17:55 | |
| Nope. Gone! 18:02 | |
| Which one are you? Send me a picture of your ass. I never forget an ass 18:03 | |
| I don't mind it, you are too old, it's not a shame to have sclerosis at your age 18:04 | She gets her 'win' |
| 😎 18:05 | I let her have it, as I walked into it |
| 😘 18:06 | Smoothed over |

When you take risks in texting, you'll make mistakes. Teasing, challenging, and mythologising all work best towards the upper limits of compliance and thus it's easy to go a step too far. This leaves a quandary. Should you apologise? Bluff it out? Escalate? Go silent? Distract? Each strategy has its merits and demerits, so you'll need to decide on the fly. I'd avoid apologies unless you have seriously mis-stepped and genuinely upset the girl. I'd also avoid going silent because it appears psychologically weak and shifty. My preferred way to repair breaches is this:

1. Agree and amplify playfully, and keep it short

2. Give her an opening to counter-attack, to score a pride-restoring 'win'

3. Let her have the victory by recognising her win

4. Smile and move forwards

Done this way you can avoid getting drawn into an argument which will make a big 'thing' out of the mistake and thus let it live longer in memory, souring the interaction. If you never let her win anything she may store up resentment and choose this hill to die on. By following the above plan you don't immediately capitulate (thus avoid weakness) but recognise your error and give her what she needs to move forwards. The mistake is lost to the mists of time.

Even something as simple as telling a girl your plans can be re-cast into a playful interaction. Girls generally like to hear a man state his intentions boldly, as it expresses positive masculine traits of pro-activity and living through your intentions. Women like men who strike out boldly into the world. You can add a parody element by imagining she (or others) are trying to stop you but you are so *determined* in your plans that you will crash through every barrier. This is humorous because at no point is anyone actually trying to stop you. You are chasing dragons.

## 13. Jelly Joke  (Ivanna)

I'm getting drunk tonight.
You can't stop me    14:34

As if she'd even tried to stop me

14:53

Her own WoMW ping.

Strange    16:23

mild challenge

What is strange?    16:24

Jelly underwear    16:24

There are even worse jellies    16:25

she folds

16:26

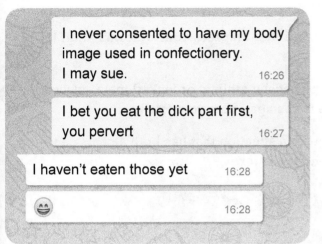

I never consented to have my body image used in confectionery.
I may sue.                                    16:26

I bet you eat the dick part first, you pervert                        16:27

I haven't eaten those yet        16:28

😁                               16:28

sexualising the conversation and teasing

allowing it

Of course this is all nudge-wink I-know-that-you-know-that-I-know. Some other hypothetical examples:

— I want a hot bath. The water is a bit cold but I shall not be thwarted in my designs!
— I was hungry. I wanted a sandwich, so I made a sandwich. That's me – I'm a man of action. Tuna sweetcorn with mayonnaise, if you're wondering.
— Listening to The Rolling Stones sing "you can't always get what you want". I beg to differ. I get what I want. I'm a winner.

Notice how her reply is to send me her own **Window On My World** ping. You'll find over time that girls adapt to your messaging style and begin to imitate your gambits. Girls often send me the thumbs up or photo pings when their initial messaging with me didn't use them. It's comfort building for her to shape herself to your outline. Girls consider themselves a mirror to their man.

There are a number of easy go-to phrases you can use when lacking inspiration which a girl will read into whatever she wants to talk about. When a girl is telling me, in positive terms, what she's doing I will often reply with:

• Living the dream

• Rock n roll

These are mostly rapport-building because they represent positive approval, yet they are not as gushing as "cool", "awesome" and so on. If I wish to throw in mild attraction, I may challenge her on her ping, such as here with "strange". It implies withheld approval, but not outright hostility.

## 14. Robbery Joke (Ivanna)

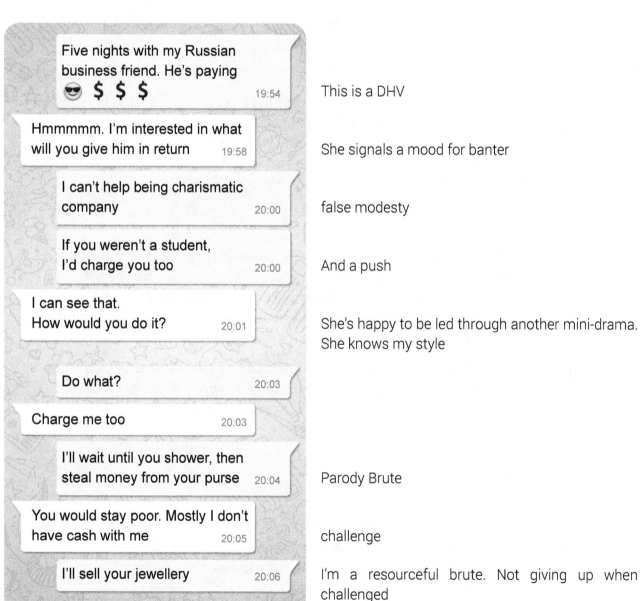

Five nights with my Russian business friend. He's paying 😎 $ $ $    19:54

This is a DHV

Hmmmmm. I'm interested in what will you give him in return    19:58

She signals a mood for banter

I can't help being charismatic company    20:00

false modesty

If you weren't a student, I'd charge you too    20:00

And a push

I can see that. How would you do it?    20:01

She's happy to be led through another mini-drama. She knows my style

Do what?    20:03

Charge me too    20:03

I'll wait until you shower, then steal money from your purse    20:04

Parody Brute

You would stay poor. Mostly I don't have cash with me    20:05

challenge

I'll sell your jewellery    20:06

I'm a resourceful brute. Not giving up when challenged

Those are in my gypsy base 20:07

Callback humour seeks rapport

I guess the clothes
is the most expensive          20:13

That could help you          20:13

She will often flip from challenge to co-operation mid-chat

Then you're walking home naked 20:13

aaaaaand it's sexualised again

Or not walking home at all     20:15

I'm not sure her nuance sexual or criminal?

That's possible          20:16

Now that I'm thinking
about you naked..... 😊     20:18

so I snip and stack towards sex

Am I look good?
Hope I'm dilapidated        20:20

challenge

You're still young. You have a few
more years before you look like
an old crone               20:21

faint praise is really a tease

😂                      20:22

I would like to know how you
imagine women few years
older than me...           20:26

20:39

double down with a funny push

You aged 25            20:39

😱                      20:39

You mad, bro?         20:58

closed loop, will go back to comfort

Note how playfully combative this exchange is. It is a hypothetical scenario in which she challenges me, I get the better of her, and we end up sexual. I lace my comments with my usual parody elements of narcissism, brutishness, avarice, and libido. She laces hers with her usual parody of challenge and looking like a gypsy. We are each trading on a shared understanding of the other and therefore this ostensibly combative exchange (attraction) is also warmly co-operation (comfort) in it's subtext. As with other fragments here, note how the whole exchange has a narrative arc and once closure is reached we move back to comfort (though I don't show them here).

**Gambit #11** – When a girl challenges you with obstacles to a stated plan, keep inventing ever more ludicrous solutions to indicate you won't be thwarted.

Generally speaking you need to accept 'no' when a girl gives it to you. However, there's no rule you need to accept the *first* 'no'. When you know a girl fancies you, let the power of your will drive you forwards. With Inga, we'd already been making out on the first two dates and this message was sent after she got home from the second. She'd almost walked back to my apartment with me. Now she was expressing reluctance because sex was becoming inevitable and she wasn't yet sure if she should take her final step off The Cliff. Having gotten her this far, it was worth nudging her further.

## 15. Refuse To Accept No (Inna)

| | |
|---|---|
| hey I've considered everything I still do think you are cool but you'd better waste no more time on me and search for smone else)22:42 | A reluctant 'no'. She's conflicted |
| hope you are okay with it    22:42 | She wants my approval. She feels accountable to me |
| Sure. We'll talk again tomorrow when you change your mind again 😊 22:43 | Brush it off as female whimsy |
| ahaha self confident as fuck but so am I    22:43 | Big hit |

| | |
|---|---|
| Sleep well 🌙    22:44 | comfort |
| you too    22:44 | she never argued the toss |

The actual gambit is simply an overt statement of what I know to be her internal forebrain-hindbrain conflict. That's why she responds so well to it: I'd demonstrated social acuity in understanding her. We'll finish with a less obvious expression of the irresistible force.

## 16. Gaming Obtuseness (Alisa)

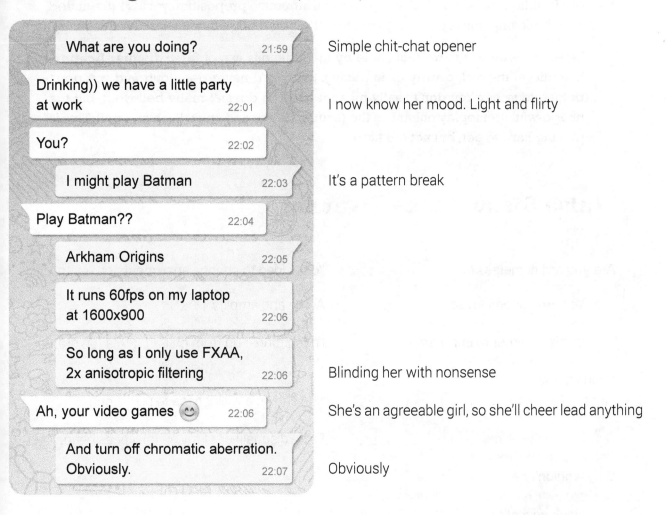

| | |
|---|---|
| What are you doing?    21:59 | Simple chit-chat opener |
| Drinking)) we have a little party at work    22:01 | I now know her mood. Light and flirty |
| You?    22:02 | |
| I might play Batman    22:03 | It's a pattern break |
| Play Batman??    22:04 | |
| Arkham Origins    22:05 | |
| It runs 60fps on my laptop at 1600x900    22:06 | |
| So long as I only use FXAA, 2x anisotropic filtering    22:06 | Blinding her with nonsense |
| Ah, your video games 😊    22:06 | She's an agreeable girl, so she'll cheer lead anything |
| And turn off chromatic aberration. Obviously.    22:07 | Obviously |

This is amusing mainly because of how it parodies a lack of social acuity. I'm sub-communicating that I'm hearty in my appetites and unyielding in my wish to follow my interests. I'm also (nudge-wink) expecting her to be as interested in my hobbies as I am, which is a solipsistic self-absorption. The phrasing, plus our shared history, means she knows not to take any of it at face value.

The usual frame between a hot girl and her admirers is that they are trying to demonstrate to her reasons why they are good enough to win her romantic interest. We call this **qualification**. Any time someone is providing reasons they are good enough, they are qualifying. It's kryptonite to seduction because it willingly places the girl above you, on a pedestal, and sub-communicates that she's better than you. Girls want to date up, not slum it.

The opposite of qualification is **disqualification**, meaning giving a girl reasons why she *shouldn't* date you. If a girl isn't at all interested in you, she'll take you at your word. However, if she *is* interested in you, she now feels challenged and her interest increases accordingly. Players must thus walk a narrow road wherein the girl is obliquely persuaded that you are an attractive proposition yet also dissuaded from believing you are trying to get her. It's the art of qualifying without qualifying.

Mystery Method squares this circle by the judicious use of **false disqualification**. You inform the girl, overtly or implicitly, that you'd never get along and you don't belong together. You don't really mean it and she doesn't really believe it, but the nudge-wink gameplay enhances the flirting. Carrot and stick. Push and pull. This is playing hard to get, but not *too* hard.

## 17. False Disqualifiers (Ivanna)

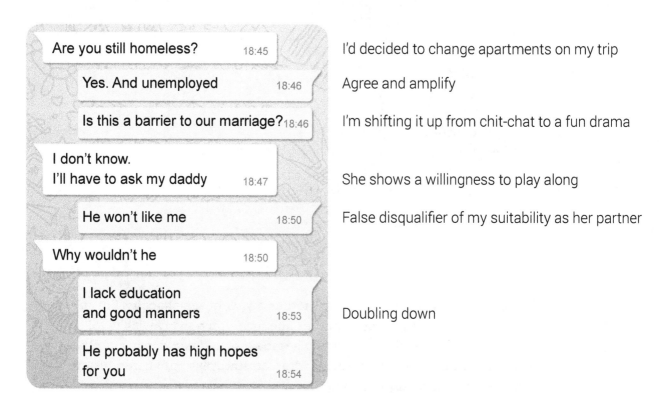

| | |
|---|---|
| Are you still homeless? 18:45 | I'd decided to change apartments on my trip |
| Yes. And unemployed 18:46 | Agree and amplify |
| Is this a barrier to our marriage? 18:46 | I'm shifting it up from chit-chat to a fun drama |
| I don't know. I'll have to ask my daddy 18:47 | She shows a willingness to play along |
| He won't like me 18:50 | False disqualifier of my suitability as her partner |
| Why wouldn't he 18:50 | |
| I lack education and good manners 18:53 | Doubling down |
| He probably has high hopes for you 18:54 | |

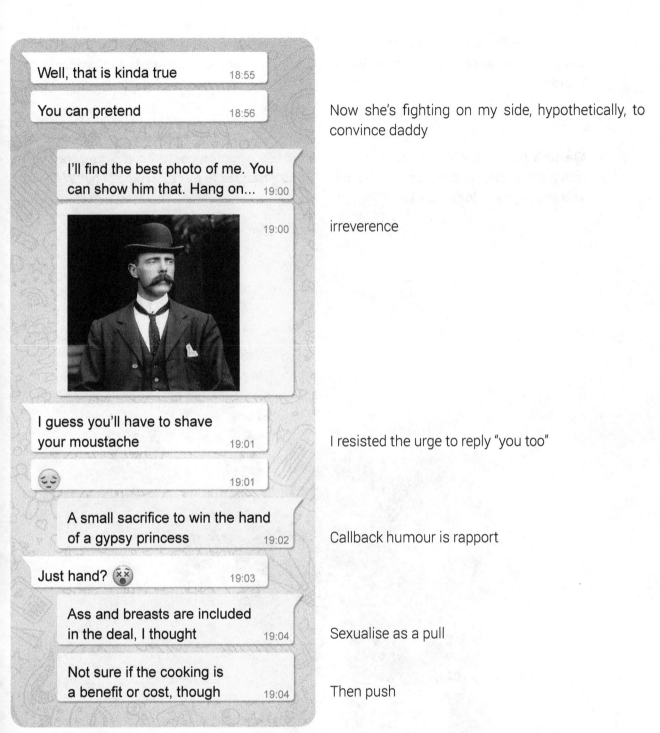

Well, that is kinda true  18:55

You can pretend  18:56

Now she's fighting on my side, hypothetically, to convince daddy

I'll find the best photo of me. You can show him that. Hang on...  19:00

19:00

irreverence

I guess you'll have to shave your moustache  19:01

I resisted the urge to reply "you too"

😔  19:01

A small sacrifice to win the hand of a gypsy princess  19:02

Callback humour is rapport

Just hand? 😵  19:03

Ass and breasts are included in the deal, I thought  19:04

Sexualise as a pull

Not sure if the cooking is a benefit or cost, though  19:04

Then push

By now you'll be familiar with a pattern to banter. It involves the creation and resolution of mini-dramas that are plucked from thin air. Think how her first question could've been answered, had I taken it at face value (as it was no doubt intended). I'd have said something like, "No, it's okay. I called a landlady today and agreed a new apartment. Phew!" and that would've been the end of it. Instead of answering her question I took it as a segue into a mini-drama to falsely disqualify and get her to fight in my corner to prove my worth to her father.

Once the little drama had played out and closed its own loop, I got real and gave her a genuine answer to her question. We were then back into chit-chat and rapport building.

**Gambit #12** – When a minor reversal in your life situation could be exaggerated into a disqualifying catastrophe, ask her "Is this a barrier to our marriage?" or "Will you still love me for who I am?"

*Daygame Mastery*

# COSTUME PINGS

Much of your attraction material is intended to build you up into a larger-than-life character, a process I call mythologising. By investing yourself with pomp and ceremony you lift yourself out of the grey faceless mass of normal men. You proffer positive labels she can hang onto you because, deep down, she wants to buy into your mythology. A fast way to support such mythologies is to photo ping her a character and link yourself to it.

It really is as simple as, "look! This is me!" Here are a few examples.

## 18. Tanning Joke  (Ivanna)

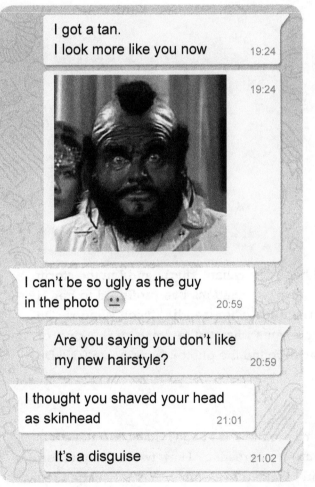

I got a tan.
I look more like you now          19:24

                                  19:24

reference to her Balkan colouring and gypsy style

I can't be so ugly as the guy
in the photo 😐          20:59

Are you saying you don't like
my new hairstyle?          20:59

deliberately misconstrue her

I thought you shaved your head
as skinhead          21:01

It's a disguise          21:02

more nonsense

At its heart this is just a dressed-up ping photo. I could've simply sent the photo without comment, just for fun. Instead I manufacture an "argument" out of nothing so that I can push-pull her. It's a very short mini-drama built upon a silly mythology ping. The next example is less irreverent.

# 19. Crusader Ping (Tamara)

| | |
|---|---|
| I am wake up! | 07:59 |
| Me too, just now | 12:28 |
| I'm wearing special protection from the storm | 18:01 |
| Wait..... let me take a selfie.... | 18:01 |
| | 18:01 |
| 😂 😂 😂 😂 😂 😂 | 22:48 |
| Where is storm?? | 22:48 |
| I am the storm | 15:16 |

Again it's all nonsense but I've now told her I'm a valiant knight and I'm the storm that smites my opponents. These are positive associations I've proffered to her at no cost. Let's consider some general principles when sending such Window On My World pings. At it's most simple, it represents what you're doing, or thinking, or something you saw that caught your interest. Found the photo? Okay, now STOP! Do not immediately send it.

Think.

How can I build a mini-mythology or drama around this image? How can I make this photo of a teddy bear next to a cheeseburger interesting? I saw two dogs get their leashes tangled up and fall over, how can I make that a funnier mental image? You never simply take a picture of your coffee or steak and say "I'm eating steak and drinking coffee". That's just step one. Step two is to dress it up and make it larger than life. Make the photo composition interesting and add something: "I'm eating the world's juiciest steak. I might sell my house and buy a ranch in Argentina. I'll make a great cowboy"

# BLURRED REALITY

I commonly make ironic use of the *blurred reality* technique by which I pretend an inability to separate fantasy from reality and thus believe myself to be the hero in my own dramas. This gives carte blanch to go off on flights of fancy, whipping up tales of vision and drama [I do this several times in later chats below] and to then introduce greater extremes of emotion than day-to-day life entails. In this case I'm so deeply immersed in my delusional fantasy world that I'm concerned about offering policy advice to the Mayor of Gotham City: as opposed to simply enjoying the game.

## 20. Batman Joke  (Ivanna)

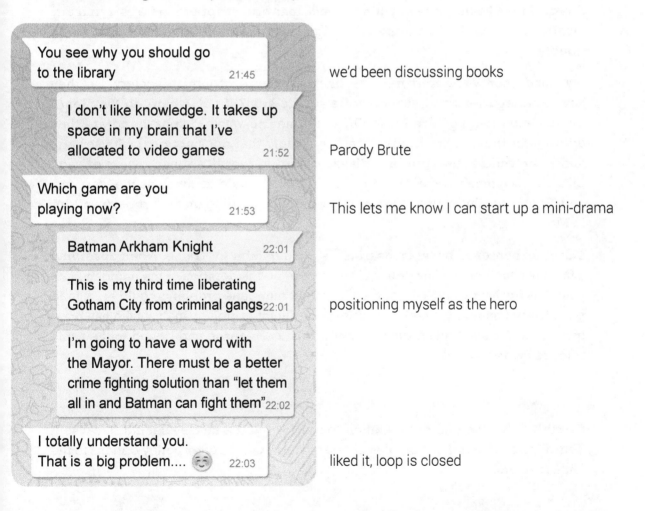

You see why you should go to the library  21:45

we'd been discussing books

I don't like knowledge. It takes up space in my brain that I've allocated to video games  21:52

Parody Brute

Which game are you playing now?  21:53

This lets me know I can start up a mini-drama

Batman Arkham Knight  22:01

This is my third time liberating Gotham City from criminal gangs 22:01

positioning myself as the hero

I'm going to have a word with the Mayor. There must be a better crime fighting solution than "let them all in and Batman can fight them" 22:02

I totally understand you. That is a big problem.... 😌  22:03

liked it, loop is closed

During the seduction of a girl you need to be careful about Parody Brute gambits because the girl may not know enough about you and your communication style to understand the parody element. As you get to know each other better and can demonstrate your intelligence, she'll know it's parody.

A second, distinct, gambit I weave into the same tale is what I call the *policy wonk* technique. It's slightly esoteric to explain but once you 'get it', you'll see comedians do it all the time and it's very easy to implement. Let me explain.

Did you ever watch Lord Of The Rings and, as the orc army stormed out of Mordor to attack the land of men, you wondered "do they have any infrastructure to support this war effort?"

I did.

"When Napoleon invaded Russia he prioritised his supply train to replenish his artillery" I thought. "His army were paid and instructed to eat from the land, such as buying from peasants in the villages they passed. This is why Russia's scorched earth policy was so effective. The French were not bringing their own food through supply lines and Russia had destroyed the ability of soldiers to procure food locally. Hmmmmm. I'm guessing the Orcs also procure locally but it certainly doesn't look like they buy anything. In fact, many don't appear to be carrying any money at all. Surely if Sauron's campaign bogs down in Winter, the orcs are in trouble."

My mind soon wandered into the likely structure of Orcish society. Do they have kindergartens and schools to raise Orc kids? If not, where do they learn the common tongue? Are some Orcs assigned to waste disposal and are they eligible for the military draft? Clearly a society that does not deal with sewage and waste will be susceptible to disease. Mordor doesn't appear to have sewage piling up so *somebody* is dealing with it. Are they paid as much as the warriors, and if not, does this cause resentment or difficulty getting on the property ladder in Mordor?

This is all nonsense but at its heart is a simple gambit for Game. When observing a fantasy situation that has deliberately avoided consideration of the mundane, put your SimCity hat on and ask yourself how their mundane problems could arise (and be solved). Imagine yourself a business consultant or policy analyst who has been hired to find a solution and that solution must be realistic and bound to the same rules as the real world.

**Gambit #13** – Pretend exasperation (or curiosity) at a fantasy setting because it doesn't appear to follow the rules of real settings. Offer better policy options to the fantasy actors.

# 21. Hitman Joke  (Ivanna)

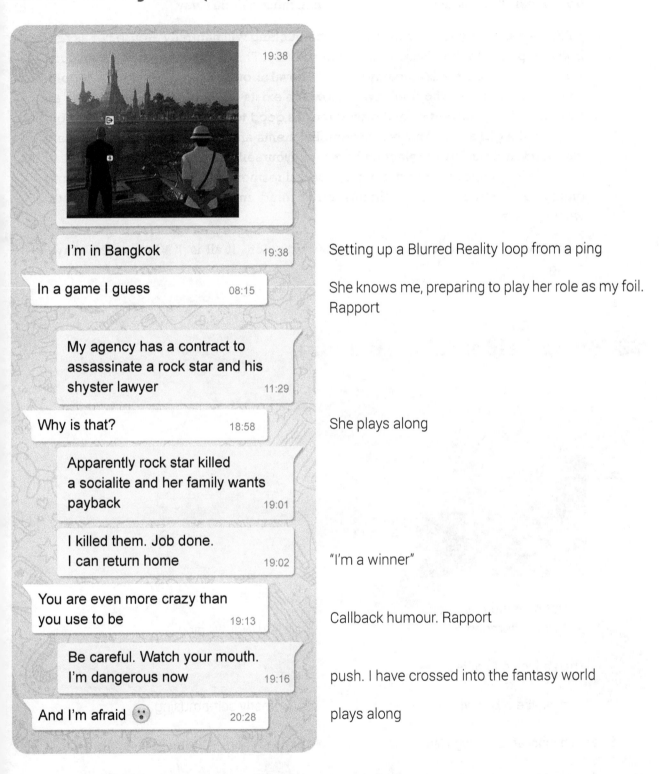

| | |
|---|---|
| **19:38** | |
| I'm in Bangkok   19:38 | Setting up a Blurred Reality loop from a ping |
| In a game I guess   08:15 | She knows me, preparing to play her role as my foil. Rapport |
| My agency has a contract to assassinate a rock star and his shyster lawyer   11:29 | |
| Why is that?   18:58 | She plays along |
| Apparently rock star killed a socialite and her family wants payback   19:01 | |
| I killed them. Job done. I can return home   19:02 | "I'm a winner" |
| You are even more crazy than you use to be   19:13 | Callback humour. Rapport |
| Be careful. Watch your mouth. I'm dangerous now   19:16 | push. I have crossed into the fantasy world |
| And I'm afraid 😮   20:28 | plays along |

This follows the same pattern as the earlier Batman story, where I ping her a window onto my world but rather than leave it there I whip up a nonsense mini-drama about being lost in the fantasy world. I guess you could call this a meta-DHV in that I'm positioning myself as an international traveller, a skilled hitman with the power of life and death, and a winner.... all within the fantasy world. It's one step removed from a real DHV about your actual life. But.... think of it this way.

Telling a girl a dirty story about you and her fucking will naturally arouse her as her body responds to the visualisations you provide. This is **direct** sexual projection. However, when she reads a steamy romance novel about two people fucking – people she's never met and who don't even know she exists – she will become aroused at that too. This in **indirect** sexual projection. It's good to learn direct DHV projection as you tell a girl about your real accomplishments and qualities. However you can also learn indirect DHV projection by writing yourself into a fantasy or hypothetical scenario. The important thing is not the logical resilience of the manoeuvre. You are engaging certain favourable circuits in her mind and linking them to you. That's what matters.

Don't think she's not aware of it, and how ridiculous it all is. It's fun, so she plays along.

## 22. Tomb Raider joke (Ivanna)

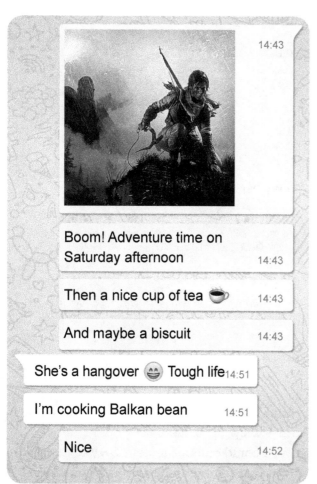

| | |
|---|---|
| 14:43 | |
| Boom! Adventure time on Saturday afternoon 14:43 | A standard WoMW ping |
| Then a nice cup of tea ☕ 14:43 | |
| And maybe a biscuit 14:43 | This is mostly self-amusing |
| She's a hangover 😄 Tough life 14:51 | |
| I'm cooking Balkan bean 14:51 | |
| Nice 14:52 | Our swapping of WoMW, rapport-building, is complete so move forwards |

This game is great. I'm breaking into ancient lost cities and stealing all their stuff                14:52

Looks just like you                14:52

Parody Brute

"that is so you" rapport

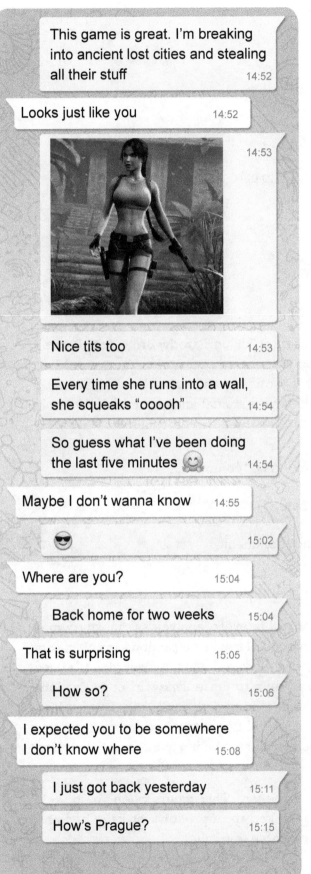
14:53

Nice tits too                14:53

Every time she runs into a wall, she squeaks "ooooh"                14:54

So guess what I've been doing the last five minutes 😊                14:54

Sexualisation

Maybe I don't wanna know                14:55

😎                15:02

The second loop of the exchange is complete

Where are you?                15:04

She stacks me forwards

Back home for two weeks                15:04

That is surprising                15:05

How so?                15:06

I expected you to be somewhere I don't know where                15:08

I just got back yesterday                15:11

How's Prague?                15:15

This is all comfort chit-chat, expressing interest in her wellbeing

| | |
|---|---|
| Cold and little bit rainy | 15:17 |
| We had frost today. Freezing | 15:22 |
| I've only been playing an hour and I've already wrecked one secret tomb of inestimable archaeological value | 15:23 |
| Now I'm in Siberia hoping to wreck another | 15:23 |
| Oooooookkkkk.... O.o | 15:24 |

Back to parody brute to liven things up

You'll spot the usual elements in this chat, of which Parody Brute and Blurred Reality are the main components. Notice also the structure of conversation. This exchange has four 'movements' in which a loop is opened and then closed and it flows smoothly because both Ivanna and I have a mutual understanding of when it is appropriate to move from one to the next. The three movements are:

1. Window on my World pings exchanged, up to my "nice" comment.

2. A Parody Brute flight of fancy, up to my smiley face.

3. A comfort-building chit-chat, up to my "Freezing" comment.

4. A reprise of the earlier Parody Brute

You don't need to think through your texting to this level of analysis as it mostly comes naturally. I merely wish to draw out the structure of social interaction to explain why a short exchange like this can be lively and flow smoothly. Awkwardness arises when the two participants are out of sync, akin to those awkward conversations where you mess up the turn-taking and keep talking over each other by accident. Texting noobs (or those trying new gambits) will frequently find their exchanges become awkward and fall apart. One possible cause is failing to manage the closing of loops and opening of new ones.

A street-stop version of this is "killing the opener". This occurs when you open a girl and a fun opener hits well and, having stacked appropriately, you keep banging on about whatever you opened with. For example (hypothetical)

> *You:* Hey, I just had to say hello because I love your flowery dress. It's very summery.
> *Her:* Oh, thank you! *smiles*
> *You:* It's so colourful, it makes my mind wander to fields of sunflowers and poppies, golden yellows and ruby reds
> *Her:* *giggles, it's hook point*
> [This is the moment you should stack forward, such as asking where she's from]
> *You:* And your bag is bright blue which is nice, like the clear sky above those fields.
> *Her:* Um, oooookay.
> *You:* I guess if you had green shoes like grass it would complete the picture.
> *Her:* Thank you. Look, I'm late to meet my friend. I have to go.

The reason the above interaction slips from quite cool to cringe is through failing to recognise that the first 'movement' or 'loop' was finished after the reference to ruby red. It should've been closed and then a new loop opened. Instead, things became awkward. The same principle applies in texting so be attuned to when it's time to move off one topic or type of energy and onto the next.

Lastly, here's an example of playing off call-back humour. Polina had been testy on our dates because she wanted to see what I was made of. One example she'd picked was that I liked Costa Coffee and she construed this as me liking it too much. I just happened to run into a great opportunity to throw this back at her (attraction) while using the shared background (comfort).

# 23. Coffee Man Exchange (Polina)

> It's time I visited a therapist.
> I may be mentally ill          10:52

Begin with attention-grabbing open

> There is now a blurring between reality and fantasy. I can't be sure what I see is real. Perhaps I'm hallucinating          10:53

patient set-up by pretending seriousness

> 10:53

he just happened to walk by me so I snapped photo

| | |
|---|---|
| Is this real, or did my imagination create it because I WISH it's real 10:53 | the punchline |
| Haha, laughed out loud even 😄 12:44 | rewards my efforts |
| But in other words I see nothing wrong with the picture, just a guy walking wearing a red sweater 12:44 | plays along to tease me, wanting banter |
| With a white logo. Maybe you are right you should talk about this to someone. 12:45 | her punchline and playful reversal |
| 😳 12:52 | I reward her by showing the effect she wanted to cause |
| Oh God! It's true! 12:52 | Agree and amplify but don't labour the point |

The world offers much raw material from which to craft mini-dramas. If you ever see something that grabs your attention, it might well have the same effect on a girl. Use your imagination and shape it to your advantage.

Men usually value their peace of mind, seeking to calm their environment and bring it under control. In contrast, women quickly tire of calm and seek to create drama. You can pre-empt this and 'fight' on your own terms by creating the drama yourself. I stress this is all playful. You are taking on roles and *simulating* drama, rather than actually becoming a histrionic moron.

In the following two examples I pick a fight over nothing. It's the seduction equivalent of "what the fuck are you looking at, pal?" but all playful. The result is to lift the girl out of her routine and reward her for engaging me.

## 24. Feminism Joke  (Ivanna)

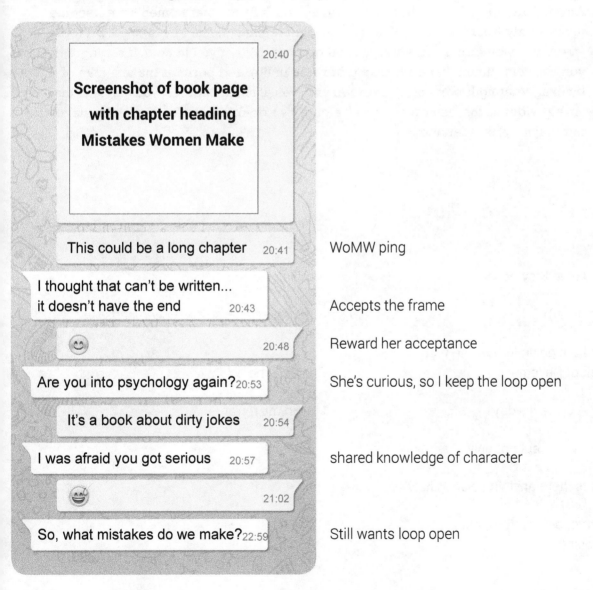

| | |
|---|---|
| Screenshot of book page with chapter heading Mistakes Women Make — 20:40 | |
| This could be a long chapter — 20:41 | WoMW ping |
| I thought that can't be written... it doesn't have the end — 20:43 | Accepts the frame |
| ☺ — 20:48 | Reward her acceptance |
| Are you into psychology again? — 20:53 | She's curious, so I keep the loop open |
| It's a book about dirty jokes — 20:54 | |
| I was afraid you got serious — 20:57 | shared knowledge of character |
| 😄 — 21:02 | |
| So, what mistakes do we make? — 22:59 | Still wants loop open |

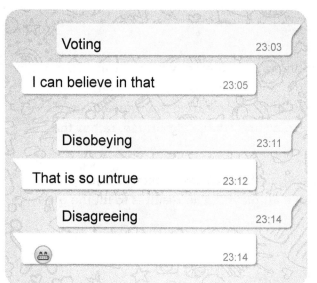

| | | |
|---|---|---|
| Voting | 23:03 | |
| I can believe in that | 23:05 | Not sure if she believes in voting, or believes voting is a mistake |
| Disobeying | 23:11 | I just plod ahead anyway |
| That is so untrue | 23:12 | She's served up a fat ball.... |
| Disagreeing | 23:14 | ... so I hit it out the park |
| 😬 | 23:14 | win |

An easy trap to suck a girl into is to open up with a frame that women have become increasingly troublesome of late, such as with feminism. The key is to pick a topic where it is women's disagreebility (real or alleged) that you lament. If she agrees, you can compliment her on knowing her role in life, and perhaps make a joke of it by exaggerating how much she agreed with you. If she disagrees, you can take that as the evidence that you were right all along. It's a double-bind for her, which makes her playfully exasperated.

## 25. Mario Joke  (Zoya)

| | | |
|---|---|---|
| I'm in Kiev now! | 15:41 | Simple ping |
| Ohh great)) | 15:50 | She's agreeable, so she cheer-leads |
| And I am going to Italy the first week of December | 15:50 | She adds her WoMW |
| A pizza holiday? | 15:51 | I begin my reframe |
| Haha yeah, but not only | 15:54 | |
| Is there anything else in Italy? | 15:58 | |
| Culture, architecture, arts, shopping | 16:11 | |

| | |
|---|---|
| Booooooooring 16:20 | Parody Brute |
| And is it more interesting in the Ukraine? 17:19 | Playful challenge |
| You're going to visit your Italian boyfriend, aren't you 17:20 | Total over-reaction in order to pick a fight |
| I've seen his photo 17:20 | |
|  17:20 | |
| Ok, I admit it. He can jump higher than me 17:21 | |
| Ahaha you are totally right. How could you guess? 17:21 | |

My last four lines are a mini-drama of their own where I've suspected infidelity, gotten jealous, and admitted defeat by a superior rival. She hasn't even gotten a word in edgeways.

Once in a while it's funny to go all Salvador Dali on her and give her a pattern-break. This works especially well if you've had a date already and been texting a while and thus she has greater understanding of your character from which to interpret the surrealism as an exaggeration thereof. The key to surrealism is to find an odd arresting image and spinning off from it with a story. Play up the self-absorption so it functions like a Parody Narcissist who is only dimly self-aware.

This first example is blatantly shoe-horning in an image I happened to come across.

## 26. Irreverence Photo Ping (Ana)

I call it "painting the target around the arrow", to mean you fire a shot and no matter where it lands you claim that's exactly where you were aiming. So any time you find a really odd photo just pretend you (or her) wanted to find exactly that. It's the absurdity of your 'search' coupled with the absurdity of the photo that creates the irreverent humour. For the next example we'll use a feigned mistake as the humour.

# 27. Oversleep Joke (Ivanna)

I got a new phone.
I've joined 2015!                     18:07

Which one?
You know it's 2016?         19:30

Wait......                        19:31

What?                          19:31

What year is this????         19:32

19:32

I SLEPT TOO LONG!!

😂 😂 😂 😗         19:33

You can roll out this gambit any time you become up to date on a current technology or trend. The humour is mostly in the timing to anticipate the punchline and then the funny photo. Any post-apocalyptic image with suffice: Planet Of The Apes, Mad Max, or in this case Army Of Darkness.

The PUA community has long grappled with the problem of re-heating cold leads. The Yes Girls never break text contact and usually come out on dates at the earliest opportunity. The No Girls usually drop off quickly. It's the Maybe Girls that frustrate the keen player and suck up most of his mental focus. We've all been in the position where a girl seemed enthusiastic but won't quite come onto a date, and then her responses slow down and ultimately stop. Usually this is because there's one or more men in the picture that she prefers to you. Your best chance at reeling this girl in is to remain on the fringes of her awareness until her circumstances change.

Given that you won't know her circumstances, you must occasionally touch base to find out where you stand. Walk that fine line of letting her know you are there when she's ready, but that you're not pining for her specifically (because you have so much going on in your life). Pinging works well here.

However, sometimes the lead has gone completely cold. For this eventuality, PUAs created the 'recovery text'. It's a short message sent to girls who've gone radio silent as a last-minute Hail Mary to entice them back into conversation. Here are some community standard recovery texts (I didn't create them):

- OMG you've been kidnapped! Tell them I'll pay the ransom! X. p.s have they been feeding you properly? I'll bring chocolate! Plain or milk?

- We are soo getting divorced, call the lawyers, cite 'Irreconcilable differences', I want the cat back.

- OMG – You've disappeared! Have I offended you? I do hope not X

- I guess I should take the hint. Seems a shame though as I actually really liked you

I happen to think they are a bit lame in execution, but the principle is solid. Now that we're in the era of WhatsApp, emojis and photo pings we can build on them. Here is my favourite, the *Krauser Crazy Police* recovery text:

## 28. Recovery (Sasha)

👮 : Hello Crazy Police. I'd like to report a crazy girl.
👮 : Describe her.
👮 : Tall, Kazakh, long legs, always laughing.
👮 : What is her craziness?
👮 : She likes me but keeps disappearing from WhatsApp.
👮 : Yes, she is crazy.  12:41

😂 😂 😂 😂 😂 😂 😂 😂 😂 19:21

It's not I crazy, youuuuu crazy!!!! 😂 😂
😂 😂 😄 😂 😄 😄 😄  19:21

🌺 🌺 🌺 🌺 🌺  19:21

This is a generic all-purpose recovery. All you need do is insert her relevant personal characteristics into the third line, being sure to keep it positive. I like to include some physical, some personality. Of the girls who respond, they usually all fill their reply with laughing emojis like that.

A different type of recovery is in order when the girl is replying to you but somewhat reluctantly. Perhaps she's agreed in principle to have a date but won't agree a time and place. In this case I like to introduce irreverence through the 'Soon' memes. It's a playful recognition that you're almost stalking her and thus defuses any discomfort. You've named the elephant in the room.

## 29. Soon (Tamara)

21 SEPTEMBER 2017

Will finish soon 😄  15:36

How are you?  15:36

Wow  19:09

Good                    19:09

Result!                 19:09

I am working            19:09                    no date solicitation

Busy busy busy          21:03                    so I don't make invite I expect to be rebuffed

22 SEPTEMBER 2017

                        12:19                    Reminders framed as jokes

**SOON**

😆 😆 😆 😆 😆 😆 😆    13:17

Horse?                  13:17                    Less pressure than direct invite. It's really a probe

                        13:17

**SOON.**

24 SEPTEMBER 2017

                        13:12

**SOON.**

You can only do this so many times before you've either gotten the date or you need to roll off a while. It does neatly avoid giving a series of refused date requests, as she knows her role is to simply tell you once she's ready. As with all recovery pings, the very fact that you are falling back onto them suggests that she's probably not going to have sex with you. Lower your expectations accordingly.

Any time a girl sends a photo of herself looking pretty it's an excellent sign: she wants you to think of her as a sexual being. How you respond depends entirely on where you are in the set with her. The general rule is you use the primary energy in the set as it's been so far:

- If she was bantering hard in the street, banter her in the photo response.

- If she was shy and demure, tease her softly then say something nice.

- If she was highly sexual, focus on the sex (or completely ignore the sexual aspect of the photo and comment on something mundane within the shot)

Here's an example of a shy demure girl, quite likely a virgin. In these cases I always ask myself "which cute fluffy animal does she remind me of?" then I search Google Images for it. As a quick guide: Big dark eyes means raccoon. Full round cheeks means hamster. Visible front teeth and smile means squirrel. Narrowed eyes means cat. Long legs means flamingo.

## 30. Selfie Riposte  (Zhanara)

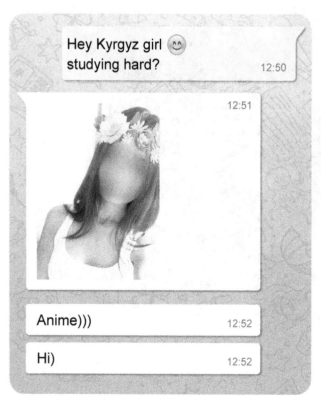

"look at me, I'm pretty"

close the loop and stack forward with comfort

The vast majority of my replies to a girl's selfie ping is to give a mild compliment and a mild tease (via comparing her to a fluffy animal). It's by far the safest option and before long you'll have a dozen pre-prepared images in your phone gallery to select from. Default to this.

Sometimes you'll change things up, especially if you're getting frustrated with a girl and thinking of just binning the lead (e.g. she's a window-shopper). The next example is *considerably* more risky so I find it more appropriate with girls you've already dated and you can each calibrate the other more accurately. I'd only send this to a girl between the street stop and first date if the set was highly sexual and she'd already responded well to earlier banter. So, be warned!

# 31. Selfie Riposte (Alyona)

"look at me, I'm pretty"

I can see your cleavage 😊   22:36          sexualise

what do you mean?   22:56

23:03

👍 🤲 😊   23:04

I took this risk because Alyona had been coquettish. We'd had several dates, made out, and I'd even had my hands up her shirt on my bed. Then she pulled away to a looser orbit. I took this to mean either she had another man, or she didn't like the casual sex deal I was offering. Either way, I wanted to force things to a head and find out where she stood, rather than go on another time-waster date. Thus it was worth taking a risk. I would not have done this if the seduction was proceeding smoothly.

You can continue to mess with girls after you've gotten sexual because it's the humour that won her over that is the humour that keeps her around. Usually my replies will be about her (e.g. framing her as a cute animal) but in this case my reply is a playful positioning of her for her role in my life.

## 32. Ass Selfie  (Dominika)

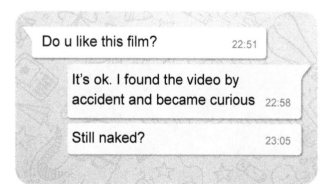

Do u like this film?   22:51

It's ok. I found the video by accident and became curious   22:58          Closing an earlier loop

Still naked?   23:05

When a girl likes you, she wanted to be claimed by you (symbolically if not literally). Therefore I'll often tell a girl that her ass belongs to me and may even admonish her for not taking due care of my property.

Some humour is hit-and-run, such as a photo ping and one-line comment. Other times it's fun to slowly suck a girl in by pretending to engage in serious conversation before dropping in the punchline. Due to the time it takes to execute, and the need to carefully calibrate specifically to that girl, I think these are best suited to the Bubble Burst period between first and second dates, or later. Doing this before a first date is usually a mistake because it conveys a level of rapport higher than you've established, and is thus over-investment.

## 33. Wictor Gambit (Ivanna)

| | |
|---|---|
| I'm always right    18:28 | A previous loop closing |
| I don't know. I never listen 🙈    18:31 | |

next day

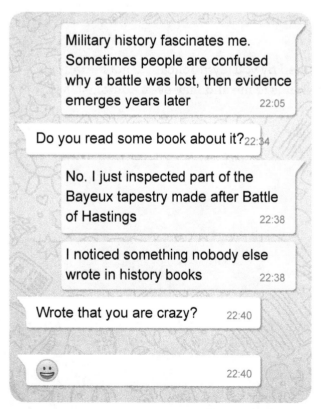

| | |
|---|---|
| Military history fascinates me. Sometimes people are confused why a battle was lost, then evidence emerges years later    22:05 | I'm setting something up, pretending to be serious |
| Do you read some book about it? 22:34 | She takes the bait |
| No. I just inspected part of the Bayeux tapestry made after Battle of Hastings    22:38 | |
| I noticed something nobody else wrote in history books    22:38 | the Wictoring begins |
| Wrote that you are crazy?    22:40 | She senses I'm actually setting up a joke so she switches gear to match my energy |
| 😀    22:40 | |

> Really, look carefully at this screenshot and see if you notice something strange    22:40

> Look carefully!    22:41

> If you can't see it, I'll explain it    22:41

Labouring the point of my seriousness

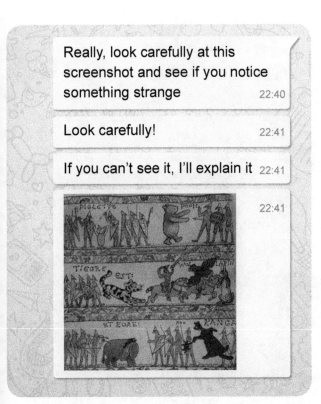
22:41

I named this after Thomas Wictor, a Twitter account known for the author's extreme attention to detail in analysing phone cam and CCTV footage to pick out important details that everyone else missed. He would raise a topic, show a video, then conduct a frame-by-frame analysis to highlight a tiny feature from which he'd extrapolate an important insight into real-world politics. He's serious, I'm not.

The humour works by the contrast between your claimed extreme attention to detail, set up with a straight face and an admonition for her to pay attention, then the punchline of an unexpected detail that nobody could've possibly missed. You can then congratulate yourself on your (delusional) perspicacity and let her know you expect appreciation for the vital secret you just shared.

## 34. Concubine False Dilemma (Alisa)

> I realised I have a problem with you.    19:45

Attention-getting, intended to distract

> Are you my groupie or concubine?    18:46

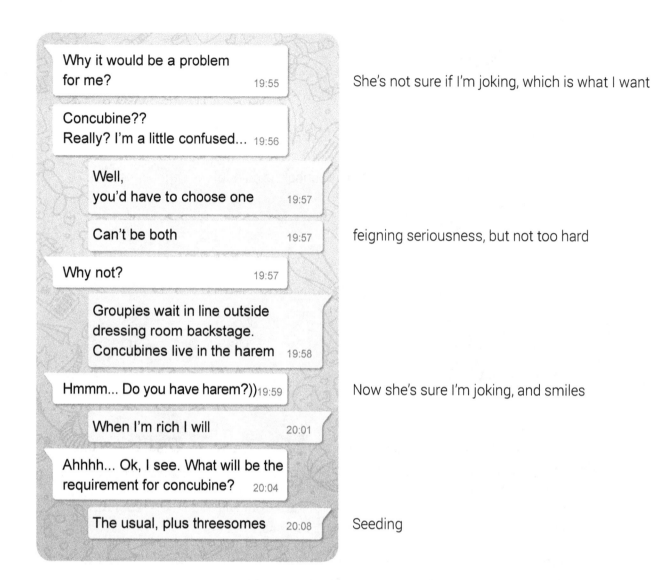

Why it would be a problem for me? 19:55 — She's not sure if I'm joking, which is what I want

Concubine??
Really? I'm a little confused... 19:56

Well,
you'd have to choose one 19:57

Can't be both 19:57 — feigning seriousness, but not too hard

Why not? 19:57

Groupies wait in line outside dressing room backstage.
Concubines live in the harem 19:58

Hmmm... Do you have harem?)) 19:59 — Now she's sure I'm joking, and smiles

When I'm rich I will 20:01

Ahhhh... Ok, I see. What will be the requirement for concubine? 20:04

The usual, plus threesomes 20:08 — Seeding

Naturally, the above example is a girl I've already established as a regular. Thus the goal of the exchange, aside from usual maintenance, is to seed the idea of a threesome that I can return to later. The final example is a bait-and-switch where I lead a girl to think I'm going to dirty-talk her but I actually want something else.

## 35. Sandwich joke (Zoya)

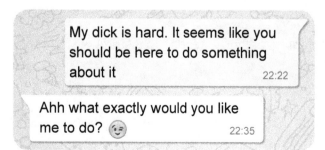

My dick is hard. It seems like you should be here to do something about it 22:22 — lure her to expect dirty talk

Ahh what exactly would you like me to do? 😉 22:35 — she's taken the bait

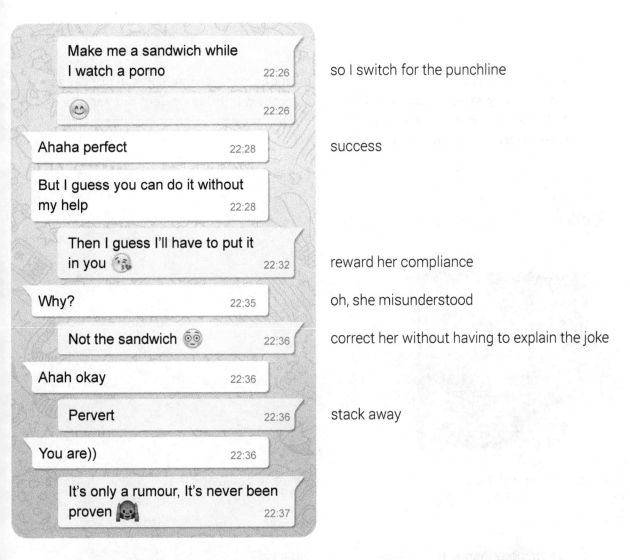

Make me a sandwich while
I watch a porno                  22:26

so I switch for the punchline

😊                               22:26

Ahaha perfect                    22:28

success

But I guess you can do it without
my help                          22:28

Then I guess I'll have to put it
in you 😚                        22:32

reward her compliance

Why?                             22:35

oh, she misunderstood

Not the sandwich 😳              22:36

correct her without having to explain the joke

Ahah okay                        22:36

Pervert                          22:36

stack away

You are))                        22:36

It's only a rumour, It's never been
proven 🙈                        22:37

A pattern you can use over-and-over again is to begin a sexual projection and then abruptly switch gears before its consummation. The girl understands you are exerting control over her mood and displaying your ability to lead. Just be careful not to overuse it because by 'crying wolf' too many times, she'll be reluctant to partake in a real sexual projection later. Use sparingly. The structure is:

1. Introduce sexual energy

2. Set up a story line she'd expect leads to sex

3. Pull her in to anticipate sex

4. Abruptly switch moods to something comically non-sexual

It's most effective if you perform (4) at or near her moment of psychological buy-in. Make sure these are short gambits, perhaps only a minute or two. They work best during the daytime when she's with company and thus couldn't begin masturbating. If you do it at night after a long build-up she'll just get angry: in those circumstances it should be an *actual* sexual projection.

# DISCARD FAILED GAMBITS

You won't always hit the target with your gambits. Sometimes you'll miscue because it's not as funny as you think it is. Other times your gambit is perfect but she's had a shitty day and is in no mood for banter. If you find yourself having a 'new Coke' moment, smoothly drop it and stack forwards.

## 36. Trump Trolling (Ivanna)

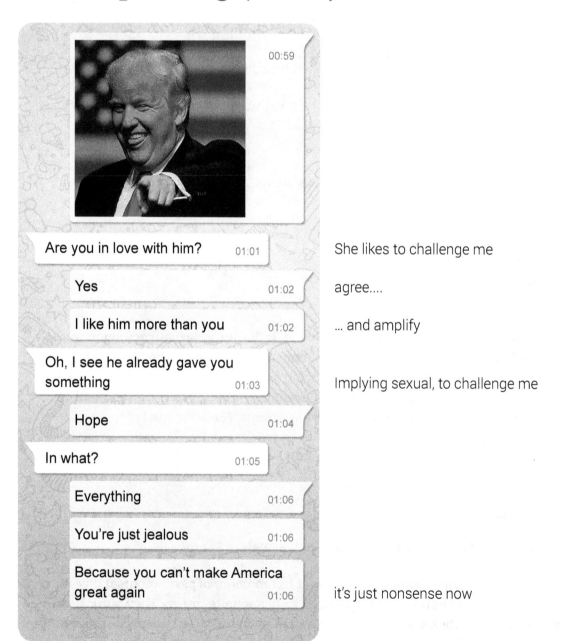

| | |
|---|---|
| 00:59 | |
| Are you in love with him? 01:01 | She likes to challenge me |
| Yes 01:02 | agree.... |
| I like him more than you 01:02 | ... and amplify |
| Oh, I see he already gave you something 01:03 | Implying sexual, to challenge me |
| Hope 01:04 | |
| In what? 01:05 | |
| Everything 01:06 | |
| You're just jealous 01:06 | |
| Because you can't make America great again 01:06 | it's just nonsense now |

There's nothing special going on here. Donald Trump had won an important vote so I was celebrating it, and she knew I'm aboard the Trump Train (but she doesn't like him or politics in general). I tried to create something out of nothing but it didn't really stick so, upon realising this wasn't going anywhere, I quickly made a fighting withdrawal and went back to routine chit-chat. Be ready to abandon gambits that don't hit.

# Continue your Player's Journey with Nick Krauser's other resources!

## The Model

Everything you need to know about street pick-up is packed into these cutting-edge textbooks. Each volume is written to match your own progress in learning the art form. *Daygame Nitro* introduces the basics of street pick-up and inner game in a simple, easy-to-follow guide. *Daygame Mastery* breaks apart the model into minute detail to help you fine-tune your method. *Daygame Infinite* unlocks your potential with extensive vibe and calibration advice.

 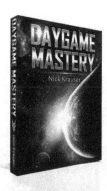 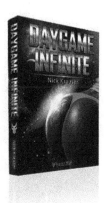

## The Journey

Dive deep into the Player's lifestyle with the most detailed and most insightful Game memoir ever written. Four massive volumes take you through every stage from zero to hero as Nick tells you his story. Higher level knowledge seeps out of every page. Live the life!

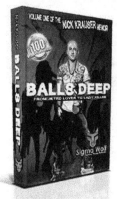   

## The Demonstration

It's one thing to understand the theory but another to watch, on video, how to run street game and master dating. *Daygame Overkill* provides a play-by-play breakdown of Nick's infield videos, showing you how to get Adventure Sex. *Black Book* explains the dating model in detail, and *Womanizers Bible* provides high-level theory on the Player's World.

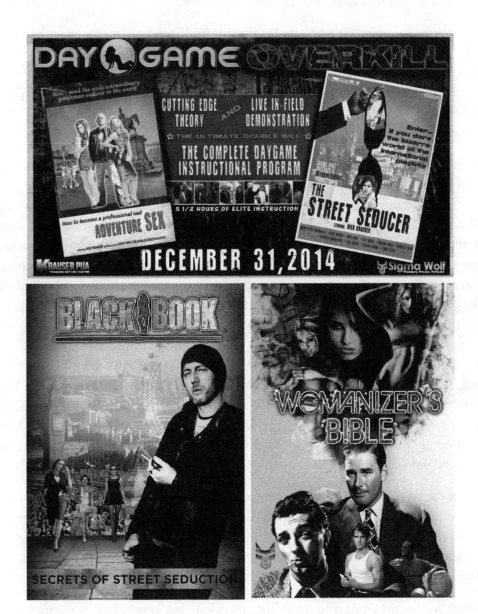

*Check out sigmawolf.com and daygameoverkill.com to access these amazing resources.*

# ACKNOWLEDGEMENTS

Readers sometimes contact me to tell me this book changed their lives. What they probably don't suspect is that it changed my life too. The unexpected critical and financial success of *Daygame Mastery* allowed me to quit my office job and devote myself full-time to writing about seduction. For this, I owe every single reader a big thank you. That includes you. Thank you for your support.

This book is a labour of love and I'm grateful for the opportunity to give it another lick of paint for the second edition. My thanks go to Alexey for his meticulous layout, Davorin for his inspired graphic design and cover art, and to Cristian for his charming caricature art of the girls. Thanks to Rob and Sam for taking additional street photos. Thanks also to Brian and Edward who reviewed drafts of the new content to clean up my usual errors and linguistic tangles.

The first edition of *Daygame Mastery* relied quite strongly upon the work of other men in the seduction community and the broader 'manosphere'. You'll remember in the introduction I first referred to this book as outlining the *London* Daygame Model, and only when introducing my own precise formulation did I change the term to *Krauser* Daygame Model. This book has presented my personal version of a more general template. I have been enormously lucky to learn my game just as the planets came into alignment in my adopted home town of London and a crucible of daygame learning existed. If I'd started a couple of years earlier things would've been so much harder. The London Daygame Model presented here is the emergent outcome of thousands of man-hours of work by perhaps a dozen dedicated and talented men. Thus I give thanks to that first generation of which I was a part: Yad, Andy, Tom, Anthony, Jon, and Sasha. We too relied on men who'd blazed the trail before us, so thanks also to the old-school PUAs such as Mystery, Style, Ross Jeffries, Gunwitch, Assanova, Tyler, and 60 Years Of Challenge. Thanks also to the intellectual pioneers of the manosphere, in particular Roissy (now Heartiste), Rollo Tomassi, Roosh, and Vox Day.

I was lucky to have excellent wings and mentors to help me develop my craft. Whether through formal consultation or mere off-hand comments, these men were a fertile source of ideas, many of which found their way into the model. So, my thanks to Jimmy Jambone, Mick, Fernando, Johnny Wisdom, Colin, Bodi, and Steve Jabba.

I look forward to hearing your thoughts on this book. Let me know at my blog krauserpua.com or fire off a comment linking a discussion or review you have about it on another website.

CPSIA information can be obtained
at www.ICGtesting.com
Printed in the USA
LVHW060146070723
751804LV00008B/67

9 781999 946210